TEACHER'S BOOK
with Digital Pack

4

CEFR
B2

AMERICAN TH!NK

SECOND EDITION

CAMBRIDGE
UNIVERSITY PRESS

Brian Hart

CONTENTS

C Conversations; Personality; Using *should*; Career paths; Decisions; Permission
D A change of lifestyle?; Reporting verbs; Negative adjectives; Another country; Changes; Regrets: *I wish … / If only …*

PRONUNCIATION	THINK!	SKILLS
Dipthongs: alternative spellings	**Train to THINK:** Thinking rationally	**Reading** Article: Surviving for seven weeks Article: How to survive in the wilderness **Writing** A diary page about an experience **Listening** Radio show: *Exam advice*
Phrasal verb stress	**Train to THINK:** Distinguishing fact from opinion **Values:** Learning from other cultures	**Reading** Article: Getting to work Blog: A Brazilian adventure **Writing** An informal email **Listening** Radio quiz about migration in nature
B2 First for Schools practice		
Adding emphasis	**Train to THINK:** Changing your opinions	**Reading** Blog: An embarrassing dad Website article: To sharent or not to sharent **Writing** An essay about parenting **Listening** Podcast about a hero dad
Pronouncing words with *gh*	**Train to THINK:** Lateral thinking **Values:** Appreciating creative solutions	**Reading** Article: A big change for artists Web post: A problem on *Your answers here* **Writing** A story beginning: "I had no idea what to do." **Listening** Talking heads – thinking imaginatively
B2 First for Schools practice		
The schwa /ə/ sound	**Train to THINK:** The PMI strategy	**Reading** Article: A digital detox Article: Great success for teenage teachers: when silver surfers get connected **Writing** Instructions **Listening** A podcast about an invention
Linking words with /dʒ/ and /tʃ/	**Train to THINK:** Exaggeration **Values:** Doing good	**Reading** Email: Comic Con Article: CoderDojo Coolest Projects International **Writing** An essay about social media **Listening** Interview: *Friendships*
B2 First for Schools practice		
Intonation: encouraging someone	**Train to THINK:** Learning to see things from a different perspective	**Reading** Blog: My takes on life, the universe, and everything Website page: Quotations for worriers **Writing** A short story ending: "Every cloud has a silver lining" **Listening** Podcast: *Silver Linings*
Weak forms with conditionals	**Train to THINK:** The "goal-setting" checklist **Values:** Lists	**Reading** Book review: *The Checklist Manifesto* by Atul Gawande Blog: Elisa's list blog **Writing** An essay: A wonder of the natural world **Listening** A talk about bucket lists
B2 First for Schools practice		
Linking: intrusive /w/ and /j/	**Train to THINK:** Jumping to a hasty conclusion	**Reading** Article: Making difficult decisions Quiz: What kind of a friend are you? **Writing** An article for the school magazine **Listening** A radio show about life choices
Linking: omission of the /h/ sound	**Train to THINK:** Recognizing the source of a statement	**Reading** Magazine article: Fake news Article: The Secret Paparazzo **Writing** A magazine article about an interview with a well-known person **Listening** An interview with a foreign correspondent
B2 First for Schools practice		
Stress on modal verbs for speculation	**Train to THINK:** Spotting flawed arguments	**Reading** Article: A mission to Mars Blog: Top four space movies of the 21st century **Writing** A report about a problem on a school trip **Listening** Podcast about space tourism
Linking: intrusive /r/	**Train to THINK:** Exploring hidden messages **Values:** Human activity and the natural world	**Reading** Article: Saving great discoveries! Article: Explorers: a friend to the native people: Cândido Rondon **Writing** A short biography **Listening** A talk about discovering new species
B2 First for Schools practice		

Welcome to **AMERICAN TH!NK**, the course that develops your students' communication and critical thinking skills, values, and life competencies so they can successfully meet the challenges ahead.

Have you ever asked yourself: "how can I be expected to prepare my students to succeed in a world that's changing so fast?" While it's impossible to predict what specific skills will be in demand by the time our students enter the workforce, there are some things that we as educators can do to ensure our students are as well prepared for their futures as they can be. We know there is an ever-increasing need for individuals to be able to work together effectively with others around the world, and to be able to think creatively and solve problems collaboratively. They also need to be able to analyze and process sources of information more critically, communicate, and support their views more effectively, and they need to maintain a positive mindset in challenging environments.

With **AMERICAN TH!NK** you can be certain you're giving your learners the tools they need to build a brighter future for themselves and a better world for us all.

What's new in the Second Edition?

We've kept everything that teachers loved about AMERICAN TH!NK First Edition:

- The high-interest, relevant, and thought-provoking topics
- The development of critical thinking, positive values, and self-esteem
- A syllabus built on the Cambridge English Learner Corpus and English Profile
- The inclusion of Cambridge Exams practice sections

The second edition builds and expands on these strengths:

- The **globally focused content** will appeal to teens' natural curiosities and interests, and feed their growing sense of the world around them.
- The **Life Competencies** strand, supported by entertaining student vlogs and correlated to the Cambridge Life Competencies Framework, will help them develop the vital capabilities they'll need to be successful throughout their lives.
- The authentic, **real-world documentary-style videos** will captivate student interest and provoke meaningful thought and lively classroom discussion.
- Powerful, all-in-one digital tools and support will empower teachers to deliver dynamic and effective lessons.

The story of AMERICAN TH!NK

AMERICAN TH!NK Second Edition was developed using the latest research into teen cognitive science and best practices and methodologies for the secondary classroom. To learn more, visit **cambridge.org/think2e** or scan this QR code with your smartphone or tablet.

Cambridge Life Competencies

A framework to develop skills for life

There have been many initiatives to address the skills and competencies our students need for the 21st century – each relating to different contexts. At Cambridge, we are responding to educators who have asked for a way to understand how all these different approaches to life competencies relate to English language programs.

The Cambridge Framework sets out to have three dimensions:

BREADTH	DEVELOPMENT	DEPTH
Complete view of transferable skills within one system	How the skills develop across stages of the learning journey	Enough detail to guide teaching and assessment in practical ways

We have grouped the different competencies into six main areas.

- Creative Thinking
- Critical Thinking
- Learning to Learn
- Communication
- Collaboration
- Social Responsibilities

These are supported by three foundation layers that underpin the Framework:

- Emotional Development
- Digital Literacy
- Discipline Knowledge

What Are "Competencies"?

We call these "competencies" rather than "skills," because competencies are more than just skills. The competencies in this Framework are complex and require development in three areas:

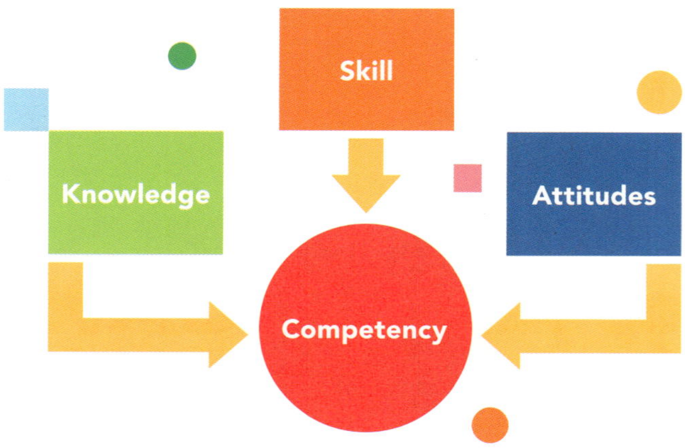

Competencies are defined as a combination of knowledge, skills, and attitudes, where:

a) knowledge is composed of the facts and figures, concepts, ideas, and theories which are already established and support the understanding of a certain area or subject;

b) skills are defined as the ability and capacity to carry out processes and use the existing knowledge to achieve results;

c) attitudes describe the disposition and mindsets to act or react to ideas, persons, or situations.

Council of the European Union, 2018, p14.

Core areas

Core area				
Creative Thinking	Participating in creative activities	Creating new content from own ideas or other resources	Using newly created content to solve problems and make decisions	
Critical Thinking	Understanding and analyzing links between ideas	Evaluating ideas, arguments, and options	Synthesizing ideas and information	
Learning to Learn	Practical skills for participating in learning	Taking control of own learning	Reflecting on and evaluating own learning success	
Communication	Using appropriate language and register for context	Managing conversations	Participating with appropriate confidence and clarity	
Collaboration	Taking personal responsibility for own contribution to a group task	Listening respectfully and responding constructively to others' contributions	Managing the sharing of tasks in a project	Working towards a resolution related to a task
Social Responsibilities	Understanding personal responsibilities as part of a group and in society – including citizenship	Taking active roles including leadership	Understanding and describing own and others' cultures	Understanding and discussing global issues – environmental, political, financial, and social

Foundational layers

Emotional Development

Digital Literacy

Discipline Knowledge

cambridge.org/clcf

For a full correlation to the Cambridge Life Competencies Framework, visit **cambridge.org/americanthink2e**

AMERICAN TH!NK and the Cambridge Life Competencies Framework

Although **AMERICAN TH!NK** focuses on both the *Social Responsibilities* and the *Emotional Development* competencies in the *Cambridge Life Competencies Framework*, all of the six Life Competencies are explored throughout the course.

The table below shows, at a glance, where you can find an activity which concentrates on a particular Core Area.

The following table shows which *competencies* are developed in this level.

Competency	Core Area	U1	U2	U3	U4	U5	U6	U7	U8	U9	U10	U11	U12
Social Responsibilities	Understanding personal responsibilities as part of a social group						✔						
	Understanding global issues												✔
	Showing intercultural awareness		✔							✔	✔		
Emotional Development	Managing own emotions							✔					
	Understanding emotions / Supporting others				✔						✔		
	Showing empathy for the feelings of others							✔					
	Empathy and relationship skills												✔
Critical Thinking	Evaluating ideas and arguments			✔	✔				✔			✔	✔
	Understanding and analyzing ideas and arguments		✔				✔		✔	✔	✔	✔	
	Solving problems and making decisions	✔				✔							
Learning to Learn	Practical skills for participating in learning	✔	✔	✔	✔	✔	✔	✔	✔	✔	✔	✔	✔
	Taking control of own learning	✔							✔				
	Setting goals and planning		✔										
Communication	Using appropriate language and register for context						✔						✔
Creative Thinking	Generating ideas / Preparing for creativity				✔			✔	✔				
Collaboration	Listening respectfully and responding constructively to others' contributions	✔	✔	✔	✔	✔	✔	✔	✔	✔	✔	✔	✔

Here are a few examples of how activities can help your students develop particular Can Do Statements:

THE ART OF THINKING UNIT 4

A big change for artists

The National Gallery in Trafalgar Square in London has a collection of paintings that stretches from hundreds of years ago right up to the present day. You can plan a walk that goes chronologically through the centuries – 16th, 17th, 18th century, and so on. As you go through the first rooms, you get used to seeing paintings in dark, heavy colors of brown and black, deep reds and blues, with subjects that are indoors or in huge landscapes that were created by imaginative painters. But something happens [1]__________ in the middle of the 19th century. Suddenly, after about 1845, you start to see paintings with dazzling, bright colors and with vivid outdoor settings. How can this remarkable change be explained?

The answer is twofold. First of all, after the Industrial Revolution, artificial pigments had now begun to be used in paint, [2]__________ . The second reason was the work of a man almost no one has heard of: John Goffe Rand.

Rand was an American, born in 1801 in New Hampshire, but he moved to London when he got married. He was a practical but also a creative man: an inventor and an enthusiastic, competent painter. Like all other painters at the time, he worked mainly with oil paints. The problem with oil paint was how to store it [3]__________ . Painters used to keep the paint in animal bladders, which they could pierce to get the paint out, but these were fragile and short-lived containers. It was almost impossible to move the paint from one place to another or to store it for a long time, [4]__________ . Most artists were used to dealing with this situation, but Rand thought he could do something to improve it.

And so, in 1841, he invented … the metal tube. Taking very thin layers of tin – a metal that would not react with the oil paint, he made small tubes into which the paint could be poured. The tube could then be squeezed gently to get out as much paint as the artist needed and closed again [5]__________ . And they were small and light, so they could be taken wherever the painter wanted. These tubes changed everything for artists. Suddenly, they could go out into wide open spaces, fields, gardens, and streets, taking their paint with them and painting what they saw, not worrying about the paint itself.

The art movement known as "impressionism" partly owes its existence to Rand and his tube. One of the greatest impressionist painters, Renoir, told his son: "… without colors in tubes, there would have been no Cézanne, no Monet, no Sisley, or Pissarro, nothing of what people were to call impressionism."

John Rand patented his invention, but never became especially wealthy because of it, even though the tube that he invented went on to be used in many other ways, [6]__________ .

Train to THINK

Lateral thinking

"Lateral thinking" means solving problems by thinking in a creative way. It means not following the obvious line of thinking. Here is an example.

A man is driving down a city street at 25 km per hour. The speed limit is 30 km per hour. He passes three cars that are traveling at 20 km per hour. A police officer stops him and gives him a $100 fine. Why?

If we think too much about the speed, we may not get the answer. What does the situation NOT tell us? It doesn't tell us information like what time of day it is – so a possible reason for the $100 fine is that it is night time and the man is driving with no lights on his car. Or another possible reason for the fine is that the street is one-way, and the man is driving the wrong way.

7 SPEAKING **Here are more situations. Work in pairs and discuss possible answers.**

1 A father and son are in a bad car crash. They are both taken to the hospital. The son is taken into the operating room. The doctor there looks at the boy and says, "That's my son!" How is this possible?

2 A woman is lying awake in bed. She dials a number on the phone, says nothing, puts the phone down, and then goes to sleep. Why?

3 A man lives on the 12th floor of a building. Every morning, he takes the elevator down to the entrance and leaves the building. In the evening, he gets into the elevator and, if there is someone else in the elevator, he goes directly to the 12th floor. If the elevator is empty, he goes to the 10th floor and walks up two flights of stairs to his apartment. Why?

39

Competency: Creative Thinking

Core Area: Generating ideas

Can Do Statement: Imagines alternatives and possibilities.

In this Train to ***TH!NK*** *section, students are encouraged to ask questions to come up with their own theories and possibilities.*

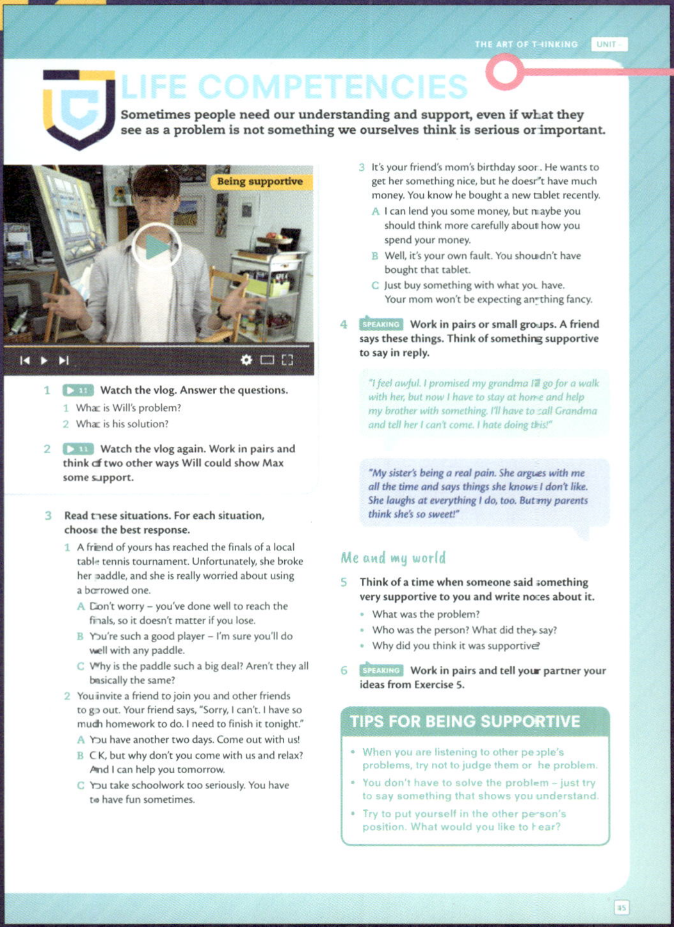

THE ART OF THINKING UNIT

LIFE COMPETENCIES

Sometimes people need our understanding and support, even if what they see as a problem is not something we ourselves think is serious or important.

Being supportive

1 ▶ 11 **Watch the vlog. Answer the questions.**

1 What is Will's problem?

2 What is his solution?

2 ▶ 11 **Watch the vlog again. Work in pairs and think of two other ways Will could show Max some support.**

3 **Read these situations. For each situation, choose the best response.**

1 A friend of yours has reached the finals of a local table tennis tournament. Unfortunately, she broke her paddle, and she is really worried about using a borrowed one.

A Don't worry – you've done well to reach the finals, so it doesn't matter if you lose.

B You're such a good player – I'm sure you'll do well with any paddle.

C Why is the paddle such a big deal? Aren't they all basically the same?

2 You invite a friend to join you and other friends to go out. Your friend says, "Sorry, I can't. I have so much homework to do. I need to finish it tonight."

A You have another two days. Come out with us!

B OK, but why don't you come with us and relax? And I can help you tomorrow.

C You take schoolwork too seriously. You have to have fun sometimes.

3 It's your friend's mom's birthday soon. He wants to get her something nice, but he doesn't have much money. You know he bought a new tablet recently.

A I can lend you some money, but maybe you should think more carefully about how you spend your money.

B Well, it's your own fault. You shouldn't have bought that tablet.

C Just buy something with what you have. Your mom won't be expecting anything fancy.

4 SPEAKING **Work in pairs or small groups. A friend says these things. Think of something supportive to say in reply.**

"I feel awful. I promised my grandma I'd go for a walk with her, but now I have to stay at home and help my brother with something. I'll have to call Grandma and tell her I can't come. I hate doing this!"

"My sister's being a real pain. She argues with me all the time and says things she knows I don't like. She laughs at everything I do, too. But my parents think she's so sweet!"

Me and my world

5 **Think of a time when someone said something very supportive to you and write notes about it.**

- What was the problem?
- Who was the person? What did they say?
- Why did you think it was supportive?

6 SPEAKING **Work in pairs and tell your partner your ideas from Exercise 5.**

TIPS FOR BEING SUPPORTIVE

- When you are listening to other people's problems, try not to judge them or the problem.
- You don't have to solve the problem – just try to say something that shows you understand.
- Try to put yourself in the other person's position. What would you like to hear?

45

Competency: Emotional Development

Core Area: Empathy and relationship skills

Can Do Statement: Showing empathy for the feelings of others.

The following exercises encourage students to show understanding of other peoples' perspectives and feelings.

Student's Book

Each unit of AMERICAN TH!NK builds students' knowledge and skills through a series of carefully constructed learning inputs and activities. Units begin with a thought-provoking question and introductory video, followed by a series of high-interest readings and abundant opportunities for personalized speaking practice.

Each sequence of exercises helps students unlock the text, while contextualized vocabulary and grammar concepts recycle and build throughout the unit, sharpening students' language proficiency.

Objectives

Learning objectives clearly show unit aims at a glance, including language functions and target vocabulary and grammar concepts.

Get THINKING

Each unit is introduced by a documentary-style video, with questions designed to pique curiosity, activate prior knowledge, and get students thinking critically.

Some units conclude with a focus on developing Life Competencies, while even-numbered units end with exams-style practice pages, ensuring students are well prepared for the challenges that lie ahead.

Train to THINK

Train to Think sections encourage students to reflect on the topics presented in the readings and to express their opinions on meaningful issues, as well as require them to work together to achieve consensus or to solve a problem.

GRAMMAR

Grammar presentations use a scaffolded inductive approach to help students understand the features and structures of English grammar.

Grammar video ▶

These short videos help illustrate and explain grammar concepts in an innovative and memorable way.

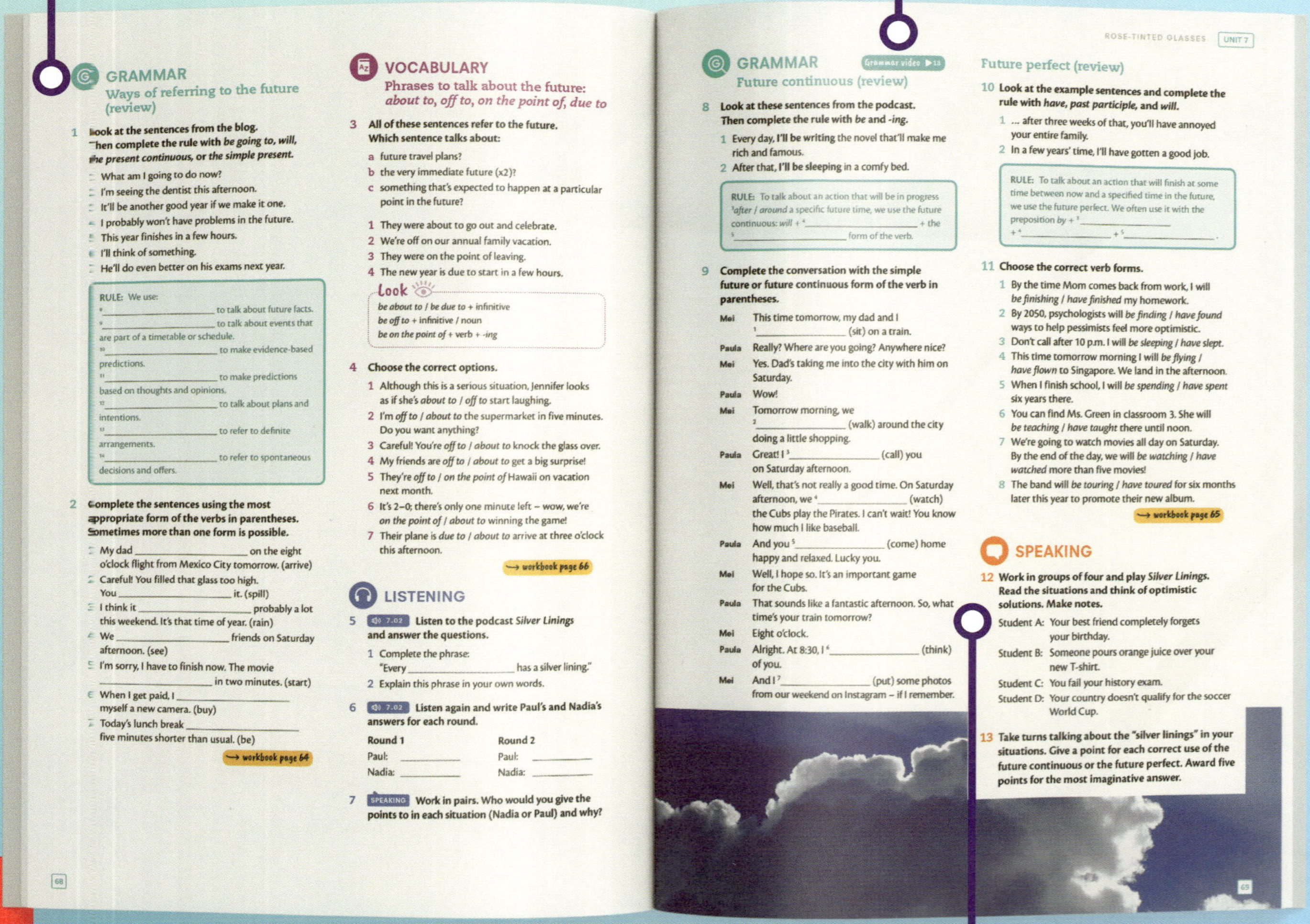

SPEAKING

Frequent opportunities for speaking practice build on students' prior knowledge and encourage them to relate the text to their own experience, personalizing the speaking tasks.

WordWise

These features provide valuable practice with words or phrases that often have multiple uses or meanings in English.

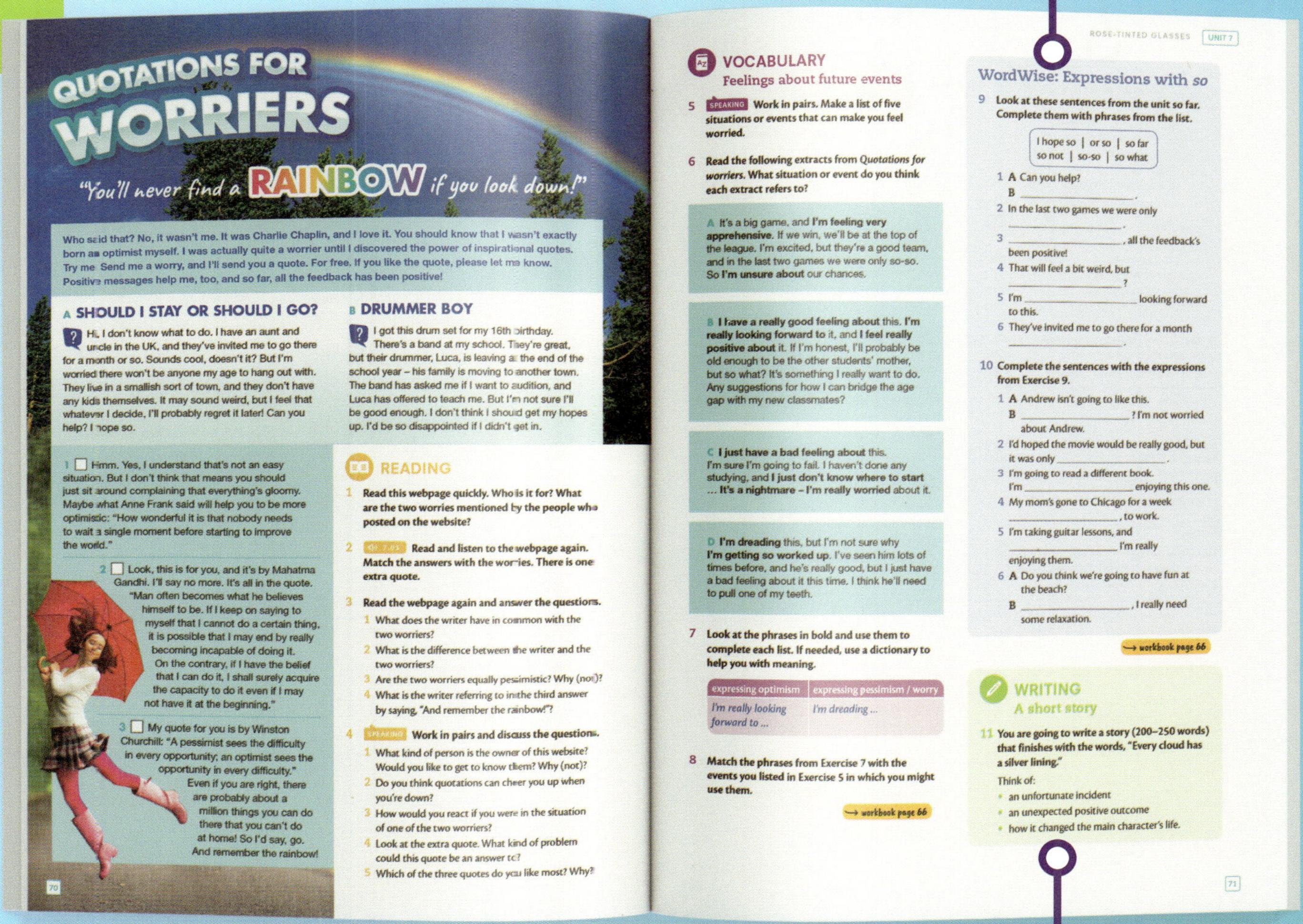

ROSE-TINTED GLASSES | UNIT 7

QUOTATIONS FOR WORRIERS

"You'll never find a RAINBOW if you look down!"

Who said that? No, it wasn't me. It was Charlie Chaplin, and I love it. You should know that I wasn't exactly born an optimist myself. I was actually quite a worrier until I discovered the power of inspirational quotes. Try me. Send me a worry, and I'll send you a quote. For free. If you like the quote, please let me know. Positive messages help me, too, and so far, all the feedback has been positive!

A SHOULD I STAY OR SHOULD I GO?

Hi, I don't know what to do. I have an aunt and uncle in the UK, and they've invited me to go there for a month or so. Sounds cool, doesn't it? But I'm worried there won't be anyone my age to hang out with. They live in a smallish sort of town, and they don't have any kids themselves. It may sound weird, but I feel that whatever I decide, I'll probably regret it later! Can you help? I hope so.

B DRUMMER BOY

I got this drum set for my 16th birthday. There's a band at my school. They're great, but their drummer, Luca, is leaving at the end of the school year – his family is moving to another town. The band has asked me if I want to audition, and Luca has offered to teach me. But I'm not sure I'll be good enough. I don't think I should get my hopes up. I'd be so disappointed if I didn't get in.

1 ☐ Hmm. Yes, I understand that's not an easy situation. But I don't think that means you should just sit around complaining that everything's gloomy. Maybe what Anne Frank said will help you to be more optimistic: "How wonderful it is that nobody needs to wait a single moment before starting to improve the world."

2 ☐ Look, this is for you, and it's by Mahatma Gandhi. I'll say no more. It's all in the quote. "Man often becomes what he believes himself to be. If I keep on saying to myself that I cannot do a certain thing, it is possible that I may end by really becoming incapable of doing it. On the contrary, if I have the belief that I can do it, I shall surely acquire the capacity to do it even if I may not have it at the beginning."

3 ☐ My quote for you is by Winston Churchill: "A pessimist sees the difficulty in every opportunity; an optimist sees the opportunity in every difficulty." Even if you are right, there are probably about a million things you can do there that you can't do at home! So I'd say, go. And remember the rainbow!

READING

1 Read this webpage quickly. Who is it for? What are the two worries mentioned by the people who posted on the website?

2 7.03 Read and listen to the webpage again. Match the answers with the worries. There is one extra quote.

3 Read the webpage again and answer the questions.
1 What does the writer have in common with the two worriers?
2 What is the difference between the writer and the two worriers?
3 Are the two worriers equally pessimistic? Why (not)?
4 What is the writer referring to in the third answer by saying, "And remember the rainbow!"?

4 SPEAKING Work in pairs and discuss the questions.
1 What kind of person is the owner of this website? Would you like to get to know them? Why (not)?
2 Do you think quotations can cheer you up when you're down?
3 How would you react if you were in the situation of one of the two worriers?
4 Look at the extra quote. What kind of problem could this quote be an answer to?
5 Which of the three quotes do you like most? Why?

70

VOCABULARY
Feelings about future events

5 SPEAKING Work in pairs. Make a list of five situations or events that can make you feel worried.

6 Read the following extracts from *Quotations for worriers*. What situation or event do you think each extract refers to?

A It's a big game, and **I'm feeling very apprehensive.** If we win, we'll be at the top of the league. I'm excited, but they're a good team, and in the last two games we were only so-so. So **I'm unsure about** our chances.

B **I have a really good feeling about** this. **I'm really looking forward to** it, and **I feel really positive about** it. If I'm honest, I'll probably be old enough to be the other students' mother, but so what? It's something I really want to do. Any suggestions for how I can bridge the age gap with my new classmates?

C **I just have a bad feeling about** this. I'm sure I'm going to fail. I haven't done any studying, and **I just don't know where to start … It's a nightmare – I'm really worried** about it.

D **I'm dreading** this, but I'm not sure why **I'm getting so worked up.** I've seen him lots of times before, and he's really good, but I just have a bad feeling about it this time. I think he'll need to pull one of my teeth.

7 Look at the phrases in bold and use them to complete each list. If needed, use a dictionary to help you with meaning.

expressing optimism	expressing pessimism / worry
I'm really looking forward to …	*I'm dreading …*

8 Match the phrases from Exercise 7 with the events you listed in Exercise 5 in which you might use them.

→ workbook page 66

WordWise: Expressions with *so*

9 Look at these sentences from the unit so far. Complete them with phrases from the list.

I hope so | or so | so far
so not | so-so | so what

1 A Can you help?
B ____________.
2 In the last two games we were only ____________.
3 ____________, all the feedback's been positive!
4 That will feel a bit weird, but ____________?
5 I'm ____________ looking forward to this.
6 They've invited me to go there for a month ____________.

10 Complete the sentences with the expressions from Exercise 9.
1 A Andrew isn't going to like this.
B ____________? I'm not worried about Andrew.
2 I'd hoped the movie would be really good, but it was only ____________.
3 I'm going to read a different book. I'm ____________ enjoying this one.
4 My mom's gone to Chicago for a week ____________, to work.
5 I'm taking guitar lessons, and ____________ I'm really enjoying them.
6 A Do you think we're going to have fun at the beach?
B ____________, I really need some relaxation.

→ workbook page 66

WRITING
A short story

11 You are going to write a story (200–250 words) that finishes with the words, "Every cloud has a silver lining."

Think of:
- an unfortunate incident
- an unexpected positive outcome
- how it changed the main character's life.

71

WRITING

Each unit includes scaffolded writing activities presented in a real-world context, as either an informal activity or a more academically focused task.

DEVELOPING SPEAKING

These modeled speaking activities provide abundant practice to help students build their speaking confidence while Phrases for Fluency tips focus on authentic language to help them sound more natural.

LIFE COMPETENCIES

These lessons focus on developing a key competency area from the Cambridge Life Competencies Framework. The competencies that students develop throughout **AMERICAN TH!NK** will serve them throughout their lives within their communities and in the world at large.

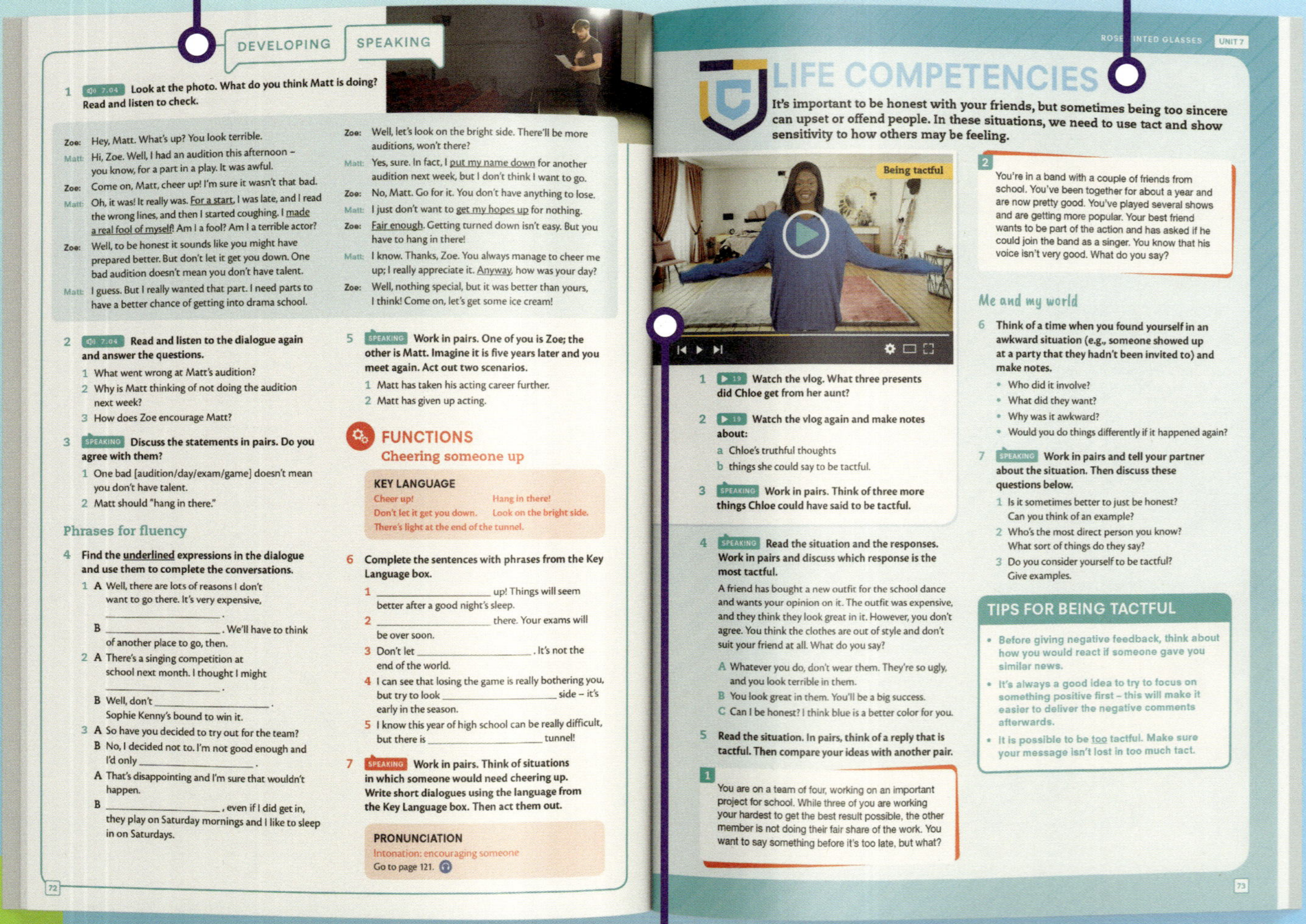

DEVELOPING SPEAKING

1 Look at the photo. What do you think Matt is doing? Read and listen to check.

Zoe: Hey, Matt. What's up? You look terrible.
Matt: Hi, Zoe. Well, I had an audition this afternoon – you know, for a part in a play. It was awful.
Zoe: Come on, Matt, cheer up! I'm sure it wasn't that bad.
Matt: Oh, it was! It really was. For a start, I was late, and I read the wrong lines, and then I started coughing. I made a real fool of myself! Am I a fool? Am I a terrible actor?
Zoe: Well, to be honest it sounds like you might have prepared better. But don't let it get you down. One bad audition doesn't mean you don't have talent.
Matt: I guess. But I really wanted that part. I need parts to have a better chance of getting into drama school.
Zoe: Well, let's look on the bright side. There'll be more auditions, won't there?
Matt: Yes, sure. In fact, I put my name down for another audition next week, but I don't think I want to go.
Zoe: No, Matt. Go for it. You don't have anything to lose.
Matt: I just don't want to get my hopes up for nothing.
Zoe: Fair enough. Getting turned down isn't easy. But you have to hang in there!
Matt: I know. Thanks, Zoe. You always manage to cheer me up; I really appreciate it. Anyway, how was your day?
Zoe: Well, nothing special, but it was better than yours, I think! Come on, let's get some ice cream!

2 Read and listen to the dialogue again and answer the questions.
1 What went wrong at Matt's audition?
2 Why is Matt thinking of not doing the audition next week?
3 How does Zoe encourage Matt?

3 SPEAKING Discuss the statements in pairs. Do you agree with them?
1 One bad [audition/day/exam/game] doesn't mean you don't have talent.
2 Matt should "hang in there."

Phrases for fluency

4 Find the underlined expressions in the dialogue and use them to complete the conversations.

5 SPEAKING Work in pairs. One of you is Zoe; the other is Matt. Imagine it is five years later and you meet again. Act out two scenarios.
1 Matt has taken his acting career further.
2 Matt has given up acting.

FUNCTIONS
Cheering someone up

KEY LANGUAGE
Cheer up! Hang in there!
Don't let it get you down. Look on the bright side.
There's light at the end of the tunnel.

6 Complete the sentences with phrases from the Key Language box.

7 SPEAKING Work in pairs. Think of situations in which someone would need cheering up. Write short dialogues using the language from the Key Language box. Then act them out.

PRONUNCIATION
Intonation: encouraging someone
Go to page 121.

LIFE COMPETENCIES

It's important to be honest with your friends, but sometimes being too sincere can upset or offend people. In these situations, we need to use tact and show sensitivity to how others may be feeling.

1 Watch the vlog. What three presents did Chloe get from her aunt?
2 Watch the vlog again and make notes about:
a Chloe's truthful thoughts
b things she could say to be tactful.
3 SPEAKING Work in pairs. Think of three more things Chloe could have said to be tactful.
4 SPEAKING Read the situation and the responses. Work in pairs and discuss which response is the most tactful.
5 Read the situation. In pairs, think of a reply that is tactful. Then compare your ideas with another pair.

Me and my world

6 Think of a time when you found yourself in an awkward situation (e.g., someone showed up at a party that they hadn't been invited to) and make notes.
7 SPEAKING Work in pairs and tell your partner about the situation. Then discuss these questions below.

TIPS FOR BEING TACTFUL
- Before giving negative feedback, think about how you would react if someone gave you similar news.
- It's always a good idea to try to focus on something positive first – this will make it easier to deliver the negative comments afterwards.
- It is possible to be too tactful. Make sure your message isn't lost in too much tact.

Life Lessons videos

Each Life Competency is introduced by a Life Lessons vlog recorded by a student. These videos help introduce the competency area in a natural and accessible way and serve as a springboard to the activities that follow.

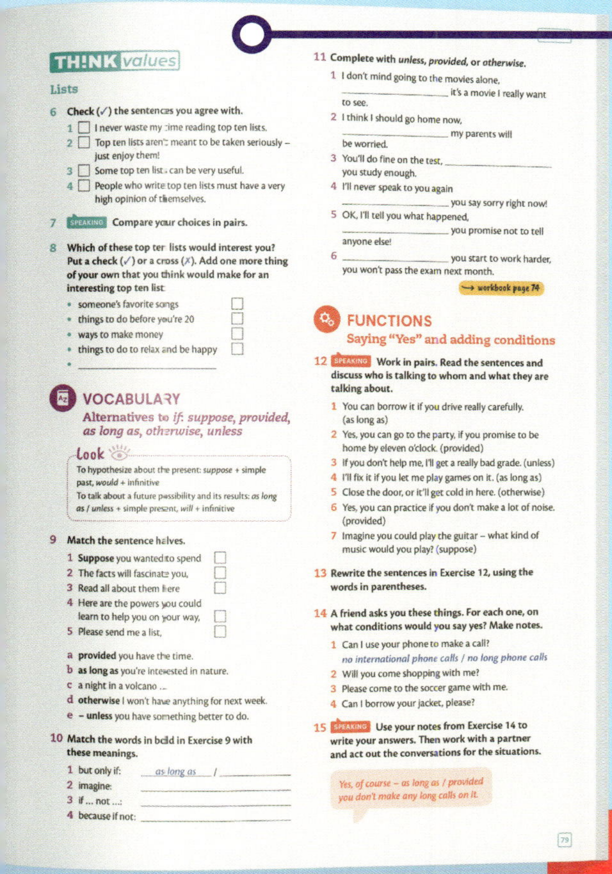

TH!NK values

This feature encourages students to reflect on and discuss a wide range of important values, helping to develop their character as well as their sensitivity to others.

Culture

The Culture sections introduce interesting topics and information about people and places around the world and spark discussion in a speaking task that requires students to make use of the information presented in the text.

WRITING

An extended writing section guides students through the writing process for a variety of text types. Students are presented with a model text for analysis of the task and purpose, and to practice the useful language they will need, before they move on to produce and share their own compositions.

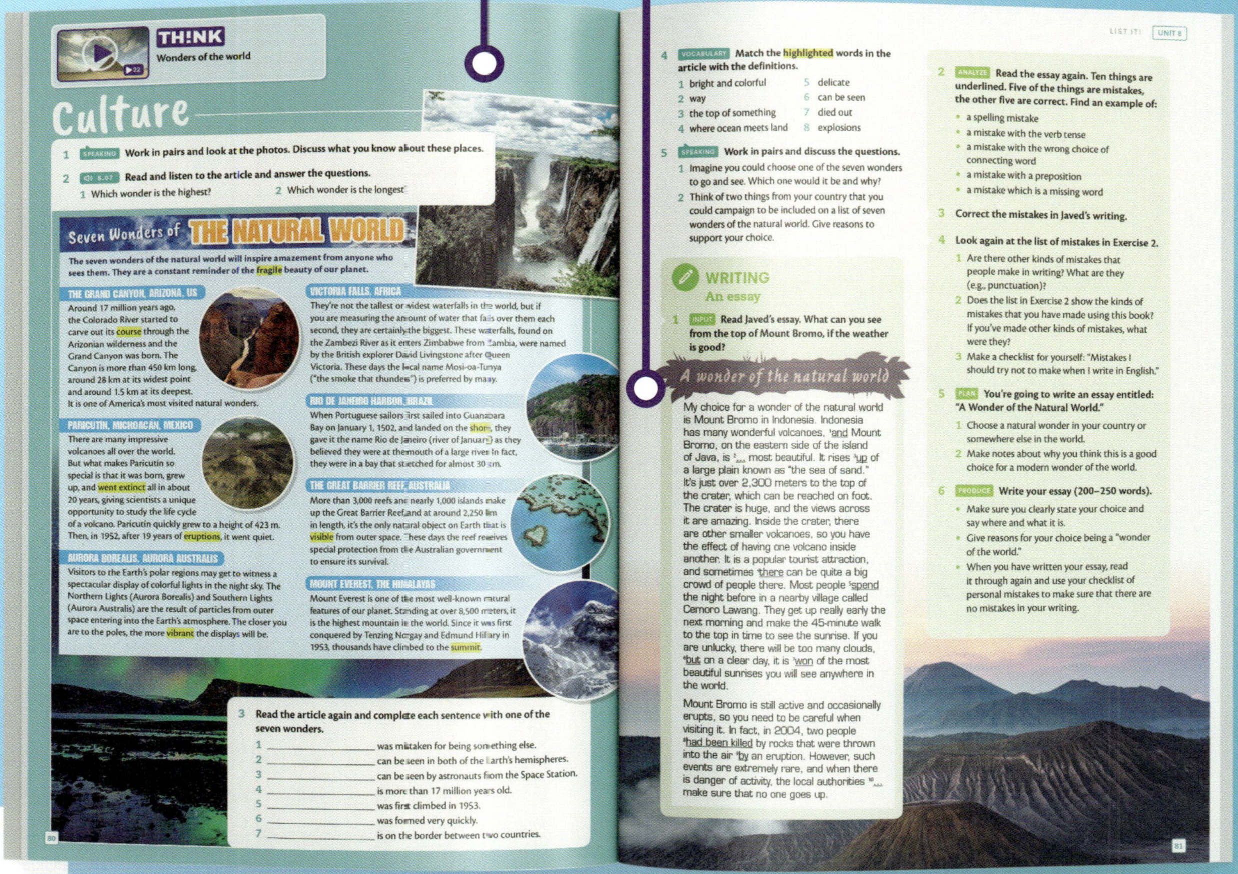

Exams

Exercises on these pages replicate the format of tasks from the Cambridge English Exams.

Cross-references to the Workbook lead to additional exams practice and useful test-taking tips.

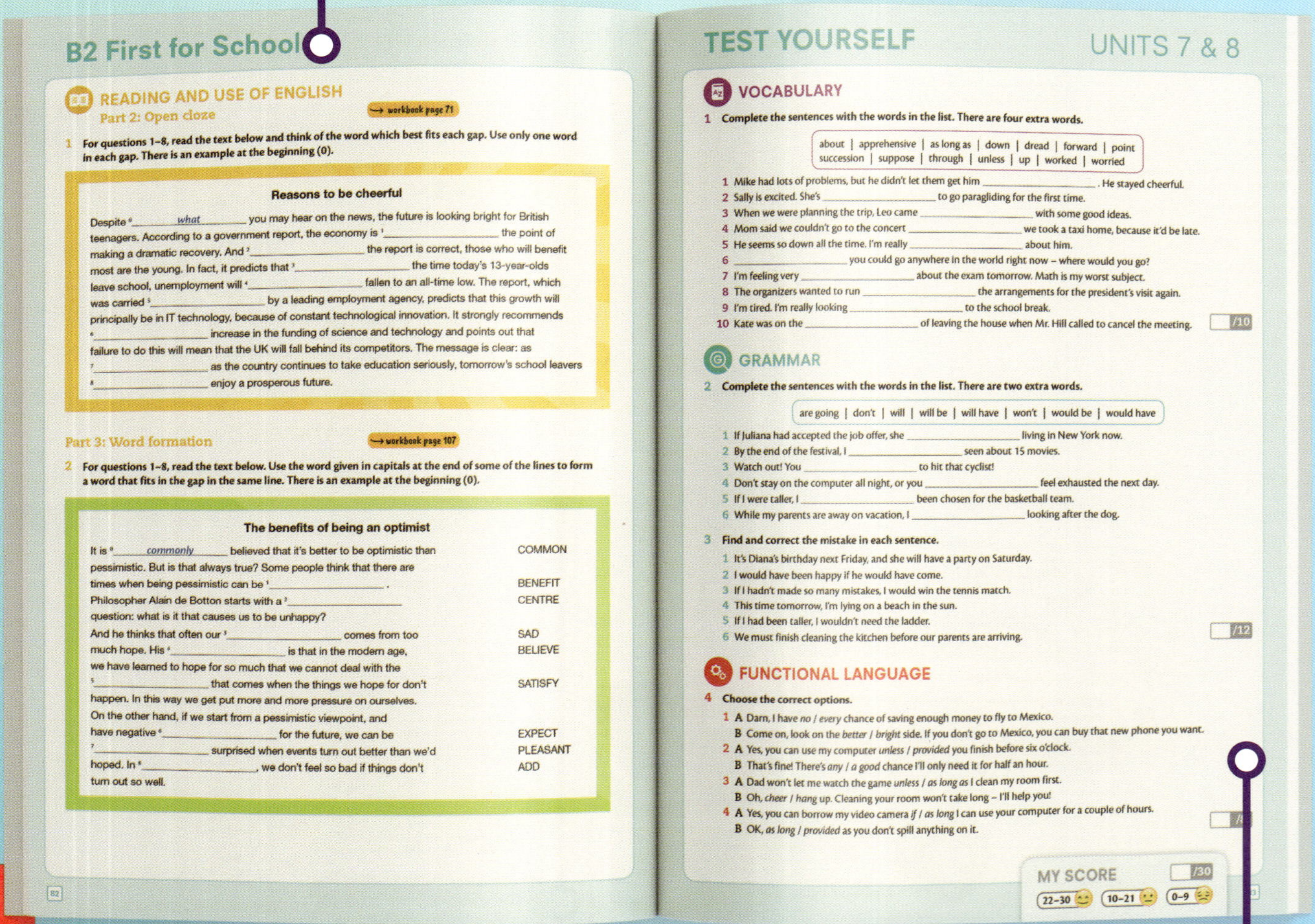

B2 First for School

READING AND USE OF ENGLISH
Part 2: Open cloze
→ workbook page 71

1 For questions 1–8, read the text below and think of the word which best fits each gap. Use only one word in each gap. There is an example at the beginning (0).

Reasons to be cheerful

Despite [0] ___*what*___ you may hear on the news, the future is looking bright for British teenagers. According to a government report, the economy is [1] ______ the point of making a dramatic recovery. And [2] ______ the report is correct, those who will benefit most are the young. In fact, it predicts that [3] ______ the time today's 13-year-olds leave school, unemployment will [4] ______ fallen to an all-time low. The report, which was carried [5] ______ by a leading employment agency, predicts that this growth will principally be in IT technology, because of constant technological innovation. It strongly recommends [6] ______ increase in the funding of science and technology and points out that failure to do this will mean that the UK will fall behind its competitors. The message is clear: as [7] ______ as the country continues to take education seriously, tomorrow's school leavers [8] ______ enjoy a prosperous future.

Part 3: Word formation
→ workbook page 107

2 For questions 1–8, read the text below. Use the word given in capitals at the end of some of the lines to form a word that fits in the gap in the same line. There is an example at the beginning (0).

The benefits of being an optimist

It is [0] ___*commonly*___ believed that it's better to be optimistic than — COMMON
pessimistic. But is that always true? Some people think that there are
times when being pessimistic can be [1] ______ . — BENEFIT
Philosopher Alain de Botton starts with a [2] ______ — CENTRE
question: what is it that causes us to be unhappy?
And he thinks that often our [3] ______ comes from too — SAD
much hope. His [4] ______ is that in the modern age, — BELIEVE
we have learned to hope for so much that we cannot deal with the
[5] ______ that comes when the things we hope for don't — SATISFY
happen. In this way we get put more and more pressure on ourselves.
On the other hand, if we start from a pessimistic viewpoint, and
have negative [6] ______ for the future, we can be — EXPECT
[7] ______ surprised when events turn out better than we'd — PLEASANT
hoped. In [8] ______, we don't feel so bad if things don't — ADD
turn out so well.

82

TEST YOURSELF — UNITS 7 & 8

VOCABULARY

1 Complete the sentences with the words in the list. There are four extra words.

about | apprehensive | as long as | down | dread | forward | point
succession | suppose | through | unless | up | worked | worried

1 Mike had lots of problems, but he didn't let them get him ______ . He stayed cheerful.
2 Sally is excited. She's ______ to go paragliding for the first time.
3 When we were planning the trip, Leo came ______ with some good ideas.
4 Mom said we couldn't go to the concert ______ we took a taxi home, because it'd be late.
5 He seems so down all the time. I'm really ______ about him.
6 ______ you could go anywhere in the world right now – where would you go?
7 I'm feeling very ______ about the exam tomorrow. Math is my worst subject.
8 The organizers wanted to run ______ the arrangements for the president's visit again.
9 I'm tired. I'm really looking ______ to the school break.
10 Kate was on the ______ of leaving the house when Mr. Hill called to cancel the meeting. /10

GRAMMAR

2 Complete the sentences with the words in the list. There are two extra words.

are going | don't | will | will be | will have | won't | would be | would have

1 If Juliana had accepted the job offer, she ______ living in New York now.
2 By the end of the festival, I ______ seen about 15 movies.
3 Watch out! You ______ to hit that cyclist!
4 Don't stay on the computer all night, or you ______ feel exhausted the next day.
5 If I were taller, I ______ been chosen for the basketball team.
6 While my parents are away on vacation, I ______ looking after the dog.

3 Find and correct the mistake in each sentence.

1 It's Diana's birthday next Friday, and she will have a party on Saturday.
2 I would have been happy if he would have come.
3 If I hadn't made so many mistakes, I would win the tennis match.
4 This time tomorrow, I'm lying on a beach in the sun.
5 If I had been taller, I wouldn't need the ladder.
6 We must finish cleaning the kitchen before our parents are arriving. /12

FUNCTIONAL LANGUAGE

4 Choose the correct options.

1 A Darn, I have *no / every* chance of saving enough money to fly to Mexico.
B Come on, look on the *better / bright* side. If you don't go to Mexico, you can buy that new phone you want.
2 A Yes, you can use my computer *unless / provided* you finish before six o'clock.
B That's fine! There's *any / a good* chance I'll only need it for half an hour.
3 A Dad won't let me watch the game *unless / as long as* I clean my room first.
B Oh, *cheer / hang* up. Cleaning your room won't take long – I'll help you!
4 A Yes, you can borrow my video camera *if / as long* I can use your computer for a couple of hours.
B OK, *as long / provided* as you don't spill anything on it.

MY SCORE /30
22–30 10–21 0–9

Test Yourself

The Test Yourself page allows students to check their progress and is based on the language presented in the previous pair of units.

The "emoji" scoring key encourages students to continuously monitor their progress as they move through each level.

Pronunciation

This handy reference at the back of the Student's Book covers sounds that are likely to pose a challenge for English learners and provides additional practice and support via the classroom audio program.

Get it Right!

Cross-references in the Teacher's Book indicate appropriate points within the unit to direct students to this section in the back of the Student's Book. Get it Right! activities help students avoid common errors as identified by the Cambridge English Learner Corpus*.

Cambridge English Corpus

*What is the Cambridge English Learner Corpus?

The Corpus comprises a 50 million-word collection of real-life learners' written and spoken English, derived from actual students taking the Cambridge English exams. We use this information to determine which word structures are more easy or more difficult for English learners, and ultimately, to determine how best to support students when they encounter them.

Workbook

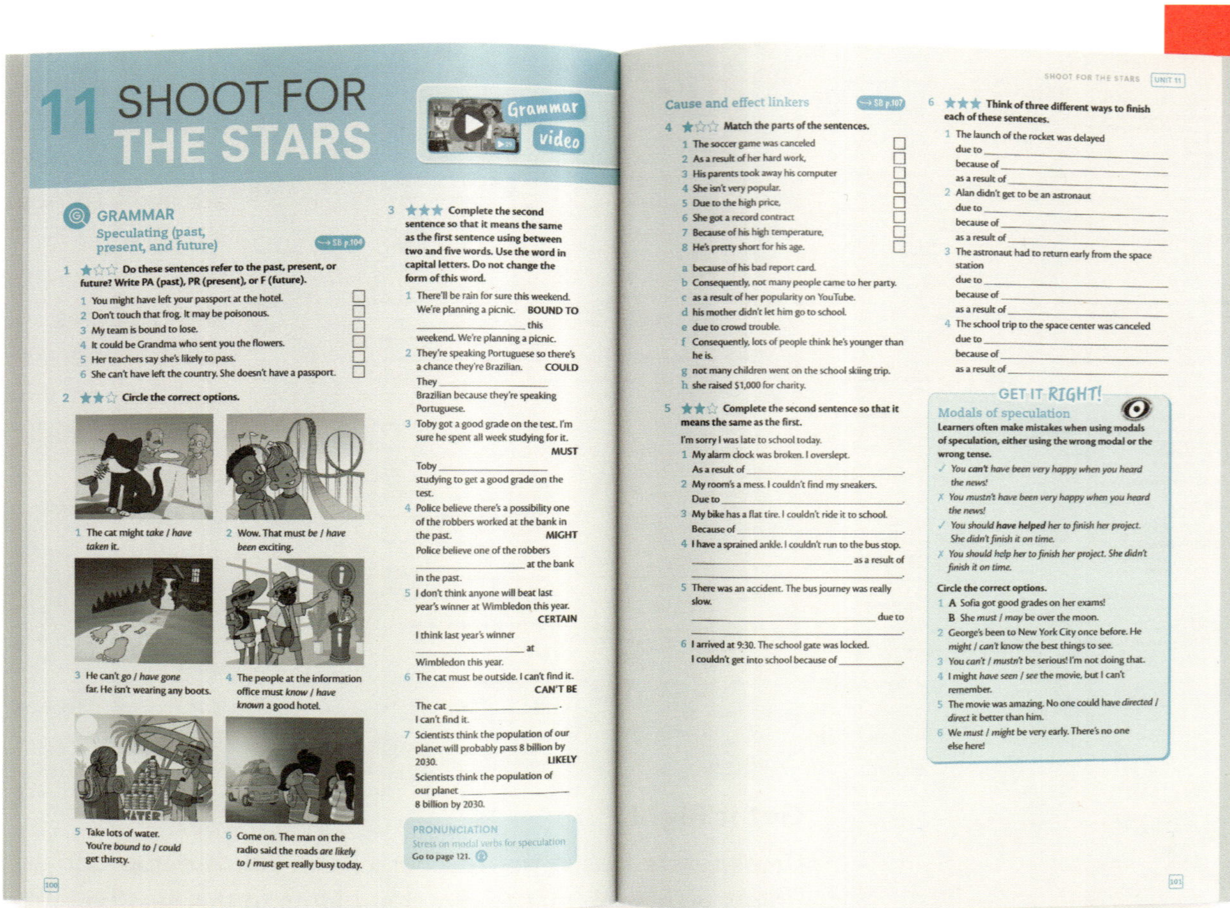

11 SHOOT FOR THE STARS

Grammar video

GRAMMAR
Speculating (past, present, and future)
→ SB p.104

1 ★☆☆ Do these sentences refer to the past, present, or future? Write PA (past), PR (present), or F (future).
1 You might have left your passport at the hotel.
2 Don't touch that frog. It may be poisonous.
3 My team is bound to lose.
4 It could be Grandma who sent you the flowers.
5 Her teachers say she's likely to pass.
6 She can't have left the country. She doesn't have a passport.

2 ★★☆ Circle the correct options.
1 The cat might *take / have taken* it.
2 Wow. That must *be / have been* exciting.
3 He can't *go / have gone* far. He isn't wearing any boots.
4 The people at the information office must *know / have known* a good hotel.
5 Take lots of water. You're *bound to / could* get thirsty.
6 Come on. The man on the radio said the roads *are likely to / must* get really busy today.

3 ★★★ Complete the second sentence so that it means the same as the first sentence using between two and five words. Use the word in capital letters. Do not change the form of this word.
1 There'll be rain for sure this weekend. We're planning a picnic. BOUND TO
___ this weekend. We're planning a picnic.
2 They're speaking Portuguese so there's a chance they're Brazilian. COULD
They ___ Brazilian because they're speaking Portuguese.
3 Toby got a good grade on the test. I'm sure he spent all week studying for it. MUST
Toby ___ studying to get a good grade on the test.
4 Police believe there's a possibility one of the robbers worked at the bank in the past. MIGHT
Police believe one of the robbers ___ at the bank in the past.
5 I don't think anyone will beat last year's winner at Wimbledon this year. CERTAIN
I think last year's winner ___ at Wimbledon this year.
6 The cat must be outside. I can't find it. CAN'T BE
The cat ___. I can't find it.
7 Scientists think the population of our planet will probably pass 8 billion by 2030. LIKELY
Scientists think the population of our planet ___ 8 billion by 2030.

PRONUNCIATION
Stress on modal verbs for speculation
Go to page 121.

100

Cause and effect linkers → SB p.107

4 ★☆☆ Match the parts of the sentences.
1 The soccer game was canceled
2 As a result of her hard work,
3 His parents took away his computer
4 She isn't very popular.
5 Due to the high price,
6 She got a record contract
7 Because of his high temperature,
8 He's pretty short for his age.
a because of his bad report card.
b Consequently, not many people came to her party.
c as a result of her popularity on YouTube.
d his mother didn't let him go to school.
e due to crowd trouble.
f Consequently, lots of people think he's younger than he is.
g not many children went on the school skiing trip.
h she raised $1,000 for charity.

5 ★★☆ Complete the second sentence so that it means the same as the first.
I'm sorry I was late to school today.
1 My alarm clock was broken. I overslept.
As a result of ___
2 My room's a mess. I couldn't find my sneakers.
Due to ___
3 My bike has a flat tire. I couldn't ride it to school.
Because of ___
4 I have a sprained ankle. I couldn't run to the bus stop.
___ as a result of ___
5 There was an accident. The bus journey was really slow.
___ due to ___
6 I arrived at 9:30. The school gate was locked.
I couldn't get into school because of ___

SHOOT FOR THE STARS UNIT 11

6 ★★★ Think of three different ways to finish each of these sentences.
1 The launch of the rocket was delayed
due to ___
because of ___
as a result of ___
2 Alan didn't get to be an astronaut
due to ___
because of ___
as a result of ___
3 The astronaut had to return early from the space station
due to ___
because of ___
as a result of ___
4 The school trip to the space center was canceled
due to ___
because of ___
as a result of ___

GET IT RIGHT!
Modals of speculation
Learners often make mistakes when using modals of speculation, either using the wrong modal or the wrong tense.
✓ *You can't have been very happy when you heard the news!*
✗ *You mustn't have been very happy when you heard the news!*
✓ *You should have helped her to finish her project. She didn't finish it on time.*
✗ *You should help her to finish her project. She didn't finish it on time.*

Circle the correct options.
1 A Sofia got good grades on her exams!
B She *must / may* be over the moon.
2 George's been to New York City once before. He *might / can't* know the best things to see.
3 You *can't / mustn't* be serious! I'm not doing that.
4 I *might have seen / see* the movie, but I can't remember.
5 The movie was amazing. No one could have *directed / direct* it better than him.
6 We *must / might* be very early. There's no one else here!

101

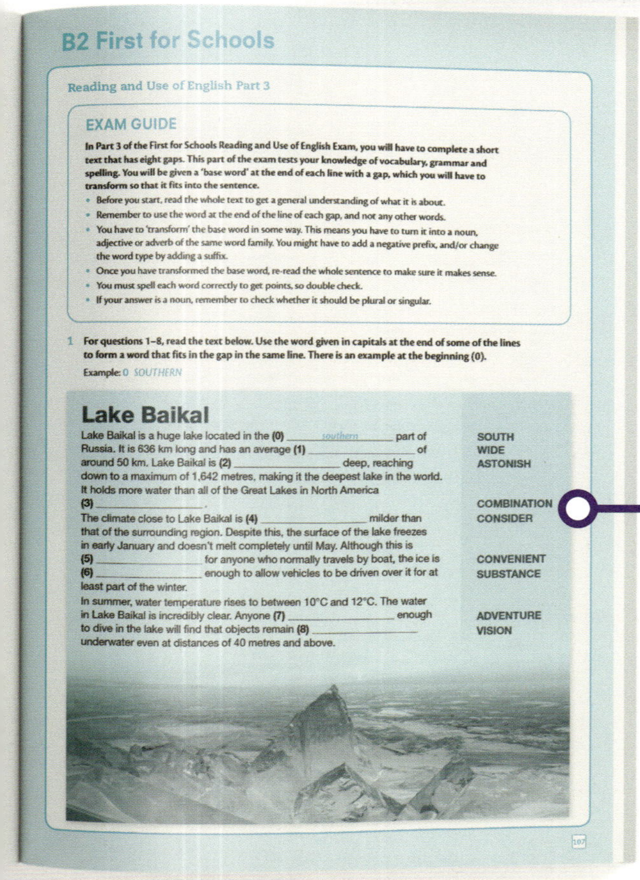

B2 First for Schools

Reading and Use of English Part 3

EXAM GUIDE
In Part 3 of the First for Schools Reading and Use of English Exam, you will have to complete a short text that has eight gaps. This part of the exam tests your knowledge of vocabulary, grammar and spelling. You will be given a 'base word' at the end of each line with a gap, which you will have to transform so that it fits into the sentence.
- Before you start, read the whole text to get a general understanding of what it is about.
- Remember to use the word at the end of the line of each gap, and not any other words.
- You have to 'transform' the base word in some way. This means you have to turn it into a noun, adjective or adverb of the same word family. You might have to add a negative prefix, and/or change the word type by adding a suffix.
- Once you have transformed the base word, re-read the whole sentence to make sure it makes sense.
- You must spell each word correctly to get points, so double check.
- If your answer is a noun, remember to check whether it should be plural or singular.

1 For questions 1–8, read the text below. Use the word given in capitals at the end of some of the lines to form a word that fits in the gap in the same line. There is an example at the beginning (0).
Example: 0 SOUTHERN

Lake Baikal
Lake Baikal is a huge lake located in the (0) *southern* part of Russia. It is 636 km long and has an average (1) ___ of around 50 km. Lake Baikal is (2) ___ deep, reaching down to a maximum of 1,642 metres, making it the deepest lake in the world. It holds more water than all of the Great Lakes in North America (3) ___.
The climate close to Lake Baikal is (4) ___ milder than that of the surrounding region. Despite this, the surface of the lake freezes in early January and doesn't melt completely until May. Although this is (5) ___ for anyone who normally travels by boat, the ice is (6) ___ enough to allow vehicles to be driven over it for at least part of the winter.
In summer, water temperature rises to between 10°C and 12°C. The water in Lake Baikal is incredibly clear. Anyone (7) ___ enough to dive in the lake will find that objects remain (8) ___ underwater even at distances of 40 metres and above.

SOUTH
WIDE
ASTONISH
COMBINATION
CONSIDER
CONVENIENT
SUBSTANCE
ADVENTURE
VISION

107

The Workbook offers extra practice of the language and skills presented in the Student's Book. Handy cross-references immediately following activities in the Student's Book direct students to corresponding pages in the Workbook, where they can get additional practice.

Cambridge Exams Practice

The Cambridge Exams sections provide useful tips and practice to help students prepare for Cambridge English as well as other high-stakes international exams.

AMERICAN TH!NK Digital Support

Presenting all your digital tools together in one place!

With **AMERICAN TH!NK**, everything you need is at your fingertips, including Presentation Plus, the powerful front-of-class presentation tool with complete course content, the entire classroom audio and video programs, Teacher's Resource Bank, and Test Generators.

Presentation Plus

- Student's Book and Workbook with interactive exercises
- Embedded links to classroom audio and video
- Additional games and activities
- Accessible online and offline.

Teacher's Resource Bank

- Online teacher resource area with support for projects, graded grammar and vocabulary practice worksheets, video worksheets, writing templates, extra speaking activities, and more!
- Test Generator: an easy-to-use tool to customize and create end of unit, end of term, and end of year tests, as well as exam practice tests.

Collaboration Plus

- Students can work together on digital projects online using the Collaboration Plus tools and teachers can set, view, support, and grade the work.
- Teachers can share students' project work with the class in the Showcase area.

Practice Extra

- Mobile-friendly platform and content
- Bite-sized learning activities with audio and video
- Performance tracking.

For updated information on **AMERICAN TH!NK**'s Digital Tools, visit **cambridge.org/americanthink2e** or scan this QR code.

How to use the Teacher's Book

The AMERICAN TH!NK wraparound Teacher's Book is designed to help you plan and deliver highly effective lessons easily and seamlessly.

White panel side notes provide guided lesson support and include model student responses in activities and answers to questions.

Light blue panel notes provide additional background information and optional suggestions for building and expanding on lessons.

Purple panels identify lesson objectives and assist with unit navigation.

Yellow panels identify potential homework and flipped-classroom ideas.

Red panels alert teachers to available teaching resources and point out areas where students are likely to struggle.

Warmer

Ideas to introduce students to the unit's topic help activate their prior knowledge and experience and encourage classroom discussion.

Get TH!NKing

Strategies to help teachers get the best use out of the Get **TH!NK**ing videos and activities ensure that students are primed to discuss the unit topic.

Resources for this unit

An at-a-glance listing of all the lesson support available for the unit appears in the bottom panel, including available teaching resources, video, digital support, and assessment tools.

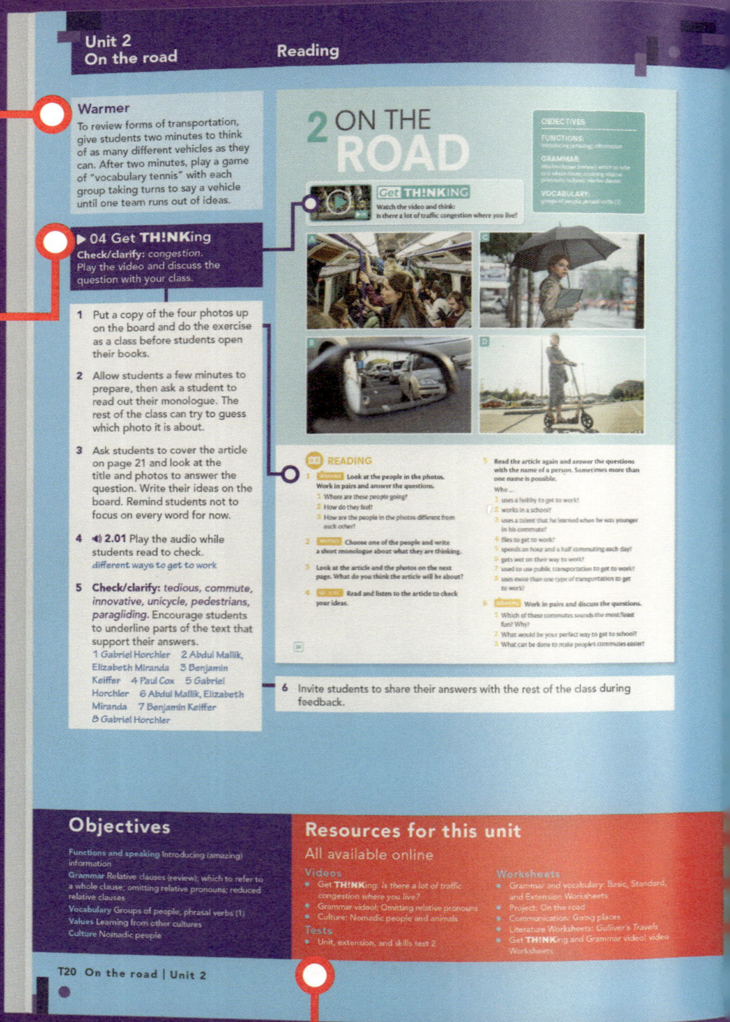

Unit 2
On the road

Reading

Warmer
To review forms of transportation, give students two minutes to think of as many different vehicles as they can. After two minutes, play a game of "vocabulary tennis" with each group taking turns to say a vehicle until one team runs out of ideas.

▶ 04 Get TH!NKing
Check/clarify: congestion.
Play the video and discuss the question with your class.

1 Put a copy of the four photos up on the board and do the exercise as a class before students open their books.

2 Allow students a few minutes to prepare, then ask a student to read out their monologue. The rest of the class can try to guess which photo it is about.

3 Ask students to cover the article on page 21 and look at the title and photos to answer the question. Write their ideas on the board. Remind students not to focus on every word for now.

4 2.01 Play the audio while students read to check.
different ways to get to work

5 Check/clarify: tedious, commute, innovative, unicycle, pedestrians, paragliding. Encourage students to underline parts of the text that support their answers.
1 Gabriel Horchler 2 Abdul Mallik, Elizabeth Miranda 3 Benjamin Keiffer 4 Paul Cox 5 Gabriel Horchler 6 Abdul Mallik, Elizabeth Miranda 7 Benjamin Keiffer 8 Gabriel Horchler

2 ON THE ROAD

6 Invite students to share their answers with the rest of the class during feedback.

Objectives

Resources for this unit
All available online

T20 On the road | Unit 2

Alternative Activities

Ideas for alternative classroom activities give teachers additional flexibility and freedom to dive deeper into rich language-building opportunities.

Homework

Useful ideas for activities that students could do at home to consolidate in-class learning and encourage independent study.

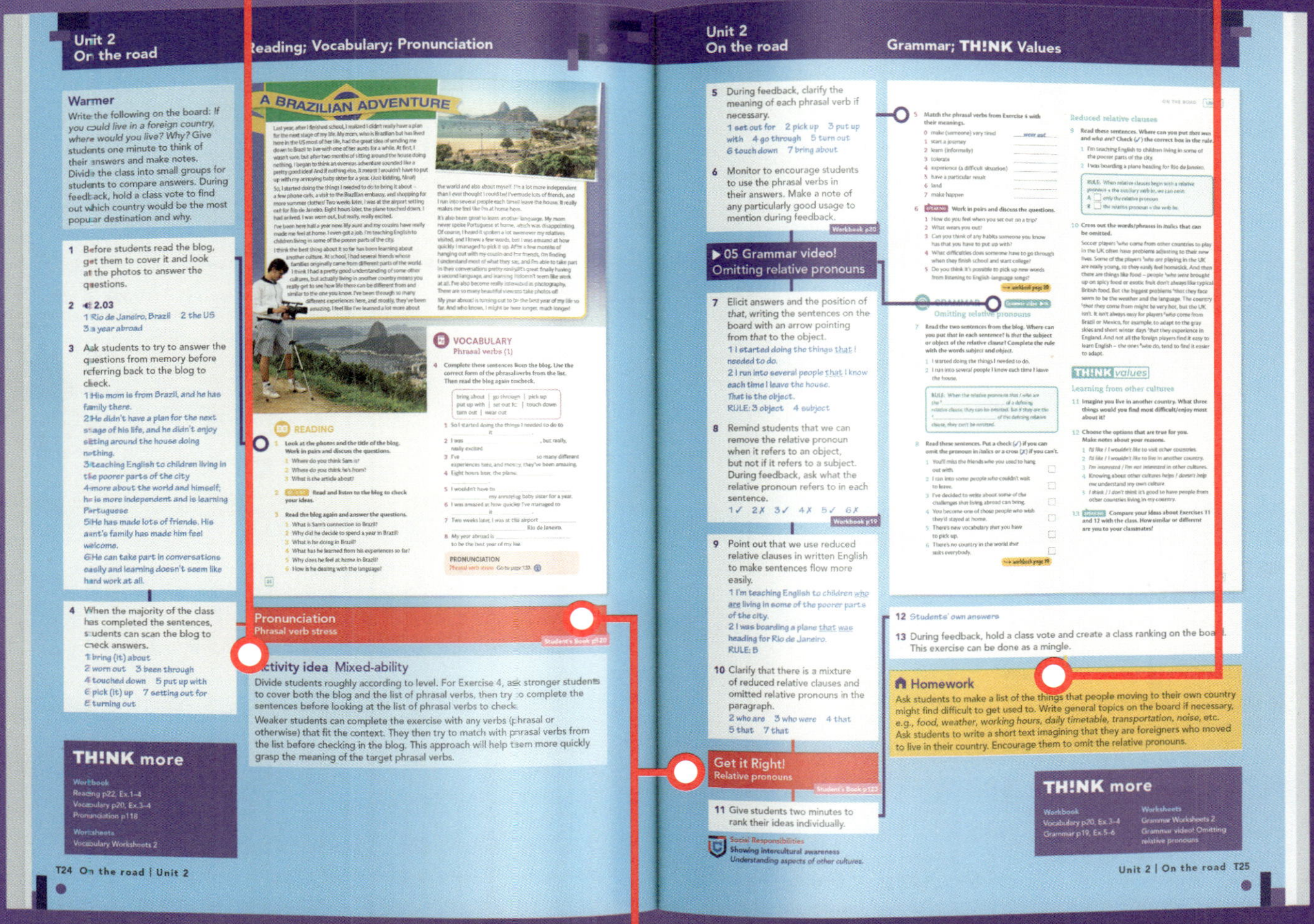

Get it Right! and Pronunciation

These notes help alert teachers to potential problem areas for English learners and offer mitigation and/or remediation strategies and tools.

Cambridge Framework for Life Competencies

This icon identifies which Life Competency is being developed and what teachers should expect students at this level to be able to do via a Can-Do statement.

WELCOME

A WHAT A STORY!

A lucky pilot

1 W.01 **Complete the conversation with the verbs from the list in the correct tense. Then listen and check your answers.**

add | ~~crash~~ | destroy | dive | end | find
hit | keep | manage | pull | scream | set

Mike So, did you see that story about the plane that [0] *crashed* into the ocean?
Finn No, I didn't. What happened?
Mike Well, this guy [1] ________ off from Florida in his plane – a small one, only one engine – to go to New Orleans.
Finn Wow – that's a long way.
Mike Right, and it's usually too far for a plane like that, but he had [2] ________ extra fuel tanks. However, after he had begun his journey, he realized he didn't have enough fuel to [3] ________ on flying, so he radioed New Orleans and told them that he was in trouble. He told them he had to land the plane in the Gulf of Mexico.
Finn In the Gulf of Mexico?!
Mike Yes, there was a fishing boat not far away that was able to pick the pilot up. But here's the incredible thing – and you can see it in a video. The plane had a parachute, but it didn't work, and the plane started to [4] ________ toward the water! But then almost at the last minute, the parachute pulled the plane horizontal, just before it [5] ________ the water. The impact almost [6] ________ the plane.
Finn And the pilot?
Mike He was OK. He [7] ________ to get out of the plane and into a life raft from the fishing boat. Then the people from the fishing boat came and [8] ________ him out of the raft and took him to the ship. He wasn't injured, so he didn't [9] ________ up in the hospital or anything. Now they're trying to [10] ________ out what went wrong.
Finn Wow – I'd have been so scared if I'd been in that plane. I'd have [11] ________ really loudly!

2 **Read the dialogue again. Answer the questions.**
1 Where was the plane flying to and from?
2 Why had the pilot added extra fuel tanks?
3 What did the pilot use to try to land the plane safely in the water?
4 How was the pilot rescued?

Descriptive verbs

3 **Match the verbs with the definitions.**
1 demolish — a to hit very hard and break
2 dive — b to run away quickly
3 flee — c to go down quickly
4 grab — d to destroy completely
5 rage — e to shout loudly in a high pitch
6 scream — f to take hold of something quickly
7 smash — g to hit
8 strike — h to spread uncontrollably

4 **Complete the sentences with the correct form of one of the verbs from Exercise 3.**
0 When the clock *struck* 12, I knew it was time to go home.
1 When war broke out, hundreds of people had to ________ the country.
2 I went back to my old school, but it wasn't there any more: it had been ________ .
3 I was late for the bus, so I just ________ my bag and ran to the bus stop!
4 The fire at the old factory ________ for over three hours.
5 She got really angry and ________ a plate against the wall.
6 They ________ , but nobody heard them.
7 She ________ off the bridge and into the river.

4

WELCOME

Phrasal verbs

5 **Complete the sentences from the dialogue on page 4. Then read again and check your answers.**
1 The pilot ________ from Florida in his plane to go to New Orleans.
2 The pilot wasn't injured so he didn't ________ in the hospital.
3 Now they're trying to ________ what went wrong with the fuel calculations.

6 **Choose the correct words.**
1 My father's health has improved so much since he *gave up* / *ended up* smoking.
2 She wanted to get fit, so she *gave up* / *took up* judo.
3 It's a bit of a problem, but I'm sure we can *sort it out* / *blow it out*.
4 If we *get on* / *keep on* walking this slowly, we won't get there before dark.
5 We're going to the big game tomorrow – I'm *looking forward to* / *looking into* it.
6 He's very tall, and he has red hair, so he really *stands out* / *looks out* in a crowd.
7 I got there really late because the bus *broke down* / *blew out*.
8 All the restaurants were closed, so we *took up* / *ended up* eating at a fast-food place.

Childhood memories

7 SPEAKING **Work with a partner. What do you remember about your first visit to a movie theater (e.g., who you went with, what the movie was, etc.)?**

8 **Read this extract from an autobiography. Which of the things that you remember are mentioned?**

Movie paradise

I'm in my seventies now, and I used to love going to the movies when I was a kid. Back in the 1950s, there used to be a thing called Children's Matinee at the movie theater in the town where we lived. It was wonderful! Every Saturday morning, the theater would show movies for kids – and only kids. They showed cartoons and cowboy movies, adventure movies, detective movies, and science fiction – everything that kids loved back then (and still do I guess!).

My brother used to take me – he was five years older than me. We'd always try to get there early so we could get seats in the front row, or at least one or two rows back. The theater sold ice cream and popcorn; we would buy as much as we could, and then sit and watch the movies while stuffing ourselves with food.

We loved the cartoons – we laughed a lot. Our favorite was always *Tom and Jerry*, and we cheered when we saw them. And then there were the adventure movies. The plots were often terrible, and the dialogue, too, but we really didn't care – after all, we were kids! We used to boo the villains and cheer on the heroes. Some kids used to throw popcorn at the screen when the villain came on – the movie theater staff sometimes tried to stop us, but usually they gave up! The ending was always completely predictable, of course – the hero always won – and we'd cheer like crazy when he did!

9 **Read the extract again and answer the questions.**
1 Who couldn't go to the Children's Matinees?
2 Who did the writer go with?
3 Why did they go early?
4 When did the children usually cheer?
5 When did they boo?

Elements of a story

10 **Complete the text with words from the list.**

characters | dialogue | ending
hero | plot | set | villain

I read a book last week called *Moscow Mystery*. It was a thriller – a kind of detective story. It is [1] ________ in Moscow. The [2] ________ of the story is a woman named Valentina, who helps many of the other [3] ________ to escape from a terrible situation – they have been kidnapped by a horrible old man named Nikolai, who's the [4] ________ of the story.
Anyway, the book's fairly good. I thought the overall [5] ________ was pretty exciting, and it had a nice unexpected twist at the end.
(I won't tell you the [6] ________ , though, in case you read the book yourself.) And I really liked the [7] ________ , too – the conversations between the different characters sound like real people talking to each other. A good read – I'd recommend it.

11 SPEAKING **In small groups, think of an example of each of these from a movie or book.**
1 a great hero
2 a terrifying villain
3 an amazing plot
4 a satisfying ending

Talking about past routines

12 **Complete the sentences from the extract "Movie paradise." Use *would* or *used to*.**
1 I ________ love going to the movies as a kid.
2 My brother ________ take me.
3 The hero always won, and we ________ cheer when he did.
4 Some kids ________ throw popcorn.

5

1 W.01
1 set 2 added 3 keep 4 dive 5 hit 6 destroyed
7 managed 8 pulled 9 end 10 find 11 screamed

2 1 from Florida to New Orleans
2 Because it's usually too far for a small plane.
3 He tried to use a parachute.
4 People from a fishing boat rescued him.

3 1 d 2 c 3 b 4 f 5 h 6 e 7 a 8 g

4 1 flee 2 demolished 3 grabbed 4 raged / was raging / had been raging 5 smashed 6 screamed / were screaming 7 dived / dove / had dived

5 1 set off 2 end up 3 find out

6 1 gave up 2 took up 3 sort it out 4 keep on 5 looking forward to 6 stands out 7 broke down 8 ended up

7 Students' own answers

8 Students' own answers

9 1 Adults couldn't go. 2 He/She went with his/her older brother. 3 They went early so they could get seats near the front. 4 They cheered when they saw the cartoon / *Tom and Jerry* and when the hero won. 5 They booed when they saw the villain.

10 1 set 2 hero 3 characters 4 villain 5 plot 6 ending 7 dialogue

11 Students' own answers

12 1 used to (*would* is not possible as the sentence is describing a state) 2 used to (*would* is also possible) 3 would (*used to* is also possible) 4 used to (*would* is also possible)

TH!NK more

Workbook
A What a story! pp4–5, Ex.1–7

B AN UNCERTAIN FUTURE

Future plans

1 W.02 **Read the conversation. Put the phrases into the correct places. Then listen and check.**

when you finish school | get a good degree | to start a family | and then travel the world | then retire | before I think about settling down

Mom So, Jordan, have you thought about which college you want to go to yet?
Jordan I told you, Mom – I'm not so sure that I want to go to college.
Mom But if you [1] ______, you'll be guaranteed a secure future. You know, maybe in ten years, you'll be managing a huge company!
Jordan But that's just it, Mom – I don't want to manage a big company or a small company either. I don't want to spend 40 years doing that and [2] ______ and wonder where my life went. That's not the future I want – I think.
Mom Well, so what are you going to do [3] ______ then?
Jordan I'm not sure yet. Maybe work, save a little money, [4] ______ for a few months, you know, get some life experience.
Mom Well, that won't do you much good. In this day and age, employers want people with work experience, not travel experience.
Jordan Well, maybe you're right, Mom. But even so, I want some time for myself [5] ______.
Mom There's nothing wrong with settling down. That's what your father and I did.
Jordan I know, Mom, and that's fine – it was fine for you and Dad, back in the last century. But the world's different now, and people have such different goals, ideas, everything!
Mom Yes, I suppose so. You're right.
Jordan But don't worry, Mom. I mean, I'd like [6] ______ at some point. So you'll be playing with your grandchildren one day – I hope.
Mom Well, I'm delighted to hear that, Jordan!

2 **Mark the sentences T (true), F (false), or DS (doesn't say).**

1 Jordan and his mom have talked about college before. ☐
2 Jordan's mother works for a big company. ☐
3 Jordan definitely wants to finish school and travel. ☐
4 Jordan's mother values work experience. ☐
5 Jordan would like to have children. ☐

Life plans

3 **Complete the sentences with the words from the list.**

career | degree | finish | promoted | retired | settled | start | travel

1 My plan was to ______ the world, but when I got to Italy, I loved it so much that I stayed.
2 I have no idea what to do when I ______ school.
3 She got an excellent ______ from Cambridge University.
4 He worked really hard, and got ______ to junior manager.
5 My uncle got sick when he was 55, so he ______ early.
6 A course in psychology is a good way to start a ______ in teaching.
7 My cousin has always moved from one place to another – he's never ______ down.
8 They feel they don't have enough money yet to ______ a family.

4 SPEAKING **Work in pairs and discuss the questions. Then compare your answers in small groups.**

1 At what age do people finish school in your country? Do you think this is the right age? Why (not)?
2 At what age can people retire in your country? Is it the same for men and for women? Do you think this is the right age? Why (not)?
3 Is it important in your country to get a degree in order to have a good career? Why (not)?

Future continuous

5 **Complete the sentences with the future continuous form of the verbs in the list.**

listen | live | study | travel | wonder | work

Five years from now,
1 I'll ______ the world.
2 I won't ______ at home anymore.
3 I'll ______ at a university.
4 Some of my friends will ______ for big international companies.
5 I'll ______ to the same kind of music as I do now.
6 I'll still ______ what to do with my life.

6 SPEAKING **Work in pairs. Which of the statements from Exercise 5 are true for you? Which statements are true for your partner?**

Future perfect

7 **Complete the text with the future perfect form of the verbs in parentheses.**

Don't worry about Jordan. He'll be fine. By the time he's 20, he [1] ______ (finish) school, and he [2] ______ (save) enough money to travel around the world. By the time he's 30, Jordan [3] ______ (be) to every continent and [4] ______ (decide) what he wants to do with his life. And by the time he's 40, Jordan [5] ______ (settle) down and [6] ______ (start) a family.

Being emphatic: *so* and *such*

8 **Complete these sentences from the dialogue on page 6.**

1 I'm not ______ sure that I want to go to college.
2 People have ______ different goals, ideas, everything!

9 **Make these statements more emphatic. Use *so* or *such*.**

0 Going to college is an important moment in your life.
Going to college is such an important moment in your life.
1 Getting a job offer is an amazing feeling.
2 Spending money that you earned and saved is satisfying.
3 It's an awful waste of time to go traveling.
4 Deciding to settle down is a huge decision.
5 Worrying about their children is terrifying for parents.

10 **Who do you think said the things in Exercise 9, Jordan or his mom? Write J or M in the boxes.**

0 *M* 1 ☐ 2 ☐ 3 ☐ 4 ☐ 5 ☐

11 SPEAKING **Work with a partner. Which of the statements in Exercise 9 do you (not) agree with?**

Extreme adjectives

12 **Look at the emphatic statements in Exercise 9 again. Find words that mean:**

1 really scary ______
2 really good ______
3 really bad ______
4 really big ______

13 **Write the words in the correct places.**

delighted | exciting | freezing | funny | great | hot | huge | interesting | miserable | scared | terrible | tiny

	Gradable adjective	Extreme adjective
1	bad	______ / awful
2	good	wonderful / ______ / amazing
3	______	fascinating
4	______	terrified
5	______	hilarious
6	happy	______
7	sad	______
8	______	thrilling
9	big	______ / enormous
10	small	______ / minute
11	cold	______
12	______	boiling / sweltering

14 **Complete the dialogues with suitable extreme adjectives.**

0 A The water's cold, isn't it?
B More than that – it's *freezing*!
1 A She's really funny, isn't she?
B Yes, she's ______.
2 A That house is pretty small.
B Small?! It's ______!
3 A I thought the movie was really good, didn't you?
B Yes, I thought it was ______.
4 A Wow! I was scared from beginning to end of that!
B Me, too! In fact, I was ______!
5 A Was the concert really so bad?
B Yes, it was. It was ______.

15 WRITING **With a partner, write three more dialogues, using words from Exercise 13 that don't appear in Exercise 14.**

1 W.02
1 get a good degree 2 then retire
3 when you finish school 4 and then travel the world
5 before I think about settling down 6 to start a family

2 1 T 2 DS 3 F 4 T 5 T

3 1 travel 2 finish 3 degree 4 promoted 5 retired
6 career 7 settled 8 start

4 Students' own answers

5 1 be traveling 2 be living 3 be studying 4 be working
5 be listening 6 be wondering

6 Students' own answers

7 1 will have finished 2 will have saved 3 will have been
4 will have decided 5 will have settled 6 will have started

8 1 so 2 such

9 1 Getting a job offer is such an amazing feeling.
2 Spending money that you earned and saved is so satisfying.
3 It's such an awful waste of time to go traveling.
4 Deciding to settle down is such a huge decision.
5 Worrying about their children is so terrifying for parents.

10 Suggested answers: 1 M 2 J 3 M 4 J 5 M

11 Students' own answers

12 1 terrifying 2 amazing 3 awful 4 huge

13 1 terrible 2 great 3 interesting 4 scared 5 funny
6 delighted 7 miserable 8 exciting 9 huge 10 tiny
11 freezing 12 hot

14 1 hilarious 2 tiny/minute 3 fantastic/wonderful/great/amazing 4 terrified 5 awful/terrible

15 Students' own answers

TH!NK more

Workbook
B An uncertain future pp5–6, Ex.1–7

Welcome
C How people behave

C HOW PEOPLE BEHAVE
Conversations

1 W.03 **Listen and match the conversations to the pictures. Write 1–3 in the boxes.**

2 W.03 **Listen again. Complete the spaces with one word.**

Conversation 1

Dev What's the matter with you?
Megan Didn't you see? I held the door open for that elderly lady; I let her go through in front of me.
Dev Yes, I saw that. It was very thoughtful of you. Very [1]__________ .
Megan But she just walked past me and didn't say thank you. She didn't even look at me! It's so [2]__________ , I think.
Dev Oh, you [3]__________ get so worked up. She was probably just thinking about something else.

Conversation 2

Milly Hi, Jack. Here are your headphones.
Jack My headphones! I've been looking for them. So, *you* took them?
Milly Yes – sorry, I should [4]__________ asked you, I know, but ...
Jack Well, give them back. You're not [5]__________ to take my things without asking!
Milly OK. I'm sorry. But you don't have to be so [6]__________ , do you?

Conversation 3

Jason I'm so upset. I just heard that Paul, one of my best friends, is going to move to Argentina.
Sarah Oh, that's disappointing. But never [7]__________ , you have other friends, don't you?
Jason Yes, I know, but I'm going to miss him a lot. He's really fun to [8]__________ out with.
Sarah Well, you don't [9]__________ to lose touch with him, do you? You can Skype.
Jason That's right. And maybe my parents will [10]__________ me go and visit him sometime.

3 SPEAKING **Work with a partner. What would you have said in these situations if you were:**

- Dev?
- Milly?
- Sarah?

Personality

4 SPEAKING **Work in pairs. Choose six of the adjectives. For each one, think of something that someone could say or do to show that quality.**

calm | cold | generous | lively | patient
polite | rude | selfish | shy | thoughtful
unfriendly | warm

If someone goes on vacation and brings you back a present – well, that's thoughtful.

Using *should*

5 **Write what you would say to reply to these people. Use a form of *should* and a personality adjective.**

0 I'm in a hurry – get out of my way.
Sure, but you shouldn't be so rude!
1 I heard you lost your pen, so I bought you a new one.
____
2 I was hungry, so I ate all the sandwiches, OK?
____
3 I had a big argument with my sister and told her I don't like her now.
____
4 I'd like to say hello to her, but I can't!
____

Career paths

6 SPEAKING **What jobs do these people have? Discuss with a partner.**

7 **Read the article quickly. Which of the jobs from Exercise 6 are mentioned?**

Home New posts Archives

TIPS FOR choosing a career

Choosing a career – something you might end up doing for the rest of your working life – isn't always easy, but equally, it doesn't have to be the agony that it turns into for some people. Here are our tips to help you make up your mind.

A Don't let other people tell you what to do!
There are always people who want you to become a doctor, or work in banking, or be a teacher. Listen to them, but remember it's your life, and it's your decision, so be sure that you're the one who makes that decision!

B Consider what you think you're good at.
It's true that things like salary are important, but don't let financial considerations lead you down the wrong path. Follow your heart and your personality – if you're a very active person, don't choose an office job, even if the pay's good. In the same way, if you don't like work that involves paying lots of attention to detail, think long and hard before you decide to do something like applying to study engineering at a university.

C Your first decision isn't forever.
Some lucky people get it right first time – they start a job, love it right away, and stick with it. But it isn't always like that, so remember – you're allowed to change your mind! Certainly, it's no good agonizing for years: maybe your first job doesn't turn out the way you had wanted it to. That doesn't mean the right job for you isn't right around the corner!

D Do something of value.
Some people choose their career simply because they think they'll earn huge amounts of money (although the careers that pay the most – acting, writing, singing – also have millions of people who never make it to the top). OK, if that's what you want. But, generally, people get more satisfaction out of their career if they feel they are doing something valuable for others. It doesn't have to be charity work – it could be a job that helps other people in the community, like a caregiver for elderly people. Just don't forget that job satisfaction isn't only about money.

8 SPEAKING **Put the four tips (A–D) from the text in order to show how useful you think each one is (1 = most useful, 4 = least useful). Compare your ideas with a partner.**

Decisions

9 **Complete the questions with the words and phrases from the list.**

come to a | long and hard
make | make up | mind

1 What do you find it difficult to __________ decisions about?
2 When do you think it's wrong to change your __________ ?
3 Can you remember a time when you couldn't __________ your mind about something?
4 Who do you talk to before you __________ decision about something?
5 What kind of things do you think __________ about before making a decision?

10 SPEAKING **Discuss the questions in Exercise 9 in pairs.**

Permission

11 **Complete the sentences with the correct form of *make, let,* or *be allowed to.***

1 You should never __________ other people make decisions for you.
2 No employer can __________ you work longer hours than the law permits.
3 My cousin has a job where she __________ work from home three days a week.
4 My grandfather left a job when the manager tried to __________ him work late.
5 In the past, factories __________ use children as workers – can you believe that?
6 This company __________ its employees dress well from Monday to Thursday, but on Friday it __________ them wear less formal clothes.

12 **Write sentences about your perfect job or career. Use *make / let / be allowed to* in some of your sentences.**
My ideal job lets me choose the times of day I work.

---

1 W.03
A 2 B 3 C 1

2 W.03
1 kind 2 rude 3 shouldn't 4 have 5 allowed
6 unfriendly 7 mind 8 hang 9 have 10 let

3 Students' own answers

4 Students' own answers

5 Suggested answers: 1 Thank you, you shouldn't have!
2 You shouldn't have been so selfish.
3 You shouldn't have been so rude.
4 You shouldn't be so shy.

6 Suggested answers: A caregiver/nurse/doctor
B engineer/miner C call center worker D pilot E teacher

7 doctor, teacher, caregiver

8 Students' own answers

9 1 make 2 mind 3 make up 4 come to a 5 long and hard

10 Students' own answers

11 1 let 2 make 3 is allowed to 4 make 5 were allowed to
6 makes; lets

12 Students' own answers

TH!NK more

Workbook
C How people behave pp7–8, Ex.1–10

D NEW THINGS
A change of lifestyle

1 W.04 **Read and listen to the dialogue.**
1 Where are Tom and Maia?
2 Who doesn't want to be there? Why?

2 W.04 **Listen again and complete the conversation.**

Tom You said it opened at eight o'clock.
Maia And I was wrong! I'm sorry. Don't be so [1] ______. It'll be open very soon.
Tom I already wish I hadn't come.
Maia Oh, come on, Tom. We [2] ______, didn't we? You said that you were frustrated with your [3] ______ lifestyle.
Tom True. And then you [4] ______ me that the best thing to do was exercise.
Maia Right. And I [5] ______ you to come with me to the gym, and you agreed, so here we are. We're going to work out for a while, and then you'll feel great.
Tom I always feel [6] ______ wearing sports gear. I have thin legs.
Maia Oh, stop complaining, Tom. There's nothing wrong with your legs.
Tom I asked you what I [7] ______ wear, and you said shorts. But I look terrible!
Maia Look, no one here cares – everyone is completely unconcerned about what other people look like; they're all too busy doing exercise.
Tom That's completely untrue!
Maia Tom, I'm beginning to wish I [8] ______ invited you. Oh, look, it's opening. Come on then, let's go in and start.

3 **Answer the questions.**
1 Why has Tom agreed to try exercising?
2 Why is Tom not happy about wearing shorts?
3 Why, according to Maia, are people not worried about other people's appearance?
4 Why do you think Maia says: "I'm beginning to wish I hadn't invited you"?

Reporting verbs

4 **Rewrite each sentence with the verbs in parentheses.**
0 "Would you like to come to the game with me, Julie?" (invite)
He invited Julie to go to the game with him.
1 "The new bakery on King Street is really good." (recommend)
He ______
2 "No – I won't tell you the answers, James." (refuse)
She ______
3 "I'm tired because I slept really badly last night." (explain)
Mark ______
4 "OK, Mabel, I'll let you use my lipstick." (agree)
She ______
5 "Go on, Alex – try the soup!" (encourage)
I ______

5 SPEAKING **Work in pairs. Tell your partner about the following things:**
1 a time someone persuaded you to do something
2 a book or movie that someone recommended to you
3 something you would not encourage another person to do
4 something you agreed to do, but regretted

Negative adjectives

6 **Write the negative form of these adjectives.**
1 important ______
2 polite ______
3 possible ______
4 concerned ______
5 responsible ______
6 legal ______

7 **Complete the sentences using the negative form of an adjective in the list.**

~~expensive~~ | formal | happy | logical | patient | regular

0 I don't like spending money unnecessarily – I'm happy to buy *inexpensive* things.
1 I'll be ready in three minutes! Don't be so ______!
2 Something bad must have happened; she looks so ______.
3 You can wear what you want here. It's a really ______ place.
4 You want to travel over summer break, but you're not saving any money! That's just ______.
5 We never know when the next bus will come – the service is very ______.

Another country

8 **Read the blog. Which of the things in the photos does Jessica not talk about?**

Jessica's blog – *from Tokyo!*

Hi everyone,

Well, those of you who read my blog regularly know that I've moved – I'm now living in Tokyo: my parents got jobs here, and they're on two-year contracts, so here we are. We got here about a month ago, and we've found a place to live, so we're starting to feel a bit more settled.

It's so different here from home. Well, that's unsurprising, of course! For one thing, there are always so many people around, and for a country girl like me who's used to peace and quiet, it isn't easy to deal with. Well, I guess I'll get used to it, but it might take a while! I just wish someone had told me in advance about the number of people on the trains to and from school! But I've made a resolution: I'm going to use my time spent traveling wisely – to learn to knit, maybe, but mainly to learn Japanese. I think I'm going to struggle, because Japanese has a different writing system and the grammar's really different, too, but I'm going to put my mind to it, and I hope I can make some progress. (It's a good thing lots of signs are in the Latin alphabet, too, otherwise I'd be completely lost!) One of my friends told me to try to learn some Japanese before coming here – if only I'd listened to him! It'd be quite a bit easier now, I guess.

One of the truly wonderful things here is the food – you may remember that I've already raved about how much I love Japanese food. My favorite restaurant at home is Japanese, so I'm used to all of the dishes with seafood and rice, and I love them. But here – wow, the flavors are out of this world. Well, that's all for now. I'll write more soon!

9 **Read the blog again. What things does Jessica have to get used to?**

10 SPEAKING **Work in pairs. Think of two more possible things that Jessica might need to get used to. Compare your ideas.**

Changes

11 **Complete the sentences with words from the list.**

break | doing well | form | give up | ~~resolution~~ | struggle | taking up | ways

0 Jessica made a *resolution* to use her travel time well.
1 She's thinking of ______ knitting.
2 She thinks she's going to ______ to learn Japanese.
3 She's started learning already, but so far she isn't ______.
4 Moving to another country is a chance to ______ some new habits.
5 I love seafood, so I could never ______ eating shrimp.
6 I need to get in shape, so I'll have to change my ______ a bit.
7 I don't think I'm ever going to ______ my bad habits.

Regrets: *I wish … / If only …*

12 **Complete the sentences from Jessica's blog. Then read again and check.**
1 I just wish someone ______ me in advance about the number of people on the trains to and from school!
2 One of my friends told me to try to learn some Japanese before coming here – if only ______ to him!

13 **Jessica wrote some emails to her friends back home. Complete the things she said. Use verbs from the list to help you.**

bring | find | know | ~~say~~ | wear

0 I didn't see Kylie before I left – I wish *I'd said* goodbye to her.
1 Electronic things here are really expensive – if only ______ a little more money!
2 I went to a party last night, and it was really hot – I wish ______ a dress, not jeans.
3 There are lots of beautiful things to see here – if only ______ a bit more about Japanese culture before we came.
4 Our apartment here is pretty small – I wish my dad ______ a bigger one.

1 W.04
1 They are at the gym.
2 Tom doesn't want to be there because he feels uncomfortable wearing sports gear.

2 W.04
1 impatient 2 agreed 3 unhealthy 4 persuaded 5 encouraged 6 uncomfortable 7 should 8 hadn't

3 1 Because he's frustrated with his unhealthy lifestyle.
2 Because he has thin legs.
3 Because they're too busy doing exercise.
4 Because Tom keeps complaining.

4 1 recommended the new bakery on King Street. / recommended (that) I (should) visit the new bakery on King Street.
2 refused to tell James the answers.
3 explained that he was tired because he (had) slept really badly (the night before).
4 agreed to let Mabel use her lipstick.
5 encouraged Alex to try the soup.

5 Students' own answers

6 1 unimportant 2 impolite 3 impossible 4 unconcerned 5 irresponsible 6 illegal

7 1 impatient 2 unhappy 3 informal 4 illogical 5 irregular

8 nature / the sights / the buildings / the temple

9 the number of people on the trains / Japanese writing and grammar

10 Possible answers: the traffic, a different currency, different subjects at school, the climate

11 1 taking up 2 struggle 3 doing well 4 form 5 give up 6 ways 7 break

12 1 had told 2 I'd listened

13 1 I'd brought 2 I'd worn 3 I'd known 4 had found

Culture notes

Tokyo was originally a small fishing village called Edo, which means "estuary." It became the capital of Japan in 1868 and changed its name. Tokyo comes from the word *to*, which means "east," and *kyo* which means "capital." Tokyo is prone to earthquakes, and much of the city was destroyed during World War II. When it was rebuilt, it was constructed to provide more earthquake protection.

TH!NK more

Workbook
D New things pp8–9, Ex.1–7

Warmer

Draw a two-column table on the board with the headings *Continents* and *Oceans*. Give student pairs two minutes to write down as many as possible. If they are struggling, you could remind them that there are seven continents and five oceans (Continents: Africa, Antarctica, Asia, Australasia/Oceania, Europe, North America, South America; Oceans: Arctic, Atlantic, Indian, Pacific, Southern). The first pair to finish can share their ideas with the class.

▶ 01 Get TH!NKing

Play the video and discuss the question with your class.

1 Put a copy of the three photos up on the board and do the exercise as a class before students open their books.
B outboard motor C tarp
the Pacific Ocean

2 Divide the class into pairs or small groups for students to discuss the question. At the end of the exercise, listen to some of the students' ideas and encourage open class discussion. Write their ideas on the board.
Students' own answers

3 **Check/clarify:** *memorial service, funeral service, clambered, disoriented, drift, crouched, raw, sip, safe and sound.*
Before students do the exercise, give them just two minutes to scan the article quickly and see how many of their ideas in Exercise 2 are mentioned. Encourage them not to focus on every word for now but just to check against the list on the board.

1 SURVIVAL INSTINCT

OBJECTIVES

FUNCTIONS: issuing and accepting a challenge

GRAMMAR: verbs followed by infinitives or gerunds; verbs that take gerunds and infinitives with different meanings: *remember, forget, regret, try, stop*

VOCABULARY: verbs of movement; adjectives to describe uncomfortable feelings

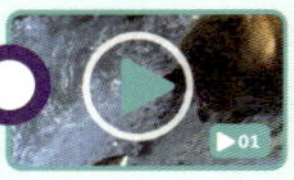

Get TH!NKING
Watch the video and think: are you adventurous?

A

B

C

READING

1 Look at the map and the photos. Which one shows an *outboard motor* and which one shows a *tarp*? Which ocean can you see?

2 SPEAKING Imagine being in a small boat in the middle of the Pacific Ocean. What would you need to think about?

3 Read the article. Seven sentences have been removed from the article. Choose from sentences A–H to complete the article. There is one extra sentence.

A The boys knew right away that they could only sit, wait, and hope.
B Tears were shed again, but this time they were tears of joy and gratitude.
C A passing fishing boat spotted them and stopped to pick them up.
D The boat had no roof to protect them.
E All they could do was watch as it continued to sail away.
F But they would be proved wrong.
G Little did they know their trip would last over seven weeks.
H This meant they had something to drink.

4 1.01 Read and listen to the article again and check your answers.

5 SPEAKING Work in pairs and discuss the statements.

1 The boys should not have tried to make the trip without an adult.
2 If the boys had taken phones with them, they would have been found earlier.
3 I don't think I could survive a situation like that.
4 I would like to meet the three boys and ask them more about their experience.
5 How do you think you would deal with a situation like this? What would you find the most difficult?

12

4 🔊 **1.01**
1 F 2 G 3 A 4 H 5 E 6 C
7 B D is the extra sentence.

5 Monitor to help with any difficulties, but do not interrupt as this is a fluency activity. You might also offer ideas if students have none.

Activity idea Mixed-ability

In Exercise 5, make similar-ability pairings. Allow weaker students some time to think about their answers before discussing them. Monitor, helping with vocabulary as required. Listen to some of their answers in open class.

Objectives

Functions and speaking Issuing and accepting a challenge
Grammar Verbs followed by infinitives or gerunds; verbs which take gerunds and infinitives with different meanings: *remember, forget, regret, try, stop*
Vocabulary Verbs of movement; adjectives to describe uncomfortable feelings; **WordWise:** Expressions with *right*
Life Competencies Giving yourself a challenge

Resources for this unit

All available online

Videos
- Get **TH!NK**ing: *Are you adventurous?*
- Grammar video!: Verbs that take gerunds and infinitives with different meanings: *remember, forget, regret, try, stop*
- Vlog: Giving yourself a challenge

Tests
- Unit, extension, and skills test 1

Worksheets
- Grammar and vocabulary: Basic, Standard, and Extension Worksheets
- Project: Survival instinct
- Communication: Survival
- Literature Worksheets: *Gulliver's Travels* and *The Yellow Wallpaper*
- Get **TH!NK**ing, Grammar video!, and Life Lessons video Worksheets

Culture note

The Pacific Ocean is the world's largest ocean. It covers more than a third of the Earth's surface and separates Asia and Australasia/Oceania from the Americas. It ranges from warm waters near the equator to icy waters where it connects with the Arctic and Southern Oceans. It also contains the Mariana Trench, the deepest place in the world at a depth of 10,984 meters. The water at the bottom is close to freezing point.

6 Do the first item with the whole class as an example. Encourage students to vote on whether it is relevant or irrelevant. Ask students to work with a partner before checking answers as a class.
Relevant facts: 1, 2, 4, 5

7 Encourage students to think of several different feelings that the boys may have had. Listen to some of their ideas.

8 Ask students to work individually to write down their ideas for situations 1–3 before dividing the class into pairs or small groups to discuss the situations. Monitor and prompt students to keep talking, but as this is a fluency activity, do not interrupt to correct mistakes. Listen to some of the students' ideas and encourage open class discussion.

Pronunciation
Diphthongs: alternative spellings
Student's Book p120

Homework

Ask students to research a survival story from around the world. They can find a picture and make notes of the details of the story in English. If students do not have access to the internet, they can create their own stories. As a follow-up, students can bring the picture to the next lesson and present their survival story to the class.

Surviving for SEVEN WEEKS

Out in the Pacific Ocean, 500 km north of Samoa, lies a small group of islands called Tokelau. The population is only about 1,400 people, but one day early in November 2010, 500 of them gathered for a memorial service for three teenagers. No one had seen 14-year-old Etueni Nasau or his two 15-year-old cousins Samuel Pelesa and Filo Filo for a month. Their boat was gone, too. When people realized that the three boys were missing, planes spent over three weeks trying to find them, but eventually they gave up. Their friends and relatives wept at their funeral service, believing that the boys were dead. [1] ________

In early October, the three boys had clambered into their small 3.5-meter boat because they felt like making a short trip to a neighboring island. They had decided to take some coconuts and water with them, enough for a couple of days.

[2] ________

Not long after they headed out to sea, the boys lost sight of land and started to become disoriented. Then they ran out of fuel for their outboard motor and started to drift. [3] ________

For days, they crouched in the boat under the fierce sun. Their water and coconuts quickly ran out. Sometimes, a small flying fish would fall into their boat and they would eat it, but this wasn't enough food for them. Once, a seabird landed on the boat – one of the boys leaped up and managed to grab it. They killed it and ate it, raw. At night, there were often heavy rainstorms that threatened to overturn the boat, and the boys had to dive to the floor, holding on as hard as they could. But the storms also left a little rainwater in their canvas tarp. [4] ________

They constantly kept watch for land or boats. One night, they saw the lights of a ship, but it was too far away to see them, and they had no lights to attract attention. [5] ________

After several weeks, the night rains stopped. The boys were desperately thirsty and, despite knowing the dangers of drinking seawater, they decided to sip some. Then, with perhaps only days, or even hours, to live, the thing they had been desperately hoping for, happened.

[6] ________

The boys were very weak, but they managed to stagger onto the fishing boat. They began to recover after having some water and some food. From the boat, Filo Filo called his father, who rushed to pass on to the other villagers the scarcely believable news that the boys were safe and sound.

[7] ________

Train to TH!NK

Thinking rationally

Solving a problem requires decision-making. In a difficult situation, we may need to make sure that we are not distracted by irrelevant ideas, so we can look at the facts that are relevant for making the right decision.

6 Which of these facts were relevant for the three boys in making their decision to drink some seawater?

1. They had no fresh water in the boat.
2. Seawater doesn't taste very good.
3. Their boat was very small.
4. There were no clouds in the sky.
5. If you don't drink anything, you can die of dehydration.

7 SPEAKING Work in pairs and discuss how the boys may have felt when they made their decision.

8 SPEAKING Read the situations. For each one, think about what you might want to do and what you should do. Then compare your ideas with a partner.

1. You have an important test tomorrow, and your friend wants you to go to a party tonight.
2. You haven't been feeling well for several days. A tells you to go to a doctor. B tells you to take some medicine. You like B better than A.
3. You borrowed a friend's bike and had a small accident – there's a scratch on the bike that isn't easy to see.

PRONUNCIATION
Diphthongs: alternative spellings Go to page 120.

Activity idea Extension

Organize a debate. Elicit the names of four famous real or fictional people who have different backgrounds, e.g., a politician, an athlete, an actor, and a cartoon character.

Tell students that the characters are in a sinking boat. Students throw the characters out, one at a time, in order for the remaining character to survive. Divide the class into groups of four and ask students to decide which characters should be thrown from the boat. They should come up with one relevant and one irrelevant reason for each character and discuss in which order the characters should go overboard and why.

TH!NK more

Workbook
Pronunciation p118

Worksheets
Project Survival instinct
Communication Survival
Get TH!NKing *Are you adventurous?*

Critical TH!NKing
Solving problems and making decisions
Identifying, gathering, and organizing relevant information.

Warmer

In pairs, students find as many infinitive and gerund forms in the article on page 13 as they can in three minutes (not including *be*/*have*). Ask the pair with the most verbs to read them out and make a list on the board. Ask other pairs to add to the list.

There are 14 infinitives and seven gerunds: *missing, trying, to find, believing, making, to take, to become, to drift, to grab, to overturn, to dive, holding, to see, to attract, drinking, to sip, to live, hoping for, to stagger, to recover, to pass.*

1 Ask students to try to complete the sentences from memory before referring back to the article to check. Point out that there are no specific rules to decide which verb is followed by which form and that verb patterns need to be learned individually.

1 making 2 to grab 3 both
4 to drink 5 to pick 6 both
RULE: 7 gerunds 8 infinitives
9 gerunds / infinitives
10 infinitives / gerunds

2 If you are short on time, assign this exercise for homework.

1 climbing 2 going 3 to show
4 reading 5 walking 6 to buy
7 helping 8 getting

Workbook p10

Get it Right!
Verb patterns

Student's Book p122

3 During feedback, ask concept-check questions, e.g., *When you dive, do your feet touch the water first?* (no, hands first); *What is another word for leap?* (jump); *If you rush, do you move quickly or slowly?* (quickly); *In what situations might a person stagger?* (when sick, exhausted, or hurt)

1 leaped 2 dive 3 stagger
4 rushed

Workbook p12

TH!NK more

Workbook
Grammar p10, Ex.1–5
Vocabulary p12, Ex.1–2
Vocabulary Extra p13, Ex.1–2

Worksheets
Grammar Worksheets 1
Vocabulary Worksheets 1

GRAMMAR
Verbs followed by infinitives or gerunds

1 **Read the sentences from the article on page 13 and choose the correct words. There are two sentences in which both options are possible. Then complete the rules with *a gerund* and *an infinitive*.**

1 They felt like *making / to make* a short trip to a neighboring island.
2 One of the boys leaped up and managed *grabbing / to grab* it.
3 All they could do was watch as it continued *sailing / to sail* away.
4 They knew all the dangers of drinking seawater, but they decided *drinking / to drink* some.
5 A passing fishing boat spotted them and stopped *picking / to pick* them up.
6 They began *recovering / to recover*.

> **RULE:** We follow the verbs:
> - *imagine, feel like, suggest, practice, miss, can't stand, enjoy, hate,* and *don't mind* with [7] ________________.
> - *manage, want, decide, refuse, hope, promise, ask, learn, expect, afford, offer,* and *choose* with [8] ________________.
> - *begin, start,* and *continue* with [9] ________________ or [10] ________________ with no difference in meaning.

2 **Complete the sentences with the verbs in the list. Use the gerund or infinitive form.**

buy | climb | get | go | help | read | show | walk

1 The weather was great on Sunday, but I didn't feel like ________________ a mountain.
2 My friend suggested ________________ on a bike ride.
3 Nobody asked us ________________ our tickets as we entered the movie theater.
4 I gave Sienna a copy of Joe Simpson's book *Touching the Void*. She says she's really enjoying ________________ it.
5 Can I borrow your umbrella? I can't stand ________________ around in the rain.
6 I wanted ________________ new skis, but I couldn't afford them.
7 I don't mind ________________ my brother with his homework.
8 Can you imagine ________________ caught in a snowstorm for hours?

→ workbook page 10

VOCABULARY
Verbs of movement

3 **Complete the sentences with the correct form of the verbs in the list. Then check your answers in the article on page 13.**

dive | leap | rush | stagger

1 One of the boys ________________ up and managed to grab it.
2 The boys had to ________________ to the floor, holding on as hard as they could.
3 The boys were very weak, but managed to ________________ onto the fishing boat.
4 He ________________ to give the incredible news to other villagers.

4 **Match the words with the definitions.**

1 climb | 2 crawl | 3 dive | 4 hop | 5 leap
6 rush | 7 stagger | 8 swing | 9 tiptoe | 10 wander

a ☐ to jump on one foot
b ☐ to walk around without any clear purpose
c ☐ to move backward and forward or side to side, often from the end of a rope
d ☐ to walk on your toes, especially in order not to make a noise
e ☐ to jump into water headfirst
f ☐ to go up or to go toward the top of something
g ☐ to (cause to) go or do something very quickly
h ☐ to make a large jump from one place to another
i ☐ to move slowly on hands and knees
j ☐ to walk or move with difficulty as if you are going to fall

5 **Complete the sentences with the correct forms of the verbs from Exercise 4.**

1 He was really hot, so he ________________ into the swimming pool right away.
2 We spent the morning ________________ around the harbor, looking at the boats.
3 At the zoo, the monkeys were ________________ from the trees and ________________ to the top of them.
4 Their daughter was asleep, so they ________________ around the house.
5 Children learn to ________________ when they are babies, but they don't learn to ________________ on one foot until they are a bit older.
6 As soon as I heard Jo was back, I ________________ to her mom's house to see her.
7 With difficulty she managed ________________ to the phone to call for help.
8 He saw the snake, and in no time, he ________________ onto the table.

→ workbook page 12

---

4 In pairs, ask students to discuss the meaning of the verbs. Listen to some of their ideas in open class, but do not comment at this stage. Tell students to use an English–English dictionary, as this will give them a description of the word and an example of it in use rather than a translation, which may not be entirely accurate.

a 4 b 10 c 8 d 9 e 3 f 1 g 6 h 5 i 2 j 7

5 **Check/clarify:** *harbor.*

1 dived / dove 2 wandering 3 swinging; climbing 4 tiptoed 5 crawl; hop
6 rushed 7 to stagger 8 leaped

Activity idea Extension

Divide the class into pairs. Ask students to make a list of situations when they might have to or want to: 1 climb, 2 crawl, 3 hop, 4 tiptoe, 5 leap, 6 rush. Listen to some of their ideas in open class.

6 🔊 **1.04** Tell students not to worry about understanding every word for now.
They are discussing exams, the stress they cause, and how to deal with it.

7 🔊 **1.04 Check/clarify:** *maintain a balance, desperate, doesn't suit you.*
Ask students to answer as much as they can from memory. During feedback, play the audio again and encourage students to think about the correct answer to the false statements.
1 T 2 T 3 T 4 F (She says it's important to keep enjoying yourself.) 5 F (She says you have to do the right amount for you.) 6 F (He says it wasn't a success.) 7 T 8 F (She says you should try to be flexible.)

8 Give students some time to discuss in pairs and then hold a class vote on which pieces of advice are the most, and the least useful.

▶ 02 Grammar video!
Verbs that take gerunds and infinitives with different meanings: *remember, forget, regret, try, stop*

9 Ask students to try to complete the sentences from memory before playing the audio again to check. Explain/elicit that some verbs can be followed by *to* + infinitive or the gerund form but with a change in meaning. During feedback, check understanding with concept-check questions (e.g., *In item 1, which sentence is giving advice? Which sentence refers to the past?*).
1 to eat; having 2 not taking; to say 3 to avoid; studying

10 Ask students to work in pairs to describe the pictures before they match them with the sentences.
A 4 B 1 C 2 D 3
RULE: 5 gerund 6 infinitive 7 gerund 8 infinitive 9 gerund 10 infinitive 11 infinitive 12 gerund 13 gerund 14 infinitive

---

LISTENING

6 🔊 1.04 **Listen to a discussion on a radio show. What are the two people discussing?**

7 🔊 1.04 **Listen again. Mark the statements T (true) or F (false). Then correct the false statements.**

1 The man says that he didn't sleep very well during his exams. ☐
2 The woman says she didn't do enough serious studying. ☐
3 She says it's important to think about diet and sleep during an exam period. ☐
4 She says you should spend more time studying than enjoying yourself. ☐
5 She says you should not do more or less studying than your friends. ☐
6 The man was happy that he studied along with his friends. ☐
7 The woman thinks you should study in whatever way is good for you. ☐
8 She thinks it's important to keep to a schedule 100% of the time. ☐

8 SPEAKING **Work in pairs and do the following:**

1 List the pieces of advice the woman gives and say which ones you agree or disagree with.
2 Add one or two more pieces of advice for dealing with pre-exam stress.

GRAMMAR
Grammar video ▶02

Verbs that take gerunds and infinitives with different meanings: *remember, forget, regret, try, stop*

9 **Complete the sentences from the listening with the verb in parentheses. Use the correct form.**

1 Remember ____________ regularly and well. (eat)
I still remember ____________ sleepless nights. (have)
2 I really regret ____________ it more seriously. (not take)
I regret ____________ that we've run out of time. (say)
3 Try ____________ comparing yourself with friends. (avoid)
I tried ____________ together with my friends. (study)

10 **Match sentences 1–4 with pictures A–D. Then complete the rule with *gerund* or *infinitive*.**

1 She should stop to rest, but she needs to finish her work today.
2 She should stop resting, but she just doesn't want to go back to work.
3 He forgot to meet Sandra.
4 He'll never forget meeting Sandra for the first time.

RULE: *Remember, forget, regret*
Remember + [5]____________ *means thinking of a past experience you've had.*
Remember + [6]____________ *means don't forget to do something.*
Forget + [7]____________ *means to no longer think of something that you did.*
Forget + [8]____________ *means to not think of doing something you should do or should have done.*
Regret + [9]____________ *means feeling sorry about something you said or did in the past.*
Regret + [10]____________ *means feeling sorry about something you are going to say or do next or in the future.*
Other verbs
Try + [11]____________ *means try hard to see if you can do something that is really not easy.*
Try + [12]____________ *means do it and see what the results are.*
Stop + [13]____________ *means to not continue doing a certain activity or action.*
Stop + [14]____________ *means make a pause in one activity in order to do a different activity.*

11 **Complete each sentence with the correct form of the verbs in parentheses.**

1 On the way to work, Dad stopped ____________ some magazines. (buy)
2 I really regret ____________ Jim. He's going to tell Martha, I'm sure. (tell)
3 When you go into town, please remember ____________ some paper for the printer. (get)
4 Don't forget ____________ food for my packed lunch tomorrow, Mom. (buy)
5 Sarah stopped ____________ the guitar a few years ago. (play)
6 I just can't solve this puzzle. I've been trying ____________ the answer for hours. (find)
7 My ankle hurts. I tried ____________ some ice on it, but it hasn't helped. (put)
8 I remember ____________ strawberry ice cream when I was very young. (love)

→ workbook page 11

---

11 If you are short on time, assign this exercise for homework.
1 to buy 2 telling 3 to get 4 to buy 5 playing 6 to find 7 putting 8 loving

Workbook p11

Get it Right!
remember, forget, regret, try, and stop

Student's Book p122

Homework
Ask students to write six positive and negative sentences about themselves and their family using some of the verb patterns. As an alternative, they could write five true sentences and one false one. As a follow-up in the next lesson, they could work in pairs, and each partner guesses which of the sentences is untrue.

TH!NK more

Practice Extra
Unit 1 Practice it!

Workbook
Listening p16, Ex.1
Grammar p11, Ex.6–9

Worksheets
Grammar Worksheets 1

Warmer

Write *to go* and *going* on the board. In open class, read out verbs from the rules on pages 14 and 15 and nominate individuals to say whether they are followed by *to go*, *going*, or both.

1 During feedback, work on pronunciation by saying the adjectives for students to repeat. Check that they're placing stress on the correct syllable (on the first in all cases except for *ashamed*, where the second syllable is stressed).
1 ashamed 2 puzzled 3 stuck
4 awkward 5 guilty 6 desperate

2 1 awkward 2 ashamed 3 guilty
4 desperate 5 puzzled 6 stuck

Workbook p12

3 At the end of the exercise, ask students to compare answers with a partner. Listen to some of their ideas in open class.

4 Give your own example to get students started on this. While students write their sentences, monitor to help with vocabulary and to encourage them to use adjectives from Exercise 1 to describe uncomfortable feelings.

5 Read the examples and point out the use of imperatives and verb patterns with *stop*, *remember*, *start*, and *try*. Monitor to make a note of any examples of good usage. Praise students who attempt to expand on their answers.

6 Before students do the task, get them to cover the article on page 17 and look at the title and picture. In pairs, give students two minutes to think about the answers to the questions. Do not give them the answers yet.

VOCABULARY
Adjectives to describe uncomfortable feelings

1 Match the adjectives from the list with their definitions.

ashamed | awkward | desperate
guilty | puzzled | stuck

1 ______________ : feeling extremely embarrassed about something you did
2 ______________ : feeling confused because you do not understand something
3 ______________ : feeling you are in a difficult situation, or unable to change or get away from a situation
4 ______________ : feeling embarrassed or uncomfortable
5 ______________ : feeling worried or unhappy because you did something wrong
6 ______________ : feeling the need for or wanting something very much

2 Complete the sentences with the adjectives from Exercise 1.

1 When I'm with Mrs. Meyer, I always feel ______________. It's difficult to find something to talk about with her.
2 Ciara ought to be ______________ of herself – talking to her mother like that!
3 Carl must have done something wrong, because he's looking so ______________.
4 After the earthquake, the people on the island were ______________ for help.
5 We're a bit ______________ as to why we haven't heard from them for weeks.
6 Without your help, we'd be ______________ and wouldn't know what to do next.

→ workbook page 12

SPEAKING

3 When you have a problem and get stuck, which of these three things apply to you? Add three more of your own.

☐ I go online and look for some advice.
☐ I stop thinking about it and listen to some music.
☐ I start feeling helpless.

4 WRITING Write three sentences to describe problems and your emotional reactions to them. Use adjectives from Exercise 1.

I have a test tomorrow, and I haven't studied enough. I'm desperate.
It was my best friend's birthday last Monday, and I forgot to give her a present. I feel guilty.

5 Work in small groups. Listen to each other's problems and tell each other what to do.

Stop feeling desperate. Maybe the test won't be very difficult. Otherwise, remember to start studying earlier next time.

Try to relax before the test. Listen to some music, or go for an early morning walk.

READING

6 Look at the photos and the headline of the article. Which of these things do you think are true about Miriam Lancewood?

☐ She is from New Zealand.
☐ She lives in a city.
☐ She sometimes hunts without a gun.
☐ She lives alone.
☐ She never eats meat.

7 1.05 Read and listen to the article to check your ideas.

8 Read the text again. Answer these questions based on your own opinions. Use evidence from the text to support your ideas.

1 How did Miriam feel about her life before 2010?
2 How does her husband feel about their lifestyle?
3 How happy is she about the way she leads her life?

16

7 1.05 Before playing the audio, give students another two minutes to read the article quickly and check their predictions. Encourage them not to focus on every word for now. Play the audio and encourage students to think about the correct answers to the false statements.
✗ She is from New Zealand. (Miriam is from the Netherlands.)
✗ She lives in a city. (She lives in the wilderness in New Zealand.)
✓ She sometimes hunts with a bow and arrow.
✗ She lives alone. (She lives with her husband.)
✗ She never eats meat. (She used to be vegetarian, but now meat is part of her diet.)

8 **Check/clarify:** *survive, nuclear attack, to recount (a story), bow and arrow.* Encourage students to justify their answers and to underline the language in the article that supports their ideas.

TH!NK more

Workbook
Vocabulary p12, Ex.3–4
Reading p14, Ex.1–4

Worksheets
Vocabulary Worksheets 1

Culture note

Miriam Lancewood was born in the Netherlands. After studying to be a PE teacher, she traveled the world. After meeting her now husband in India, they hiked together through the Himalayas and South East Asia and ended up in New Zealand. Miriam was working as a teacher when they decided to move into the Southern Alps of New Zealand with a tent and bow and arrow. They lived for seven years in the wilderness and completed the *Te Araroa* Trail. Miriam's book about their adventures, *Woman in the Wilderness*, became an international success and has been translated into Dutch, French, German, and Chinese.

9 This exercise can be done for homework or in class. Ask students to read the instructions and work in pairs or small groups to discuss the topic and write down their answers. Monitor and help students with any questions. Students work individually to expand their notes into a diary page. In the next lesson, put students back into the same groups to read each other's diaries, then correct each other's mistakes and say what they like about each other's writing.

10 With books closed, write the word *right* in the middle of the board. Ask students to think of different meanings for *right* and any words that could go before or after *right*. Write any correct answers on the board (e.g., *right away, too right, taste/feel right, turn out right, make something right, a right angle, the right side, to right a wrong, human rights, equal rights, legal rights*, etc.).

1 right away 2 right in the middle
3 Right or wrong 4 right

11 During feedback, say the phrases for students to repeat and check pronunciation.

1 right 2 right away
3 right in the middle
4 Right or wrong

Workbook p12

How to SURVIVE *in the* WILDERNESS

Miriam Lancewood, from the Netherlands, has a college degree, but she has no permanent address and no job. She doesn't have a car, or a computer, or a cell phone. She doesn't have a bed, or a clock, or a mirror. And she's very happy this way.

Miriam was living in New Zealand, in 2010, when she began to ask herself: could she survive a terrible natural disaster or a nuclear attack? Could she live without technology, electricity, or other people? She decided that she didn't have the necessary skills or experience, so she and her husband Peter set off to live in the wilderness. They left their house, filled two 85-liter backpacks with some possessions and took 12 buckets of food to last the winter. And they've never looked back.

Since then, they have lived right in the middle of the wilderness of New Zealand's North Island. They live mostly in a tent or unequipped hut, with occasional returns to a town if their supplies are low – Lancewood sometimes plays guitar and sings on the street to earn a little money. Otherwise, they don't need anything from anyone.

In 2017, Miriam published a book – *Woman in the Wilderness* – which tells her story and recounts what she learned about nature, other people, and herself. Life in the wilderness taught her how to manage with simple things, how to be alone, how to be bored, how to be afraid. She also talks about how she had to learn how to use a bow and arrow to hunt with and the first time she killed a goat with one. Afterwards, she sat and cried because she had been brought up as a vegetarian. She and her husband ate the meat, because they did not want to waste a life and because it provided protein. Meat then became part of their diet.

Miriam and her husband Peter met in India. They spent two months in the Himalayas, trekking and meeting people who lived very simply in the mountains. The lifestyle attracted them both, and once they were back in New Zealand, the idea of living in the wilderness became a possibility, and eventually a reality. She does not for one moment regret choosing this way of life. "If people don't agree with the way I live, well, it doesn't matter, does it?" she says.

WRITING
A diary page about an experience

9 **Imagine you are Miriam Lancewood. Write a page of your diary. Write about:**

- the activities you've been doing
- how you felt while you were doing them
- what you learned from them

Write 150–200 words.

WordWise: Expressions with *right*

10 **Look at these sentences from the unit so far. Complete them with phrases from the list.**

right | right away | right in the middle | right or wrong

1 The boys knew ________ that they could only sit, wait, and hope.
2 Since 2010, they have lived ________ ________ of the wilderness.
3 ________, the results of their exams will determine what they do next.
4 But you survived, ________?

11 **Complete the sentences with an expression with *right*.**

1 You're the new girl at school, ________?
2 Look at the time! We're late. We have to leave ________.
3 There's going to be a new supermarket ________ of town.
4 ________, we have to turn off our phones before class starts.

→ workbook page 12

Homework

Students could do the writing for homework. If they have access to mobile devices, you could ask them to write a diary page about themselves and send it to another member of the class. Ask them to check that all the points in the task have been covered. Finally, ask students to write comments about their partner's diary entry. What interested/surprised them most?

Activity idea Extension

Ask students to work in pairs and make a list of movies, books, or television shows which deal with people surviving in the wild. Regroup students into different groups for them to compare their lists, discuss what happens in each one, and make recommendations.

TH!NK more

Workbook
Reading p14, Ex.1–4
Developing Writing p15
WordWise p12, Ex.5

Warmer

Review phrases with *right* by giving students a sentence and eliciting a phrase with *right*, e.g., *Do it immediately – Do it right away.; Please sit in the center – Please sit right in the middle.; BTS is thought to be the best band in the world, whether you think so or not. – BTS is thought, right or wrong, to be the best band in the world.*

1 **1.06** Tell students to cover the dialogue and discuss the question in pairs before listening to check their answers.
Students' own answers

2 **1.06** Ask students to underline the answers in the dialogue.
1 survive three days without her phone
2 She will pay for Ava's meal at the burger place.
3 Paloma gets a message on her phone.
4 She thinks that she will not be able to do the challenge.

3 At the end of the exercise, listen to some of the students' ideas and encourage open class discussion.

4 Write the underlined phrases from the dialogue on the board. Ask students for an L1 translation before they complete the sentences in English.
1 something or other 2 Same here 3 give me a heads up 4 It's a deal 5 You know what 6 where were we

5 Before students do Exercise 5, drill the dialogues in Exercise 4 for students to repeat together, paying attention to the intonation of sentences and questions. Give students time to practice saying the dialogues with a partner.

DEVELOPING SPEAKING

1 1.06 **Look at the photo. What do you think the two girls are doing? Read and listen to check.**

Ava: Sunday afternoon … I'm pretty bored.
Paloma: Same here. I think I'll just play some games on my phone.
Ava: Oh, phone, phone, phone. You know what, Paloma? You're addicted to that phone! You're always using it for something or other.
Paloma: Of course I'm not addicted to it. I could stop using it right now if I wanted to!
Ava: Really? OK, I challenge you, Paloma. I bet you can't survive three days without your phone.
Paloma: Seriously? Three days? That's too easy. You're on.
Ava: OK then. You'll have to give me your phone, though, and promise not to use anyone else's either.
Paloma: No problem.
Ava: You'll never manage to do this, Paloma, and you know it.
Paloma: Oh, I'll manage it, Ava, don't worry. And if I don't, we'll go to the burger place. You order whatever you want, and I'll pay. Agreed?
Ava: It's a deal! I can't believe I'm … .
Paloma: Oh, just a minute, Ava. A message from Mary. Give me two seconds … yes, replied. Sorry about that. Now, where were we?
Ava: We were talking about you not using your phone – until you started using your phone!
Paloma: Oh, you're right! I'm having second thoughts about this challenge. I think you're probably right. I can't do it!
Ava: I knew it! But we had a deal, so I still want my burger!
Paloma: Fair enough. Give me a heads up when you know what day you want it.

2 1.06 **Read and listen to the dialogue again and answer the questions.**
1 What does Ava challenge Paloma to do?
2 What does Paloma promise to do if she loses?
3 How is their conversation interrupted?
4 Why does Paloma change her mind?

3 SPEAKING **Discuss the statements in pairs. Do you agree with them?**
1 It's possible to be addicted to your cell phone.
2 Ava is being unfair when she challenges Paloma to not use her phone.

Phrases for fluency

4 **Find the underlined expressions in the dialogue and use them to complete the conversations.**
1 A I was really busy over the weekend. No time to relax! I always had [1]______ to do.
B [2]______! I didn't stop for a moment.
2 A Listen, if you find the homework difficult, [3]______ and I can try to help you. Then maybe you can make us a snack later.
B [4]______! Thanks a lot, Georgia.
3 A This exercise is exhausting.
B You're right. [5]______? We should take a break.
4 A Agreed. I think we should do that.
B Hang on, let me answer this phone call … Sorry about that. Right, [6]______?

5 SPEAKING **Work in pairs. You are two friends who are bored and who are trying to find things to do. Try to use as many of the phrases from Exercise 4 as you can.**

FUNCTIONS
Issuing and accepting a challenge

KEY LANGUAGE

I bet you can't …	I think you're (probably) right.
Of course I can.	You'll never manage to …
I challenge you to …	No problem.
That's too easy.	I bet (you) I can …

6 **Read the phrases in the Key Language box. Which are used to issue a challenge? Which are used to accept or turn down a challenge?**

7 SPEAKING **Work in pairs. Write short dialogues where one person challenges the other. Use these ideas or one of your own. Then act them out for the class.**
- eat a donut without licking your lips
- stay awake for 24 hours
- walk 20 kilometers in four hours
- finish this exercise before the pair next to us
- speak only in English during break times and lunch for a whole week
- ______

18

6 During feedback, say the phrases for students to repeat and check pronunciation.
Issue a challenge: I bet you can't … I challenge you to … You'll never manage to …
Accept a challenge: Of course I can. That's too easy. No problem. I bet (you) I can …
Turn down a challenge: I think you're (probably) right.

7 Allow students six to eight minutes to prepare their dialogues. Monitor to make sure all students are on task. Encourage them to use the key language.

Activity idea Mixed-ability

In Exercise 7, weaker students can write and practice their dialogues before trying to act them out without looking at their notes. Stronger students can perform dialogues spontaneously.

Activity idea Extension

Ask students to work in pairs and give each other challenges that could be done in class, e.g., say the alphabet in English, backwards, in less than one minute; think of a word in English with no vowels (*rhythm*, *shyly*, *myth*).

Life Competencies

Warmer

Write *giving yourself a challenge* on the board and elicit what it might mean. Encourage students to try to clarify its meaning through examples or explanation, rather than through a translation. Ask students to read the introductory paragraph to check their ideas. Elicit examples of people giving themselves a challenge in Unit 1.

▶ 03 Life Lessons: Giving yourself a challenge

1 ▶03 Ask students to compare their ideas with a partner.
the audience: to count the number of woodpeckers appearing on screen
herself: to learn Spanish

2 ▶03 Ask students to try to answer the questions about Chloe's challenge from memory before watching the video again to check.
Obstacles: She's never been very good at languages; Pronunciation can be so hard!
Rewards: She could go to so many parts of the world; She'll be able to talk and people will understand her; She'll make friends; Maybe she'll go and live in Mexico.

3 **Check/clarify:** *charity, disabled, wheelchairs, marathon, sponsors.* Give students three minutes to read the blog post and find the answers. Encourage them not to focus on every word.
1 She wanted to raise money for a charity that needed money to buy new wheelchairs.
2 She had never done any running before.
3 She managed to complete the marathon in five hours and ten minutes but was taken to the hospital. The charity got the wheelchairs.
4 Students' own answers

4 This exercise can be done as a mingle activity with students changing partners every few minutes.

5 Allow students six to eight minutes to prepare ideas. Help with any vocabulary and monitor to make sure all students are on task.

Learning to Learn
Taking control of own learning
Sets goals and plans for learning.

SURVIVAL INSTINCT UNIT 1

LIFE COMPETENCIES

It can be important to try to do new things – it's by taking on challenges that we learn new skills and grow as people. But it's also important to be realistic about what you can achieve.

1 ▶ 03 **Watch the vlog. What challenge does Chloe set the audience? What challenge does she set herself?**

2 ▶ 03 **Watch the vlog again and make notes about:**
a the obstacles to the challenge
b the rewards of the challenge.

3 SPEAKING **Read the blog post. Work in pairs and answer the questions.**
1 Why did Sara decide to run a marathon?
2 Why was it a hard challenge for her?
3 What were the results of her running the marathon – for herself, and for others?
4 Was it a good idea for her to set herself this challenge? List positive and negative things.

4 **Imagine you are one of Sara's friends on the day that she told you she was going to run the Boston Marathon. What would you say to her?**

Me and my world

5 **Think of a time when you set yourself a challenge and make notes.**
- What was it?
- What did you do?
- What was the outcome?

6 SPEAKING **Work in pairs and tell your partner about your challenge.**

Last year, I started doing some volunteer work for a charity in my town that helps disabled children. I found out that the charity needed to buy some new wheelchairs, but that they really didn't have the money. So, I started to think about what I could do to raise money.

When I mentioned this to my friends, they said, "Well, why don't you run the Boston Marathon?!" They laughed and so did I – we all know that I'm not an athlete at all. I've never done any running before. But later, I started to think that it might not be a bad idea.

I talked to the charity people, and they agreed to put my name forward. I bought some gear and started running. I went out every night for a run, and after a month or so, I found I could do almost five kilometers. The problem, though, is that the marathon is 42 kilometers!

The race was only five months away. I practiced as hard as I could – I had to run and finish the race, because if I did, I would raise enough money from my sponsors to buy four new wheelchairs.

Well, when the big day came, I was not at all sure that I was ready. During my training, I'd managed to run 25 kilometers in one session, but 42? Could I do it? Fortunately, it wasn't a hot day, and the people running with me helped a lot. Nevertheless, after about 34 kilometers, I was exhausted, and I nearly stopped, but the people watching cheered me on, and I managed to struggle on to the finish line. My time was five hours and ten minutes. But I was in pretty bad shape, and I was taken to the hospital. I had to stay there overnight to recover, but they let me go home the next day.

It was hard, but I'm so proud that I did the marathon and got the wheelchairs for the charity.

TIPS FOR GIVING YOURSELF A CHALLENGE

- When you set yourself a challenge, think about the possible outcomes – if you succeed and if you don't succeed.
- Think about outcomes not only for yourself, but for other people, too.
- If you think it's a tough challenge, talk to other people you trust before making a decision about whether or not to accept the challenge.

19

6 You may like to give your own example first. Listen to some of the students' ideas and encourage open class discussion.

Homework

Ask students to keep a journal for two or three days, with a record of challenges they have had, what they did about them, and what the outcomes were. If this is too sensitive a topic, they could make up some ideas.

Culture note

The Boston Marathon is an annual running race in Boston, Massachusetts. It first took place in 1897 and is the oldest annual marathon race in the world. It is traditionally held on Patriots' Day, on the third Monday of April. Around 30,000 athletes compete in the race, which attracts nearly half a million spectators each year.

TH!NK more

Practice Extra
Unit 1 Master it!

Worksheet
Life Lessons: Giving yourself a challenge

Tests
Unit, extension, and skills test 1

Warmer

To review forms of transportation, give students two minutes to think of as many different vehicles as they can. After two minutes, play a game of "vocabulary tennis" with each group taking turns to say a vehicle until one team runs out of ideas.

▶ 04 Get TH!NKing

Check/clarify: *congestion.*
Play the video and discuss the question with your class.

1 Put a copy of the four photos up on the board and do the exercise as a class before students open their books.

2 Allow students a few minutes to prepare, then ask a student to read out their monologue. The rest of the class can try to guess which photo it is about.

3 Ask students to cover the article on page 21 and look at the title and photos to answer the question. Write their ideas on the board. Remind students not to focus on every word for now.

4 🔊 **2.01** Play the audio while students read to check.
different ways to get to work

5 **Check/clarify:** *tedious, commute, innovative, unicycle, pedestrians, paragliding.* Encourage students to underline parts of the text that support their answers.
1 Gabriel Horchler 2 Abdul Mallik, Elizabeth Miranda 3 Benjamin Keiffer 4 Paul Cox 5 Gabriel Horchler 6 Abdul Mallik, Elizabeth Miranda 7 Benjamin Keiffer 8 Gabriel Horchler

2 ON THE ROAD

OBJECTIVES

FUNCTIONS: introducing (amazing) information

GRAMMAR: relative clauses (review); *which* to refer to a whole clause; omitting relative pronouns; reduced relative clauses

VOCABULARY: groups of people; phrasal verbs (1)

Get TH!NKING
Watch the video and think: is there a lot of traffic congestion where you live?

A

C

B

D

READING

1 SPEAKING **Look at the people in the photos. Work in pairs and answer the questions.**
1 Where are these people going?
2 How do they feel?
3 How are the people in the photos different from each other?

2 WRITING **Choose one of the people and write a short monologue about what they are thinking.**

3 **Look at the article and the photos on the next page. What do you think the article will be about?**

4 🔊 2.01 **Read and listen to the article to check your ideas.**

5 **Read the article again and answer the questions with the name of a person. Sometimes more than one name is possible.**
Who …
1 uses a hobby to get to work?
2 works in a school?
3 uses a talent that he learned when he was younger in his commute?
4 flies to get to work?
5 spends an hour and a half commuting each day?
6 gets wet on their way to work?
7 used to use public transportation to get to work?
8 uses more than one type of transportation to get to work?

6 SPEAKING **Work in pairs and discuss the questions.**
1 Which of these commutes sounds the most/least fun? Why?
2 What would be your perfect way to get to school?
3 What can be done to make people's commutes easier?

20

6 Invite students to share their answers with the rest of the class during feedback.

Objectives

Functions and speaking Introducing (amazing) information
Grammar Relative clauses (review); *which* to refer to a whole clause; omitting relative pronouns; reduced relative clauses
Vocabulary Groups of people; phrasal verbs (1)
Values Learning from other cultures
Culture Nomadic people

Resources for this unit

All available online

Videos
- Get **TH!NK**ing: *Is there a lot of traffic congestion where you live?*
- Grammar video!: Omitting relative pronouns
- Culture: Nomadic people and animals

Tests
- Unit, extension, and skills test 2

Worksheets
- Grammar and vocabulary: Basic, Standard, and Extension Worksheets
- Project: On the road
- Communication: Going places
- Literature Worksheets: *Gulliver's Travels*
- Get **TH!NK**ing and Grammar video! video Worksheets

Culture notes

The Anacostia River and its tributaries are part of the approximately 455 km^2 of the Anacostia watershed – an area of land that drains rainfall into rivers and eventually to the ocean. The area is home to over 70 species of fish, 200 species of birds, and more than 800,000 people. More than 300 years of neglect and overuse has resulted in pollution, loss of habitat, sedimentation, flooding, and destruction of these wetlands. However, in recent years, private organizations, local businesses, and governments have come together to reduce pollution levels and protect the ecology of the area.

Malappuram is a city in Kerala in southwest India. Situated at the top of a mountain and largely surrounded by the Kadalundi Puzha river, it was a military headquarters in ancient times. Malappuram is the first Indian municipality to provide free Wi-Fi to all residents. According to a 2020 survey by *The Economist*, it is the fastest-growing city in the world. Despite this, Malappuram has won several awards for cleanliness and was one of only two cities in India to achieve "low pollution" status.

7 Point out the use of *Does that mean that …?* and *What evidence is there that …?* to start the questions. Elicit the answer from the class.

The purpose of question B is to check if statement A is true.

8 Monitor and help if students are having difficulties thinking of questions. Listen to some of their ideas in open class and write good answers on the board.

ON THE ROAD UNIT 2

GETTING TO WORK

Most people's commute to work or school is usually pretty simple – a short ride in a car or on public transportation. If you're very lucky, you might be able to walk or cycle. Of course, for some commuters, it can be more tedious. Their workplace might not be so far from home, but heavy traffic can make it take much longer than it should. Their employer won't be happy if they're late. Suddenly, the commute becomes very stressful, which is not a great way to start the day.

However, there are some people who have found innovative ways to get to work.

Gabriel Horchler, who works in Washington, D.C., noticed that most of his commute took him alongside the Anacostia River. Being an avid rower, Gabriel realized that he didn't need to be sitting still in his car for hours, along with all the other drivers. So, he exchanged his car for a row boat and two bikes (one on each end). His commute, which now takes him 90 minutes, also helps him to keep in shape.

Elsewhere in the US, Benjamin Keiffer beats the traffic by hopping on his unicycle and weaving his way through the New York traffic. It's a skill he learned as a boy at circus school. Benjamin says that it's the best part of his day and much better than when he used to travel on crowded subway trains or had to share the sidewalk with hundreds of other pedestrians who were all fighting for space.

But maybe the most exciting commute of all belongs to Paul Cox. On vacation in Spain, Paul tried out paragliding and loved it. Now, when the weather allows him, he makes the 16-km trip from his home in North Wales to work by paramotor!

However, there are some people who have to go to even greater lengths to get to work.

Abdul Mallik is a teacher in Malappuram, India. He teaches in an elementary school that is only 12 km from his home. It used to take him three hours to get there by bus, as his home and the school are separated by a river. But Abdul has found a unique way to get to work faster – he walks across the river, even though the water is neck-high. Once on the other side, he changes into dry clothes and continues to the school.

This is nothing, however, compared to Elizabeth Miranda from the Philippines. Elizabeth is also a teacher, but her trip to join the rest of the staff at her school takes several hours and involves crossing five rivers. This means getting her feet and legs wet. It can be dangerous at times, but nothing will stop Elizabeth from getting to school so that she can teach her students.

Train to TH!NK

Distinguishing fact from opinion

People often have disagreements because they confuse opinions with facts. A fact is something true for which there is usually proof. An opinion is a thought or belief and may not be true. When you want to know if what someone is saying is really true, it's important to ask the right questions to help you separate opinions from facts.

7 Read the two statements (A). What is the purpose of the question (B) that follows each of them?

1 A *Teenagers never want to travel anywhere with their parents.*
  B Does that mean that there has never been a young person who liked traveling with their parents?

2 A *I'm convinced listening to music keeps you healthy.*
  B What evidence is there that proves you are right?

8 SPEAKING Here are things people said about their commute to work. Work in pairs and think of good questions that you could ask to separate facts from opinions.

1 I spend half my life in my car.
2 The government needs to spend a lot more money on public transportation.
3 Commuting is bad for your mental health.
4 People would be healthier if they could work from home.
5 People are too selfish to use public transportation.

21

Homework

Ask students to write a short text describing a trip that they have made. It could be a trip that was part of a vacation, a trip to visit family, or a trip they take daily, perhaps as part of their commute to school or work. Encourage them to use as much language from the text as possible. As a follow up, students can present their travel experiences to the class in the next lesson. After each presentation, encourage the rest of the class to ask questions and, finally, hold a class vote to decide which was the most interesting trip.

Activity idea Mixed-ability

In Exercise 8, stronger students can write questions for all five statements. Weaker students can focus on just the first three statements.

TH!NK more

Worksheets
Project On the road
Communication Going places
Get **TH!NK**ing *Is there a lot of traffic congestion where you live?*

Critical **TH!NK**ing
Understanding and analyzing ideas and arguments
Identifying and classifying information.

Warmer

Write the following on the board: *My cousin, who lives in Paris, is a lawyer; My cousin who lives in Paris is a lawyer.* Ask students to work out the difference in meaning between these sentences (in the first sentence, the speaker has just one cousin, whereas in the second, the speaker has a number of cousins, one of whom lives in Paris).

1 At this level, students will have seen relative clauses before, but may still make mistakes when using them, particularly with the use of commas in non-defining clauses. During feedback, read the sentences without the relative clause to show that B and C define the noun and A and D add extra information.
RULE: 1 B 2 C 3 A 4 D

2 Give students some time to discuss the subjects in small groups. Then hold a class vote to decide which they agree or disagree with.
1 who/that 2 who/that 3 who/that 4 that They are all defining relative clauses.

3 If you are short on time, assign this exercise for homework. Remind students that we do not use *that* as a relative pronoun in non-defining relative clauses.
1 The commuter, who was driving too fast, shouted at me.
2 Los Angeles, which is where I work, is a busy city.
3 I've been reading a book by William Boyd, who is one of my favorite writers, on my commute.
3 Juan, who is from Spain, has been working here for ten years.

4 Explain that *which* can be used to refer to specific things or to whole clauses.
the fact that the commute can become very stressful

THINK more

Workbook
Grammar p18, Ex.1–4
Vocabulary p20, Ex.1–2
Vocabulary Extra p21, Ex.1–3

Worksheets
Grammar Worksheets 2
Vocabulary Worksheets 2

GRAMMAR
Relative clauses (review)

1 **Read the sentences from the article on page 21. Look at the underlined parts. Then complete the rule by writing A, B, C, or D.**

A His commute, which now takes him 90 minutes, also helps him to keep in shape.
B He teaches at an elementary school that is only 12 km from his home.
C He had to share the sidewalk with other pedestrians who were all fighting for space.
D Gabriel Horchler, who works in Washington, D.C., noticed that …

RULE: We use a defining relative clause to identify an object (*that*), a person (*who/that*), a place (*where*), or a possession (*whose*). Without this information, it's hard to know who or what we're talking about (e.g., sentences [1]___ and [2]___).
We use a non-defining relative clause to add extra information. We don't need this information to understand the sentence. We put commas around it (e.g., sentences [3]___ and [4]___).

2 SPEAKING **Complete each sentence with *who* or *that*. Are they defining or non-defining relative clauses? Then discuss the statements in pairs.**

1 I don't understand people __________ decide to drive to work instead of walking.
2 I don't like people __________ eat their lunch next to me on a bus.
3 A commuter is just someone __________ is trying to get to work.
4 It's buses being dirty __________ makes me not want to use them.

3 **Join the sentences to make one sentence with a non-defining relative clause. Put commas in the correct places.**

0 The workers were tired. They had traveled a long way to work.
The workers, who had traveled a long way, were tired.
1 The commuter was driving too fast. The commuter shouted at me.
2 Los Angeles is a busy city. It is where I work.
3 I've been reading a book by William Boyd on my commute. Boyd is one of my favorite writers.
4 Juan has been working here for ten years. He is from Spain.

which to refer to a whole clause

4 **Read the sentence from the article on page 21. What does *which* refer to?**

Suddenly, the commute becomes very stressful, which is not a great way to start the day.

5 **What does *this* refer to in these sentences? Rewrite them as one sentence.**

0 A lot of commuters use their car. This is bad for the environment.
A lot of commuters use their car, which is bad for the environment.
1 Some people at my office commute for over an hour. This is tiring.
2 I have to be at work by eight o'clock. This can be difficult.
3 My boss doesn't mind if I'm late sometimes. This makes life easier.
4 People can get very stressed in heavy traffic. This often leads to arguments.

→ workbook page 18

VOCABULARY
Groups of people

6 **Complete each sentence with a word from the list.**

~~commuters~~ | drivers | employees | employers | immigrants | inhabitants | pedestrians | politicians | refugees | residents | the crew | the staff

0 People who travel to work are *commuters*.
1 People who walk on a street or sidewalk are called __________.
2 A group of people who work for an organization are __________.
3 People who drive cars are called __________.
4 A group of people who work on a plane or ship are __________.
5 __________ are people or animals that live in a specific place.
6 People who are paid to work for other people are called __________.
7 People who work in politics are called __________.
8 __________ are people who have to leave their own country because it's too dangerous to live there.
9 __________ pay others to work for them.
10 People who live in a certain place are the __________.
11 __________ are people who go to a different country to live there permanently.

→ workbook page 20

22

5 Point out that *which* is used to join the two sentences and makes the language sound more fluent and interesting.
1 Some people at my office commute for over an hour, which is tiring.
2 I have to be at work by eight o'clock, which can be difficult.
3 My boss doesn't mind if I'm late sometimes, which makes life easier.
4 People can get very stressed in heavy traffic, which often leads to arguments.

Workbook p18

Get it Right!
that and *which* in relative clauses

Student's Book pp122–123

6 If students are struggling with this, encourage them to use English–English dictionaries to complete the exercise, as there may not be a direct translation in their own language.
1 pedestrians 2 the staff 3 drivers 4 the crew 5 Inhabitants 6 employees 7 politicians 8 Refugees 9 Employers 10 residents 11 Immigrants

Workbook p20

7 Check/clarify: *migration, caribou /ˈkær.ɪ.buː/, a bar-tailed godwit, freshwater eel /iːl/.*
Put a copy of the photos up on the board and do the exercise as a class before students open their books. Make a note of students' ideas on the board, but do not give the answers at this stage.

8 🔊 **2.02** Tell students not to worry if they don't understand every word, but to just focus on checking that they've matched the right journey with the right animal.
A 2 B 3 C 1

9 🔊 **2.02** Before playing the audio again, ask students to answer as much as they can from memory.
1 A 2 C 3 B 4 A

10 Monitor to help with any difficulties, but do not interrupt as this is a fluency activity. If students are struggling to answer question 1, you could ask them to come up with a list for question 2 first, to give them more to discuss.

11 🔊 **2.02** Pause after each phrase and ask students to repeat the phrase using suitable intonation. Encourage students to sound enthusiastic!
1 not 2 know 3 believe
4 impressive

12 Give some of your own examples before students do the exercise. Encourage them to continue the conversation where possible. This exercise can be done as a mingle activity, with students changing partners after each dialogue.

LISTENING

7 SPEAKING Work in pairs. Look at the photos and the maps. Which animals in the photos make which journeys on the maps?

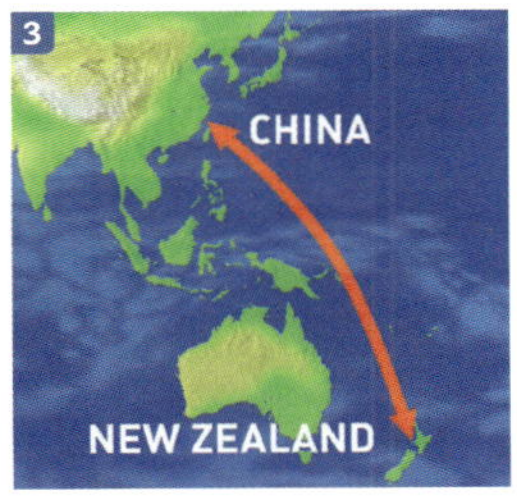

8 🔊 2.02 Listen to the radio quiz to check your ideas. Write 1–3 in the boxes.

9 🔊 2.02 Listen again and choose the correct answer, A, B, or C.

1 What is this quiz round about?
  A animal migration
  B famous animals
  C animals in nature
2 What's the most amazing fact about the bar-tailed godwit's migration?
  A It's the longest migration of any bird.
  B It does it in a day.
  C It does it without stopping.
3 How many times in their life do freshwater eels find themselves in the Sargasso Sea?
  A one
  B two
  C three
4 What makes the caribou's journey more difficult?
  A They make it on foot.
  B They have to do it through heavy snows.
  C They make it four times a year.

10 SPEAKING Work in pairs and discuss the questions.

1 Which of these animals do you think is the most amazing and why?
2 What animals migrate to and from your country?

FUNCTIONS
Introducing (amazing) information

11 🔊 2.02 Listen again to the radio quiz. Complete the phrases used to introduce information with the missing words.

1 Believe it or ______________ …
2 Did you ______________ that …?
3 Would you ______________ me if I told you …?
4 What's most ______________ about … is …

12 SPEAKING Work in pairs. Student A thinks of something amazing that they know. (Invent something if you want!) Student A gives the information to Student B, using one of the expressions in Exercise 11. Then A and B change roles.

Activity idea Extension

Ask students to add further examples of groups of people to the list in Exercise 6 (e.g., *army, association, committee, congregation, crowd, household, jury, movement, network, team, tribe, unit*). They could think of words in their own language and use dictionaries to translate, if that helps.

Homework

Ask students to write five sentences about members of their family and include non-defining relative clauses. Give them an example to get them started, e.g., *My father, who was born in France, moved to Canada in 1984.*

TH!NK more

Workbook
Listening p24, Ex.1–2

Warmer

Write the following on the board: *If you could live in a foreign country, where would you live? Why?* Give students one minute to think of their answers and make notes. Divide the class into small groups for students to compare answers. During feedback, hold a class vote to find out which country would be the most popular destination and why.

1 Before students read the blog, get them to cover it and look at the photos to answer the questions.

2 🔊 **2.03**
1 Rio de Janeiro, Brazil 2 the US 3 a year abroad

3 Ask students to try to answer the questions from memory before referring back to the blog to check.
1 His mom is from Brazil, and he has family there.
2 He didn't have a plan for the next stage of his life, and he didn't enjoy sitting around the house doing nothing.
3 teaching English to children living in the poorer parts of the city
4 more about the world and himself; he is more independent and is learning Portuguese
5 He has made lots of friends. His aunt's family has made him feel welcome.
6 He can take part in conversations easily and learning doesn't seem like hard work at all.

4 When the majority of the class has completed the sentences, students can scan the blog to check answers.
1 bring (it) about 2 worn out 3 been through 4 touched down 5 put up with 6 pick (it) up 7 setting out for 8 turning out

A BRAZILIAN ADVENTURE

Last year, after I finished school, I realized I didn't really have a plan for the next stage of my life. My mom, who is Brazilian but has lived here in the US most of her life, had the great idea of sending me down to Brazil to live with one of her aunts for a while. At first, I wasn't sure, but after two months of sitting around the house doing nothing, I began to think an overseas adventure sounded like a pretty good idea! And if nothing else, it meant I wouldn't have to put up with my annoying baby sister for a year. (Just kidding, Nina!)

So, I started doing the things I needed to do to bring it about – a few phone calls, a visit to the Brazilian embassy, and shopping for more summer clothes! Two weeks later, I was at the airport setting out for Rio de Janeiro. Eight hours later, the plane touched down. I had arrived. I was worn out, but really, really excited.

I've been here half a year now. My aunt and my cousins have really made me feel at home. I even got a job. I'm teaching English to children living in some of the poorer parts of the city.

I think the best thing about it so far has been learning about another culture. At school, I had several friends whose families originally came from different parts of the world. I think I had a pretty good understanding of some other cultures, but actually living in another country means you really get to see how life there can be different from and similar to the one you know. I've been through so many different experiences here, and mostly, they've been amazing. I feel like I've learned a lot more about the world and also about myself. I'm a lot more independent than I ever thought I could be! I've made lots of friends, and I run into several people each time I leave the house. It really makes me feel like I'm at home here.

It's also been great to learn another language. My mom never spoke Portuguese at home, which was disappointing. Of course, I heard it spoken a lot whenever my relatives visited, and I knew a few words, but I was amazed at how quickly I managed to pick it up. After a few months of hanging out with my cousin and her friends, I'm finding I understand most of what they say, and I'm able to take part in their conversations pretty easily. It's great finally having a second language, and learning it doesn't seem like work at all. I've also become really interested in photography. There are so many beautiful views to take photos of!

My year abroad is turning out to be the best year of my life so far. And who knows, I might be here longer, much longer!

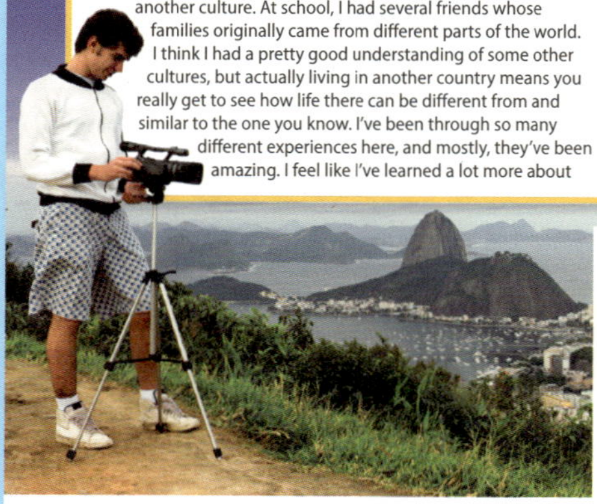

READING

1 Look at the photos and the title of the blog. Work in pairs and discuss the questions.
1 Where do you think Sam is?
2 Where do you think he's from?
3 What is the article about?

2 🔊 2.03 **Read and listen to the blog to check your ideas.**

3 Read the blog again and answer the questions.
1 What is Sam's connection to Brazil?
2 Why did he decide to spend a year in Brazil?
3 What is he doing in Brazil?
4 What has he learned from his experiences so far?
5 Why does he feel at home in Brazil?
6 How is he dealing with the language?

24

VOCABULARY
Phrasal verbs (1)

4 Complete these sentences from the blog. Use the correct form of the phrasal verbs from the list. Then read the blog again to check.

bring about | go through | pick up
put up with | set out for | touch down
turn out | wear out

1 So I started doing the things I needed to do to ________ it ________.
2 I was ________ ________, but really, really excited.
3 I've ________ ________ so many different experiences here, and mostly, they've been amazing.
4 Eight hours later, the plane ________ ________.
5 I wouldn't have to ________ ________ ________ my annoying baby sister for a year.
6 I was amazed at how quickly I've managed to ________ it ________.
7 Two weeks later, I was at the airport ________ ________ ________ Rio de Janeiro.
8 My year abroad is ________ ________ to be the best year of my life.

PRONUNCIATION
Phrasal verb stress Go to page 120.

Pronunciation
Phrasal verb stress

Student's Book p120

Activity idea Mixed-ability

Divide students roughly according to level. For Exercise 4, ask stronger students to cover both the blog and the list of phrasal verbs, then try to complete the sentences before looking at the list of phrasal verbs to check.

Weaker students can complete the exercise with any verbs (phrasal or otherwise) that fit the context. They then try to match with phrasal verbs from the list before checking in the blog. This approach will help them more quickly grasp the meaning of the target phrasal verbs.

TH!NK more

Workbook
Reading p22, Ex.1–4
Vocabulary p20, Ex.3–4
Pronunciation p118

Worksheets
Vocabulary Worksheets 2

Grammar; TH!NK Values

5 During feedback, clarify the meaning of each phrasal verb if necessary.
1 set out for 2 pick up 3 put up with 4 go through 5 turn out 6 touch down 7 bring about

6 Monitor to encourage students to use the phrasal verbs in their answers. Make a note of any particularly good usage to mention during feedback.

Workbook p20

▶ 05 Grammar video!
Omitting relative pronouns

7 Elicit answers and the position of *that*, writing the sentences on the board with an arrow pointing from *that* to the object.
1 I started doing the things that I needed to do.
2 I run into several people that I know each time I leave the house.
That is the object.
RULE: 3 object 4 subject

8 Remind students that we can remove the relative pronoun when it refers to an object, but not if it refers to a subject. During feedback, ask what the relative pronoun refers to in each sentence.
1 ✓ 2 ✗ 3 ✓ 4 ✗ 5 ✓ 6 ✗

Workbook p19

9 Point out that we use reduced relative clauses in written English to make sentences flow more easily.
1 I'm teaching English to children who are living in some of the poorer parts of the city.
2 I was boarding a plane that was heading for Rio de Janeiro.
RULE: B

10 Clarify that there is a mixture of reduced relative clauses and omitted relative pronouns in the paragraph.
2 who are 3 who were 4 that 5 that 7 that

Get it Right!
Relative pronouns

Student's Book p123

11 Give students two minutes to rank their ideas individually.

Social Responsibilities
Showing intercultural awareness
Understanding aspects of other cultures.

5 **Match the phrasal verbs from Exercise 4 with their meanings.**

0 make (someone) very tired *wear out*
1 start a journey ______
2 learn (informally) ______
3 tolerate ______
4 experience (a difficult situation) ______
5 have a particular result ______
6 land ______
7 make happen ______

6 SPEAKING **Work in pairs and discuss the questions.**

1 How do you feel when you set out on a trip?
2 What wears you out?
3 Can you think of any habits someone you know has that you have to put up with?
4 What difficulties does someone have to go through when they finish school and start college?
5 Do you think it's possible to pick up new words from listening to English-language songs?

→ workbook page 20

GRAMMAR
Grammar video ▶05
Omitting relative pronouns

7 **Read the two sentences from the blog. Where can you put *that* in each sentence? Is *that* the subject or object of the relative clause? Complete the rule with the words *subject* and *object*.**

1 I started doing the things I needed to do.
2 I run into several people I know each time I leave the house.

> **RULE:** When the relative pronouns *that* / *who* are the [3] ______ of a defining relative clause, they can be omitted. But if they are the [4] ______ of the defining relative clause, they can't be omitted.

8 **Read these sentences. Put a check (✓) if you can omit the pronoun in *italics* or a cross (✗) if you can't.**

1 You'll miss the friends *who* you used to hang out with. ☐
2 I ran into some people *who* couldn't wait to leave. ☐
3 I've decided to write about some of the challenges *that* living abroad can bring. ☐
4 You become one of those people *who* wish they'd stayed at home. ☐
5 There's new vocabulary *that* you have to pick up. ☐
6 There's no country in the world *that* suits everybody. ☐

→ workbook page 19

Reduced relative clauses

9 **Read these sentences. Where can you put *that was* and *who are*? Check (✓) the correct box in the rule.**

1 I'm teaching English to children living in some of the poorer parts of the city.
2 I was boarding a plane heading for Rio de Janeiro.

> **RULE:** When relative clauses begin with a relative pronoun + the auxiliary verb *be*, we can omit:
> A ☐ only the relative pronoun
> B ☐ the relative pronoun + the verb *be*.

10 **Cross out the words/phrases in *italics* that can be omitted.**

Soccer players [1]*who* come from other countries to play in the UK often have problems adjusting to their new lives. Some of the players [2]*who are* playing in the UK are really young, so they easily feel homesick. And then there are things like food – people [3]*who were* brought up on spicy food or exotic fruit don't always like typical British food. But the biggest problems [4]*that* they face seem to be the weather and the language. The country [5]*that* they come from might be very hot, but the UK isn't. It isn't always easy for players [6]*who* come from Brazil or Mexico, for example, to adapt to the gray skies and short winter days [7]*that* they experience in England. And not all the foreign players find it easy to learn English – the ones [8]*who* do, tend to find it easier to adapt.

TH!NK values
Learning from other cultures

11 **Imagine you live in another country. What three things would you find most difficult/enjoy most about it?**

12 **Choose the options that are true for you. Make notes about your reasons.**

1 *I'd like* / *I wouldn't like* to visit other countries.
2 *I'd like* / *I wouldn't like* to live in another country.
3 *I'm interested* / *I'm not interested* in other cultures.
4 Knowing about other cultures *helps* / *doesn't help* me understand my own culture.
5 *I think* / *I don't think* it's good to have people from other countries living in my country.

13 SPEAKING **Compare your ideas about Exercises 11 and 12 with the class. How similar or different are you to your classmates?**

12 Students' own answers

13 During feedback, hold a class vote and create a class ranking on the board. This exercise can be done as a mingle.

Homework

Ask students to make a list of the things that people moving to their own country might find difficult to get used to. Write general topics on the board if necessary, e.g., *food, weather, working hours, daily timetable, transportation, noise*, etc. Ask students to write a short text imagining that they are foreigners who moved to live in their country. Encourage them to omit the relative pronouns.

TH!NK more

Workbook
Vocabulary p20, Ex.3–4
Grammar p19, Ex.5–6

Worksheets
Grammar Worksheets 2
Grammar video! Omitting relative pronouns

Warmer

Call out either the verb or the particle from the phrasal verbs in Exercise 4 on page 24 and elicit the whole phrasal verb. For example, you say *bring* or *about* and students say *bring about*. Once you've demonstrated this with one or two examples, pairs take turns testing each other in the same way.

▶ 06 TH!NK

Nomadic people and animals

1 **Check/clarify:** *nomadic.* Put a copy of the three photos up on the board and do the exercise as a class before students open their books.

2 🔊 **2.06** Tell students not to try to understand every word, but to focus on checking their answers to Exercise 1.

1 the Tlingit – on islands between Canada and Alaska 2 the Bedouin – Northern Africa and the Arabian peninsula 3 the Nukak-Maku – Amazon rainforest in Colombia

Culture notes

The Tlingit people are believed to date back as long as 11,000 years ago. They are divided into three groups known as the Eagle, Raven, and Wolf. Women have always been the dominant family members in a Tlingit household. Both women and men can assume leadership roles.

The use of the Tlingit language was discouraged when Americans controlled the Alaskan frontier. However, in the late twentieth century, language revitalization programs were introduced by the 1,100 native Tlingit speakers left.

TH!NK
Nomadic people and animals

Culture

NOMADIC PEOPLE

1 SPEAKING Work in pairs and look at the photos and the title. Where do you think the groups of people live?

2 🔊 2.06 Read and listen to the text to check your ideas.

Most of us are used to living in the same place – every day, all year round, we go "home." But for some people around the world, home is a place that moves, often across international borders. Here are three groups of people who have or had a nomadic way of life.

1 THE TLINGIT

The Tlingit are found on the islands and the shores between Canada and Alaska. They were once a much larger group of people, but the arrival of Europeans in the 1770s brought the Tlingit into contact with diseases, such as smallpox, against which they had no immunity. Many of them died.

They have their own language, in which their name translates to "people from the tides." Unsurprisingly, the sea has played a huge role in their lives, particularly as a source of food. Their diet consists of a lot of fish, seal meat, and seaweed. They also hunt deer, bears, and goats while collecting berries and other plants from the forests.

Today, around 15,000 Tlingit still live in the area, and although most of them have a modern way of life, some still live off the land in the way that their ancestors did.

2 THE BEDOUIN

The Bedouin are one of the most well-known nomadic tribes, and there are an estimated 21 million Bedouin in the world today, split into many different clans. In Arabic, their name means "desert dwellers," as they have lived in the dry regions of Northern Africa and the Arabian peninsula for over 1,000 years. Their search for water sources means they are always on the move, taking their herds of goats and camels with them. These two animals are essential to the Bedouin for food, dairy products, and for trading with other clans.

Many Bedouin have left their nomadic lifestyle behind them and have settled in the towns and cities of the region. However, they are eager to keep their culture alive and organize annual festivals to celebrate their heritage and introduce it to new audiences.

3 THE NUKAK-MAKU

The Nukak-Maku are a nomadic tribe that lives deep inside the Amazon rainforest in Colombia. For hundreds of years, they lived unknown to the outside world. They were only discovered in 1981. Unfortunately, contact with civilization meant they were exposed to new illnesses, and many died from these diseases. Their land is also under threat from people wanting to grow crops. These days, fewer than 1,000 Nukak-Maku are thought to remain there, and they are at risk of becoming extinct.

They live in very small groups and are always on the move, staying in one place for only a few days before moving on to their next destination. They are true masters of survival and use poisoned darts and blowguns to hunt animals such as monkeys, birds, and wild pigs.

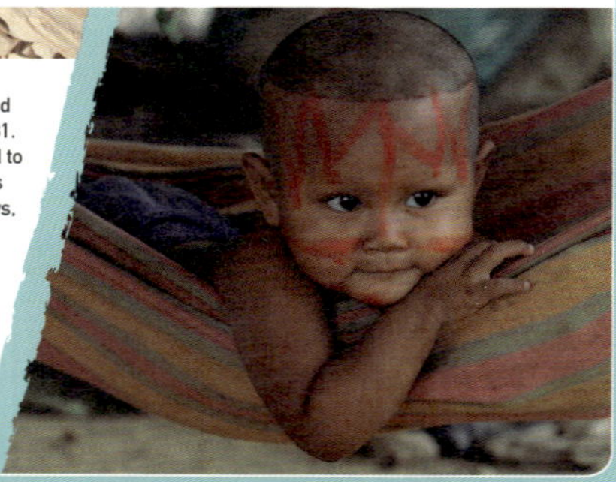

26

The Bedu, or Bedouin people, are thought to have been established since 850 BCE. Divided into many tribes, they herd goats and camels as a source of dairy products, meat, and wool. Others are herdsmen that practice farming and agriculture. More than three or four generations of Bedouins live together as a single unit. In the 1950s and 1960s, huge numbers of the Bedouin people left their traditional nomadic life and settled in cities.

The Nukak live in southeast Colombia. They are one of six groups known as the "Maku" peoples, all nomadic hunter-gatherers living in the northwest Amazon. Traditionally, they live in groups of nine to thirty people in the forest away from the rivers. The Nukak avoided regular contact with outsiders until 1988 when about 40 Nukak people unexpectedly arrived at a newly-created town called Calamar, creating a sensation in the international press. In 1993, the Colombian government recognized the tribe's right to their ancestral land and created the Nukak Reserve. Today that land is occupied by coca growers (the raw material for cocaine). Many Nukak have been forced to flee their homes and seek refuge in towns. The Nukak are one of at least 32 tribes in Colombia believed to be at "imminent risk of extinction."

Culture; Writing

3 Check/clarify: *rely on.*
Before students read the article again, get them to identify the key information that they need to look for in each question. Tell students to underline information in the text that helped them answer each question.
1 the Tlingit 2 the Nukak-Maku 3 the Bedouin 4 the Bedouin 5 the Nukak-Maku 6 the Tlingit

4 Check/clarify: *defense, died out.*
Ask students to cover the definitions. Give them two minutes to find the highlighted words in the article and to try to deduce meaning from context.
1 borders 2 destination 3 diet 4 immunity 5 clans 6 extinct 7 annual 8 remain

5 Monitor and write down any common errors to review at the end. Listen to some of the students' ideas in open class discussion.

1 Set a two-minute time limit to encourage students to read quickly for gist and to focus on the questions.
1 ten days 2 a couple of days ago 3 Their patience. Inuit hunting involves a lot of waiting in the cold.

2 *1 a lot 2 here I am at last 3 said I could go along with them 4 I'm over the moon 5 how I'm getting on with things 6 a couple of days ago*

3 *She is writing an informal email to someone she knows well. The phrases in Exercise 2 are more formal.*

4 Give students time to make notes in preparation for writing an email. Monitor to help with any questions. Encourage them to use some of the vocabulary and expressions from the email and the article on page 26.

5 If you are short on time, assign this exercise for homework.

3 **Read the article again and answer the questions.**
According to the article, which group (or groups):
1 relies heavily on the sea?
2 has only recently become known to the world?
3 has seen many of their people move to towns?
4 lives in an area where water is difficult to find?
5 is in danger of not surviving?
6 has modernized the way they live?

4 VOCABULARY **Match the highlighted words in the article with the definitions.**
1 the places where one country ends and another begins
2 on a journey or trip, the place you want to get to
3 all the things that you eat
4 defense against a disease
5 small groups of people
6 having died out completely
7 happening once every year
8 stay

5 SPEAKING **Work in pairs and discuss the questions.**
1 Do you know of any other groups of people who are nomadic? What do you know about their culture?
2 What do you think might be the advantages and disadvantages of a nomadic lifestyle?
3 The article says that the Nukak-Maku may die out. What do you think could be done to protect these people?

WRITING
An informal email

1 INPUT **Read Giulia's email and answer the questions.**
1 How long has she been with the Inuit people?
2 When did she try to catch a seal?
3 What does she say strikes her most about the Inuit?

2 ANALYZE **Match words or phrases from the email with these meanings.**
1 a great deal
2 I have finally arrived
3 agreed that I could accompany them
4 I am extremely happy
5 my experiences here
6 one or two days ago

3 **Why does Giulia not use the phrases in Exercise 2 in her email?**

4 PLAN **Imagine you are spending two weeks living with one of the nomadic tribes mentioned in the article on page 26 and make notes.**
- Choose which of the three groups you are living with.
- Decide what things in general have been good/not so good about your experiences so far.
- Decide on one specific thing about their life that has really impressed you.

5 PRODUCE **Write an email to an English-speaking friend (about 200 words).**
- Make sure to start and end your email appropriately.
- Talk generally about your experiences first; then move on to more specific details.
- Check your writing to make sure that your language is not too formal.

Giulia
Giulia@thinkmail.com

Hi James,
How are you doing? Hope you're OK!
Well, here I am at last – living in northern Canada with nomadic Inuit people. You know that I've been wanting to do this for years, and my dream has finally come true. I'm over the moon to be here.
I got here ten days ago, and I'm staying with a family who said I could go along with them to hunt. I've already done some amazing things – sleeping in an igloo, for example, and watching people go hunting for fish and small animals.
The most difficult thing to deal with, of course, is the cold. There's also the fact that you have to keep moving every few days to find food. The way they hunt is interesting. They make a hole in the ice and hope that a seal will appear so that they can catch it. I went hunting with my host dad a couple of days ago – he showed me how to make a hole and then we stood for six hours in the freezing cold, waiting for a seal to appear. It never came. I got so frustrated. But then I thought, "Hey, Inuit people do this all the time, sometimes waiting for ten hours. And sometimes they catch a seal, and sometimes they don't. What's my problem?" What amazes me most about them is their patience, and my own is getting a lot better!
Well, I'll write and tell you more about how I'm getting along with things when I can. Hope you're well!
All the best,
Giulia

Homework
If you are short on time, students can do Writing Exercise 5 for homework. If you have done this in class, ask students to exchange their emails with another student for them to read and give feedback on content and structure. Students could check if the email uses the same structure as the plan. They should also decide which the most/least interesting part of the email is.

Activity idea Extension
On completion of Exercise 5, ask students to exchange their emails with another student. Ask them to evaluate on the basis of **content** (Were all points included? How interesting were the ideas?), **organization** (Did each paragraph include a clear and distinct idea?), **communicative purpose** (Were you convinced by it?), and **language**.

TH!NK more
Practice Extra
Unit 2 Practice it!
Unit 2 Master it!

Workbook
Developing Writing p23

Tests
Unit, extension, and skills test 2

1 In B2 First Reading and Use of English Part 4, candidates read six questions. Each question contains three parts: a lead-in sentence, a key word, and a second gapped sentence. Candidates fill the gap in the second sentence so that when complete it has a similar meaning to the lead-in sentence. This part of the exam tests lexical and grammatical structures and the ability to paraphrase.

Encourage your students to do the following:

- Read the first sentence to understand the meaning.
- Pay attention to any verb in the second sentence, as it will often indicate whether to use a singular or plural noun.
- Write only the words that fill the gap.
- Check that the answer has between two and five words, including the key word.
- Check that the key word has been used in the same form as it was given.
- Read the completed sentence again to make sure it is similar to the first one.

1 has worn/tired me 2 regret going 3 which (really) annoyed 4 should put up with 5 don't forget to lock 6 can't stand getting

B2 First for Schools

READING AND USE OF ENGLISH

Part 4: Key word transformations

1 For questions 1–6, complete the second sentence so that it has a similar meaning to the first sentence, using the word given. Do not change the word given. You must use between two and five words, including the word given. Here is an example (0).

0 I think taking the 8 pm train is the best idea.
PREFER
I'd *prefer to take* the 8 pm train.

1 I've been studying all day and I'm really tired.
ME
Studying all day ____________________ out.

2 I wish I hadn't gone to bed so late.
REGRET
I ____________________ to bed so late.

3 I got really annoyed by Paul and Dave laughing all the time.
WHICH
Paul and Dave kept laughing, ____________________ me.

4 That kind of behaviour should not be tolerated by anyone.
PUT
No-one ____________________ that kind of behaviour.

5 Please make sure you lock the door.
FORGET
Please ____________________ the door.

6 Getting up early in the morning is the worst thing.
STAND
I ____________________ up early in the morning.

Part 1: Multiple-choice cloze

→ workbook page 97

2 For questions 1–8, read the text below and decide which answer (A, B, C or D) best fits each gap. There is an example at the beginning (0).

The Great Migration of wildebeest in Africa is [0] *C* the world's most impressive wildlife [1]___. Every year, around two million of these strange animals [2]___ a huge, circular journey of 3,000 kilometres or so, [3]___ grass and water. The exact [4]___ they follow depends very much on the seasons and where there is rainfall. At one point on their journey, the animals get to the Grumeti and Mara rivers and they need to [5]___ the fast-flowing and crocodile-infested waters in order to [6]___. Usually, they are very hesitant to go in, and can wait for hours or days at the river bank, but [7]___, one wildebeest jumps into the water and all the others follow. Thousands are taken by the crocodiles, but the survivors have the [8]___ of fresh grass on the other side. They won't have to face the crocodiles for another year!

	A	B	C	D
0	at	in	(among)	around
1	views	glimpses	incidents	spectacles
2	make	do	have	participate
3	searching	seeking	looking	viewing
4	way	direction	map	route
5	overtake	walk	cross	leave
6	proceed	run on	prolong	carry out
7	ultimately	eventually	lastly	lately
8	review	release	reward	reassurance

WRITING

Part 1: An essay

→ workbook page 43

3 Write your answer in 140–190 words in an appropriate style.

In your English class, you have been talking about inventions. Now your English teacher has asked you to write an essay for homework. Write your essay using **all** the notes and giving reasons for your point of view.

Technological or scientific inventions are responsible for some of the biggest changes we can see in the world today. What do you think?

Notes

Write about:

1 transport
2 communication
3 ____________________ (your own idea)

28

2 In B2 First Reading and Use of English Part 1, candidates read a text containing eight gaps representing a word or phrase. Candidates will also find eight sets of four words or phrases which correspond with each gap. Candidates choose one of four options, A, B, C, or D, that best fits the gap. This part of the exam tests the candidates' lexical knowledge and understanding of collocations and set phrases.

Encourage your students to do the following:

- Read the text to find out more about the context.
- Read the whole of each gapped sentence, not just the part that goes before the gap.
- Compare each option with the sentence before choosing an answer.
- Read the sentence again to confirm the correct answer.

1 D 2 A 3 B 4 D 5 C 6 A 7 B 8 C

Workbook p97

3 In B2 First Writing Part 1, candidates write an essay of about 170 words. There will be a statement or question which students have to give their opinion about and two prompts to help give students some ideas. This part of the exam tests the candidates' ability to write well-organized texts with a real communicative purpose.

Encourage your students to do the following:

- Read the question/statement and the two prompts carefully, to identify what is required, who it is for, and what kind of information is needed.
- Plan the answer and respond to both prompts.
- Students will need to think of a third idea of their own which is different from the two given prompts. Brainstorm some ideas for this.
- Write a rough draft of the essay before writing the final answer. Check that it is well-organized and has a range of tenses, expressions, and vocabulary.
- Read the essay again to check that it makes sense and that all the content points have been included.

Students' own answers

Workbook p43

1 1 wandering 2 ran into 3 refugees 4 go through 5 guilty 6 staff 7 residents 8 crawl 9 puzzled 10 turned out

2 1 to go 2 falling 3 to do 4 to live 5 doing 6 living

3 1 I really like that guy ~~which~~ who plays Sam on TV.
2 My brother Julian ~~that,~~ who lives in New York, is coming to stay with me.
3 It isn't a movie that makes everyone laugh.
4 The man ~~what~~ who plays the drums in the band is on the left in the photo.
5 My brother broke my phone, ~~what~~ which means he has to buy me a new one.
6 She's the runner who / that won the gold medal.

4 1 quite a; amazing 2 phenomenal; incredible 3 bet; can't 4 will; dare

TEST YOURSELF UNITS 1 & 2

VOCABULARY

1 **Complete the sentences with the words in the list. There are four extra words.**

crawl | drivers | go through | guilty | puzzled | ran into | refugees
residents | rushing | staff | stuck | turned out | wandering | worn out

1 Sally was ________________ slowly around the store looking for a present for her uncle's birthday.
2 I hadn't seen Marie for ages, but yesterday I ________________ her at the movie theater.
3 I saw a documentary about ________________ fleeing across borders to escape the war.
4 I'm so happy that I passed my driving test. It was awful, and I wouldn't want to ________________ that again!
5 You haven't done anything wrong – you don't have to feel ________________ about anything, OK?
6 Mr. Sawyer runs a small business. He has a ________________ of four people.
7 They are all local ________________. Most of them live in the streets near us.
8 My little sister can't walk yet, but she can ________________ really fast!
9 I was ________________ by my friend's reaction – I couldn't understand why she laughed.
10 The beginning of the movie was very sad, but it all ________________ OK in the end. /10

GRAMMAR

2 **Complete the sentences. Use the verbs in the list, with *to* + infinitive, or with a gerund (*-ing* form). Use two of the verbs twice.**

do | fall | go | live

1 Yesterday, my friends decided ________________ to the beach to play volleyball.
2 My brother says he remembers ________________ out of bed when he was two years old.
3 Jack always forgets ________________ his homework and then gets in trouble.
4 I want ________________ in Paris one day.
5 I don't mind ________________ the dishes at home.
6 I hate being in an empty house. I can't imagine ________________ alone.

3 **Find and correct the mistake in each sentence.**

1 I really like that guy which plays Sam on TV.
2 My brother Julian that lives in New York is coming to stay with me.
3 It isn't a movie makes everyone laugh.
4 The man what plays the drums in the band is on the left in the photo.
5 My brother broke my phone, what means he has to buy me a new one.
6 She's the runner won the gold medal. /12

FUNCTIONAL LANGUAGE

4 **Choose the correct options.**

1 A Next week Rebecca's going to run a 15-kilometer race. That's *quite a / really* distance.
B Yes, it is. And she only started running a couple of months ago, too. That's *amazing / daring*.
2 A I heard that you got 95%. That's *OK / phenomenal*. Well done!
B Thanks. I could hardly believe it. And my parents thought it was *incredible / quite*.
3 A *I'm betting / bet* you can't say "good morning" in five different languages.
B Well, you're right – of course I *can / can't*.
4 A You *can / will* never manage to stay off the internet for two days.
B Hmm. I think you're right, but I *dare / can dare* you to stop using Whatsapp for a week! /8

MY SCORE /30
22–30 10–21 0–9

29

The Cambridge Life Competencies Framework

Learning to Learn
Setting goals and planning
Watch this video for a tip on developing your students' ability to learn. Scan the QR code here.

Warmer

Ask students to work with a partner and brainstorm a list of typical outfits that people wear to costume parties to check how familiar students are with the theme of the unit.

▶ 07 Get TH!NKing

Play the video and discuss the question with your class.

1 Give a couple of your own examples before students do the exercise.

2 Before students do the task, get them to cover the blog on page 31 and look at the title and photos, as well as the photos on page 30. Give student pairs two minutes to think about the answer to the question.

3 🔊 **3.01** Before playing the audio, give students another two minutes to read the blog quickly and to check ideas. The focus here is on understanding the gist. Encourage students not to focus on every word for now.

4 Encourage students to underline the parts of the blog that helped them find the answers.

1 They waved from the doorstep.
2 180 days
3 Rain's brother and his mom
4 American football player, pirate
5 $50
6 He used the family costume collection, and friends and neighbors helped.
7 He was embarrassed at the beginning, but thought he was pretty cool in the end.
8 He was there again in costume.

3 GROWING UP

OBJECTIVES

FUNCTIONS: emphasizing

GRAMMAR: quantifiers; *so* and *such* (review); *do* and *did* for emphasis

VOCABULARY: costumes and uniforms; bringing up children

Get TH!NKING

Watch the video and think: what's the hardest part of being a teenager?

A

C

B

D

READING

1 SPEAKING **Look at the photos and discuss the questions in pairs.**
1 Do you enjoy dressing up? Why do you think people enjoy wearing costumes?
2 Do you think costumes are just for kids?
3 Do you think it's OK to make animals wear costumes? Why (not)?

2 SPEAKING **Look again at the photos and look at the title and the photo on the next page. What do you think the blog will be about?**

3 🔊 3.01 **Read and listen to the blog to check your ideas.**

4 **Read the blog again and answer the questions.**
1 What did Rain's parents do on his first day of high school?
2 How many days did Rain's dad, Dale, wave at the bus?
3 Which other family members got involved?
4 What were the first and last costumes that Dale wore?
5 How much did Dale spend on the costumes?
6 How did he keep the cost so low?
7 What did Rain think about his dad dressing up at the beginning? And at the end?
8 What happened at the beginning of the next school year?

5 SPEAKING **Work in pairs and discuss the questions.**
1 Does Dale sound like a good dad? Explain your reasons.
2 How would you feel if your dad was like Dale? Why?
3 Why do you think Dale wanted to dress up?

30

5 As this is a fluency activity, do not interrupt to correct errors unless they impede communication. Listen to some of the students' ideas in open class as feedback, encouraging them to react to and debate with each other.

Objectives

Functions and speaking Emphasizing
Grammar Quantifiers; *so* and *such* (review); *do* and *did* for emphasis
Vocabulary Costumes and uniforms; bringing up children
Literature *About a Boy*

Resources for this unit

All available online

Videos
- Get **TH!NK**ing: *What's the hardest part of being a teenager?*
- Grammar video!: Quantifiers

Tests
- Unit, extension, and skills test 3
- End of term test 1

Worksheets
- Grammar and vocabulary: Basic, Standard, and Extension Worksheets
- Project: Growing up
- Communication: The next generation
- Literature Worksheets: *Gulliver's Travels*
- Get **TH!NK**ing and Grammar video! video Worksheets

6 Ask students to find all the people mentioned in the blog and write them on the board as prompts (Rain, Dale (Rain's dad), Rochelle (Rain's mom), Rain's younger brother, Rain's friends).
1 Rain 2 Rain's friends 3 Rochelle

7 Point out the use of *Initially* and *with time*. Encourage students to find evidence in the article to justify their answers.

8 Give a couple of your own ideas as examples before students work in pairs. At the end of the exercise, listen to some of the students' ideas and encourage open class discussion.

Homework

Ask students to write a short text about an embarrassing moment that they have had. If they haven't had any, or the subject is too personal, they can interview someone or make up some ideas. As a follow-up, students can present their text to the class in the next lesson. After each presentation, encourage the rest of the class to ask questions and finally hold a class vote to decide which was the most embarrassing.

Culture notes

Makani Rain Price is from Utah, USA. He has an older sister, Rikki, and a younger brother, Ryatt. In 2011, when his school bus changed routes and drove past his house, he became the focus of his dad Dale's prank of dressing up and waving at the bus.

Dale Price is a stay-at-home dad who previously owned a chain of paintball stores in the USA. On Rain's last day of school, Dale chose a pirate costume for his final send-off. Other costumes included a giant chicken and The Little Mermaid. He even brought an old toilet bowl onto the street and sat on it, reading a newspaper. The family's blog received more than two million page views.

GROWING UP UNIT 3

AN EMBARRASSING DAD

If you think you have the world's most embarrassing dad, then think again.

American teenager Rain Price was waved off to school from the bus stop outside his house, by his dad, every day for a whole school year. OK, so that doesn't sound too bad, but this was no ordinary goodbye, because each day, Rain's dad did it while wearing a different costume!

It all started on 16-year-old Rain's first day of high school. Like many proud parents, Rochelle and Dale, Rain's mom and dad, sent Rain off to school with a big wave from the doorstep. That evening Rain made the mistake of complaining about how embarrassing they were, which gave Dale a great idea.

The next morning, as Rain stepped onto the bus outside his house, he could hear all of his school friends laughing at something. He turned around, and to his horror, there was his dad waving goodbye, dressed as an American football player, complete with ball and helmet. But that was just the beginning. For the next 180 school days, come rain or shine, Dale waved goodbye to his son dressed in a different costume. One day he was a king waving his sword and shield, the next a chef in his hat and apron, the following a pirate. Then there was Elvis and Wonder Woman.

Dale even got other members of the family involved, using Rain's younger brother to play Batman alongside his Robin.

Amazingly, Dale only spent $50 on all of the costumes. He got lots of costumes from the family costume collection, and there were several friends and neighbors who were happy to help.

Some of Rain's friends didn't find it funny, but most of them looked forward to seeing what Dale would be wearing every day. And Dale found an international audience for his dressing up, too, as each day, Rochelle took a photo of her husband in costume and put it on their blog, waveatthebus.blogspot.com, which became a hit on the internet. Even Rain was eventually able to see the funny side and realized that his dad was pretty cool after all.

For the final farewell on the last day of school, Dale dressed up as a pirate and stood next to a sign that said, "It's been fun waving at the bus. Have a great summer." But all good things don't always come to an end. The new school year began, and Dale was there again, in costume, to wave at the bus.

Train to TH!NK

Changing your opinions

It can be a mistake to believe something just because it's based on an opinion you have. Becoming a critical thinker means continually reflecting on your opinions and being willing to change them if they aren't based on evidence.

6 **Which people from the story may have had these opinions at some point? Write their names.**
1 "My dad is the most embarrassing person in the world." ____________
2 "Rain's dad is really silly." ____________
3 "I don't think Dale should do this – it's going to cost a lot of money." ____________

7 SPEAKING **Work in pairs and discuss how the people's opinions in Exercise 6 changed throughout the school year and why.**

Initially, Rain thought that his dad was the most embarrassing dad in the world. But with time, he realized that maybe that wasn't true. He learned to appreciate his dad's sense of humor.

8 SPEAKING **Work in groups and discuss some opinions that you or family members have had that have changed. Think about music, school, fashion, friends, etc.**

31

Activity idea Extension

Write the following statements on the board:

Cycling should not be allowed in the city center.

People who write graffiti on walls should go to prison.

If students do not pass a test, they should do extra classes on Saturdays.

Divide the class into two groups: A and B. Group A agrees with the statements. Group B disagrees. Give students three minutes to brainstorm with a student from their own group reasons why they might agree or disagree. Regroup students into A/B pairs to debate the statements and to try to change each other's opinions. Ask volunteers to report back on their discussions during open-class feedback.

TH!NK more

Worksheets
Project Growing up
Communication The next generation
Get **TH!NK**ing *What's the hardest part of being a teenager?*

Critical TH!NKing
Evaluating ideas and arguments
Drawing appropriate conclusions.

Warmer

To review clothes, give students two minutes to think of as many different items of clothing as they can. After two minutes, play a game of "vocabulary tennis" with each group taking turns to say a piece of clothing until one team runs out of ideas.

1 Ask students to try to complete sentences from memory before looking back at page 31 to check their answers. This encourages students to notice language and helps activate their curiosity around the target language.
1 many 2 all 3 lots
4 several 5 Some; most
RULE: 6 none 7 a little
8 several 9 lots of 10 all

2 *1 lots of 2 a lot of 3 most*
4 Most 5 Most 6 hardly any

3 Monitor and encourage students to answer in full sentences.

Workbook p28

▶ 08 Grammar video! Quantifiers

Get it Right!
much vs. many

Student's Book p123

Get it Right!
much and most

Student's Book p123

4 If you have access to the internet, find pictures of the items in the list. Ask students to match the items in the list with the pictures in order to check/clarify *sword, shield, wig, snorkel,* and *poncho.* Say the words for students to repeat and check pronunciation.
Suggested answers: sword and shield – gladiator, foot soldier, knight, warrior
leather jacket – biker
wig – clown
snorkel – diver
poncho – cowboy, hippy
helmet – astronaut, police officer, engineer
bathrobe – boxer, wizard, monk, hospital patient, angel, king or queen
mask – Batman, surgeon; apron – chef, baker; football jersey – football player

5 Give students two minutes to discuss the difference between a costume and a uniform (a costume is worn to create the appearance of a particular period or character, e.g., a cowboy costume; a uniform is worn by members of an organization or a sports team, e.g., an army uniform).
A uniform B costume C uniform

6 At the end of the exercise, listen to some of the students' ideas and encourage open class discussion.

Workbook p30

GRAMMAR
Quantifiers

Grammar video ▶08

1 **Look at the blog on page 31 and complete the sentences. Then complete the rule with *lots of, a little, all, several,* and *none.***

1 Like ______ proud parents …
2 He could hear ______ of his school friends laughing at something.
3 He got ______ of costumes from the family costume collection.
4 There were ______ friends and neighbors happy to help.
5 ______ of his friends didn't find it funny, but ______ of them looked forward to seeing what Dale would be wearing every day.

RULE: Quantifiers are words and expressions that we use to talk about amount.

0%
6 ______
hardly any
a few / 7 ______,
not many / much, a small number of
some / 8 ______
9 ______ / *a lot of,*
plenty, much / many, a good deal of
most, almost all, the vast majority of
10 ______
100%

2 **Choose the correct words.**

1 I have *a few / lots of* followers on my YouTube channel – more than 20,000.
2 I spend *a lot of / hardly any* time with my friends – we meet up every day after school and most weekends, too.
3 I spend *most / hardly any* of my time on my tablet. It's the most important thing I have.
4 *A small number / Most* of my teachers are really nice. I really like this school.
5 *Most / All* of my family lives near me, but I have an uncle who lives in Australia.
6 I spend *almost all / hardly any* money on downloads. I don't really care about music.

3 SPEAKING **Work in pairs and discuss the sentences in Exercise 2. Which of them are true for you?**

→ workbook page 28

VOCABULARY
Costumes and uniforms

4 SPEAKING **Look at the list of clothes and accessories. What costumes might people use these items for? Discuss in pairs.**

- sword and shield
- leather jacket
- wig
- snorkel
- poncho
- helmet
- bathrobe
- mask
- apron
- football jersey

5 **Look at the photos. Who is wearing a costume? Who is wearing a uniform?**

A

B

C

6 SPEAKING **Work in pairs and discuss the questions.**

1 Do you or anybody you know wear a uniform for work? Describe it.
2 Can you list five jobs in which people wear uniforms?
3 Describe a sports uniform to your partner, but don't say what sport it's for. Can your partner guess?
4 Describe your perfect costume to wear to a costume party.

→ workbook page 30

32

Activity idea Extension

For further work with quantifiers, write the following on the board: *Lots of students … , Hardly any students … , Almost all students … , The vast majority of students …*

Ask students to complete the sentences to describe students in their school.

TH!NK more

Workbook
Grammar p28, Ex.1–4
Vocabulary p30, Ex.1–2

Worksheets
Grammar Worksheets 3
Grammar Video! Quantifiers
Vocabulary Worksheets 3

Listening; Speaking

7 Invite students to share their ideas with the rest of the class, but do not give the answers yet.

8 🔊 **3.02 Check/clarify:** *tragic, heart warming.*
Ask students to read the statements before they listen. Tell them not to worry about understanding every word for now, but to focus on listening for the answers. Encourage them to think about the correct answer to the false statements.
1 F (It doesn't have a tragic ending.) 2 T 3 T 4 F (He competes in triathlons with her.) 5 T

9 🔊 **3.02 Check/clarify:** *moving (story), cerebral palsy, devoted, triathlons, heavy smoker, a buggy, diagnosed, sprint, intense, devotion.*
1 B 2 A 3 B 4 B 5 C

10–11 Check/clarify: *sacrifice.*
Give a couple of your own examples before students do the exercises.

Homework

Ask students to research someone from around the world who has made a sacrifice / raised a lot of money / done good for other people. As a follow-up, students can present this person to the class in the next lesson. After each presentation, encourage the rest of the class to ask questions and finally hold a class vote to decide which was the most interesting presentation.

LISTENING

7 Look at the photos. What do you think the podcast will be about?

8 🔊 3.02 Listen to the podcast. Mark the sentences T (true) or F (false).

1 This is a story with a tragic ending. ☐
2 This is a heartwarming story of a father's love for his daughter. ☐
3 We learn how a father is motivated by his daughter's love of the outdoors. ☐
4 Ricky van Beek regularly competes in the Paralympics with his daughter, Maddy. ☐
5 Many people are inspired by watching the father and daughter duo compete in triathlons. ☐

9 🔊 3.02 Listen again and choose the correct answers.

1 What is unusual about Maddy and her father, Ricky van Beek, competing together in outdoor races?
A Ricky finds walking difficult.
B Maddy has a condition that means she is unable to walk.
C Maddy has a fear of water.

2 What was a major challenge for Ricky when they began racing?
A He smoked heavily, and he was not very fit.
B He couldn't give up smoking.
C He didn't like running on bumpy roads.

3 What is the main motivation for Ricky?
A the feeling of freedom that running gives him
B seeing the joy that it gives his daughter
C being an inspiration to others

4 What will Ricky do if Maddy can no longer race with him?
A He will give up racing.
B He will continue to race with her in his heart.
C He will find another sport for her to participate in.

5 How does seeing them race together make people feel?
A They are inspired to take part in future marathons.
B They wish that they could race with their daughters.
C They feel moved by the love Ricky's actions show for his daughter.

SPEAKING

10 Work in pairs and discuss the questions.

Look at the examples below. Have your parents or your siblings ever made a similar sacrifice for you or a good cause you are passionate about?

- done a sponsored swim or walk with you
- baked cookies to help you raise money for charity
- climbed a mountain with you
- helped you when you were scared
- given up their time to teach you to play a musical instrument

11 Have you ever done any of these things, or something similar, for a brother or sister, or a friend?

Culture note

Cerebral palsy is the name for a group of lifelong conditions that affect coordination and movement. It is caused by a problem with the brain that develops before, during, or soon after birth. The severity of symptoms can vary significantly. Some people only have minor problems, while others may be severely disabled.

The triathlon is a multi-discipline endurance sport consisting of swimming, cycling, and running. The three disciplines are completed consecutively with athletes transitioning between events as quickly as possible. Although the distances in different contests can vary, a standard triathlon always has the same order. The triathletes compete for the fastest completion time over the three events.

Activity idea Mixed-ability

To increase the challenge in Exercise 9 for stronger students, give them the questions without the multiple-choice options. Give weaker students just two options for each question by identifying one incorrect option in each.

TH!NK more

Workbook
Listening p34, Ex.1–3

Reading; Speaking

Warmer

Write the following on the board: *motel, emoticon, spork, hangry*. Ask: *Which two words have been combined to make these?* Elicit *motor* + *hotel*, *emotion* + *icon*, *spoon* + *fork*, and *hungry* + *angry*. Hold a brainstorming session to see if students can come up with other portmanteau words (see Language note). Write some of their ideas on the board.

Alternatively, ask students to research other portmanteau words and then play "portmanteau tennis." One student says a portmanteau word, and the other person must reply with the two words that make it up as quickly as possible. Examples could be: *chillax, motel, hangry, emoticon, frenemy, spork, skort, glamping, ginormous, guesstimate, moped, staycation, jeggings, kideo*.

1 *Students' own answers*

2 🔊 **3.03** Tell students not to worry about understanding every word for now, but to focus on listening for the answer.
"Sharenting" is when parents share photos of their children online.

3 **Check/clarify:** *familiar, digital footprint, consent, lawsuits, violating, respect.*
Encourage students to underline the answers in the text.
1 Apple Martin 2 Christie Tate 3 Ray 4 Sam 5 Jack 6 Jenny

4 At the end of the exercise, listen to some of the students' ideas and encourage open class discussion.

5 Give your own examples before students do the task. Encourage them to think about reasons for their choices.

6 If space allows, encourage students to walk around the classroom to find someone who agrees with their statements. Ask students to report their findings back to the class and encourage them to use the phrase "So does he/she/[student's name]."

TO SHARENT OR NOT TO SHARENT

"I can't believe you put that photo of me on Instagram!"

Does this sound familiar? Do your parents post photos of you online? Are there photos out there that you really don't want the world to see?

We all know that parents just want to do their best for their children. However, parents around the world are creating a digital footprint for their children before they can give consent. Future employers might be able to access those images online.

French police have warned that parents could face future lawsuits from their children for violating their privacy. Under French privacy law, you are currently not allowed to publish a photo of someone without their consent.

Some children have publicly asked their parents not to share photos on Instagram or on their blogs. Children grow up fast, and parents must respect that.

"Mom, we've discussed this. You may not post anything without my consent." Apple Martin famously wrote the above comment under a selfie taken by her famous mother, Gwyneth Paltrow, of the two of them skiing, and a media storm followed.

The daughter of Christie Tate, a mommy blogger, found lots of essays and photos of herself online when she googled herself. She did ask her mother if the content could be taken down, but her mother refused.

Ray Fitzgerald, a parenting coach, advises his followers to stick to the "three P rules of posting":

- **PRIVACY** – Make sure private images stay private and check that your privacy settings are as tight as possible.
- **PERCEPTION** – If you were a teenager, would you like your parents to share that picture of you online? If the answer is no, then don't post it.
- **PERMISSION** – Always ask a teenager's permission before posting an image.

I asked some teenagers, and here are some of their comments:

"I don't usually mind. My mom and dad have given me a very happy childhood. They've been great parents. But then last week my mom shared a picture of me and her in the park. It was such a bad picture. I was so embarrassed. Sharenting is bad news." SAM

"My mom has so few followers, I don't mind. But it's different if your parents are famous or have thousands of followers. Gwyneth Paltrow is very famous, and so many people saw that skiing picture. I think her daughter was right to be angry." JACK

"I did see the picture, and I do follow Gwyneth Paltrow. I didn't think the picture itself was so terrible. However, I do understand her daughter's anger." JENNY

After much discussion, most people seem to agree that it's time to stop sharenting when your children are about 12 or 13. The pictures can be so embarrassing, and they're out there forever. Where do you stand on this issue?

34

READING

1 Work in pairs. Look at the photos and the title of the article. What do you think "sharenting" is?

2 🔊 3.03 Read and listen to the article to check your ideas.

3 Read the article and the comments again. Who said or did these things? Write the name.

1 ______________ had previously discussed the issue of sharenting with her mother.
2 ______________ made the decision to continue sharenting against her daughter's wishes.
3 ______________ said parents should think carefully before they share.
4 ______________ thinks it was OK to share some pictures and not others.
5 ______________ thinks it's OK to sharent when very few people will see the photos.
6 ______________ thinks parents should respect their children's wishes.

4 SPEAKING Work in pairs and discuss the questions.

1 Have your parents ever shared a photo of you that you wish they hadn't?
2 What are your opinions on sharenting? Do you think parents should ask for your consent before posting a picture on Instagram or on other social media?

SPEAKING

5 Read each sentence and choose a number from 1–5 (1 = I strongly agree, 5 = I strongly disagree).

1 Teenagers should always be supported by their parents. 1 2 3 4 5
2 Parents are not the most important people in teenagers' lives. 1 2 3 4 5
3 Parents should give teenagers freedom of choice in everything. 1 2 3 4 5
4 Teenagers should spend as much time as possible with parents/family. 1 2 3 4 5

6 Discuss your answers in groups. Which question(s) do almost all of you agree on? And which one(s) do almost all of you disagree on? Why?

Language note Portmanteau words

Sharenting is an example of a portmanteau word /pɔːrt'mæn.toʊ ˌwɜːrd/ – a word that is formed by combining two other words (here *share* and *parenting*). Other portmanteau examples are *jeggings* (*jeans* and *leggings*), *Schnoodle* (from *Schnauzer* and *Poodle*), *cosplay* (from *costume* and *play*), *smog* (from *smoke* and *fog*), *floordrobe* (from *floor* and *wardrobe*), *Nintendonitis* (from *Nintendo* and *tendonitis*). Portmanteau words differ from compounds, which have both words in full, by having only a part of one or both of the words.

Culture note

In the UK, around 88% of secondary school children use social networks to broadcast information about themselves and publicly communicate with friends and commercial bodies. All children have Personal, Social, Health, and Economic education (PSHE) which covers all the key areas of personal information and internet safety:

What personal data is and why it's important
How personal information is used
How to keep personal and private information safe
What our rights are

TH!NK more

Workbook
Reading p32, Ex.1–4

7 Ask students to complete sentences 1–2 before finding the sentences in the article to check their answers.
1 so 2 such
RULE: 3 such 4 so

8 Divide the class into pairs for students to compare answers. Listen to some examples in open class as feedback.
1 so 2 such 3 so 4 such

Workbook p28

9 Before students look at the rule, you could ask them to consider the effect of *do* and *did* in the example sentences (they create emphasis).
1 do 2 did

10 During feedback, refer to the rules and read through the *Look* box and check understanding.
1 were so few chairs (that) / weren't enough chairs 2 doesn't save enough 3 too boring to 4 did like

Workbook p29

Pronunciation
Adding emphasis

Student's Book p120

11 Check/clarify: *do their best, get ahead in life, bring up, grow up, do well.*
Before doing the exercise, ask students to read the text to answer the following question: *Does the text suggest that parenting is easy or difficult?* (difficult) The aim of this is to encourage students to read a text first to understand the gist, which will help them to complete the task. Elicit the meaning of the completed phrases as you check answers.
1 do 2 get 3 bring 4 childhood 5 grow 6 do 7 strict 8 lenient

12 Check/clarify: *make advances.*
a get ahead in life b bring up c grow up d do well e lenient f do their best g strict h childhood

Workbook p30

Homework
Ask students to write three more statements for the speaking task in Exercise 5. They can bring them to the next class for partners to read and respond to.

GRAMMAR
so and such (review)

7 Write the correct words to complete the sentences. Check in the article on page 34; then complete the rule with *so* and *such*.
1 I was ___________ embarrassed.
2 It was ___________ a bad picture.

RULE: We use *so* and *such* to emphasize.
[3] ___________ (a/an) + (adjective) + noun
[4] ___________ + adjective
We often follow *so* and *such* with a *that* clause to talk about consequences.
It was such a difficult question that I didn't know what to say.
It was so hot that I couldn't sunbathe.

8 Complete the sentences with *so* or *such* and your own ideas.
0 It was *such* a hot day that *we stopped working and went to the beach*.
1 The homework was ___________ difficult that …
2 He's ___________ a good friend that …
3 The train was ___________ late that …
4 It was ___________ an exciting book that …

→ workbook page 28

do and did for emphasis

9 Complete the sentences from the article on page 34 with the missing word; then read the rule.
1 I ___________ understand her daughter's anger.
2 She ___________ ask her mother if the content could be taken down, but her mother refused.

RULE: We can use the auxiliaries *do, does,* and *did* to add emphasis to what we want to say, often when we're contradicting someone.
A: *You didn't like the movie, did you?*
B: *I did like it!*
A: *She doesn't want to go to the party.*
B: *She does want to go – she's just shy.*

Look
too* and *not enough
To say something is more than we need, we use *too*, and to say that it's less, we use *not enough*.
too + adjective
too + *many* + countable noun
too + *much* + uncountable noun
not + adjective + *enough*

10 Complete the second sentence so it has a similar meaning to the first, using the word given and *so/such, did* for emphasis, or *too/not enough*. Write between two and five words.
1 There were too many people at the meeting. Some people had to stand.
There ___________ at the meeting, so some people had to stand. (chairs)
2 He spends too much money.
He ___________ money. (save)
3 This book isn't interesting enough. I'm not going to finish it.
This book is ___________ finish. (boring)
4 You're wrong. I thought the book was really, really good.
I ___________ the book. (like)

→ workbook page 29

PRONUNCIATION
Adding emphasis Go to page 120.

VOCABULARY
Bringing up children

11 Complete the phrases in the text with the words in the list.

bring | childhood | do (x2) | get | grow | lenient | strict

The toughest job in the world
Most parents want to [1] ___________ *their best* for their children and help them [2] ___________ *ahead in life*. They try to [3] ___________ their children *up* well and give them a happy [4] ___________. But it's not always so easy. Children [5] ___________ *up* so fast these days, and it can be difficult to get it right all the time. Of course, parents know the importance of school, and they want their children to [6] ___________ *well*, but what happens when the child doesn't want to try? If they are too [7] ___________, their children might rebel. If they are too [8] ___________, then the children might only do the things they want to do. It's a difficult balancing act and, of course, parents get it wrong sometimes. After all, they're only human.

12 Match phrases 1–8 from Exercise 11 with their meanings.
a ☐ make advances in life
b ☐ raise
c ☐ get older
d ☐ be a success
e ☐ to describe a parent who has very few (or no) rules
f ☐ be as good as you can
g ☐ to describe a parent who has lots of rules
h ☐ the time of being a child

→ workbook page 30

Activity idea Mixed-ability
In Exercise 12, you could ask stronger students to cover the definitions (a–h) and to work with a partner to try to work out the meanings from context.

TH!NK more
Practice Extra
Unit 3 Practice it!

Workbook
Grammar p28, Ex.5–6
Pronunciation p118
Vocabulary p30, Ex.3–4
Vocabulary Extra p31, Ex.1–3

Worksheets
Grammar Worksheets 3
Vocabulary Worksheets 3

Warmer

In pairs, give students two minutes to brainstorm a list of movies about teenagers. Write the titles on the board. Divide the class into pairs for students to take turns describing the plot of the movies listed for their partners to guess the title. Listen to some examples in open class and write any repeated themes on the board.

1 **Check/clarify:** *depression, bullied.*
Before reading the introduction, focus attention on the movie poster and ask students to discuss the question. Ask them to read the introduction to check.

2 🔊 **3.06** Tell students not to worry about difficult vocabulary at this stage and encourage them just to concentrate on answering the question.
Marcus has to decide whether to trust his mother's ideas or to do what he thinks is best.

3 **Check/clarify:** *fashion-conscious.*
Tell students to underline key information in the extract that helped them to decide whether each sentence is true or false. During feedback, ask students to justify their answers by quoting the text they have underlined.
1 F (He buys him new sneakers.)
2 F (She says, "Kids wear what they put on in the mornings," implying that they don't need to think about it.)
3 T 4 F (She says, "We're doing all right our way.")
5 F (Marcus thinks there were many kids in school who stole, swore too much, and bullied other kids.) 6 T

Literature

1 Look at the poster and then read the introduction to the extract. Who do you think the people on the poster are?

2 🔊 3.06 Read and listen to the extract. What two choices does Marcus have?

About a Boy

by Nick Hornby

Marcus is a schoolboy who lives with his mom, who has depression. Marcus has a hard time at school – he gets bullied a lot, especially because of the clothes his mom makes him wear. Recently, Marcus has started to become friends with Will, a rich, lazy man who buys him new sneakers.
Here, Marcus and his mom are going home after visiting Will at his apartment.

"You're not going round there again," she said on the way home.
Marcus knew she'd say it, and he also knew that he'd take no notice, but he argued anyway.
"Why not?"
"If you've got anything to say, you say it to me. If you want new clothes, I'll get them."
"But you don't know what I need."
"So tell me."
"I don't know what I need. Only Will knows what I need."
"Don't be **ridiculous**."
"It's true. He knows what things kids wear."
"Kids wear what they put on in the mornings."
"You know what I mean."
"You mean that he thinks he's **trendy**, and that [...] he knows which trainers are fashionable, even though he doesn't know the first thing about anything else."
That was exactly what he meant. That was what Will was good at, and Marcus thought he was lucky to have found him.
"We don't need that kind of person. We're doing all right our way."
Marcus looked out of the bus window and thought about whether this was true, and decided it wasn't, that neither of them were doing all right, **whichever way** you looked at it.
"If you are having trouble, it's nothing to do with what shoes you wear, I can tell you that for nothing."
"No, I know, but –"
"Marcus, trust me, OK? I've been your mother for twelve years. I haven't made too bad a job of it. I do think about it. I know what I'm doing."
Marcus had never thought of his mother in that way before, as someone who knew what she was doing.
He had never thought that she **didn't have a clue** either; it was just that what she did with him (for him? to him?) didn't appear to be anything like that. He had always looked on being a mother as **straightforward**, something like, say, driving: most people could do it, and you could **mess it up** by doing something really obvious, by driving your car into a bus, or not telling your kid to say "please" and "thank you" and "sorry" (there were loads of kids at school, he **reckoned**, kids who stole and swore too much and bullied other kids, whose mums and dads had a lot to answer for). If you looked at it that way, there wasn't an awful lot to think about. But his mum seemed to be saying that there was more to it than that. She was telling him she had a plan.
If she had a plan, then he had a choice. He could trust her, believe her when she said she knew what she was doing [...] Or he could decide that, actually, she was **off her head** [...] Either way it was scary. He didn't want to put up with things as they were, but the other choice meant he'd have to be his own mother, and how could you be your own mother when you were only twelve?
He could tell himself to say "please" and "thank you" and "sorry," that was easy, but he didn't know where to start with the rest of it. He didn't even know what the rest of it was. He hadn't even known until today that there was a rest of it.

3 Read the extract again. Mark the sentences T (true) or F (false). Then correct the false sentences.

1 Will buys Marcus a new jacket. ☐
2 Marcus's mom is very fashion-conscious. ☐
3 Marcus doesn't agree that he and his mom are doing OK. ☐
4 His mother doesn't think she's a good mother. ☐
5 The other kids at school never did anything wrong. ☐
6 Marcus didn't think he was capable of being his own mother. ☐

British English	American English
go round there	go around there
trainers	sneakers
mum	mom

36

Culture notes

Nick Hornby (born April 17, 1957) is an English novelist and screenwriter. His novels include *Fever Pitch* (1992), *High Fidelity* (1995), *About a Boy* (1998), and *Just like You* (2020), several of which have been made into movies. His novels mainly focus on music, sports, and the difficulties of human relationships.

About a Boy was adapted as a movie in 2002, starring Hugh Grant as a rich, lazy man who lives off the royalties from his father's music. Nicholas Hoult plays a young boy who is bullied at school, and he is brought up by his single mother (Toni Collette). The movie focuses on the difficulties of growing up, both for the young boy, and the adult man. It is an excellent movie to show to teenagers in class and can lead to a lot of discussion about relationships, bullying, parenthood, life as a teenager, and so on.

Functions; Writing

4 Before students do the exercise, write the highlighted words on the board. Tell students to find the words in the extract and to try to work out the meaning of the phrases from the context. Ask them to compare their ideas with the definitions in the book.
1 trendy 2 mess it up
3 didn't have a clue 4 whichever way
5 reckoned 6 ridiculous
7 off her head 8 straightforward

5 Make a note of any nice expressions or lexical errors to refer to during feedback.

6 Ask: *Which words can we use to make sentences more emphatic?* Elicit answers and write *so/such/do/did* on the board. During feedback, say the sentences for students to repeat and check pronunciation. Encourage them to be emphatic!
1 He's such a good father.
2 She gets along so well with children.
3 She's so patient.
4 My dad did try his best.
5 My parents did make some mistakes.
6 She's so lenient with her children.

7 *Students' own answers*

8 In pairs, allow students six to eight minutes to prepare their dialogues.
Students' own answers, including a sentence they have selected from Exercise 6

9 Give an example of your own. Use emphasis when describing the person's personality and anecdotes to show how the person is good with children.

1–2 This could be done as a collaborative writing activity in class, or planning for this exercise can be done in class with the writing assigned for homework.
Two embarrassing things: dressing differently, being affectionate in public
Two ways having a teenager can be hard: they have lost an adoring child, their support is being rejected

3 *1 e 2 a 3 d 4 c 5 b*

4 *Second on my list, Now, First, Second, To conclude*

---

4 VOCABULARY Match the **highlighted** words in the extract with the definitions.
1 up-to-date with modern fashion
2 do it in a really bad way
3 had no idea
4 no matter how
5 thought
6 silly, stupid
7 crazy
8 simple, not complicated

5 SPEAKING Work in pairs and discuss the questions.
1 What do you learn about Marcus in the passage? What is he like?
2 What are your mom and dad good at? Think of the positive things about them.

FUNCTIONS
Emphasizing

6 Add *so, such, do,* or *did* to the sentences to make them more emphatic. Make any other necessary changes.
1 He's a good father.
2 She gets along well with children.
3 She's patient.
4 My dad tried his best.
5 My parents made some mistakes.
6 She's lenient with her children.

7 SPEAKING Work in pairs. Who might be talking to whom in each of the sentences in Exercise 6? What was said before?

Parents can be really embarrassing sometimes!

Our parents have always been a shoulder to cry on, but now we've reached an age where we want to be more independent. At this stage in our lives, we find some of their actions embarrassing, and they find some of our reactions upsetting.

First, let's look at what embarrasses us. At the top of my list is dressing differently, which applies to my mom. In fact, my friends think she's cool, but I just wish she would dress like the other mothers. Second on my list is being affectionate in public. My dad is guilty of this. He called out, "I love you" from the car as he dropped me at school, and all my friends heard him. It was so uncool.

Now, let's look at it from our parents' point of view. First, they have lost an adoring child, who once thought of them as heroes. Second, they've spent many years taking care of you, and now you're rejecting their support. They find this difficult.

To conclude, I think parents should understand that teenagers want to be more independent, and teenagers should understand that parents can feel rejected and that this can be hurtful.

8 WRITING Choose a sentence from Exercise 6 and develop it into a six-line dialogue. The sentence you choose could appear at the beginning, middle, or end.

9 SPEAKING Think about someone you know who is really good with children or teenagers. Then talk to your partner about your person. Give examples and use emphasis when you can.

WRITING
An essay

1 INPUT Read the essay and find two embarrassing things parents sometimes do and two ways in which having a teenager can be hard for parents.

____
____
____
____

2 In pairs, think of more embarrassing things your parents or other people's parents do. Write a list.

3 ANALYZE Find these phrases in the essay and match them with their meanings.

1	a shoulder to cry on	a	has done something wrong/bad
2	guilty of	b	in front of other people
3	feel rejected	c	showing your love
4	being affectionate	d	feel sad and pushed away
5	in public	e	someone who listens to you and is sympathetic

4 List some of the ways the author introduces a point.
First, At the top of my list, ________, ________, ________, ________, ________

5 PLAN You're going to write your own essay about the same topic. Make notes for each of the four paragraphs:
- a short introduction
- two or three things from your point of view as a teenager
- two or three things from your parents' point of view
- a conclusion, giving your final opinion

6 PRODUCE Write your essay: Parents can be really embarrassing sometimes! Use your notes from Exercise 5 (about 200 words).

---

5 Divide the class into small groups to share ideas and make notes before writing individually (they could do this for homework). Prompt students to use the introductions (from Exercise 4) and emphatic language.

6 Students should expand on the notes they wrote in Exercise 5 and follow the same paragraph format.

Homework

If you are short on time, students can do Exercise 6 for homework. If you have done this in class, ask students to exchange their essays with another student for them to read and give feedback on content and structure. Students could check that the essay uses the same structure as the template.

TH!NK more

Practice Extra
Unit 3 Master it!

Workbook
Developing Writing p33

Tests
Unit, extension, and skills test 3
End of term test 1

Warmer

Ask the class to stand up. Nominate a student to say the name of an artist or artistic movement. Students who like images by this artist / in this style sit down. Keep going until everybody is sitting down.

▶ 09 Get TH!NKing

Play the video and discuss the question with your class.

1 Give your own example to get students started on this.

2 After a few minutes, invite students' reactions in open class, prompting them to try to explain their answers.

3 Set a two-minute time limit to encourage students to read quickly and to focus on the task rather than on trying to understand every word.
Photo C is a tube of paint. Its invention is one of the main reasons for the change in painting style between the earlier painting in photo A, which is mainly dark in color, and the later painting in photo B, which is much brighter.

4 This exercise is similar to Reading and Use of English Part 6. Encourage students to read the whole text first to understand the main idea. After choosing a sentence, they should check the other options and decide why they are wrong.
1 D 2 G 3 B 4 E 5 F 6 C
(extra phrase: A)

5 🔊 **4.01 Check/clarify:** *bladders, impressionism, dazzling, artificial pigments, competent, pierce, short-lived.*

4 THE ART OF THINKING

OBJECTIVES

FUNCTIONS: expressing frustration

GRAMMAR: *be/get used to (doing)* vs. *used to (do)*; adverbs and adverbial phrases

VOCABULARY: personality adjectives; common adverbial phrases

Get TH!NKING
Watch the video and think: are you a creative thinker?

A

B

C

READING

1 Look at the paintings in photos A and B. Make a list of as many differences between them as you can think of. Then compare with a partner.

2 SPEAKING Work in pairs or small groups. Discuss how photo C might be connected to the differences between paintings A and B.

3 Read the article quickly and check your ideas from Exercise 2.

4 Read the article again. Six phrases have been removed. Choose the correct phrases A–G to complete the article. There is one extra phrase.
A without using more colors than they actually needed
B and stop it from drying out
C transforming various aspects of life forever
D when you go from Room 41 to Room 42
E and so painters mostly worked indoors, in studios
F to stop the rest from drying out
G meaning the range of colors available to artists increased dramatically

5 🔊 4.01 Read and listen to the article again. Mark the statements T (true) or F (false). Then correct the false statements.
1 The National Gallery does not have modern paintings. ☐
2 John Goffe Rand was a good painter. ☐
3 Things like animal bladders did not last very long as containers. ☐
4 Most artists were accustomed to the problems with oil paint. ☐
5 Rand used tin for the tubes because it was cheap. ☐
6 Artists using the tubes still had to worry about the paint inside them. ☐
7 Rand's tubes were an important factor in the appearance of impressionism. ☐
8 Rand became rich and famous through his inventions. ☐

6 SPEAKING Work in pairs and do the following.
1 On a scale of 1–5, agree on how impressive you think John Goffe Rand's invention was (1 = not impressive at all, 5 = amazing!). Say why your group gave this score.
2 The last sentences says that the tube "went on to be used in many other ways." List all of the other ways you can think of.

38

1 F (It has paintings from the present day.) 2 T 3 T 4 T 5 F (He used tin because it doesn't react with oil paint.) 6 F (The tubes could be closed after being used.) 7 T 8 F (He never became especially wealthy.)

6 Give students four minutes to brainstorm other important uses of Rand's metal tube and to rank them in order of importance.

Objectives

Functions and speaking Expressing frustration
Grammar *be/get used to (doing)* vs. *used to (do)*; adverbs and adverbial phrases
Vocabulary Personality adjectives; common adverbial phrases; **WordWise:** Expressions with *good*
Values Appreciating creative solutions
Life Competencies Being supportive

Resources for this unit

All available online

Videos
- Get **TH!NK**ing: *Are you a creative thinker?*
- Grammar video!: *be/get used to (doing)* vs. *used to (do)*
- Vlog: Being supportive

Tests
- Unit, extension, and skills test 4

Worksheets
- Grammar and vocabulary: Basic, Standard, and Extension Worksheets
- Project: Lateral thinking
- Communication: Thinking outside the box
- Grammar presentation: *be / get used to (doing)* vs. *used to (do)*
- Literature Worksheets: *Anne of Green Gables*
- Get **TH!NK**ing, Grammar video!, and Life Lessons video Worksheets

Culture notes

The National Gallery in central London is one of the most-visited art museums in the world. It was founded in 1824 and has over 2,300 paintings from between 1250 and 1900.

John Goffe Rand was born in New Hampshire, USA in 1801, and lived and worked in Boston, London, and New York as a portrait painter and inventor. Rand invented and patented the first collapsible artist's paint tube, which allowed unused paint to be stored and used later without drying out. These tubes also made oil painting more affordable, which especially benefited art students and amateur artists.

The Impressionist painters were very radical for their time, studying the effects of light, and painting mostly *en plein air* (outside). Their work broke from tradition by showing an "impression" of what the person, light, atmosphere, object, or landscape looked like to them using quick, obvious, and often messy brushstrokes. Artists include Auguste Renoir, Paul Cézanne, and Berthe Morisot.

7 Check/clarify: *operating room.* Remind students that there may be more than one possible solution and encourage them to come up with as many ideas as they can.

Possible answers: 1 The doctor is the boy's mother. 2 The woman is in a hotel room, and the person in the next room is snoring loudly. She calls the number to wake them up and to stop the snoring. 3 The man is not tall enough to reach the button for the 12th floor.

Homework

Ask students to research a lateral thinking problem or to come up with their own. They can bring them to the next lesson for their partners to read and respond to them.

A big change for artists

The National Gallery in Trafalgar Square in London has a collection of paintings that stretches from hundreds of years ago right up to the present day. You can plan a walk that goes chronologically through the centuries – 16th, 17th, 18th century, and so on. As you go through the first rooms, you get used to seeing paintings in dark, heavy colors of brown and black, deep reds and blues, with subjects that are indoors or in huge landscapes that were created by imaginative painters. But something happens [1] ______________________ in the middle of the 19th century. Suddenly, after about 1845, you start to see paintings with dazzling, bright colors and with vivid outdoor settings. How can this remarkable change be explained?

The answer is twofold. First of all, after the Industrial Revolution, artificial pigments had now begun to be used in paint, [2] ______________________ . The second reason was the work of a man almost no one has heard of: John Goffe Rand.

Rand was an American, born in 1801 in New Hampshire, but he moved to London when he got married. He was a practical but also a creative man: an inventor and an enthusiastic, competent painter. Like all other painters at the time, he worked mainly with oil paints. The problem with oil paint was how to store it [3] ______________________ . Painters used to keep the paint in animal bladders, which they could pierce to get the paint out, but these were fragile and short-lived containers. It was almost impossible to move the paint from one place to another or to store it for a long time, [4] ______________________ . Most artists were used to dealing with this situation, but Rand thought he could do something to improve it.

And so, in 1841, he invented … the metal tube. Taking very thin layers of tin – a metal that would not react with the oil paint, he made small tubes into which the paint could be poured. The tube could then be squeezed gently to get out as much paint as the artist needed and closed again [5] ______________________ . And they were small and light, so they could be taken wherever the painter wanted. These tubes changed everything for artists. Suddenly, they could go out into wide open spaces, fields, gardens, and streets, taking their paint with them and painting what they saw, not worrying about the paint itself.

The art movement known as "impressionism" partly owes its existence to Rand and his tube. One of the greatest impressionist painters, Renoir, told his son: "… without colors in tubes, there would have been no Cézanne, no Monet, no Sisley, or Pissarro, nothing of what people were to call impressionism."

John Rand patented his invention, but never became especially wealthy because of it, even though the tube that he invented went on to be used in many other ways, [6] ______________________ .

Train to TH!NK

Lateral thinking

"Lateral thinking" means solving problems by thinking in a creative way. It means not following the obvious line of thinking. Here is an example.

A man is driving down a city street at 25 km per hour. The speed limit is 30 km per hour. He passes three cars that are traveling at 20 km per hour. A police officer stops him and gives him a $100 fine. Why?

If we think too much about the speed, we may not get the answer. What does the situation NOT tell us? It doesn't tell us information like what time of day it is – so a possible reason for the $100 fine is that it is night time and the man is driving with no lights on his car. Or another possible reason for the fine is that the street is one-way, and the man is driving the wrong way.

7 SPEAKING **Here are more situations. Work in pairs and discuss possible answers.**

1. A father and son are in a bad car crash. They are both taken to the hospital. The son is taken into the operating room. The doctor there looks at the boy and says, "That's my son!" How is this possible?
2. A woman is lying awake in bed. She dials a number on the phone, says nothing, puts the phone down, and then goes to sleep. Why?
3. A man lives on the 12th floor of a building. Every morning, he takes the elevator down to the entrance and leaves the building. In the evening, he gets into the elevator and, if there is someone else in the elevator, he goes directly to the 12th floor. If the elevator is empty, he goes to the 10th floor and walks up two flights of stairs to his apartment. Why?

Activity idea Extension

Here are two more lateral thinking problems:

- *A cowboy rode into town on Friday, spent one night there, then left on Friday. How is that possible? (His horse is named Friday.)*
- *A woman had two sons, Billy and Bobby, who were born at the same hour on the same day of the same year, but they were not twins. How is this possible? (They were two of a set of triplets.)*

Divide the class into A/B pairs and give each student a different problem with the solution. Ask students to exchange problems. Students ask each other questions to find the solution to each problem. Tell them they can only ask *yes/no* questions (not *Who, What, Why,* etc.) to maximize language practice.

Critical TH!NKing
Evaluating ideas and arguments
Evaluating arguments as a whole.

Creative TH!NKing
Generating ideas
Imagining alternatives and possibilities.

TH!NK more

Worksheets
Project Lateral thinking
Communication Thinking outside the box
Get TH!NKing *Are you a creative thinker?*

Warmer

To review personality adjectives, give students two minutes to think of as many different adjectives as they can. After two minutes, play a game of "vocabulary tennis," with each group taking turns to say a personality adjective until one team runs out of ideas.

▶ 10 Grammar video! *be/get used to (doing)* vs. *used to (do)*

1 *1 seeing 2 keep 3 dealing*
RULE: 4 used to do
5 be used to doing
6 get used to doing

2 *1 make 2 traveling 3 travel 4 be 5 seeing 6 not having*

3 *1 am 2 get 3 got 4 get 5 Are 6 weren't*

4 Monitor and make a note of common errors with *used to* and *be/get used to + -ing*. Write these on the board to correct during feedback.

Workbook p36

Get it Right!
used to

Student's Book p124

Language note *be/get used to (doing)* vs. *used to (do)*

Students often make the following mistake due to L1 interference: *I am used to get up early.* Point out that we use the gerund form to talk about something familiar, not to describe something as a regular or habitual event: *I am used to getting up early.* = Getting up early is normal for me; it's not particularly difficult.

TH!NK more

Workbook
Grammar p36, Ex.1–4
Vocabulary p38, Ex.1–2

Worksheets
Grammar Worksheets 4
Grammar presentation: *be / get used to (doing)* vs. *used to (do)*
Grammar video! *be/get used to (doing)* vs. *used to (do)*
Vocabulary Worksheets 4

GRAMMAR
be / get used to (doing) vs. used to (do)

Grammar video ▶10

1 **Complete these sentences from the article on page 39 with the words from the list. Then complete the rule by choosing the correct options.**

dealing | keep | seeing

1 You get used to ________ paintings in dark, heavy colors.
2 Painters used to ________ the paint in animal bladders.
3 Most artists were used to ________ with this situation.

RULE: We use:
[4]*used to do / be used to doing* to talk about situations that were true in the past but are not true now.
[5]*used to do / be used to doing* to talk about something that is familiar.
[6]*be used to doing / get used to doing* to talk about the process of something becoming familiar.

2 **Choose the correct words.**

1 In the past, people used to *make / making* roads from earth.
2 The roads were bumpy, but people got used to *travel / traveling* on them.
3 Before cars, people used to *travel / traveling* in horse-drawn carriages.
4 The streets in cities used to *be / being* very dirty and smelly.
5 Many people are used to *see / seeing* roads being repaired.
6 Soon, we'll get used to *not have / not having* holes in our roads.

3 **Complete with the correct form of *be* or *get*.**

1 I'm from Canada, so I ________ used to cold weather.
2 Did it take you long to ________ used to the food here?
3 I lived in the UK for years, but I never ________ used to driving on the left.
4 I think I'll never ________ used to summer in January!
5 ________ you used to life here now?
6 We didn't like the food in Vietnam at first because we ________ used to it.

4 SPEAKING **Work in pairs and think of these things:**

- two things that both you and your partner used to do
- two things you are used to doing
- two things that you have gotten used to doing this year

→ workbook page 36

40

VOCABULARY
Personality adjectives

5 **Which adjective from the list is used in the article to describe John Goffe Rand? Which one is used to describe some artists working indoors? What do they mean? What do the other adjectives mean?**

arrogant | bad-tempered | bright | cautious | confident | decisive | dull | imaginative | impatient | organized | practical | responsible

6 **Read about these people Jane met at her new school. Check (✓) the people she likes. Put a cross (✗) for the people she doesn't like. Put a question mark (?) where it isn't clear.**

0 Rico gets angry all the time, and he complains a lot. He's pretty *bad-tempered*. ✗
1 Barbara understands quickly and has lots of good ideas. She's very ________. ☐
2 Clara doesn't like taking risks. She's a very ________ person. ☐
3 Dana's great because she makes her mind up really quickly – a really ________ girl. ☐
4 Derek never has anything interesting to say – he's so ________! ☐
5 Imogen always has wonderful ideas – she's very ________. ☐
6 Ian wants everything, and he wants it now! He's pretty ________. ☐
7 Oscar always knows where things are and what he has to do – he's very ________. ☐
8 Ria is someone you can trust, who makes good decisions – she's ________. ☐

7 **Complete the sentences in Exercise 6 with the words from Exercise 5.**

→ workbook page 38

SPEAKING

8 **Work in pairs. Think of five different people and write sentences to describe them. Don't include an adjective.**

Leah is waiting for her friend, who's two minutes late. She calls her to see where she is.

9 **Change partners and read your sentences from Exercise 8. Can they guess the adjective you were thinking of?**

impatient

10 **Ask your partner extra questions about their adjective.**

Do you often get impatient in this kind of situation?

5 *The adjective practical (able to provide effective solutions to problems) is used to describe John Goffe Rand.*
Imaginative (good at thinking of new original and clever ideas) is used to describe the artists.
arrogant: proud and unlikeable bad-tempered: gets angry easily bright: intelligent cautious: unwilling to take risks confident: being sure of one's abilities decisive: makes decisions easily dull: boring impatient: not patient organized: able to make plans easily responsible: able to make important decisions or do important things

6 *1✓ 2? 3✓ 4✗ 5✓ 6? 7✓ 8✓*

7 *1 bright 2 cautious 3 decisive 4 dull 5 imaginative 6 impatient 7 organized 8 responsible*

Workbook p38

8 Be alert to students describing other members of the class negatively.

9 Encourage students to sit facing each other to force students to speak and listen, rather than just read each other's sentences.

10 Give weaker students time to work with a partner to think of further questions first.

11 Put a copy of the two pictures up on the board and do the exercise as a class before students open their books.

12–13 🔊 **4.02 Check/clarify:** *coasters, candle, wax, Frisbees.*
1 use them as coasters, put them under a candle to catch wax, draw a circle with them and use them as Frisbees 2 a tree, two faces looking at each other, broccoli, and a human brain

14 🔊 **4.02** This exercise is closely modeled on Listening Part 2 of the Cambridge English: First exam.
1 don't drip 2 get your dog
3 see broccoli 4 so hard
5 any tests on 6 to buy

15 Tell students that there isn't only one correct answer. Nominate one or two students to give reasons for their choice.

16–17 Remind students to think about what is important for themselves, not for people in general. Encourage them to write down the reasons for their choices. Students discuss the statements as a class and come up with a definitive list.

18 With books closed, write *good* on the board. In pairs, ask students to make a list of as many expressions with *good* as they can in three minutes.
1 So far, so good 2 It's a good thing
3 it's no good 4 for good

19 During feedback, say the phrases for students to repeat and check pronunciation.
a for good (4) b it's no good (3)
c it's a good thing (2) d so far, so good (1) e not very good at (0)

Workbook p38

LISTENING

11 SPEAKING **Look at the two tasks. Think of ideas for both. Then compare with a partner.**

How imaginative are YOU?

Try these two tasks to see how **imaginative** you are.

1 Look at these CDs. How many different uses can you think of for old CDs? Make a list of at least six things.
2 Look at the picture. How many different things can you see in it?

1

2

12 🔊 4.02 **Lewis and Phoebe did the tasks. Listen and do the following:**

1 Note the things they thought of for the CDs.
2 Note the things they saw in the picture.

13 SPEAKING **In groups, compare Lewis and Phoebe's ideas with your own ideas from Exercise 11.**

14 🔊 4.02 **Listen again and complete each sentence with no more than three words.**

1 Lewis says that candles ______ nowadays.
2 Lewis thinks you can throw the CD and ______ to bring it back.
3 Phoebe isn't really sure if she can ______ in the picture.
4 Phoebe says that Lewis shouldn't be ______ on himself.
5 The two of them are happy that there aren't ______ creative thinking.
6 Lewis says that he doesn't want ______ the magazine now.

TH!NK values

Appreciating creative solutions

15 **Choose the best way to finish this sentence.**

I think the tasks in Exercise 11 tell us that …

1 it's important to be imaginative.
2 being imaginative is better than being practical.
3 you can be an imaginative person, even if you're not good at these tasks.
4 not everybody is as imaginative as everybody else.
5 everybody's imagination is different.

16 **Now put these in order of importance for you (1 = most important, 5 = least important).**

☐ being practical
☐ being imaginative
☐ knowing a lot of things
☐ being responsible
☐ being organized

17 SPEAKING **Work in pairs. Compare your answers. How similar are your ideas?**

WordWise: Expressions with *good*

18 **Look at these sentences from the unit so far. Complete them with phrases from the list.**

for good | it's a good thing | it's no good | ~~not very good at~~ | so far, so good

0 I'm *not very good at* them, so I guess I'm not very imaginative.
1 Yes, three. ______. But I'm not sure I can think of three more.
2 ______ there aren't any tests on creative thinking, isn't it?
3 But ______, I can't see anything at all.
4 I'm going to stop buying it ______.

19 **Match the phrases in Exercise 18 with these meanings.**

a for ever ☐
b there are no positive results ☐
c I'm / We're / You're lucky that … ☐
d We have started but not finished, but everything has been OK until now. ☐
e have no talent for ☐

→ workbook page 38

Activity idea Extension

Write the following questions on the board:

1 In which school subjects do you have to be imaginative? Do you like those subjects? Why (not)?

2 Do scientists need to be imaginative? Why (not)?

3 What would a society full of very imaginative people be like? What about a society where nobody had any imagination?

Ask students to discuss the questions in pairs or small groups, then listen to some of their ideas, and encourage further debate and discussion.

Activity idea Fast finishers

Ask students to write sentences about famous people with *used to* and *be/get used to* + *-ing*, e.g., *Lionel Messi used to live in Argentina. When he arrived in Barcelona, he found the language quite different, but now he's used to speaking Catalan.*

Creative TH!NKing
Generating ideas
Imagining alternatives and possibilities.

TH!NK more

Workbook
Listening p42, Ex.1–2
WordWise p38, Ex.4–5

Warmer

Draw the following diagram on the board:

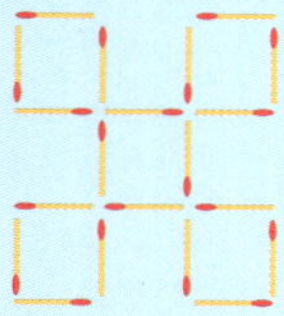

Ask: *Can you move four sticks to create six squares instead of five?* Set a three-minute time limit, and students discuss with a partner. If they are struggling, tell them that the new squares can be different sizes. The solution is to move the sticks shown to each of the four sides.

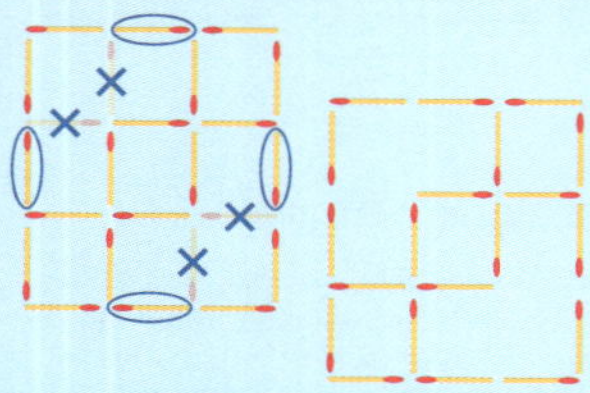

1 Draw students' attention to the text in the green box and give them one minute to scan it to find the answer.
What does "thinking outside the box" mean, and how can you learn to do it?

2 Give a couple of your own ideas as examples before students work in pairs.

3 Give students just two minutes to scan the main text quickly. Encourage them not to focus on every word for now, but just to find ideas similar to their own.

4 4.03 Tell students to underline key information in the text that helped them to decide whether each sentence is true or false. During feedback, ask students to justify their answers by quoting the text they have underlined.
1 T 2 F (She says it isn't easy, but it can be done.) 3 T 4 F (She says you shouldn't evaluate your ideas.) 5 F (She says that people can write articles to make money.) 6 T 7 T 8 F (She says kids are good at thinking outside the box.)

READING

1 **Read the post from Jake on the "Your answers here" website. What does he want to know?**

I had a problem recently, so I asked a friend to help me. She immediately said, "Think outside the box." I've heard that expression so many times, but what does it really mean? And how can you learn to do it? Thanks!

2 SPEAKING **Work in pairs and think of ways to help Jake.**

3 **Read what Soraya replies to Jake. How similar are her ideas to yours?**

4 4.03 **Read and listen to both posts again. Mark the statements T (true) or F (false). Then correct the false statements.**

1 Soraya uses a puzzle to illustrate thinking outside the box. ☐
2 She thinks it isn't very difficult to change how you think. ☐
3 She advises not staying in the same place when you want to think creatively. ☐
4 She thinks you should make a list of ideas, but throw out the ones that aren't good. ☐
5 She says that Jake should write and sell articles. ☐
6 She believes that doing a lot of different kinds of thinking makes us better thinkers. ☐
7 She thinks that it can be useful to talk to older people. ☐
8 She thinks children often know the right answer. ☐

5 SPEAKING **Work in pairs and discuss the questions.**

1 Do you think Soraya's answer is helpful? Why (not)?
2 Which of her tips do you like most? Which do you like least?

PRONUNCIATION
Pronouncing words with *gh* Go to page 120.

WRITING
A story

6 **Write a story. The story must start with these words:**
"I had no idea what to do."
Write 150–200 words.

42

HOME NEW POSTS ARCHIVES

Hi Jake,

Great question! To understand "thinking outside the box," we need to start by asking what the "box" is. We can demonstrate this in an interesting way by looking at the puzzle here.

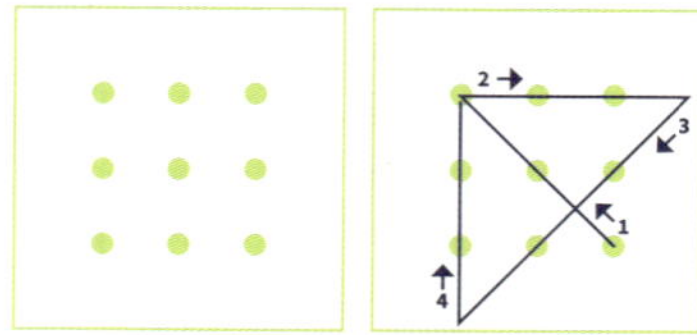

You have to join all nine dots using only four lines and not lifting the pen from the paper. In the answer, the idea of "outside the box" is illustrated nicely. No one said you have to stay inside the "box" of the nine dots, but if you do, you can't solve the problem. Go "out of the box" and you can solve it easily.

So, "thinking outside the box" means moving away from your usual way of thinking. It means thinking creatively, thinking in a different way. Now, what about tips on how to do it?

Changing your way of thinking isn't easy; you have to work hard at it. But it can be done. My first tip is, if you're a little stuck – get out of your box, physically. Leave the room, go for a walk, take a shower, run – anything that takes you away from that paper or screen in front of you. Steve Jobs did it, so did Tchaikovsky, and most likely many other successful people.

Second: try brainstorming, i.e., thinking of as many alternatives as you can without judging or evaluating them. Imagine you want to earn some money – you'll probably think of things you could do like washing cars or working in people's gardens. But sit down and make a list of other things people do that can make money – write articles for online publications, make lemonade and sell it to passersby, whatever. Keep a completely open mind, and you could find some great answers.

Third, in order to think creatively, you need to do a lot of, well … thinking! Play word games, do puzzles like Sudoku, anagrams, crosswords, whatever you prefer. Like a muscle, the more you use it, the stronger your brain becomes. You can also give yourself challenges like thinking of different uses for household objects (books, old shoes, plates you don't want any more). It trains you to look at things from a different angle. So, make sure you train your brain!

Last but not least – talk to a lot of people, including kids. Older people have experience that could help you think of something you would never think of. Kids can think outside the box because they're too young to know what the box is. Have fun!

5 At the end of the exercise, listen to some of the students' ideas.

Pronunciation
Pronouncing words with *gh*

Student's Book p120

6 The planning for this exercise can be done in class, and the writing can be assigned for homework.

Culture note

Brain-training apps appear to be a great way to improve memory and brain function. However, more proof is required that they are effective before the medical community can reach a firm conclusion. While apps have been shown to produce changes in users' brains, research has not yet established whether these changes are any different from those that occur when we learn a new skill: a new "real-life" activity. If you are using a brain-training app rather than watching TV, there may be some benefit, but it may be better to spend time on activities that offer social, environmental, or physical benefits or boost your health and well-being.

TH!NK more

Workbook
Reading p40, Ex.1–5
Pronunciation p119
Developing Writing p41

7 Check/clarify whether other adverbs that do not appear in the exercise (e.g., *finally, happily, outside*, and *certainly*, or *clearly*) are adverbs of time, manner, place, or certainty.
1 T 2 C 3 C 4 P 5 M 6 P
7 C 8 T 9 M

8 **Check/clarify:** *qualify*.
1 said 2 solve 3 thinking
4 work 5 open

9 Explain to students that an adverbial phrase is a group of words that act in the same way as an adverb, i.e., they qualify a verb. Refer to the sentences in Exercise 9 for examples of the two types of adverbial phrase. Put the adverbial phrases into sentences for further clarification, e.g., *He completed the exercise without difficulty.*
1–3 friendly; interesting; strange
4–6 enthusiasm; fear; surprise
RULE: 7 adjective 8 noun

10 If you are short on time, assign this exercise for homework.
1 interest / enthusiasm / excitement
2 a friendly way / a strange way / a horrible way 3 difficulty / interest / enthusiasm 4 a horrible way / an interesting way / a strange way / a different way 5 excitement / interest / enthusiasm 6 enthusiasm / excitement / interest

Workbook p37

11 During feedback, say the adverbial phrases for students to repeat. Pay particular attention to the pronunciation of *row* /roʊ/ and *purpose* /ˈpɜːrpəs/.
1 in public 2 in private
3 on purpose 4 by accident
5 in a panic 6 in a hurry 7 in a row

12 **Check/clarify:** *behaved, staring*.
1 in private 2 on purpose
3 in public 4 in a row 5 in a hurry
6 in a panic 7 by accident
8 in secret

13 As these questions are difficult to answer spontaneously, give students some thinking time to make notes on their answers.

Workbook p38

Activity idea Fast finishers

Ask students to close their books and write down all of the adverbs and adverbial phrases from page 43 that they can remember. When they have completed their lists, students open their books to check.

GRAMMAR
Adverbs and adverbial phrases

7 For each sentence, put a letter in the box to say if the underlined adverb is an adverb of time (T), manner (M), place (P), or certainty (C).

0 Keep a completely open mind. [M]
1 I read about it recently. [ ]
2 This is definitely the best album they've ever made. [ ]
3 He'll probably win the prize. [ ]
4 You can buy most of the things you need locally. [ ]
5 You are capable of thinking creatively. [ ]
6 We go home at nine o'clock. [ ]
7 This is possibly the best work I've ever done. [ ]
8 You can choose the best ideas later. [ ]
9 I applied for the course, and surprisingly, they accepted me! [ ]

8 Look back at the posts on page 42. What verbs do these words qualify?

1 immediately
2 easily
3 creatively
4 hard
5 completely

9 Sometimes we use adverbial phrases instead of an adverb. Add the words below to lists A and B. Then choose the correct words to complete the rule.

enthusiasm | fear | friendly
interesting | strange | surprise

A	B
in an enjoyable way	with / without difficulty
in a horrible way	with / without excitement
in a different way	with / without interest
in a [1] ________ way	with / without [4] ________
in an [2] ________ way	with / without [5] ________
in a [3] ________ way	with / without [6] ________

RULE: We often form adverbial phrases with:
- in a/an + [7] noun / adjective + way
- with/without + [8] noun / adjective

10 Complete the sentences. Use phrases from Exercise 9. Sometimes more than one answer is possible.

1 I really like music, so I went to the concert with …
2 The first time I met her, she looked at me in …
3 The run was easy – I finished it without …
4 Some of the people at the party were dressed in …
5 It was a great documentary, and I watched it with …
6 I don't really like sports, so I went to the game without …

→ workbook page 37

VOCABULARY
Common adverbial phrases

11 Use the words from the list to complete the definitions.

by accident | in a hurry | in a panic
in a row | in private | in public
~~in secret~~ | on purpose

If you do something …
0 without other people knowing, you do it *in secret*.
1 that other people can hear or see, you do it ________.
2 that other people can't hear or see, you do it ________.
3 that you intended to do, you do it ________.
4 that you didn't want to do, you do it ________.
5 feeling stressed and without thinking properly, you do it ________.
6 quickly, you do it ________.
7 three times without a break, you do it three times ________.

12 Choose the correct words.

1 The two of us went into a room, alone, so that we could talk *in a hurry / in private*.
2 He broke my phone, and I'm really angry. I'm sure he did it *on purpose / in a panic*.
3 You shouldn't have behaved that way *in public / in private*. Everyone was staring.
4 I woke up late four days *in a row / in secret*!
5 I was very late, so I had to leave the house *on purpose / in a hurry*.
6 He was *in secret / in a panic* because he couldn't find his phone.
7 I'm so sorry that I lost your papers – I left them on the bus *on purpose / by accident*.
8 She did it late at night *in secret / in a panic*. No one knew anything.

13 SPEAKING Work in pairs and discuss the questions.

1 When were you last in a hurry?
2 What can you do five times in a row?
3 Give an example of something you did on purpose and wish you hadn't.
4 Give an example of something you got right by accident.
5 When was the last time you were in a panic?

→ workbook page 38

Homework

If you are short on time, students can do Exercise 6 for homework. If you have done this in class, ask students to exchange their stories with another student for them to read and to give feedback on content and structure. Students could check if the story uses the opening words. They should also decide which the most/least interesting part of the story is.

Activity idea Extension

Divide the class into A/B pairs. Ask As to close their books and Bs to read sentences from Exercise 12 at random, replacing the adverbial phrases with "beep" for A to guess them. After three minutes, ask students to switch roles and repeat.

TH!NK more

Practice Extra
Unit 4 Practice it!

Workbook
Grammar p37, Ex.5–8
Vocabulary p38, Ex.3
Vocabulary Extra p39, Ex.1–3

Worksheets
Grammar Worksheets 4
Vocabulary Worksheets 4

Developing Speaking; Phrases for fluency; Functions

Warmer

Review common adverbial phrases by giving students a noun from the common adverbial phrases in Exercise 11 on page 43 and eliciting the adverbial phrase, e.g., *hurry – in a hurry. Correct.* Students continue in pairs.

1 4.06 Tell students to cover the dialogue and discuss the question in pairs before listening to check their answers.
Students' own answers

2 4.06
1 write something creative
2 He is always putting himself down.
3 She uses the phrase "think outside the box," which Alex says is a cliché.
4 to write a poem from nature's perspective called "I am the ocean"

3 At the end of the exercise, listen to some of the students' ideas and encourage open class discussion.

4 During feedback, say the sentences for students to repeat.
1 again 2 can't be serious
3 Calm down
4 give it a rest; out of order
5 That's just it

5 Allow students six to eight minutes to prepare their role-plays. Monitor to make sure all students are on task. If students have access to a recording device (their cell phones, for example), they could record their conversation and play it back to check their own pronunciation and intonation. They can then repeat the exercise and listen for improvements.

6 During feedback, ask students for an L1 translation.
I can't do that. This is hopeless! I give up.
They're said by people who think they can't do something.

7 To introduce the concept of frustration, tell a story about something frustrating that happened to you, e.g., running for a flight only to find that it has been delayed. Monitor to check that students are using the sentence stems appropriately. During feedback, ask students to share their ideas with the class and review any common errors.

DEVELOPING SPEAKING

1 4.06 **Look at the photo. How do you think Paulo is feeling? Read and listen to check.**

Paulo: This is terrible. The teacher told us she wants us to write something creative! "A poem about the natural world." How am I going to do that? And she wants it by Tuesday! There's no way …
Sarah: Calm down, Paulo! All you need is one idea.
Paulo: That's just it – I don't have any ideas. Not one! I'm hopeless at this kind of thing. I could sit and think for days, but it's pointless. I'll never come up with anything.
Alex: Oh, give it a rest, Paulo! You're always putting yourself down. "I can't do this, I'm no good at that!" It's ridiculous!
Sarah: Hang on, Alex. That's a bit harsh. We're supposed to be helping him, not making him feel worse. It would be nice if you could be a bit more supportive!
Paulo: No, he's right. I *am* being ridiculous. And bad-tempered, too.
Sarah: Whatever. Let's think. You have to write a poem about … what was it again?
Paulo: "The natural world." But listen, guys, it's my problem, not yours. You don't have to help me.
Sarah: But we want to! Well, I want to, at least. Look, I always think it's useful to try to think outside the box.
Alex: Oh, Sarah! Think outside the box? That's such a cliché.
Paulo: No, she might be right. I mean, maybe … instead of writing a poem *about* nature, I could write something from nature's point of view.
Sarah: Like, a poem written by the ocean, about having plastic bags floating around inside it.
Alex: Oh, no! You can't be serious, Sarah!
Paulo: It's a good idea! I'll call it: "I am the ocean."
Alex: Good luck, Paulo – you're going to need it!

2 4.06 **Read and listen to the dialogue again and answer the questions.**
1 What does Paulo have to do?
2 Why does Alex get irritated by Paulo?
3 Why does Alex get irritated by Sarah?
4 What idea does Sarah give Paulo?

3 SPEAKING **Work in pairs. Say how you felt about each person in the conversation.**

Phrases for fluency

4 **Find the underlined expressions in the dialogue and use them to complete the conversations.**
1 Sorry, I forgot. What's your name ________ ?
2 A Let's go for a run.
B A run? You ________ ! It's really cold out there!
3 A Come on, we're late!
B ________ , we're not late at all, we have another fifteen minutes.
4 A That shirt doesn't suit you.
B Oh, ________ , Jack. I'm tired of you criticizing me all the time. You're really ________ , you know?
5 A Let's watch a movie on TV – if there's anything good.
B ________ . The movies on TV are terrible!

5 SPEAKING **Work in groups of three. You are Paulo, Sarah, and Alex. Paulo has written his poem, and the teacher has graded it. Sarah and Alex talk to him to find out more.**

FUNCTIONS
Expressing frustration

KEY LANGUAGE
I can't (do that).
I'm hopeless (at …)
This is hopeless!
There's no way …
I give up.
I'll never (come up with anything).
(It's) pointless.

6 **Read the conversation again. Which phrases from the Key Language box does Paulo not say? What do all the phrases have in common?**

7 WRITING **Think of a frustrating situation you have been in. Write three things you might have thought using the phrases in Exercise 6. Compare your notes with a partner.**
I'll never finish this.

44

Activity idea Extension

Disappearing sentences: Write out the dialogues on the board or project them on the interactive whiteboard (IWB). Divide the class into A/B pairs. Students practice the conversations from Exercise 4 in pairs. Cover a small section of the dialogue, beginning from the right-hand side of the board. Students repeat the dialogues in pairs, trying to remember the whole thing, including the parts they can no longer see. Cover more and more of the dialogue, with students practicing at each stage, until eventually nothing is left on the board. Ask for volunteers to perform for the class or have all As and all Bs perform in unison. This activity involving lots of repetition is a good way for students to memorize useful lexical chunks.

Life Competencies

Warmer

Write *being supportive* on the board and elicit what it might mean. Encourage students to try to clarify its meaning through examples or explanation, rather than through a translation. For example, in the dialogue on page 44, Sarah was being supportive when she tried to help Paulo with his poem. Ask students to read the introductory paragraph to check their ideas.

▶ 11 Life Lessons: Being supportive

1 ▶ 11 Ask students to compare their ideas with a partner.
1 His best friend is really bad at painting, but Will wants to be supportive.
2 He is going to suggest his friend try an abstract style of painting.

2 ▶ 11 Invite students to share their answers with the rest of the class during feedback.

3 **Check/clarify:** *paddle, fancy.*
Students' own answers.

4 Monitor, but avoid error correction. The focus of this task is on fluency, not on practice of structures or lexis. Instead, make a note of common errors. Write a mix of correct and incorrect sentences on the board, ensuring anonymity, and ask students to identify and correct the mistakes during feedback.

5 You may like to give your own example to get students started on this.

6 Monitor to help with any difficulties, but do not interrupt as this is a fluency activity.

Homework

Have the students keep a journal for two or three days, with a record of when they were supportive or someone was supportive towards them. What was the support needed for? Did you/they accept it? If not, why not?

Emotional Development
Supporting others
Works at maintaining healthy relationships.

THE ART OF THINKING UNIT 4

LIFE COMPETENCIES

Sometimes people need our understanding and support, even if what they see as a problem is not something we ourselves think is serious or important.

1 ▶ 11 **Watch the vlog. Answer the questions.**
1 What is Will's problem?
2 What is his solution?

2 ▶ 11 **Watch the vlog again. Work in pairs and think of two other ways Will could show Max some support.**

3 **Read these situations. For each situation, choose the best response.**

1 A friend of yours has reached the finals of a local table tennis tournament. Unfortunately, she broke her paddle, and she is really worried about using a borrowed one.
A Don't worry – you've done well to reach the finals, so it doesn't matter if you lose.
B You're such a good player – I'm sure you'll do well with any paddle.
C Why is the paddle such a big deal? Aren't they all basically the same?

2 You invite a friend to join you and other friends to go out. Your friend says, "Sorry, I can't. I have so much homework to do. I need to finish it tonight."
A You have another two days. Come out with us!
B OK, but why don't you come with us and relax? And I can help you tomorrow.
C You take schoolwork too seriously. You have to have fun sometimes.

3 It's your friend's mom's birthday soon. He wants to get her something nice, but he doesn't have much money. You know he bought a new tablet recently.
A I can lend you some money, but maybe you should think more carefully about how you spend your money.
B Well, it's your own fault. You shouldn't have bought that tablet.
C Just buy something with what you have. Your mom won't be expecting anything fancy.

4 SPEAKING **Work in pairs or small groups. A friend says these things. Think of something supportive to say in reply.**

"I feel awful. I promised my grandma I'd go for a walk with her, but now I have to stay at home and help my brother with something. I'll have to call Grandma and tell her I can't come. I hate doing this!"

"My sister's being a real pain. She argues with me all the time and says things she knows I don't like. She laughs at everything I do, too. But my parents think she's so sweet!"

Me and my world

5 **Think of a time when someone said something very supportive to you and write notes about it.**
- What was the problem?
- Who was the person? What did they say?
- Why did you think it was supportive?

6 SPEAKING **Work in pairs and tell your partner your ideas from Exercise 5.**

TIPS FOR BEING SUPPORTIVE

- When you are listening to other people's problems, try not to judge them or the problem.
- You don't have to solve the problem – just try to say something that shows you understand.
- Try to put yourself in the other person's position. What would you like to hear?

45

Activity idea Extension

Students could role-play a dialogue being supportive about a problem. Divide the class into two groups A (Problem) and B (Supportive). Ask group A to think of some problems and ask group B to brainstorm phrases to sound supportive. Monitor to make sure all the students are making notes and help with ideas if necessary. Put the students in A/B pairs and give them time to act out the role-play.

TH!NK more

Practice Extra
Unit 4 Master it!

Worksheets
Life Lessons: Being supportive

Tests
Unit, extension, and skills test 4

1 4.07 In B2 First for Schools Listening Part 1, there are eight short recordings, each with a question and three answer options. Candidates have to listen, then choose the option which best answers the question. This part of the exam requires candidates to listen for specific information.

Encourage your students to do the following when they approach this task:

- Read the question and the options for each question.
- During the first listening, listen for specific information, choosing the best option.
- During the second listening, check that the answer is correct, focusing on the key information.

1 C 2 C 3 B 4 A 5 B 6 B 7 C 8 A

Workbook p79

2 4.08 In B2 First for Schools Listening Part 3, candidates have to listen to five short related texts, each with a different speaker. Candidates must choose the option from a set of eight that matches what each speaker says. This task tests listening for gist, detail, attitude, and opinion.

Encourage your students to do the following when they approach this task:

- Read and listen to the instructions to understand the context of the conversations.
- On the first listening, try to understand the gist and choose the best option for each speaker.
- On the second listening, check all the answers carefully.

Speaker 1 F Speaker 2 B Speaker 3 H Speaker 4 A Speaker 5 E

Workbook p35

B2 First for Schools

LISTENING

Part 1: Multiple choice

→ workbook page 79

1 4.07 **You will hear people talking in eight different situations. For questions 1–8, choose the best answer (A, B or C).**

1 You hear two people talking at a theatre.
Why has the man never been to the theatre before?
A It's too expensive.
B He hated plays at school.
C He prefers films.

2 You hear a voicemail message.
What is the reason Julia called?
A to invite Sally to her party
B to ask Sally about a party in Germany
C to say that Ralf needs Sally's phone number

3 You hear two people talking about a restaurant.
What problem does the woman mention?
A the quality of the food
B the slow waiters
C the high prices

4 You hear an actor talking about his latest film.
Why was he pleased to be given this role?
A His part is different from what he's done recently.
B He had forgotten what it was like to be in a film.
C People will know that he's good at playing bad guys.

5 You hear a woman talking on the radio.
What kind of broadcast is it?
A an advertisement for a supermarket
B a shopping programme
C a programme about healthy eating

6 You hear part of a radio phone-in.
What is the man complaining about?
A his neighbours
B the roads
C his taxes

7 You hear the manager of a football team after the match.
What is she disappointed about?
A the weather
B the referee
C the score

8 You overhear a man talking about his holiday.
What did he like most about it?
A how quiet the location was
B not receiving phone calls
C being near birds and trees

Part 3: Multiple matching

→ workbook page 35

2 4.08 **You will hear five short extracts in which people are talking about an after-school art club. Choose from the list (A–H) what each speaker likes most about the club. Use the letters only once. There are three extra letters which you do not need to use.**

A Practising different forms of art is enjoyable.
B It's a good opportunity to meet people with the same interest.
C It's a welcome break from academic subjects.
D It provides information about future career possibilities.
E It's interesting to find out about painters from other times.
F The teacher is very inspiring.
G The other students are brilliant artists.
H Discovering a new talent is rewarding.

Speaker 1 ☐
Speaker 2 ☐
Speaker 3 ☐
Speaker 4 ☐
Speaker 5 ☐

46

1 1 strict 2 organized 3 helmets 4 bad-tempered 5 well 6 public 7 imaginative 8 panic 9 secret 10 grow

2 1 enthusiasm 2 None 3 live 4 few 5 living 6 little

3 1 The test was ~~such~~ so difficult that nobody got everything right.
2 Ollie was used to ~~be~~ being alone in the old house, so he wasn't worried.
3 Sara was ~~much~~ too (OR much too) scared to stay there after dark.
4 Manuel listened with ~~interesting~~ interest to the interview with the local politician.
5 There was hardly any ~~of~~ space on the shelf, so I couldn't put the books there.
6 My grandmother always preferred her laptop. She never ~~used~~ got used to using a tablet.

4 1 'll never; so 2 such; I can't 3 so; such 4 hopeless; so

TEST YOURSELF UNITS 3 & 4

VOCABULARY

1 Complete the sentences with the words in the list. There are four extra words.

accident | bad-tempered | best | grow | helmets | imaginative | lenient | organized | panic | public | row | secret | strict | well

1 My parents were pretty ________ when I was young. I couldn't do everything I wanted to do.
2 My mother was very ________. The house was always clean with everything in the right place.
3 She always had our school things ready for us, even our bike ________.
4 I had five brothers, and although we were often very difficult, she was never ________.
5 Both my parents did everything they could to help us do ________ in life.
6 They kept any arguments for when they were alone. They never argued in ________.
7 My dad invented great games for us. He really was very ________.
8 He was very calm. I never saw him in a ________.
9 Once we helped him prepare a surprise party for my mom. Everything had to be done in ________ so she wouldn't find out.
10 I think we were lucky to ________ up in such a family.

/10

GRAMMAR

2 Complete the sentences with the words in the list. There are two extra words.

enthusiasm | few | little | live | living | most | none | surprise

1 Josh doesn't like volleyball much, so he went to the volleyball game without much ________.
2 ________ of my friends could come to the party. They were all away on vacation.
3 When I was a child, I used to ________ in Texas.
4 Kyle has seen a lot of movies, but he's only read a ________ books.
5 Penny has never gotten used to ________ away from her family.
6 Samya wanted to spend a ________ more time practicing her speech.

3 Find and correct the mistake in each sentence.

1 The test was such difficult that nobody got everything right.
2 Ollie was used to be alone in the old house, so he wasn't worried.
3 Sara was much scared to stay there after dark.
4 Manuel listened with interesting to the interview with the local politician.
5 There was hardly any of space on the shelf, so I couldn't put the books there.
6 My grandmother always preferred her laptop. She never used to using a tablet.

/12

FUNCTIONAL LANGUAGE

4 Choose the correct options.

1 A I'll *never* / *give up* write a novel.
B Don't be *so* / *such* pessimistic! I'm sure you can do it.
2 A But you're *so* / *such* a good writer. Can't you write one for me?
B *There's no way* / *I can't* do that – but I'll help.
3 A Ugh! This project is *so* / *such* difficult.
B What's the problem? You're usually *so* / *such* an imaginative person.
4 A Oh! I'm *give up* / *hopeless* at drawing. This dog looks more like a bear!
B Come on! Don't get *so* / *such* angry! Why don't you find a dog on the internet and copy it?

/8

MY SCORE /30

22–30 😊 10–21 😐 0–9 😣

47

The Cambridge Life Competencies Framework

Critical THINKing
Evaluating ideas and arguments
Watch this video for a tip on developing your students' critical thinking skills.
Scan the QR code here.

Warmer

Ask: *On an average day, how long do you spend looking at a screen?* Ask students to write down their answers and discuss them in small groups. Listen to some of their answers and find out who spends the longest, and who spends the least amount of time looking at screens.

▶ 12 Get TH!NKing

Play the video and discuss the question with your class.

5 TOO MUCH TECH?

OBJECTIVES

FUNCTIONS: advice and obligation

GRAMMAR: obligation, permission, and prohibition (review); necessity: *didn't need to / needn't have*; ability in the past (*could, was/were able to, managed to, succeeded in*)

VOCABULARY: technology (nouns); technology (verbs)

Get TH!NKING
Watch the video and think:
what type of technology is most important to you?

A

B

C

D

E
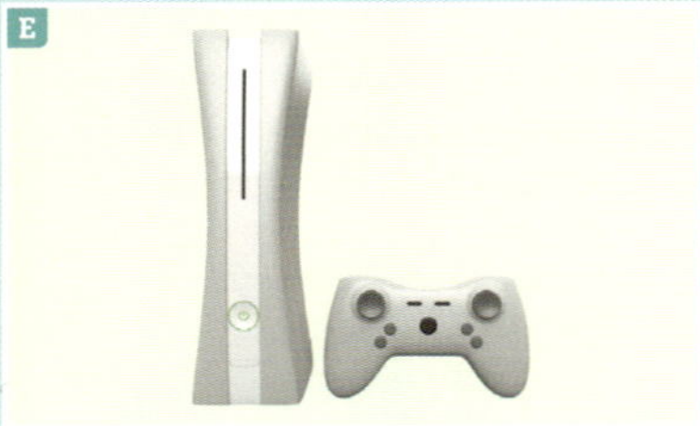

READING

1 What types of personal technology can you see in the photos? What other hi-tech items do you use? Make a list.

2 SPEAKING Work in pairs and choose three items from your lists. Think of some advantages and disadvantages each of the items may have.

3 🔊 5.01 Read and listen to the article. Discuss the questions.
   1 Which of the statistics do you find most interesting? Why?
   2 Which piece of advice do you find most useful? Why?

4 Read the article again. Match the tips with the titles. There are four extra titles.
   A Be realistic
   B Let others know about your plans
   C Focus on others
   D Don't exchange your phone for the latest model
   E Leave your phone at home
   F Get a good night's sleep
   G Make a list
   H Don't text it – say it instead!
   I Start tomorrow
   J It's easier with a friend
   K One goal at a time

5 SPEAKING Work in pairs and discuss the questions.
   1 Do you think you use too much technology? Explain your reasons.
   2 What other advice would you give to someone who wants to use their phone less?

48

1 Put a copy of the photos up on the board and do the exercise as a class before students open their books.
A smart watch B smart speaker
C virtual reality (VR) headset
D wireless charging pad
E gaming console
Students' own answers

2 Make sure students are thinking about the advantages and disadvantages of the individual types of technology, rather than technology in general, by eliciting one advantage and one disadvantage of the first item as a class.

3 🔊 **5.01** Before listening, ask students to underline key information they will need to listen for (1 statistics, 2 advice). Write these on the board at the top of two columns. Ask students to make notes as they listen. Before students discuss, elicit some ideas and write them under each column.

4 **Check/clarify:** *wireless router, intensive, self-absorbed, detox.*
1 G 2 A 3 K 4 C 5 J 6 E
7 B Extra titles: D, F, H, I

5 Give students time to reflect and make notes. Monitor and help as necessary, encouraging students to expand on and justify their opinions in English. At the end of the exercise, listen to some of the students' ideas and encourage open class discussion.

Objectives

Functions and speaking Advice and obligation
Grammar Obligation, permission, and prohibition (review); necessity: *didn't need to/needn't have*; ability in the past (*could, was/were able to, managed to, succeeded in*)
Vocabulary Technology (nouns); technology (verbs)
Culture Smart cities

Resources for this unit

All available online

Videos

- Get **TH!NK**ing: *What type of technology is most important to you?*
- Grammar video!: Necessity: *didn't need to / needn't have*
- Culture: Smart cities

Tests

- Unit, extension, and skills test 5

Worksheets

- Grammar and vocabulary: Basic, Standard, and Extension Worksheets
- Project: Tech habits
- Communication: Screen time
- Grammar presentation: Necessity: *didn't need to / needn't have*
- Literature Worksheets: *Anne of Green Gables*
- Get **TH!NK**ing and Grammar video! video Worksheets

6 Refer students back to Exercise 2 on page 48 and emphasize the need to weigh advantages and disadvantages before making decisions. Divide the class into pairs and ask students to add as many ideas to each column as they can. To focus on the importance of asking questions before making decisions and considering the consequences of different decisions, stress the particular relevance of the third column. Listen to some of their ideas in open class and encourage further discussion.

7 Divide the class into three groups and ask students to find a partner within their group. Assign one of the three situations to each group. Students use the PMI strategy to come to a decision on their situation in pairs. When the majority of students have reached a decision, regroup students into the original three larger groups for them to discuss their ideas and to agree on the best decision for their situation.

Homework

Ask students to write a paragraph about the situation they discussed in Exercise 7, including pluses, minuses, and any interesting points.

Activity idea Extension

Divide the class into two groups, one supporting the idea of banning books from schools and the other opposing it. Ask students to work in small groups and debate the pluses and minuses of their group's position. They should also discuss any questions in the "interesting" category. Make new groups of four students with two in favor and two against and get them to debate.

A DIGITAL detox

On average, we look at our phones 200 times a day. That's more than 12 times for every hour we're awake! A quarter of all people spend more time on their phone than they do asleep in bed. Nearly three-quarters of teenagers prefer texting to actually speaking with other people, and presumably, most of those teens also think that having a good wireless router in the house is more important than having a fridge. On average, a teenager will send 3,400 messages from their bed each month!

These are just a few of the frightening statistics that show how addicted we have become to technology. And the effects of this are just as scary. Research has shown that our intensive phone usage means we are finding it harder to get a good night's sleep. Our addiction to social media means we are becoming more self-absorbed and screens are making our children less caring people, as they are less likely to think about the impact of what they might post on social media. Clearly, we must do something about this. But what?

More and more experts are recommending a digital detox – an amount of time every day when we don't allow ourselves to look at our phones and other screens. Most people would probably agree this is a good idea, but putting it into practice is not that easy. That's why we've come up with a seven-step plan to help you put away your phone and get back to the business of living your life.

1 ________________
Write down all the things that you like doing, but never find the time to do. By cutting down your online activity, you will start to free up some time to do these things.

2 ________________
Don't expect to be able to just put down your phone and never touch it again. Instead, give yourself a time limit of how long you can use it each day. Even better, say exactly when you will allow yourself to use it and stick to that plan.

3 ________________
Decide on one change you want to make. Always leave your charger at home, so that you have to use your phone less to save the battery and work toward achieving this. When you're comfortable with that change, move on to another.

4 ________________
When you're with others, you should always give them your attention. If you keep looking at your phone, then you are not. This is a sign that it's time to start putting your phone away.

5 ________________
Find someone to start your detox with. That way, you can offer each other support and help each other through those difficult times. And if you need help, try to talk to them face to face rather than via text or video calls.

6 ________________
It's simple. If you don't have your phone with you, then you can't use it. Don't be scared – you'll soon find lots of other things to do. You may even start to notice things you never noticed before.

7 ________________
Tell friends and family members what you're doing. Let them know you won't always be answering their messages the minute you get them. Who knows – they might even be tempted to join you.

Train to TH!NK

The PMI strategy

A good brainstorming strategy you can use when making decisions is the PMI strategy. On a piece of paper, draw three columns and label them "plus," "minus," and "interesting." Write down the positive consequences (plus) and negative consequences (minus) of making the decision and also what would be "interesting" about carrying it out.

6 **Look at the example below. Can you think of any more ideas for each column?**

Phones should be banned from schools		
plus	**minus**	**interesting**
Students would focus more on their classes.	*Students wouldn't be able to communicate with parents if they needed to.*	*How would this change teachers' lives?*

7 SPEAKING **Work in groups and choose one of these situations. Use the PMI strategy to come to a decision.**

- Your group has been asked to take part in a reality TV show. It involves living without any technology for a month. You are not sure whether you should take part.
- Your group has been invited to make a recommendation to your town's public transportation service on whether cell phones should be forbidden on buses and trains.
- Your group has been asked to make a report on whether cell phones should only be used by people over 18.

Activity idea Extension

Students work in four (or eight) small groups and think of their own situation. Ask them to write their situation at the top of a piece of paper and draw the three PMI columns underneath.

Students hand their situation to another group and give them time to add an idea to one of the columns. Pass the paper to another group for them to add an idea to one of the remaining columns. Repeat once more until all the columns are filled, and the groups have seen each situation, at which stage the situation returns to the original group. Give students time to read all of the ideas and then nominate one student from each group to respond to the ideas in open class.

TH!NK more

Worksheets
Project Tech habits
Communication Screen time
Get **TH!NK**ing *What type of technology is most important to you?*

Critical TH!NKing
Solving problems and making decisions
Evaluating options and recommendations to come to a decision.

Warmer

Write the letters *l, m, s, n t,* and *n a t* on the board. Tell students that they are the initial letters of five modal and semi-modal forms (*let, must, should, need to,* and *not allowed to*). Elicit the forms and write them on the board.

1 1 must 2 should
RULE: 3 must 4 should
5 need to 6 let 7 not allowed to

2 Read through the information in the *Look* box in open class. Point out that *we had* contracts to *we'd* but should not be confused with *we would*.
1 isn't allowed to 2 're supposed to
3 don't let 4 'd better turn

Workbook p46

Get it Right!
should

Student's Book p124

3 **Check/clarify:** *exchange student*.

4 Ask pairs to read out the most important rule and the best piece of advice they came up with.

5 During feedback, say the words for students to repeat. Pay attention to the unstressed schwa in the final syllable of *adapter, charger, power,* and *router*.
A 8 B 4 C 1 D 9 E 5 F 3
G 2 H 6 I 7 J 10

6 **Check/clarify:** *out of battery*.
1 "at" symbol 2 adapter 3 charger
4 wireless router 5 USB port
6 power cord 7 headset 8 plug

Workbook p48

Language note Obligation, permission, and prohibition

Explain the difference between *have to* and *must*. In the present affirmative form, you can use either. However, there is a slight distinction in the first person.

GRAMMAR
Obligation, permission, and prohibition (review)

1 **Complete the sentences from the article on page 49. Then complete the rule with *let, must, should, need to,* and *not be allowed to*.**

1 Clearly, we ______________ do something about this.
2 When you're with others, you ______________ always give them your attention.

RULE: To express obligation or necessity, we can use *have to* or [3] ______________ (as in sentence 1).
- To say something is (or isn't) a good idea, we can use [4] ______________ (as in sentence 2).
- To express no obligation or necessity, we can use *don't have to* or *don't* [5] ______________.
- To express permission, we can use [6] ______________ and to say that something is not permitted, we use [7] ______________.

Look
- *had better* = something is a good idea and is often used as a warning. The form is always *had better* + the base form of verb, even when talking about the present.
- *be supposed to* = there's an obligation to do something, but in reality, people don't always do it. It is always used in the passive form (like *be allowed to*).

2 **Complete the second sentence so that it has a similar meaning to the first sentence. Use the word in parentheses. Use between two and five words including the word given.**

1 Their son can't go out after 8 p.m. (allowed)
Their son ______________ go out after 8 p.m.
2 Our teacher expects us to raise our hands if we want to ask a question. (supposed)
We ______________ raise our hands if we want to ask a question.
3 Their young daughter isn't allowed to watch TV all day. (let)
They ______________ their young daughter watch TV all day.
4 You should really turn off the TV if you don't want to get a headache. (better)
You ______________ off the TV if you don't want to get a headache.

→ workbook page 46

FUNCTIONS
Advice and obligation

3 WRITING **Imagine an exchange student is coming to your school for a few weeks. Write down three rules and three pieces of advice to help them.**

You have to arrive at school by 9 a.m.

4 SPEAKING **Work in pairs and compare your sentences.**

VOCABULARY
Technology (nouns)

5 **Match the words with the photos. Write the numbers in the boxes.**

1 adapter | 2 "at" symbol | 3 charger | 4 headset
5 plug | 6 power cord | 7 protective case
8 USB port | 9 webcam | 10 wireless router

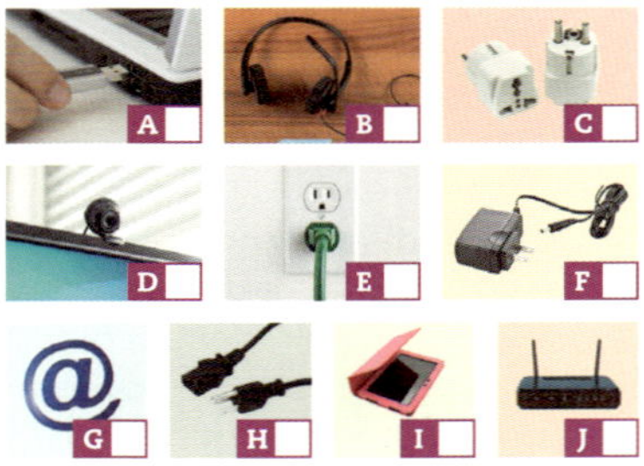

6 **Complete the sentences using the words from Exercise 5.**

1 There's something wrong with that email address. There's no ______________ in it.
2 I forgot to bring a UK ______________, so I couldn't plug in my laptop.
3 I left the ______________ for my phone at home, and the battery is almost dead. Can I borrow yours?
4 You can't get a Wi-Fi signal? Have you checked if the ______________ is turned on?
5 My laptop only has one ______________, so I can't plug in my mouse and my phone at the same time.
6 I couldn't use my laptop. I left the ______________ at home, and the battery was dead.
7 I'm going to plug in my ______________. I don't want everyone to hear what you're saying.
8 It's the wrong ______________. You need an adapter.

→ workbook page 48

50

To describe an internal obligation (an order we give ourselves), use *must*, e.g., *My sneakers are too small. I must get some new ones.* To describe an external obligation or rule (one given by somebody else), use *have to*, e.g., *My PE teacher said my sneakers are too small, so I have to get some new ones!*

In both cases the negative form is *mustn't*, e.g., *You must arrive by 9 a.m.* = *You mustn't arrive late; I have to arrive by 9 a.m.* = *I mustn't arrive late.* ~~*I don't have to arrive late.*~~

To describe an obligation to not do something, use *mustn't*. To say that there is no obligation, use *don't have to*, e.g., *You mustn't do that!* (It is not permitted.) *You don't have to do that.* (There is no obligation to do it, but you can if you want to.) Reinforce that *don't have to* expresses a lack of obligation in a similar way to *don't need to*.

When orders are official, like on notices or documents, we usually use *must*, e.g., *Passengers must keep their bags with them at all times.*

TH!NK more

Workbook
Grammar p46, Ex.1–4
Vocabulary p48, Ex.1–3

Worksheets
Grammar Worksheets 5
Vocabulary Worksheets 5

Culture note

The "at" sign (@) does not have a singular English word unlike French (*arobase*) or Spanish and Portuguese (*arroba*). On some social media forums, usernames (or "handles") are in the form *@johnsmith*.

7 Give a couple of your own ideas as examples before students work in pairs.

8 🔊 **5.02**
The shoes tell you what direction to go in.

9 🔊 **5.02**
1 sense of direction
2 inspired by the shoes
3 the heel of the left shoe
4 the direction you need to go
5 how close you are to your destination
6 using wireless technology

▶ 13 Grammar video! Necessity: *didn't need to / needn't have*

10 During feedback, draw students' attention to the words that follow *need to* and *needn't have*. Students may produce statements like *He needn't has bought a new bicycle.* Remind them that because *have* follows an auxiliary, it does not change in the third person, e.g., *He needn't have bought …*
1 Yes 2 No
RULE: 3 needn't have
4 didn't need to do

11 *1 A 2 B 3 B 4 A 5 B 6 A*

Workbook p47

12 During feedback, say the phrases for students to repeat and check pronunciation. Draw attention to the stress on the second syllable of up<u>grade</u> (as a verb) and point out that as a noun *an <u>up</u>grade* is stressed on the first syllable. This is the same for *update* (*an <u>up</u>date, to up<u>date</u>*).
1 streaming 2 connect to the Wi-Fi
3 browsing the internet 4 upgrading
5 sync devices 6 plugged in
7 posted an update 8 save

Workbook p48

13 You could move on to pronunciation at this stage prior to doing the speaking task. Invite students to share their answers with the rest of the class during feedback.

Pronunciation
The schwa /ə/ sound

Student's Book p120

LISTENING

7 Look at the photo. What do you think this invention does?

8 🔊 5.02 **Listen to the podcast to check your ideas.**

9 🔊 5.02 **Listen again and complete the sentences.**
1 Shauna says that Aaron has a really bad ______.
2 Dominic Wilcox was ______ from *The Wizard of Oz.*
3 The GPS system is in ______.
4 The left shoe shows you ______.
5 The right shoe shows you ______.
6 The shoes communicate with each other ______.

GRAMMAR
Necessity: *didn't need to / needn't have*

Grammar video ▶ 13

10 Look at the examples from the listening and answer the questions. Then complete the rule with *didn't need to do* or *needn't have*.

I needn't have downloaded that GPS app for my phone.
They're so simple to use that I didn't need to read the manual.

1 Did Aaron download a GPS app for his phone?
2 Did Shauna read the manual?

RULE: When we use [3] ______, it means that someone did something, but in fact it wasn't necessary.
When we use [4] ______, it often means that someone didn't do something because it wasn't necessary.

11 Choose the correct sentence (A or B) to follow sentences 1–6. You must use all of the sentences.
1 Dad cooked a big meal for us, but we'd already eaten.
2 Dad came and ate with us at the restaurant.
A He needn't have cooked.
B He didn't need to cook.
3 I spent ages doing my homework last night, and now Mr. Peters isn't here to collect it.
4 Mr. Peters told us we had a choice about whether to do the homework or not.
A I didn't need to do it.
B I needn't have done it.
5 She took her umbrella, but it was a really sunny day.
6 The forecast said that it was going to be a sunny day. So she left her umbrella at home.
A She didn't need to take it.
B She needn't have taken it.

→ workbook page 47

VOCABULARY
Technology (verbs)

12 Rewrite the sentences, replacing the words in *italics* with the correct form of the phrases in the list.

to browse the internet | to plug (a laptop) in
to sync devices | to post an update
to save (a document) | to stream (a video)
to connect to the Wi-Fi | to upgrade (your system)

1 Jack's *watching* yesterday's game *on the internet without downloading it.*
2 I can't *access the internet without using a cable.* There's no signal here.
3 I'm a little bored so I'm *looking at various websites on the internet.*
4 I think you should spend some money *on improving* your operating system. It's very old.
5 You should *make sure different devices (laptop, tablet, etc.) contain the same information* so you always have a backup.
6 The printer's not working. Oh! It's not *connected to the electrical outlet.*
7 Mia hasn't *added any new content to her vlog* for a week. I hope she's OK.
8 Sam is always losing files because he often forgets to *store* information *on an electronic device.*

→ workbook page 48

SPEAKING

13 Work in pairs. Discuss the questions.
1 How often do you post updates on social media?
2 Which devices do you sync?
3 What was the last TV show you streamed?

PRONUNCIATION
The schwa /ə/ sound Go to page 120.

Homework
Ask students to keep a journal for two or three days and to make a note of the technology they use, or if they don't use much technology, what technology their family uses and how long they spend on it.

Activity idea Fast finishers
Ask students to make a list of any other nouns that collocate with the verbs in Exercise 12. Alternatively, they could make a list of any other English verbs related to technology that are used in their language.

TH!NK more

Workbook
Listening p52, Ex.1–2
Grammar p47, Ex.5–6
Vocabulary p48, Ex.4–5
Vocabulary Extra p49, Ex.1–3
Pronunciation p119

Worksheets
Grammar Worksheets 5
Grammar presentation: Necessity: *didn't need to / needn't have*
Grammar video! Necessity: *didn't need to / needn't have*
Vocabulary Worksheets 5

Warmer

Ask: *How well do older people that you know understand technology? What technology do they use?* Divide the class into pairs for students to discuss these questions.

1 Put a copy of the photo up on the board and do the exercise as a class before students open their books.

2 Set a two-minute time limit to encourage students to read quickly and to focus on gist rather than specific information.
1 an elderly lady and a teenage IT teacher – possibly grandmother and granddaughter
2 The teenager is teaching the elderly lady how to use a computer and how to use the internet.

3 🔊 **5.05 Check/clarify:** *witnessing, proficient, enthusiastic, silver surfers, emigrated, newly acquired.*
Skype, Facebook, email, get ideas for traveling, music lessons, recipes, YouTube cooking tutorial, making videos, reuniting with friends and family members

4 Ask students to underline the language in the text that helped them answer.
1 It's a documentary. 2 It shows the story of teenagers teaching elderly people to use the internet. 3 Poppy and Amy Raynes 4 witnessing how the internet had changed their grandparents' lives 5 friends 6 in a local home for elderly people 7 using Facebook, getting ideas for traveling, learning how to play an instrument, or cooking 8 making a YouTube cooking tutorial, making a rap video, and reconnecting with people

5 Give students three minutes to read the questions and make notes to refer to in their discussions.

Great success for teenage teachers

– when silver surfers get connected

A new documentary called *Silver Surfers* shows the inspiring story of a group of teens helping elderly people to improve the quality of their lives by teaching them how to make use of the internet. The people were between 76 and 93 years old.

Rosemary Raynes, the director of the documentary, got the idea for the movie while talking to her sisters Poppy and Amy about a project the two of them had started several years before in Kingston, Canada. The two teenagers and a group of friends had a clear goal: they wanted to help elderly people to feel more connected to other people, through the use of the internet.

They started the project after witnessing how the internet had changed their own grandparents' lives. Their grandparents could use the internet at a basic level but wanted to become more proficient. After the two girls had given them a few basic IT lessons, they were able to use the computer confidently and became enthusiastic users of Skype, Facebook, and email.

The two students were so motivated by that success that they got several of their friends to join them. Together, they started to visit a local home for elderly people. Many of the people there couldn't even turn on a computer without help. But the young people were amazed by how much they had learned after only a few lessons.

It's fascinating to see how the silver surfers featured in the movie all had very different interests. Some of them wanted to use Facebook to stay in touch with family members who had emigrated to countries as far away as Australia. Others were eager to get ideas for traveling, learning how to play an instrument, or cooking.

The outcomes of the project were amazing: 89-year-old Sheila, managed to create a YouTube cooking tutorial with her friend; 93-year-old Marilyn succeeded in making a rap video; Albert, 89, initially wanted to learn how to use the web to find old friends, and in doing so he was struck by how easy it was to reconnect online with people he hadn't seen in decades. He even managed to use his newly acquired skills to reunite with his daughter, who he had lost touch with.

The documentary has been met with great enthusiasm in several countries, and a number of follow-up projects have been launched. They are all aimed at helping elderly people explore the benefits of technology, have fun, and stay in touch with others – thanks to a wonderful initiative by two teenage girls.

READING

1 SPEAKING **Work in pairs. Look at the photo and answer the questions.**
1 What do you think the relationship between the people is?
2 What do you think they are doing?

2 **Read the article quickly to check your ideas.**

3 🔊 5.05 **Read and listen to the article again. Find examples in the article of how elderly people learned to use technology.**

4 **Read the article again and answer the questions.**
1 What is *Silver Surfers*?
2 What does it show?
3 Who started the project?
4 What inspired them to start the project?
5 Who did they get to join them?
6 Where did they start giving lessons?
7 What were some of the elderly people's interests?
8 What were some of their achievements?

5 SPEAKING **Work in pairs and discuss the questions.**
1 What do you think of the *Silver Surfers* project?
2 Would you be interested in joining such a project? Why (not)?
3 Which example of the seniors' achievements do you find most impressive?
4 Have you ever tried to help someone you know with technology? Did you manage to teach them successfully?

TH!NK more

Workbook
Reading p50, Ex.1–4

Grammar; Speaking

6 You might like to point out the use of *even* in sentence 1. Elicit/explain that it is used to emphasize something surprising.
RULE: 5 could 6 managed 7 succeeded 8 couldn't

7 Go through the first sentence as an example, making sure students are clear on why that particular modal form is used.
1 B 2 A 3 B 4 B 5 B 6 C

8 **Check/clarify:** *geometry, dash, tapping, obstacle.*
1 could 2 couldn't 3 managed 4 able 5 couldn't

9 If you are short on time, assign this exercise for homework.

Workbook p47

10 Give your own example before students do the task. Encourage students to reflect on whether they admire the things the person does, their personality, or both. Monitor and help with ideas for people and qualities.

11–12 To prompt students to think, write the following on the board: *Why would that quality be useful to you?* Encourage students to go into detail and think of examples. Ask students to compare ideas in pairs and think of alternative/additional ways in which their partner might develop these qualities.

13 Make different pairs or put pairs together to form groups of four and tell students to discuss their ideas.

GRAMMAR

Ability in the past: *could, was / were able to, managed to, succeeded in*

6 **Read the examples from the article on page 52 and then complete the rule with *managed, succeeded, could,* and *couldn't.***

1 Many of the people there couldn't even turn on a computer without help.
2 After [...] a few basic IT lessons, they were able to use the computer confidently.
3 The outcomes of the project were amazing: 89-year-old Sheila [...] managed to create a YouTube cooking tutorial.
4 93-year-old Marilyn succeeded in making a rap video.

> **RULE:** To talk about ability generally in the past, we use [5] ________ /*couldn't.*
> To talk about ability at specific moments in the past, we use *was/were able to* ([6] ________ *to* + infinitive, or [7] ________ *in* + gerund).
> To talk about a lack of ability at specific moments in the past, we use [8] ________ /*wasn't (weren't) able to.*

7 **Choose the correct answers.**

1 Her cell phone broke a week ago. She ___ to access any social networks since then.
A couldn't
B hasn't been able
C hasn't succeeded

2 He was so moved by the award he received that he ___ continue with his speech.
A wasn't able to B succeeded in C could

3 He played soccer again for the first time after his injury, but he only ___ play for 20 minutes.
A could
B managed to
C succeeded in

4 She had to ask several people until she finally ___ in finding some help.
A managed B succeeded C could

5 My little brother ___ to walk when he was ten months old.
A could
B was able
C succeeded

6 I tried to climb that mountain once, but I ___ to get to the top because of the bad weather.
A couldn't
B didn't succeed
C didn't manage

8 **Complete the text with one word for each line.**

> When I was eight, my older brother introduced me to a game on his phone called Geometry Dash. He was amazing. He [1] ________ complete all the levels. He let me try it. It was simple. You had to make a little block jump over things by tapping the screen. At first, I was terrible. I [2] ________ even jump over the first obstacle. But I kept trying, and after about three hours I [3] ________ to complete the first level. I spent the rest of the day playing it, and by the end of the day, I was [4] ________ to do the first three levels. That night in bed, I [5] ________ sleep because I kept on playing Geometry Dash in my head!

9 WRITING **Write a short text about some things you couldn't do when you were younger, but that you can do now.**

When I was really young, I couldn't ride a bike, but I was able to do it by the time I was five.

→ workbook page 47

SPEAKING

10 **You're going to talk about an elderly person who has qualities that you admire. Make notes on why you admire this person.**

11 **Which of the qualities you have written down would you like to have in your own life?**

12 **What could you do to develop those qualities?**

13 **Discuss your ideas with a partner.**

Homework

Ask students to write their own paragraph summarizing their notes from Exercises 10–13.

Activity idea Extension

Divide the class into small groups. Ask students to decide on the three most important things that we can learn from elderly people. Nominate a student from each group to report their findings to the rest of the class and have a quick class vote to decide on the most important qualities.

Language note

You may like to tell students that *managed to* and *succeeded in* are usually used to describe the ability to do something difficult, e.g., *On his fourth attempt, he finally managed to pass / succeeded in passing his driver's test.*

Activity idea Fast finishers

In Exercise 7, ask students to write sentences of their own describing difficult things they managed to do or succeeded in doing in the past two years.

TH!NK more

Practice Extra
Unit 5 Practice it!

Workbook
Grammar p47, Ex.7

Worksheets
Grammar Worksheets 5

Warmer

Give student pairs two minutes to write down as many modern cities as possible. Go through the alphabet, asking students to name a city beginning with each letter. Students vote on which city they think is the most modern.

▶ 14 TH!NK
Smart cities

1 Allow time for pairs to discuss and put the items in order of importance. Hold a class vote to decide which they feel are the most and the least important.

2 🔊 5.06
Singapore: keeping an eye on its citizens San Francisco: transportation and road congestion Barcelona: cutting down carbon emissions Oslo: caring for old people

3 **Check/clarify:** *sensors, Alzheimer's.*
1 The government is making all of the data it collects open to the public.
2 They have a system which checks the water levels on the ground and predicts future rainfall.
3 It guides people to the nearest free parking spot.
4 They allow caregivers to check in regularly and remind elderly people of daily tasks via spoken messages.

Culture notes

Singapore is both a city and a country. Located on Singapore Island between the Indian Ocean and the South China Sea, it is only slightly larger than Chicago. Despite the high population density, it is one of the world's greenest cities. The skyscrapers are filled with trees and vertical gardens, housing developments are connected by parks, and environmentally sound buildings have been mandatory since 2008. In 2015, the Botanic Gardens were made a UNESCO World Heritage site.

San Francisco is a city on the west coast of the United States. It is a cultural and financial center. The steep streets offer fantastic views across the bay, the Pacific Ocean, and the Golden Gate Bridge.

TH!NK Smart cities

Culture

FOUR OF THE SMARTEST CITIES

1 SPEAKING **Work in pairs and decide which of these things you think will be the most important for cities of the future.**

1 caring for old people
2 transportation and road congestion
3 cutting down carbon emissions
4 keeping an eye on its citizens
5 reducing the number of inhabitants

2 🔊 5.06 **Read and listen to the article. Which of the issues above does it talk about?**

SINGAPORE – AN EYE ON EVERYTHING

Singapore has plans to become the world's first smart country, and it is already a nation of sensors. They are everywhere. One area that is highly controlled by the sensors is transportation. They are on all buses, trains, and taxis and are used to help make sure the traffic runs smoothly. They can also predict where accidents are likely to happen. But the sensors are also used to monitor other areas of Singaporean life. For example, they can detect if someone is littering or smoking in a public place. And for those who are worried about their privacy, the government has promised to make most of the data it collects open to the public, meaning you will be able to access the footage yourself.

SAN FRANCISCO – KEEPING THE TRAFFIC FLOWING

It's not surprising that the new "capital" of Silicon Valley is also one of the US's smartest cities, and it has implemented a number of impressive technologies to make life easier, such as an app that will guide drivers in the city to the nearest free parking spot. This app can detect how many people are in the car and charge accordingly. The more passengers, the cheaper it is. As a result of the tech boom, San Francisco has also seen a big rise in traffic congestion, as more and more people are coming to the city to work. Smart transportation is now a top priority for city planners as they hope to free up their highways and get their citizens moving around more freely.

BARCELONA – GOING GREEN

Barcelona prides itself on being a hub for environmentally friendly smart technology. It has sensors to help monitor the levels of air and noise pollution and to turn its street lighting on and off, making sure no energy goes to waste. But where Barcelona is really leading the way is with its green technology and measures for reducing carbon emissions. For example, it has a system that checks the water levels in the ground and predicts future rainfall, which allows it to control the city's water consumption more effectively. It also has a smart waste disposal system. Citizens throw their waste into special bins where it is sucked into underground storage. Here it is sorted and recycled, and some is burned, producing energy for heating systems.

OSLO – TAKING CARE OF THE ELDERLY

Oslo is another city with big green ambitions, and it plans to be 95 percent carbon neutral by 2030. However, it also uses smart technology to help take care of its aging population as efficiently as possible. For example, it has installed sensors in the homes of citizens suffering from Alzheimer's disease. The technology allows caregivers to check in regularly with their patients to make sure all is well. It also reminds the patients of daily tasks, such as taking their medicine, via spoken messages. Motion sensors can also detect whether the patient has left the oven on or left the front door open and send out a warning alarm if the person is in danger. Such technology means more elderly people can continue living in their own homes for longer.

3 **Read the article again and answer the questions.**

1 How is the Singapore government going to address privacy concerns?
2 How is Barcelona able to manage its water usage more efficiently?
3 What does San Francisco's parking technology do?
4 How do sensors in the home help people with Alzheimer's in Oslo?

54

Barcelona is a city in northeastern Spain. It is a major cultural center famous for its examples of Modernist and Art Nouveau architecture, and the Sagrada Família church, designed by Antoni Gaudí, is a UNESCO World Heritage Site.

Oslo, formerly known as Kristiania, is the capital of Norway. According to Viking stories, Oslo was founded in 1049 by Harald Hardrada, but archaeological research has found evidence of earlier settlement. Situated high in the Northern Hemisphere, the amount of daylight varies greatly throughout the year, with more than 18 hours in midsummer, and it never gets completely dark at night.

4 During feedback, take this opportunity to work on pronunciation by saying the adjectives for students to repeat. Check that they're placing stress on the correct syllable.
1 efficiently 2 implemented 3 congestion 4 hub 5 footage 6 sensors 7 consumption 8 monitor

5 Encourage students to express themselves in English and to use any vocabulary they have learned from the article.

1 Allow students to compare answers in pairs before feedback.
Suggested answer: It has been written for people who do not know how to save a file on a computer so that they do not lose files.

2 During feedback, point out that the words in the blanks are commonly used when giving instructions.
1 If; then 2 first thing 3 To do 4 To 5 This means 6 Finally

3 1 first thing 2 If; then 3 this means 4 To 5 Finally

4 Ask students to make notes on why they think each of the tips is important. Put them into pairs or small groups to compare ideas.

5 Divide the class into small groups so that they can share ideas before writing individually (they could do this for homework). Students make notes in preparation for writing their text.

6 Students should organize their stages in the same way as the example in Exercise 1. They should use words and phrases from Exercises 2 and 3.

4 VOCABULARY **Match the highlighted words in the article with the definitions.**
1 in the quickest and most organized way possible
2 to put an idea into practice
3 overcrowding
4 a center for something
5 a video recording
6 instruments used to detect something
7 the amount you use something
8 to check and control

5 SPEAKING **Work in pairs and discuss the questions.**
1 What smart technology does your town or city use? Are these initiatives a good idea? Why (not)?
2 What other types of smart technology would you like to see used in your town or city? Why?

WRITING
Instructions

1 INPUT **Read the instructions on how to save a Word file. Who do you think it has been written for and why?**

One of the most important things you need to learn to do when using a computer to write documents is to learn how to save a file.

1 If your file is a written document, then you will be using a word-processing program such as Microsoft Word. The first thing you need to do is to create a new file. To do this, open up the program by clicking on the icon.
2 When the program has opened, click on the icon "file" in the top left-hand corner of the screen and choose "new" from the drop-down menu. This will create a new document for you.
3 I would recommend saving this document before you have written anything. This means that if your computer shuts down unexpectedly, you won't lose the file. To save the file, click on "file" again. From the drop-down menu, choose "save."
4 A dialogue box or window will open asking you to type in the name of your document. You will also need to choose a location for the file. Select "desktop" from the list on the left-hand side of the box. This means you will be able to find your file easily when you start your computer.
5 Finally, when you close your document, a dialogue box will appear asking if you want to save any changes. Click "yes," and this will ensure you never lose any of your work.

2 ANALYZE **Complete the sentences. Then read the instructions again to check.**
1 __________ your file is a written document, __________ you will be using a word-processing program.
2 The __________ you need to do is to create a new file.
3 __________ this, open up the program.
4 __________ save the file, click on "file" again.
5 __________ you will be able to find your file easily.
6 __________, when you close your document, a dialogue box will appear.

3 **Use a word or phrase from the list to complete each sentence.**

finally | first thing | if | then | this means | to

1 To take photos, the __________ you need is a camera.
2 __________ you're serious about photography, __________ buy the best camera you can afford.
3 Choose a camera with a high number of pixels – __________ that you'll have good quality images.
4 __________ find out which are the best cameras, do research on the internet.
5 __________, get out of here and have fun!

4 PLAN **In pairs, discuss why the following tips are important when writing instructions.**
- Think carefully about who you are writing for.
- Use clear language that is easy to understand.
- Give the instructions in a logical order.
- Use a friendly, informal style.

5 **Choose one of the computing processes below and make notes for each stage.**
- how to create a folder
- how to change the font
- how to cut and paste
- how to rename a file

6 PRODUCE **Write a text (about 200 words) describing the process you chose in Exercise 5. Remember to do these things.**
- Decide who you are writing these instructions for (a child? a beginner? a fairly experienced user?).
- Give your instructions in a logical order.
- Think about the tips from Exercise 4.

Activity idea Mixed-ability
In Culture Exercise 4, stronger students could look at the eight words in the article and try to deduce meaning from context before referring back to the definitions and completing the exercise. With weaker classes, you could give students the first letter of each word to guide them.

Homework
If you are short on time, students can do Exercise 6 for homework. If you have done this in class, ask students to exchange their texts with another student for them to read and to give feedback on content and structure. Students could check if the text uses the same structure as the example. They should also decide which the most/least interesting part of the text is.

TH!NK more
Practice Extra
Unit 5 Master it!

Workbook
Developing Writing p51

Tests
Unit, extension, and skills test 5

Warmer

Write *efistalv* in the center of the board. Ask: *Which word has been mixed up?* Elicit *festival*. Ask: *How many festivals can you name?* Write some of their ideas on the board.

▶ 15 Get TH!NKing

Play the video and discuss the question with your class.

1 Write the words from the box on the board and check understanding. Put a copy of the two photos up on the board and do the exercise as a class before students open their books.

2 Ask a student to read out their notes. The rest of the class can try to guess which photo it is.

3 🔊 **6.01** Before students listen, ask them to cover the email on page 57, look at the subject line and photo, and answer the question.

4 *1 comics and graphic novels*
2 by their costumes
3 because you have more fun if you do
4 by taking selfies together
5 by competing (and not just watching)
6 because they need enough time to make costumes

5 Encourage students to express themselves in English and to use any vocabulary they have learned from the email. Monitor to help with any difficulties, but do not interrupt as this is a fluency activity.

6 BETTER TOGETHER

OBJECTIVES

FUNCTIONS: using intensifying comparatives

GRAMMAR: comparatives; linkers of contrast

VOCABULARY: ways of speaking; friendship idioms

Get TH!NKING Watch the video and think: what festivals are celebrated in your town or city?

A

B

READING

1 SPEAKING **Work in pairs. Look at the photos. What kind of festival do you think these people are attending? How do they feel?**

dull | enthusiastic | excited
miserable | self-confident | terrified

2 SPEAKING **Choose one of the two people and imagine their thoughts. Make notes. Tell your partner the person's thoughts for your partner to guess who it is.**

3 🔊 6.01 **Look at the subject line Ashley put in her email. Why do you think Ashley chose this subject line? Read and listen to the email to check your ideas.**

4 **Read the email again and answer the questions.**
1 What kind of reading material are you most likely to come across at a Comic Con?
2 How can you tell that someone likes the same show as you?
3 Why should Matteo wear a costume?
4 In what way(s) do people connect with each other?
5 How can you enjoy the Cosplay Contest more?
6 Why does Matteo have to make a quick decision?

5 SPEAKING **Work in pairs and discuss the questions.**
1 Why do you think wearing a costume gives people self-confidence?
2 Have you ever acted in a play or dressed as a superhero? How did it make you feel?
3 In what situations do you feel most self-confident?

The missing suitcase

ROLE PLAY **Work in groups of four. Students A and C: go to page 127. Students B and D: go to page 128.**

Imagine you are going to L.A. Comic Con with three friends. You traveled to Los Angeles by train. Your suitcase with your costumes was lost. Agree together on what you should do.

56

ROLE-PLAY Allow students six to eight minutes to prepare their role-plays. Monitor to make sure all students are on task. If students have access to a recording device (their cell phones, for example), they could record their conversation and play it back to check their own pronunciation and intonation. They can then repeat the exercise and listen for improvements.

Objectives

Functions and speaking Using intensifying comparatives; **Role-play**: The missing suitcase
Grammar Comparatives; linkers of contrast
Vocabulary Ways of speaking; friendship idioms
Values Doing good
Literature *Little Women*

Resources for this unit

All available online

Videos
- Get **TH!NK**ing: *What festivals are celebrated in your town or city?*
- Grammar video!: Linkers of contrast

Tests
- Unit, extension, and skills test 6
- End of term test 2

Worksheets
- Grammar and vocabulary: Basic, Standard, and Extension Worksheets
- Project: Comics
- Communication: Bringing people together
- Grammar presentation: Linkers of contrast
- Literature Worksheets: *Anne of Green Gables, Bill the Bloodhound,* and *The Yellow Wallpaper*
- Get **TH!NK**ing and Grammar video! video Worksheets

Reading; Train to TH!NK; Pronunciation

Culture note

L.A. Comic Con is a three-day annual convention that focuses on comics, anime, cult horror and science fiction shows, and gaming. It started in 2011 as a showcase for local talent, but has now expanded to attract over 100,000 visitors.

6 To introduce the topic, tell students the same story twice. The first time you tell it, use ordinary adjectives (*good, nice, not bad,* etc.), e.g., *I went on vacation last year. It was nice. The food was OK, and the weather was good.*

When you repeat the story, use language of exaggeration, stressing the adjectives, e.g., *I went on the best vacation of my life last year. It was absolutely fantastic. The food was delicious, and the weather was incredible.*

Ask: *What was the difference between the two stories?* Elicit that the second included more exaggeration and was possibly more interesting to listen to.

1 five
2 ride was terrible; worst trip of my life; stopped for ages; middle of nowhere; so bored I thought I was going to go crazy
3 ride was terrible: ride was annoying/inconvenient
worst trip of my life: it wasn't a good trip
stopped for ages: stopped for quite a long time
middle of nowhere: not at a station / in the country
so bored I thought I was going to go crazy: bored with having to wait

7 Allow students six to eight minutes to prepare their stories. Encourage students to make notes rather than write long sentences. If students have access to a recording device (their cell phones, for example), they could record their conversation and play it back to check their own pronunciation and intonation. They can then repeat the exercise and listen for improvements.

Pronunciation
Linking words with /dʒ/ and /tʃ/

Student's Book p120

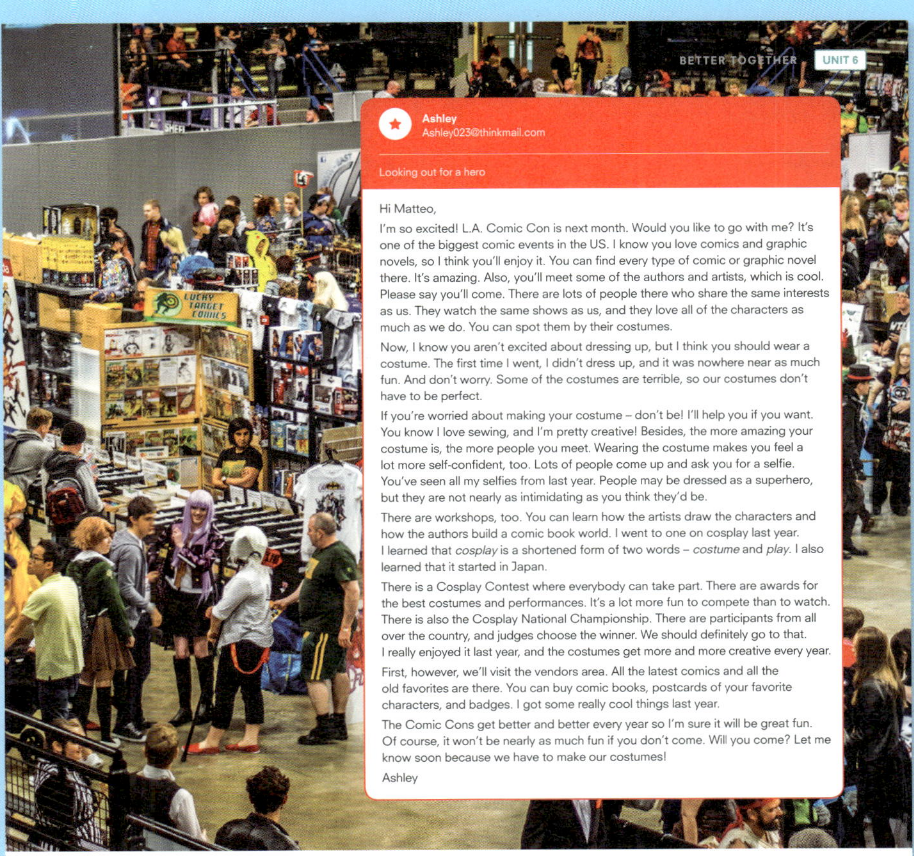

BETTER TOGETHER UNIT 6

Ashley
Ashley023@thinkmail.com

Looking out for a hero

Hi Matteo,

I'm so excited! L.A. Comic Con is next month. Would you like to go with me? It's one of the biggest comic events in the US. I know you love comics and graphic novels, so I think you'll enjoy it. You can find every type of comic or graphic novel there. It's amazing. Also, you'll meet some of the authors and artists, which is cool. Please say you'll come. There are lots of people there who share the same interests as us. They watch the same shows as us, and they love all of the characters as much as we do. You can spot them by their costumes.

Now, I know you aren't excited about dressing up, but I think you should wear a costume. The first time I went, I didn't dress up, and it was nowhere near as much fun. And don't worry. Some of the costumes are terrible, so our costumes don't have to be perfect.

If you're worried about making your costume – don't be! I'll help you if you want. You know I love sewing, and I'm pretty creative! Besides, the more amazing your costume is, the more people you meet. Wearing the costume makes you feel a lot more self-confident, too. Lots of people come up and ask you for a selfie. You've seen all my selfies from last year. People may be dressed as a superhero, but they are not nearly as intimidating as you think they'd be.

There are workshops, too. You can learn how the artists draw the characters and how the authors build a comic book world. I went to one on cosplay last year. I learned that *cosplay* is a shortened form of two words – *costume* and *play*. I also learned that it started in Japan.

There is a Cosplay Contest where everybody can take part. There are awards for the best costumes and performances. It's a lot more fun to compete than to watch. There is also the Cosplay National Championship. There are participants from all over the country, and judges choose the winner. We should definitely go to that. I really enjoyed it last year, and the costumes get more and more creative every year.

First, however, we'll visit the vendors area. All the latest comics and all the old favorites are there. You can buy comic books, postcards of your favorite characters, and badges. I got some really cool things last year.

The Comic Cons get better and better every year so I'm sure it will be great fun. Of course, it won't be nearly as much fun if you don't come. Will you come? Let me know soon because we have to make our costumes!

Ashley

Train to TH!NK

Exaggeration

When we feel strongly about something, we tend to exaggerate – we call something "a great idea," "the best (movie) ever," "an amazing journey," etc. But we often don't mean that literally. As a listener, you need to be aware of exaggeration and understand what the speaker is really saying.

6 Read the example and answer the questions.

Last night's train ride was terrible. It was the worst trip of my life. The train was two hours late, and then it stopped for ages in the middle of nowhere. I was so bored I thought I was going to go crazy. I hope today's trip won't be as bad.

1 How many exaggerations does the speaker make?
2 What are they?
3 What does he or she really mean in each case?

7 SPEAKING **Work in pairs and tell your partner about something really good or really bad that happened to you recently. Use exaggeration.**

PRONUNCIATION
Linking words with /dʒ/ and /tʃ/
Go to page 120.

57

Homework

Ask students to write their story from Exercise 7 with lots of exaggeration.

Activity idea Extension

During feedback, read the example text (in the speech bubble in Exercise 6) for students to repeat and check stress/intonation. Point out that we put a strong stress on words which we use to exaggerate meaning, e.g., *terrible – worst; two hours – ages.* Ask students to take turns telling the story to a partner using suitable stress and intonation.

Critical TH!NKing
Understanding and analyzing ideas and arguments
Interpreting and drawing inferences from arguments and data.

Communication
Using appropriate language and register for context
Using a variety of language and communication strategies to achieve a desired effect.

TH!NK more

Worksheets
Project Comics
Communication Bringing people together
Get TH!NKing *What festivals are celebrated in your town or city?*

Workbook
Pronunciation p119

Grammar; Functions; Vocabulary

Warmer

In pairs, ask students to describe their best friend to their partner.

1 Ask students to try to match the sentence halves from memory before referring back to page 57 to check.

1 c 2 d 3 e 4 b 5 a
RULE: 6 Sentence 2
7 Sentence 3 8 Sentence 5
9 Sentence 4 10 Sentence 1

2 This exercise is closely modeled on Reading and Use of English Part 4 of the Cambridge English: First exam.

1 nowhere near as difficult
2 practice, the better 3 more and more expensive 4 the less

Workbook p54

3 With books closed, write the first column on the board. Elicit reasons for each statement. Encourage students to use comparative forms in their answers before checking on page 58. During feedback, draw attention to the phrases in italics. Point out that primary stress is often placed on the intensifying comparatives and that they are often used to exaggerate information in stories.

1 b ii 2 c i 3 a iii

4 Nominate two or three students to share their favorite piece of advice with the class.

5 Sentence 5

6 1 e 2 c 3 a 4 d 5 f 6 b

7 Explain that we can form nouns from the verb roots using the suffixes in the list. Also point out that we can make verb phrases using *make* or *give* + noun, e.g., *make an enquiry*.

2 introduction 3 definition
4 suggestion 5 praise 6 criticism

GRAMMAR
Comparatives

1 Match the sentence halves. Then complete the rule with 1–5.

1 The more amazing your costume is, ☐
2 It's a lot more fun to compete ☐
3 I didn't dress up, and it was nowhere near ☐
4 The costumes get more and ☐
5 People are not nearly as ☐

a intimidating as you think they'd be.
b more creative every year.
c the more people you meet.
d than to watch.
e as much fun.

RULE:
A Use *a lot / far / much* + comparative to make a comparative stronger. Sentence [6] ____________.
B Use *just as, not nearly as,* and *nowhere near as* + adjective + *as* to intensify a comparison. Sentences [7] ____________ and [8] ____________.
C Use comparative *and* comparative + short adjectives, e.g., *hotter and hotter* to talk about how something or someone is changing or increasing. Use *more and more* + longer adjectives, e.g., *more and more interesting*. Sentence [9] ____________.
D Use *the* + comparative, *the* + comparative with short adjectives, or *the more* + adjective, *the more* + adjective + clause with long adjectives to show how two events affect each other. Sentence [10] ____________.

2 Complete the second sentence so that it has a similar meaning to the first. Use the words in parentheses. You must use between two and five words, including the word given.

1 Today's test was much easier than yesterday's test. (nowhere)
Today's test was ____________ as yesterday's test.
2 I'm practicing the piano a lot, and I'm getting much better. (practice)
The more I ____________ I get at playing the piano.
3 I'm sure the price of food is going up each month. (and)
Food is getting ____________ each month.
4 I've been seeing John a lot recently, and I'm beginning not to like him so much. (less)
The more I see John, ____________ I like him.

→ workbook page 54

FUNCTIONS
Using intensifying comparatives

3 Look at what the writer recommends to tourists traveling to the US. Match the three parts.

1 You should visit New York.	a *It's easily the best* time to visit.	i And *it's a whole lot* cheaper than the train.
2 You should travel on the subway.	b *It's far and away* the most beautiful city in the US.	ii And *it's tons less* expensive than London.
3 You should come back in the fall.	c It's the easiest way to travel *by far*.	iii And *it's even* nicer than it is now.

4 SPEAKING **Make recommendations to visitors to your country, using the sentences in Exercise 3 to help you. Compare your ideas with a partner.**

VOCABULARY
Ways of speaking

5 Which one of these sentences would probably *not* be said about the festival in the email on page 57?

1 "The costumes this year were amazing."
2 "The first time I went, I didn't make my own costume."
3 "This man dressed as Iron Man is my friend Jake."
4 "I think you should enter the Cosplay Contest."
5 "The food is terrible."
6 "*Con* is short for *convention*. It means a large meeting of people for an event."

6 Match the sentences in Exercise 5 with the speaker's communicative aim.

a to introduce ☐ d to suggest ☐
b to define ☐ e to praise ☐
c to admit ☐ f to criticize ☐

7 Write the words with the suffixes from the list. One word does not have a suffix.

-ion | -ism | -ition | -ssion | -tion

1 to admit to make an *admission*
2 to introduce to make an ____________
3 to define to give a ____________
4 to suggest to make a ____________
5 to praise to give ____________
6 to criticize to express ____________

8 Write an example for three of the functions above. Read them to a partner to guess.

You should go and see the new Batman movie. It's amazing.

You're making a suggestion.

→ workbook page 56

58

8 Give students time to write three sentences.

Workbook p56

Get it Right!
Comparatives

Student's Book p124

Language note Ways of speaking

While Exercise 6 does not focus on reported speech, you might like to point out to stronger classes that some of these verbs can be used to report what has been said. Give the following examples:

He enquired about the train. (*enquire about* + noun)
She recommended visiting New Orleans. (*recommend* + *-ing*)
He complained about the lack of free seats. (*complain about* + noun)
He confessed to eating the last piece of cake. (*confess to* + *-ing*)

Activity idea Fast finishers

Ask students to make a list of more nouns that include the suffixes in the list in Exercise 7.

TH!NK more

Workbook
Grammar p54, Ex.1–4
Vocabulary p56, Ex.1–3

Worksheets
Grammar Worksheets 6
Vocabulary Worksheets 6

Unit 6
Better together

Listening; Vocabulary

9 Ask students to work individually before comparing their ideas in pairs.

10 🔊 **6.04** Tell students not to worry about understanding every word for now, but to focus on listening to check their ideas and to put the pictures in order.
A 3 B 4 C 1 D 2

11 🔊 **6.04 Check/clarify:** *kindergarten, ponytail, paddle, panicked, inside out.*
This exercise is closely modeled on Listening Part 2 of the Cambridge English: First exam. Ask students to predict the words or type of words that could go in each space before they listen a second time. Tell students not to worry about other difficult vocabulary at this stage, as this will come up later.
1 ponytails 2 shoulder 3 everything 4 fault 5 excited 6 dragon 7 swim 8 trust

12 At the end of the exercise, listen to some of the students' ideas and encourage open class discussion.

13 Check/clarify: *pod, hatchet, hip.* Ask students to try to match the phrases before playing the audio again to hear them in context. During feedback, ask: *Is there a similar phrase in your language?*
1 d 2 c 3 e 4 g 5 f 6 b 7 h 8 a

14 Check/clarify: *identical, upset, choir.*
1 look like two peas in a pod
2 get along like a house on fire
3 know each other inside and out
4 have a shoulder to cry on
5 had a falling out
6 clear the air
7 bury the hatchet
8 joined at the hip

15 This exercise can be done as a mingle activity with students changing partners every few minutes.

Workbook p56

Homework
Ask students to write five sentences comparing themselves to a member of their family using some of the comparative structures in the rule box.

LISTENING

9 Put the pictures in order to make a story about Carlotta and Lily. Write 1–4 in the boxes.

10 🔊 6.04 Listen to the interview to check your ideas.

11 🔊 6.04 Listen again and complete the sentences.

1 In kindergarten, both Carlotta and Lily wore their hair in ________________.
2 If Carlotta was upset, Lily was always a ________________ to cry on.
3 They were best friends, and they did ________________ together.
4 It was Carlotta's ________________ that they had a falling out.
5 Lily was very ________________ about the costume competition.
6 Carlotta stole Lily's idea for the ________________ costume.
7 Lily was the only person who knew that Carlotta couldn't ________________.
8 It took a long time for Lily to ________________ Carlotta again.

12 SPEAKING Work in pairs and answer the questions in pairs.

1 Do you agree that Lily was right to be angry with Carlotta?
2 Do you understand why Carlotta did what she did?
3 Have you ever had a big fight with a good friend? Are you friends again now?

VOCABULARY
Friendship idioms

13 Match the idioms with the definitions.

1 to look like two peas in a pod ☐
2 to get along like a house on fire ☐
3 to have a shoulder to cry on ☐
4 to bury the hatchet ☐
5 to know someone inside and out ☐
6 to be joined at the hip ☐
7 to clear the air ☐
8 to have a falling out ☐

a to have an argument and not be friends any more
b to do everything together
c to get along with someone really well
d to be so similar that you can't tell one from the other
e to have someone to listen to your problems
f to know somebody very well
g to become friends again after an argument
h to forget the bad feelings between you

14 Complete the story with the correct form of the idioms from Exercise 13.

My identical twin sister, Ana, and I [1] ________________. People often call me Ana by mistake because we look so similar. As well as looking like each other, we have the same interests, too, and we [2] ________________. We spend a lot of time together. We are in the same class at school, and we know everything about each other. We [3] ________________. When I'm upset, I know I [4] ________________. Ana always knows how to cheer me up. We sometimes argue, but we have never [5] ________________ with each other. If we did, I think Ana would be the one to talk things over to [6] ________________. She hates arguments, and she's always the one to [7] ________________ and make friends again.
Ana and I do everything together. We are both in the school choir, and we both love swimming. My grandma says we're [8] ________________.

15 SPEAKING Work in pairs. Think of some characters in a movie or a book who are good friends. Describe their friendship to another pair using the idioms from Exercise 13.

→ workbook page 56

Activity idea Fast finishers
Ask students to close their books and write as many of the Vocabulary phrases from page 59 as they can remember. They can then open their books to check.

TH!NK more

Workbook
Listening p60, Ex.1–3
Vocabulary p56, Ex.4–5
Vocabulary Extra p57, Ex.1–3

Worksheets
Vocabulary Worksheets 6

Reading

Warmer

Call out a verb from Exercise 7 on page 58 and elicit the whole phrase. For example, you say *to admit*, students say *(to make) an admission*. They get two points for the whole phrase and just one if they can only remember the noun. Once you've demonstrated this with one or two examples, pairs take turns testing each other in the same way.

1 Ask students to cover the article and look at the pictures to answer the questions. Write their ideas on the board, but do not give the answers at this stage.

2 🔊 **6.05** Before playing the audio, set a two-minute time limit to encourage students to read quickly and to focus on checking ideas rather than on trying to understand every word.
Suggested answers: 1 through a coding club / through a CoderDojo event – James Whelton set up a coding club for children in Ireland and the girl is probably attending an event. 2 at a coding club / at a CoderDojo event / at a school / at the RDS in Dublin, Ireland

3 Tell students to underline key information in the article that helped them to decide whether each sentence is true or false. During feedback, ask students to justify their answers by quoting the text they have underlined.
1 T 2 F (At the first event in 2012, there were 100 attendees, but in 2018, 10,000 people attended.) 3 DS 4 T 5 DS 6 F (CoderDojo is run by volunteers.) 7 T 8 T

4 Encourage students to speak at length and to try to use vocabulary from the article in their answers.

CoderDojo COOLEST PROJECTS INTERNATIONAL

Every year, kids from all over the world come to the RDS in Dublin to demonstrate the apps, websites, games, and hardware projects they have developed in their local Dojo. At the first event in 2012, there were 19 projects and 100 attendees, but in 2018, 10,000 people attended the event, from 114 countries, and 1,000 kids showcased their projects.

Back in 2011, James Whelton, the founder of CoderDojo, set up the first coding club at his school in Cork, in Ireland. He had only just turned 18.

After that, James became well known and was invited to speak at the Dublin Web Summit. He spoke about how he had hacked his iPod Nano to turn it into a watch. James had won the iPod Nano at an awards ceremony, and bored on the plane ride home, he had started to play around with it and accidentally hacked it. Then, before he went to bed that night, he wrote about it on his blog. When he woke up, he saw that a quarter of a million people had viewed the blog. After that, all his classmates wanted to know how he had done it and asked if he would teach them to code, too. He agreed to set up a coding club at his school, and he started to teach basic HTML and CSS to his fellow students. Later that year, he met Bill Liao, an entrepreneur who saw what a great idea this club was. Bill wanted to expand the project to other cities and to other countries, too, and the pair set up CoderDojo.

CoderDojo is run by volunteers, and it can be set up anywhere. There is no set curriculum at the clubs. Children from seven to 17 work on what interests them, and they learn far more than just coding skills. They also develop problem-solving skills and learn how to manage a project, work on a team, and design something they feel passionate about.

And what's really amazing is that many of the kids' inventions have had a significant social impact. Here are two examples from the event in Dublin:

- The Best International Prize was won by a Romanian team, for their project AZ-Tech Teddy. Their e-health project aims to help prevent childhood obesity. Tech Teddy is a teddy bear for a child to feed and take care of. Children who play with the teddy bear need to track its eating habits carefully. The young coders believe this will teach young children about healthy eating habits.
- Freddie from Wales won the Openet Innovator Prize for his facial recognition door entry system which he designed for elderly people with dementia. "Safe" people can register their face so that when they come to the door, they will be recognized. The system will then tell the homeowner who is at the door and whether or not to let them in.

READING

1 SPEAKING **Work in pairs. Look at the photos and answer the questions.**
1 How do you think the people know each other?
2 Where do you think they are?

2 🔊 6.05 **Read and listen to the article to check your ideas.**

3 **Read the article again and mark the sentences T (true), F (false), or DS (doesn't say). Then correct the false sentences.**
1 Coolest Projects International is a great opportunity to meet children from all over the world. ☐
2 Over the years, fewer people have attended Coolest Projects International. ☐
3 James Whelton was great at math in school. ☐
4 James Whelton became famous after he hacked his iPod Nano. ☐
5 Bill worked with James's father and agreed to help James. ☐
6 Teachers are paid a lot of money to run CoderDojo clubs. ☐
7 Children are free to invent and design whatever they like. ☐
8 The Romanian students' project aimed to teach children to eat more healthily. ☐

4 SPEAKING **Work in pairs and discuss the questions.**
1 Is there a CoderDojo in your town or in your country?
2 Do you think they are a good idea? Why (not)?
3 Are there any similar clubs in your area?
4 What kind of community club would you set up in your area?

60

Culture notes

CoderDojo is a volunteer-based global community for free programming workshops for young people between 7 and 17 years old. There are an estimated 1,250 CoderDojos spread across almost 70 countries.

The Royal Dublin Society (RDS) was founded in 1731 as the "Dublin Society" and is an Irish philanthropic organization created to promote the cultural and economic flourishing of Ireland.

Web Summit is the largest technology conference in the world. Originally held in Dublin, and now annually in Lisbon, Portugal, it gathers founders and CEOs of technology companies, fast-growing start-ups, policy makers, and heads of state to discuss where technology is heading next.

The iPod Nano is a now-discontinued portable media player designed in 2005 by Apple Inc.

HTML and CSS are coding languages. All websites are, in part, built using these languages.

Bill Liao is an Australian entrepreneur and philanthropist, engaged in not-for-profit work. He is the founder of WeForest.org. *The Financial Times* records him as one of the world's top 100 ethnic minority leaders in technology.

The Openet Innovator Prize is one of several prizes awarded at Coolest Projects International – a world-leading showcase for young digital creators, innovators, and entrepreneurs.

TH!NK more

Workbook
Reading p58, Ex.1–4

▶ 16 Grammar video!
Linkers of contrast

5 Ask students to try to answer the questions from memory before referring back to page 60 to check.
RULE: 7 in spite of 8 even though 9 nevertheless

6 Remind students to check the position of the linker and punctuation with the rule box in Exercise 5.
1 Despite studying hard for the test, I failed it.
2 He doesn't earn a lot of money. However, he gives a lot of it to charity.
3 Although I'd seen the movie before, I still really enjoyed it.
4 In spite of starting to eat less, I didn't lose any weight. / I didn't lose any weight, in spite of starting to eat less.
5 It wasn't very warm. Nevertheless, we had a good time at the beach.
6 Even though I don't speak a word of Chinese, I understood what he said. / I understood what he said, even though I don't speak a word of Chinese.

7 Tell students that there is more than one possibility for each answer.
Suggested answers: 1 I felt really tired. However, I stayed up until midnight to celebrate the New Year. / I stayed up until midnight to celebrate the New Year, in spite of feeling really tired.
2 Although I didn't sleep well the night before the test, I still got a good score. / I got a good score, even though I didn't sleep well the night before the test.
3 Although he doesn't like basketball, he plays it with his children because they enjoy it. / Even though he doesn't like basketball, he plays it with his children because they enjoy it.

Workbook p55

Get it Right!
Linkers of contrast

Student's Book p124

8–9 You may like to ask students to consider using visual cues as part of their presentation. Give students some time to practice.

GRAMMAR
Linkers of contrast

Grammar video ▶16

5 Look at these sentences about the article on page 60. Then complete the rule.

1 The children are very young. **Nevertheless**, they invent projects with a huge social impact.
2 **Although** James was no good at academic subjects at school, he was good at programming.
3 **In spite of** their young age, the kids design some amazing projects.
4 James set up the club himself **even though** he was just a student.
5 **However** young you are, you can still learn to code.
6 **Despite** having no set curriculum, students learn how to code.

> **RULE:** To contrast ideas and facts, we use these linking words: *although, even though, however, despite, in spite of*, and *nevertheless*.
> 7 *Despite* and ______ are followed by a noun phrase or a gerund. They can be used at the beginning or in the middle of a sentence.
> 8 *Although* and ______ are followed by a full clause. They can be used at the beginning or in the middle of a sentence.
> 9 *However* and ______ introduce the contrasting idea and come at the beginning of a new sentence. They are followed by a comma.

6 Rewrite the sentences using the words in parentheses.

0 I didn't know anyone at the party, but I still had a good time. (in spite of)
In spite of not knowing anyone at the party, I still had a good time.
1 I studied hard for the test. I failed it. (despite)
2 He doesn't earn a lot of money. He gives a lot of it to charity. (However)
3 I'd seen the movie before. I still really enjoyed it. (although)
4 I started to eat less. I didn't lose any weight. (in spite of)
5 It wasn't very warm. We had a good time at the beach. (Nevertheless)
6 I don't speak a word of Chinese. I understood what he said. (even though)

7 Rewrite these sentences using words from the rule box.

1 I felt really tired. I stayed up until midnight to celebrate the New Year.
2 I didn't sleep well the night before the test, so I was really tired. I still got a good score.
3 He doesn't like basketball. He plays it with his children because they enjoy it.

→ workbook page 55

TH!NK values
Doing good

8 Work in groups of four. You are going to think of a project that will be good for your community or your school. Use the points below to help you organize your ideas.

1 **Decide on a project**
What does your community or school need?
How will it be good for your community or school?
2 **Plan the details of the project**
What do you need? (a meeting space, computers, a garden, etc.)
Who can help you to set it up?
3 **Think of a famous person to get involved**
Why this person?
What do you want them to do?
4 **Extras**
What other things can you do to make the project a success (write a blog about it, invite a local newspaper to write about it, hold a competition, etc.)?

9 SPEAKING **Present your ideas to the class. Each person in your group should talk about one of the points above.**

10 SPEAKING **As a class, vote on the projects with the most potential. Could you actually do these projects?**

10 Ask students to think of one question to ask the group presenting. Allow time for questions after each presentation. Hold a class vote to decide on the best idea.

Homework
Ask students to rewrite the sentences in Exercise 6 using different linkers of contrast.

Language note
In spite of and *despite* can be followed by a negative gerund, e.g., *In spite of / Despite not having an umbrella, he walked home in the rain.*

TH!NK more

Practice Extra
Unit 6 Practice it!

Workbook
Grammar p55, Ex.5–7

Worksheets
Grammar Worksheets 6
Grammar presentation: Linkers of contrast
Grammar video! Linkers of contrast

Social Responsibilities
Understanding personal responsibilities as part of a social group
Fulfilling responsibilities within a social group.

Warmer

Write the words *strong female characters* on the board. Elicit or give the meaning and ask students to brainstorm all the strong female characters that they can think of from literature (or from movies if students are struggling). Discuss some of the characters as a class.

1 Ask students to cover the extract and look at the pictures. Give them a minute to discuss the question in pairs.

2 **6.06** Encourage students not to focus on every word for now, but just to find the answer to the question.

a (cabinet) piano

Culture notes

Louisa May Alcott was born in 1832 in Pennsylvania, USA. Educated by her father, the family usually had little money, and she took on sewing and writing work to help support them. When the American Civil War broke out in 1861, she began to work as a volunteer army nurse in a Union Hospital. Her first book, *Hospital Sketches* (1863) was written at this time, but it was the publication of *Little Women* in 1868 that resulted in her becoming the best-selling American author of the century. Her work introduced readers to educated, strong, female heroines. As a result, her writing style greatly impacted American literature. Throughout her life, she suffered greatly from ill health aggravated by early deprivation and overwork. She died in Boston in 1888.

Literature

1 Look at the pictures and read the introduction to the extract. What do you think Mr. Laurence sent Beth as a gift?

2 6.06 Read and listen to the extract to check your ideas.

Little Women by Louisa May Alcott

Little Women follows the lives of the four March sisters, Jo, Beth, Meg, and Amy, who grew up during and after the American Civil War (1861–1865). Mr. Laurence, a wealthy old gentleman who lives next door to the family, is especially fond of Beth, as she reminds him of his little granddaughter. In this extract, Mr. Laurence has sent Beth a gift, and the sisters and Hannah, their only servant, are all very excited.

Beth hurried on in a flutter of **suspense**. At the door, her sisters seized and bore her to the parlor in a triumphal procession, all pointing and all saying at once, "Look there! Look there!" Beth did look, and turned pale with delight and surprise, for there stood a little cabinet piano, with a letter lying on the **glossy** lid, directed like a sign board to "Miss Elizabeth March."

"For me?" gasped Beth, holding onto Jo and feeling as if she should tumble down, it was such an **overwhelming** thing altogether.

"Yes, all for you, my precious! Isn't it splendid of him? Don't you think he's the dearest old man in the world? Here's the key in the letter. We didn't open it, but we are **dying to** know what he says," cried Jo, hugging her sister and offering the note.

"You read it! I can't, I feel so queer! Oh, it is too lovely!" and Beth hid her face in Jo's apron, quite upset by her present.

Jo opened the paper and began to laugh, for the first words she saw were …

"Miss March:

"Dear Madam--"

"How nice it sounds! I wish someone would write to me so!" said Amy, who thought the old-fashioned address very elegant.

"I have had many pairs of slippers in my life, but I never had any that suited me so well as yours," continues Jo. "Heartsease is my favorite flower, and these will always remind me of the gentle giver. I like to pay my debts, so I know you will allow 'the old gentleman' to send you something which once belonged to the little granddaughter he lost. With hearty thanks and best wishes, I remain 'Your grateful friend and **humble** servant, JAMES LAURENCE.'"

"There, Beth, that's an honor to be proud of, I'm sure! Laurie told me how fond Mr. Laurence used to be of the child who died, and how he kept all her little things carefully. Just think, he's given you her piano. That comes of having big blue eyes and loving music," said Jo, trying to **soothe** Beth, who trembled and looked more excited than she had ever been before.

"See the **cunning** brackets to hold candles, and the nice green silk, puckered up, with a gold rose in the middle, and the pretty rack and stool, all complete," added Meg, opening the instrument and displaying its beauties.

"'Your humble servant, James Laurence.' Only think of his writing that to you. I'll tell the girls. They'll think it's splendid," said Amy, much impressed by the note.

"Try it, honey. Let's hear the sound of the baby pianny," said Hannah, who always took a share in the family joys and sorrows.

So Beth tried it, and everyone pronounced it the most remarkable piano ever heard. It had evidently been newly tuned and put in **apple-pie order**, but, perfect as it was, I think the real charm lay in the happiest of all happy faces which leaned over it.

62

3 Check/clarify: *flutter, triumphal procession, cabinet piano, tumble down, splendid, hug, apron, slippers, heartsease, trembled, brackets, puckered up, rack, stool, humble, sorrows, pronounced, charm.*
Tell students not to worry about other difficult vocabulary at this stage as this will come up later.
1 a piano 2 what the letter says 3 Mr. Laurence's granddaughter's 4 the tone of the letter 5 it made everybody happy

4 During feedback, take this opportunity to work on pronunciation by saying the words for students to repeat. Check that they're placing stress on the correct syllable.
1 cunning 2 humble 3 overwhelming 4 soothe 5 suspense 6 apple-pie order 7 dying to 8 glossy

5 Encourage students to speak at length and to try to use vocabulary from the extract in their answers. At the end of the exercise, listen to some of the students' ideas and encourage open class discussion.

1 Let students compare their answers with a partner before feedback.
agree ("social media is a fantastic way to keep in touch with old friends and even to make new friends")

2 Point out that in a well-structured piece of writing, each paragraph should have its own purpose, which is exactly why it is written as a separate paragraph.
1 B 2 D 3 C 4 A

3 During feedback, elicit other linkers that could also fit into the sentences. If students find any of the linkers difficult, take the opportunity to go back to page 61 and review them.
1 As a consequence 2 As a result 3 Nevertheless 4 Furthermore 5 Therefore 6 However

4–5 If you are short on time, students can do the preparation in class and complete the writing at home. Alternatively, this could be done as a collaborative writing activity in class with pairs of students of a similar level working together.

BETTER TOGETHER UNIT 6

3 Read the extract again and answer the questions.
1 What has arrived and caused such excitement?
2 What do the sisters all want to know?
3 Whose piano was it?
4 What does Amy like about the letter?
5 What does the writer say was the best thing about receiving the piano?

4 VOCABULARY Match the highlighted words in the extract with the definitions.
1 clever
2 being modest, and not thinking of oneself as important or better than others
3 very great or very large
4 to gently calm somebody
5 feeling of excitement over what may happen next
6 a perfect state
7 really want to, urgently want to
8 shiny, beautifully polished

5 SPEAKING Work in pairs and discuss the questions.
1 Jo and Beth are sisters. What do you learn about their relationship in the extract?
2 What do you learn about Beth's character in this extract?

WRITING
An essay

1 INPUT Read the essay quickly. Does the author agree or disagree with the essay title? Why?

Social media is the best way to keep in touch with friends

A These days social media is a huge part of almost everyone's life. Furthermore, it's often the fastest and easiest way to keep in touch with old friends. Therefore, it's no surprise that more and more people are using social media to keep in touch.

B Social media is a great way to stay in touch with a friend who has moved to another town or another country. In the past, it was more difficult to stay in touch. As a consequence, after your friend left, you probably would not see them for months or even years. These days you can see them regularly online. A Skype, FaceTime, or WhatsApp video call is almost the same as being in the room with your friend.

C In the past, people spoke to each other on the phone, but nowadays, people prefer to communicate with friends via text messages and emails. However, despite this being a fast and easy way to communicate, there is a negative side to it. It is easier to write mean and hurtful things to someone than it is to say them to someone face to face. As a result, teenagers may be more vulnerable to being bullied nowadays.

D Nevertheless, I still believe that social media is a fantastic way to keep in touch with old friends and even to make new friends. We just need to be careful how we use it.

2 ANALYZE Match paragraphs A–D of the essay with functions 1–4.
1 argument supporting the idea ☐
2 the writer's final opinion ☐
3 argument against the idea ☐
4 introduction ☐

3 Complete the sentences with the missing linkers. Then read the essay to check.
1 ________, after your friend left, you probably would not see them for months or even years.
2 ________, teenagers may be more vulnerable to being bullied nowadays.
3 ________, I still believe that social media is a fantastic way to keep in touch with old friends and even to make new friends.
4 ________, it's often the fastest and easiest way to keep in touch with old friends.
5 ________, it's no surprise that more and more people are using social media to keep in touch.
6 ________, despite this being a fast and easy way to communicate, there is a negative side to it.

4 PLAN You're going to write your own essay with the following title. Make notes for each paragraph.
Social media brings people together
Introduction: ________
For: ________
Against: ________
My conclusion: ________

5 PRODUCE Write your essay using your notes from Exercise 4 (200–250 words).

63

Homework
If you are short on time, students can do Writing Exercise 5 for homework. If you have done this in class, ask students to exchange their essays with another student for them to read and to give feedback on content and structure. Students could check if the essay uses the same structure as the template. They should also decide what the most/least interesting part of the essay is.

Activity idea Extension
There have been several movie adaptations of *Little Women* that you could watch in class. The most recent was with Saoirse Ronan as Jo and Emma Watson as Meg, released in 2019.

TH!NK more
Practice Extra
Unit 6 Master it!

Workbook
Developing Writing p59

Tests
Unit, extension, and skills test 6
End of term test 2

1 In B2 First Reading and Use of English Part 7, candidates have to read a longer text, or up to six shorter ones, and ten questions. Candidates have to match the specific information in the text with the questions. This part of the exam tests whether candidates can recognize opinion and attitude and locate specific details.

Encourage your students to do the following when they approach this task:

- Skim the text to find out the topic and general meaning.
- Read each question carefully.
- Check that the answer to the question is reflected in the text.
- Do not assume an answer must be correct simply because it contains a word that is also in the text. Some of the options may be correct for more than one question.
- After choosing an answer, check the other options and decide why they are wrong.

1C 2B 3D 4A 5B 6A 7C 8D 9C 10A

Workbook p53

B2 First for Schools

READING AND USE OF ENGLISH

Part 7: Multiple matching

→ workbook page 53

1 You are going to read an article in which four teenagers talk about how they met their best friend. For questions 1–10, choose from the teenagers (A–D). The teenagers may be chosen more than once.

Which teenager

1 feels that they met their best friend at the perfect time? ☐
2 has changed their attitudes to best friends several times? ☐
3 has known their best friend for most of their life? ☐
4 felt an instant connection with their best friend? ☐
5 thinks that having a small number of very close friends is a positive thing? ☐
6 gets on with their best friend because they can discuss topics he doesn't talk about with his other friends? ☐
7 feels that their best friend made forming relationships with other children at school easier? ☐
8 thinks that distance helps keep a relationship healthy? ☐
9 likes having a best friend who is a different gender? ☐
10 thinks it's a good thing that their best friend doesn't know their other friends? ☐

A Dom

My best friend is Liam and I've only known him for about three months. I met Liam at a youth club and I knew immediately that he was going to be a great friend. We share exactly the same sense of humour. We like the same bands. I'm quite interested in politics and he shares exactly the same concerns as I do. It was great to finally be able to talk about something other than football and girls. Don't get me wrong, I still like talking about those things, but it's good to have a change. Also, because Liam doesn't go to the same school as me, it means that we don't waste time talking about other people.

B Gianna

I've had a lot of best friends. I remember when I was a kid, I'd have a new best friend every week. Then, when I was a bit older, I thought it was silly to have one best friend and just tried to have as many friends as I could. Recently, though, I have realised that although it's good to have lots of friends, it's even better to have one or two extra special ones that you know will always be there for you no matter what. I guess at the moment Chloe would be that friend. I really haven't known her very long, probably about a year at the most. She was the new kid in school and at first, I wasn't very friendly to her at all, probably because I already had my gang of friends. But she was in lots of my classes and I started to get to know her better and realised she was really cool.

C Anna

I still remember the first time I met Robin. I must have been about ten or eleven. I was at school when the teacher introduced him as the new student and told him to sit next to me. We were a bit shy at first, but eventually we started talking, and we've hardly stopped since. Mum says I didn't have a lot of friends at that age and I found it difficult to get on with the other kids. She says that Robin helped me find the confidence I needed to make new friends. If I hadn't met him at that point, I think I would have been quite lonely. Now we're at secondary school and we still spend lots of time together. Of course, some people think it's strange that I'm best friends with a boy, but it works for me and feels completely normal – and anyway, I tend to hang out with the girls at school and I meet up with him after school or at the weekend.

D Colin

I've known my best friend Tom since I was two. Of course, I don't remember him from then, but we met because our dads took us to the same park to play when we were toddlers. They became best friends and we grew up almost as brothers. When I was about seven, Mum and Dad moved away but they kept in touch with Tom's parents, so Tom and I would still see each other most holidays. These days, we keep in touch on Snapchat and we text each other loads. It's great having someone who knows you so well and I think the fact that we live more than 100 km apart has meant that we've become even better friends because we really value the time we have together. We don't get tired of each other because we're not living in each other's pockets.

64

1 1 shoulder 2 peas
3 definitions 4 introduced
5 zip 6 upgrade 7 backup
8 house 9 protective case
10 criticized

2 1 even though 2 succeeded in
3 wasn't allowed to
4 nowhere near as
5 needn't have 6 been able

3 1 We ran as fast as we could, but we didn't manage to get there in time.
2 Despite ~~he earns~~ earning a good salary, Mario says he never has enough money.
3 Nicole's parents weren't as strict with her brother ~~than~~ as they were with her.
4 ~~Nevertheless~~ Although / Even though George's French isn't great, he understood a lot of the movie.
5 It is very kind of you, but you don't need to pick me up at my house. I can walk to the restaurant.
6 James always does well on tests, ~~although~~ despite / in spite of never studying. / James always does well on tests, although ~~never studying~~ he never studies.

4 1 far and away; even
2 must; don't need to
3 let; have 4 easily; whole

TEST YOURSELF UNITS 5 & 6

VOCABULARY

1 Complete the sentences with the words in the list. There are four extra words.

access | backup | criticized | definitions | hatchet | house | introduced
peas | protective case | shoulder | stream | sync | upgrade | zip

1 Jake is feeling really down. He could really use a ________________ to cry on.
2 My friends Emma and Nina get along like two ________________ in a pod. They have the same hairstyle and dress very similarly.
3 A good way to remember new words is to learn their ________________ .
4 I know who Paul is, but I've never been ________________ to him.
5 The file was so big that I had to ________________ it to send it by email.
6 My computer runs my new graphics program very slowly. I need to ________________ it.
7 I almost lost everything when my computer crashed, but luckily, I had a ________________ of most of it.
8 The little boy and his cousin are getting along like a ________________ on fire.
9 I'm really clumsy, so the first thing I do when I get a new phone is buy a ________________ .
10 The politician was heavily ________________ for not admitting his mistake.

/10

GRAMMAR

2 Complete the sentences with the phrases in the list. There are two extra phrases.

been able | didn't need to | even though | managed to | needn't have
nowhere near as | succeeded in | wasn't allowed to

1 I've never visited the museum, ________________ I live very close to it.
2 My uncle took driving lessons, but he never ________________ learning to drive.
3 My mom ________________ go out with her friends until she was 16.
4 The sequel is ________________ good as the first movie.
5 Dax had already asked Mom about the trip, so I ________________ asked her.
6 My aunt hurt her hand last month. She hasn't ________________ to play the piano since then.

3 Find and correct the mistake in each sentence.

1 We ran as fast as we could, but we didn't manage get there in time.
2 Despite he earns a good salary, Mario says he never has enough money.
3 Nicole's parents weren't as strict with her brother than they were with her.
4 Nevertheless George's French isn't great, he understood a lot of the movie.
5 It is very kind of you, but you don't need pick me up at my house. I can walk to the restaurant.
6 James always does well on tests, although never studying.

/12

FUNCTIONAL LANGUAGE

4 Choose the correct options.

1 A I think Selena Gomez's latest album is *far and away / tons* the best album she's ever released.
B I agree. It's *lot / even* better than her second album.
2 A I *must / need* go home now – I still have homework to finish for tomorrow.
B No, don't be silly! You *mustn't / don't need to* do it for tomorrow – today is a holiday.
3 A Do your parents *let / allow* you stay out as late as you want?
B Yes, but only on the weekends, and I *have / must* to tell them what time I'll be home.
4 A I love this game – it's *easily / even* the best game I've ever played.
B No way! *Prince of Shadows* is a *whole / good* lot better than this.

/8

MY SCORE /30
22–30 | 10–21 | 0–9

65

The Cambridge Life Competencies Framework

Communication
Using appropriate language and register for context
Watch this video for a tip on developing your students' communication skills.
Scan the QR code here.

Warmer

Draw a glass on the board with a line halfway up. Ask: *Is the glass half-full or half-empty?* Have a show of hands and ask: *Does your answer to this question reflect your attitude to life in general?* Get students to discuss in pairs and listen to some of their ideas in open class.

▶ 17 Get TH!NKing

Play the video and discuss the question with your class.

1 You may like to put a copy of the three photos up on the board before students open their books.

2 Give students time to read the two statements before they begin their discussions in pairs.

3 **Check/clarify:** *optimist, pessimist, kidney.*
Give students two minutes to scan the blog quickly to find the answer to the question. Encourage them not to focus on every word for now, but just to find the ideas that are mentioned.
1 He had a kidney operation, he had to retire, their son was in a car accident, and he had to buy a new car. 2 She's an optimist.

4 🔊 **7.01** Before playing the audio again, ask students to answer as much as they can from memory. During feedback, you could play the audio again to check.
1 F (It's to explain that we can choose to be optimistic.) 2 T 3 F (He was badly hurt but didn't die.) 4 T 5 F (He won't have any pain any more.) 6 T 7 F (The blogger says we can control how we look at things.) 8 F (She doesn't like spending time with him.)

7 ROSE-TINTED GLASSES

OBJECTIVES

FUNCTIONS: cheering someone up

GRAMMAR: ways of referring to the future (review); future continuous (review); future perfect (review)

VOCABULARY: phrases to talk about the future: *about to, off to, on the point of, due to*; feelings about future events

Get TH!NKING
Watch the video and think: is it important to look at things from different angles?

A

B

C

READING

1 **Look at the photos. What do they mean to you? Can you relate them to any real-life situations?**

2 SPEAKING **Read statements A and B. Discuss them in pairs. Then say who is more like you: the person who wrote statement A or the one who wrote B.**

A My best friend moved to another country. I'll never get over it. I won't find anybody that I like as much as her, so I won't even try to find a new friend. Imagine I finally find someone, and then she moved away, too!

B My best friend moved to another country. That's great for her. I'm definitely going to stay in touch, and I'm looking forward to hearing stories of her new life. And who knows, one day I might even be able to visit her.

3 **Read the blog quickly and answer the questions.**
1 What are the four things the husband didn't like about the past year?
2 Is the wife an optimist or a pessimist?

4 🔊 7.01 **Read and listen to the blog again. Mark the statements T (true) or F (false). Then correct the false statements.**
1 The main reason the blogger wrote this post is to share an exciting story. ☐
2 The man had to stop working last year. ☐
3 The couple's son died in a car accident. ☐
4 The car was very badly damaged in the accident. ☐
5 The woman says her husband will still have some kidney pain. ☐
6 Their son wants to study to become a doctor. ☐
7 The blogger thinks we can't control how we react to events. ☐
8 The blogger is looking forward to spending time with her brother on vacation. ☐

5 SPEAKING **Work in pairs and discuss the questions.**
1 Do you agree with the woman's opinion about what happened during the year? Or with the man's opinion?
2 Do you think a story like this could change people's attitudes? Why (not)?

66

5 At the end of the exercise, listen to some of the students' ideas and encourage open class discussion.

Objectives

Functions and speaking Cheering someone up
Grammar Ways of referring to the future (review); future continuous (review); future perfect (review)
Vocabulary Phrases to talk about the future: *about to, off to, on the point of, due to*; feelings about future events; **WordWise:** Expressions with *so*
Life Competencies Being tactful

Resources for this unit

All available online

Videos
- Get **TH!NK**ing: *Is it important to look at things from different angles?*
- Grammar video!: Future continuous (review)
- Vlog: Being tactful

Tests
- Unit, extension, and skills test 7

Worksheets
- Grammar and vocabulary: Basic, Standard, and Extension Worksheets
- Project: Understanding different perspectives
- Communication: Always look on the bright side
- Literature Worksheets: *Poetry*
- Get **TH!NK**ing, Grammar video!, and Life Lessons video Worksheets

6 Give students time to read the two paragraphs.

First text: A teacher helped them by telling them a useful saying.
Second text: Their best friend helped them by advising them to ignore the person making fun of them.

7 Monitor and help with vocabulary and ideas. After students have discussed in pairs, regroup them into small groups for students to report back on their discussions and share opinions.

Homework

Ask students to interview someone in their family or, alternatively, research someone famous who has an optimistic attitude and write a short text. As a follow-up, students can give a presentation about this person, with any good ideas for how to be more positive to the class in the next lesson.

Activity idea Extension

Students could act out an interview with the husband or the wife from the blog. Divide the class into four groups: A (husband), B (wife), C (reporter to husband), and D (reporter to wife). Ask groups C and D to look at the relevant parts of the blog again and write down five questions to ask the husband / the wife. Ask groups A and B to look at the blog again and find key information about the husband or the wife in preparation for an interview. Monitor to make sure all the students are making notes and help with ideas if necessary. Put the students in A/C and B/D pairs and give them time to act out the interview.

My takes on life, the universe,
AND EVERYTHING

Take #21: It depends on how you look at it

Hi again! My take today is about a choice we have: the choice to look at things from a positive point of view or a negative one. How we see things matters – it affects our well-being. And here's a story I found recently that illustrates my point.

It was New Year's Eve, and a couple was about to go out to celebrate. They were on the point of leaving when the man said to his wife, "This year ends in a few hours, and I'm glad. It's been a terrible year."

His wife asked him, "Why do you say that last year was terrible? I don't understand!" The man was very surprised and replied, "You don't understand? Think about what happened last year. First of all, I had an operation to remove my kidney, and now I only have one kidney, and I was in bed for weeks. Remember? And then last month, I turned 65, and I was told I had to leave my job at the newspaper to make room for someone younger. Huh! I loved that job and didn't want to retire. What am I going to do now? And then there was our son's accident! You haven't forgotten that, have you? Three weeks in the hospital, and that meant he couldn't take his exams to get into medical school. And we had to buy a new car. Terrible year! I'm so happy it's over."

His wife didn't say much – she went out of the room, but a few minutes later, she came back in and said, "OK, I heard what you said, but this is how I see things. Your kidney had been bothering you for years, and now you won't have that pain ever again. Now that you don't have to go to work every day, you can spend more time in the garden and make it beautiful, the way you've always wanted. And yes, the car was destroyed, but our son came out alive. And now he has more time to study, so he'll do even better on his exams next year. So, I think it was a good year. But anyway, it's over, and the new one is due to start in a few hours – it'll be another good year if we make it one."

So there you are. We can't control the things that happen to us or to other people, but we can control how we look at them. You can take a pessimistic attitude or an optimistic one – it's up to you. Some things are difficult to deal with. For example, I'm seeing the dentist this afternoon, which I'm not looking forward to, but then I think about my grandpa and his awful teeth, and I think, "Going to the dentist now means I probably won't have problems in the future." And if it hurts a little? Well, nothing's forever, right?

OK, I won't be here next week, we're off on our annual family vacation. Now, how can I find a way to think positively about two weeks with my brother around all the time? I'll think of something!

Train to TH!NK

Learning to see things from a different perspective

How we see a situation influences how we feel about it and how we behave in it. Learning to look at things from a more optimistic perspective can have a positive influence on the outcome of a situation.

6 **Read about what these people experienced when trying to look at things from a different perspective. In pairs, discuss what and who helped them change their attitude.**

For a long time, I used to worry about everything all the time. I even used to worry about not finding anything to worry about. Then we had this discussion in class, and one of my teachers told us about this saying that I'll never forget. It may sound ridiculous, but it really helped me change my attitude. It basically says, "For every problem under the sun, there is either a solution or there is none. If there is one, think until you find it. If there is none, then never mind it."

I never used to believe in myself. I always thought everybody else was better than me. One day, I went out with a group of friends, and we met this guy who seemed really nice. But then I noticed that he was starting to make fun of the things I said. I became quiet and started to feel bad about myself. When I spoke to my best friend afterwards, she just said, "So what? That guy's strange, but that's him, not you." So I decided to ignore the guy, and he soon stopped making fun of me. More importantly, I felt better about myself.

7 SPEAKING **Work in pairs and discuss any difficult situations where you could usefully apply either of the two perspectives above.**

Activity idea Extension

Write the following situations on the board:

A young man on your street has bought a very expensive car.

Eaden passes exams easily and never seems to study.

George says: "I'm not smart enough to go to college."

Ask students to think of different ways people might react to the situations. What could be a positive reaction and what could be a negative reaction? For example, positive: *What a great car – he must have worked really hard to get the money for that*; negative: *He only has an expensive car to show other people how rich he is.*

Creative TH!NKing
Preparing for creativity
Considering multiple perspectives.

Emotional Development
Managing own emotions
Regulating emotions.

TH!NK more

Worksheets
Project Understanding different perspectives
Communication Always look on the bright side
Get **TH!NK**ing *Is it important to look at things from different angles?*

Warmer

Ask: *What quiz shows have you watched on TV? What are the rules?* Students discuss with a partner. To make this more challenging, ask them to imagine they are explaining the rules to a person who has never seen the show. Elicit a few examples of rules in open class and see if other students can guess the show.

1 During feedback, draw attention to the use of time expressions: *now, this afternoon, in the future, in a few hours, next year.*
RULE: 8 will 9 simple present 10 be going to 11 will 12 be going to 13 present continuous 14 will

2 Where more than one answer is possible, ask students to explain any subtle differences in meaning.
1 arrives 2 'll spill / 're going to spill 3 's going to rain 4 're seeing / 're going to see 5 starts 6 'm going to buy 7 will be

Workbook p64

3 Refer to the *Look* box to clarify the forms of the phrases.
1 b 2 a 3 b 4 c

4 If you are short on time, assign this exercise for homework.
1 about to 2 off to 3 about to 4 about to 5 off to 6 on the point of 7 due to

Workbook p66

5 🔊 **7.02** Before playing the audio, ask students to read and try to complete question 1.
1 cloud 2 Students' own answers

6 🔊 **7.02**
Round 1
Paul: he's going to get his family to take care of him
Nadia: she's going to be writing a novel
Round 2
Paul: he's going to spend the time to learn 20 Italian words
Nadia: she's going to enjoy the night in a nice hotel and spending time in Rome

TH!NK more

Workbook
Grammar p64, Ex.1–4
Vocabulary p66, Ex.1–3
Vocabulary Extra p67, Ex.1–3
Listening p70, Ex.1–2

Worksheets
Grammar Worksheets 7
Vocabulary Worksheets 7

GRAMMAR
Ways of referring to the future (review)

1 Look at the sentences from the blog. Then complete the rule with *be going to, will, the present continuous,* or *the simple present.*

1 What am I going to do now?
2 I'm seeing the dentist this afternoon.
3 It'll be another good year if we make it one.
4 I probably won't have problems in the future.
5 This year finishes in a few hours.
6 I'll think of something.
7 He'll do even better on his exams next year.

RULE: We use:
[8] ____________ to talk about future facts.
[9] ____________ to talk about events that are part of a timetable or schedule.
[10] ____________ to make evidence-based predictions.
[11] ____________ to make predictions based on thoughts and opinions.
[12] ____________ to talk about plans and intentions.
[13] ____________ to refer to definite arrangements.
[14] ____________ to refer to spontaneous decisions and offers.

2 Complete the sentences using the most appropriate form of the verbs in parentheses. Sometimes more than one form is possible.

1 My dad ____________ on the eight o'clock flight from Mexico City tomorrow. (arrive)
2 Careful! You filled that glass too high. You ____________ it. (spill)
3 I think it ____________ probably a lot this weekend. It's that time of year. (rain)
4 We ____________ friends on Saturday afternoon. (see)
5 I'm sorry, I have to finish now. The movie ____________ in two minutes. (start)
6 When I get paid, I ____________ myself a new camera. (buy)
7 Today's lunch break ____________ five minutes shorter than usual. (be)

→ workbook page 64

VOCABULARY
Phrases to talk about the future: *about to, off to, on the point of, due to*

3 All of these sentences refer to the future. Which sentence talks about:

a future travel plans?
b the very immediate future (x2)?
c something that's expected to happen at a particular point in the future?

1 They were about to go out and celebrate.
2 We're off on our annual family vacation.
3 They were on the point of leaving.
4 The new year is due to start in a few hours.

Look
be about to / be due to + infinitive
be off to + infinitive / noun
be on the point of + verb + *-ing*

4 Choose the correct options.

1 Although this is a serious situation, Jennifer looks as if she's *about to / off to* start laughing.
2 I'm *off to / about to* the supermarket in five minutes. Do you want anything?
3 Careful! You're *off to / about to* knock the glass over.
4 My friends are *off to / about to* get a big surprise!
5 They're *off to / on the point of* Hawaii on vacation next month.
6 It's 2–0; there's only one minute left – wow, we're *on the point of / about to* winning the game!
7 Their plane is *due to / about to* arrive at three o'clock this afternoon.

→ workbook page 66

LISTENING

5 🔊 7.02 **Listen to the podcast *Silver Linings* and answer the questions.**
1 Complete the phrase: "Every ____________ has a silver lining."
2 Explain this phrase in your own words.

6 🔊 7.02 **Listen again and write Paul's and Nadia's answers for each round.**

Round 1		Round 2	
Paul:	______	Paul:	______
Nadia:	______	Nadia:	______

7 SPEAKING **Work in pairs. Who would you give the points to in each situation (Nadia or Paul) and why?**

68

---

7 Give students some time to discuss in pairs and then hold a class vote to decide who should get the points in each situation.

Language note Phrases to talk about the future: *about to, off to, on the point of, due to*

Clarify that *about to* and *on the point of* are often used to describe actions in the near future, but these may not be very immediate; it all depends on context. For example:

We're about to buy a new house. (in the next few days or weeks)

They are on the point of splitting up. (It's going to happen soon.)

Activity idea Extension

Ask students to write sentences containing mistakes with future forms. Students pass their sentences to a partner. The partner has to act as a teacher, explain the problems with the sentences and elicit the correct answer from the student.

▶ 18 Grammar video!
Future continuous (review)

8 If necessary, use the examples and a timeline like the one below to clarify the rule.

now

on Tuesday afternoon

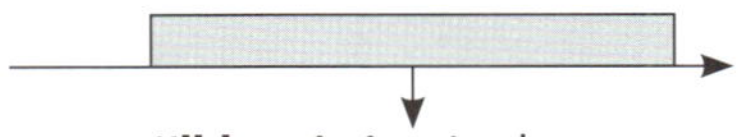

I'**ll be sitting** in the new restaurant.

RULE: 3 around 4 be 5 -ing

9 During feedback, explain/elicit that we use the future continuous to talk about an action happening around a specific future time, and the simple future is used to describe promises, predictions, and offers. Check that students are contracting *will* to *'ll*, and that they are placing the main stress on the principal verb rather than equally stressing all three words.

1 'll/will be sitting 2 'll/will be walking
3 'll/will call 4 'll/will be watching
5 'll/will come 6 'll/will be thinking
7 'll/will put

Get it Right!
Future continuous

Student's Book p125

10 During feedback, use the example sentences and the timeline below to show the difference between the future perfect and future continuous.

now

by the time we leave London

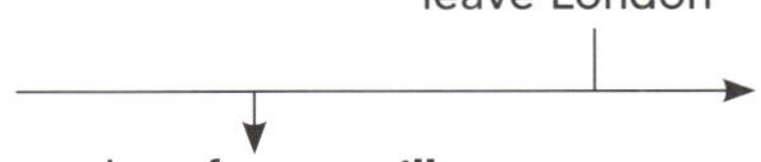

a lot of snow **will have fallen** in Italy

RULE: 3 will 4 have 5 past participle

11 If you are short on time, assign this exercise for homework. Go through the first item to make sure students are clear on what they have to do. During feedback, ask students to explain why they chose their answers and why another form is not a possible answer in each case.

1 have finished 2 have found
3 be sleeping 4 be flying
5 have spent 6 be teaching
7 have watched 8 be touring

Workbook p65

GRAMMAR
Grammar video ▶18

Future continuous (review)

8 Look at these sentences from the podcast. Then complete the rule with *be* and *-ing*.

1 Every day, **I'll be writing** the novel that'll make me rich and famous.
2 After that, **I'll be sleeping** in a comfy bed.

> **RULE:** To talk about an action that will be in progress [3]*after / around* a specific future time, we use the future continuous: *will* + [4]__________ + the [5]__________ form of the verb.

9 Complete the conversation with the simple future or future continuous form of the verb in parentheses.

Mei This time tomorrow, my dad and I [1]__________ (sit) on a train.
Paula Really? Where are you going? Anywhere nice?
Mei Yes. Dad's taking me into the city with him on Saturday.
Paula Wow!
Mei Tomorrow morning, we [2]__________ (walk) around the city doing a little shopping.
Paula Great! I [3]__________ (call) you on Saturday afternoon.
Mei Well, that's not really a good time. On Saturday afternoon, we [4]__________ (watch) the Cubs play the Pirates. I can't wait! You know how much I like baseball.
Paula And you [5]__________ (come) home happy and relaxed. Lucky you.
Mei Well, I hope so. It's an important game for the Cubs.
Paula That sounds like a fantastic afternoon. So, what time's your train tomorrow?
Mei Eight o'clock.
Paula Alright. At 8:30, I [6]__________ (think) of you.
Mei And I [7]__________ (put) some photos from our weekend on Instagram – if I remember.

Future perfect (review)

10 Look at the example sentences and complete the rule with *have, past participle,* and *will.*

1 … after three weeks of that, you'll have annoyed your entire family.
2 In a few years' time, I'll have gotten a good job.

> **RULE:** To talk about an action that will finish at some time between now and a specified time in the future, we use the future perfect. We often use it with the preposition *by* + [3]__________ + [4]__________ + [5]__________.

11 Choose the correct verb forms.

1 By the time Mom comes back from work, I will *be finishing / have finished* my homework.
2 By 2050, psychologists will *be finding / have found* ways to help pessimists feel more optimistic.
3 Don't call after 10 p.m. I will *be sleeping / have slept.*
4 This time tomorrow morning I will *be flying / have flown* to Singapore. We land in the afternoon.
5 When I finish school, I will *be spending / have spent* six years there.
6 You can find Ms. Green in classroom 3. She will *be teaching / have taught* there until noon.
7 We're going to watch movies all day on Saturday. By the end of the day, we will *be watching / have watched* more than five movies!
8 The band will *be touring / have toured* for six months later this year to promote their new album.

→ workbook page 65

SPEAKING

12 Work in groups of four and play *Silver Linings*. Read the situations and think of optimistic solutions. Make notes.

Student A: Your best friend completely forgets your birthday.
Student B: Someone pours orange juice over your new T-shirt.
Student C: You fail your history exam.
Student D: Your country doesn't qualify for the soccer World Cup.

13 Take turns talking about the "silver linings" in your situations. Give a point for each correct use of the future continuous or the future perfect. Award five points for the most imaginative answer.

12 Divide the class into four groups (A, B, C, and D). You might like to pair students within their groups (A/A, B/B, C/C, etc.) for this preparation stage. Point out that students should try to use the future perfect and future continuous in their answers, where possible.

13 Monitor and make a note of any future forms being used correctly to highlight and praise during feedback. Also write down any examples where a future form could have been used but wasn't, for students to transform during feedback.

Homework

Ask students to write five true sentences and one false sentence about themselves and members of their family using future tenses. Give examples of your own to get them started. In the next lesson, they could work in pairs, and each partner guesses which of the sentences is false.

TH!NK more

Practice Extra
Unit 7 Practice it!

Workbook
Grammar p65, Ex.5–8

Worksheets
Grammar Worksheets 7
Grammar video! Future continuous (review)

Warmer

Write the following three situations on the board:

You have an important test tomorrow.

You are going to perform in the school play this evening.

You are going to visit your cousins this weekend.

Ask students to grade from 1 (not worried at all) to 10 (very worried) how worried they would feel in each of these situations. Discuss in pairs and, after a few minutes, invite students' reactions, prompting them to try to explain their answers.

1 Set a three-minute time limit and tell students to read quickly and not worry about understanding every word.
It's for people who worry. The worries mentioned are about a decision to take a trip and being good enough to play drums in a band.

2 🔊 **7.03** Ask students to underline the parts of the webpage that helped them decide on their answers.
A 3 B 2

3 **Check/clarify:** *inspirational, hang out with, weird, drummer, audition, gloomy, acquire the capacity.*
1 The writer used to be a worrier, too. 2 The writer can see the positive in their situations. 3 Worrier A is less pessimistic seeing both positive and negative sides of the situation. 4 the Charlie Chaplin quote

4 Give students time to read the questions. Clarify any difficult vocabulary. When students have completed the exercise, regroup and ask them to repeat the exercise with new partners.

QUOTATIONS FOR WORRIERS

"You'll never find a RAINBOW if you look down!"

Who said that? No, it wasn't me. It was Charlie Chaplin, and I love it. You should know that I wasn't exactly born an optimist myself. I was actually quite a worrier until I discovered the power of inspirational quotes. Try me. Send me a worry, and I'll send you a quote. For free. If you like the quote, please let me know. Positive messages help me, too, and so far, all the feedback has been positive!

A SHOULD I STAY OR SHOULD I GO?

Hi, I don't know what to do. I have an aunt and uncle in the UK, and they've invited me to go there for a month or so. Sounds cool, doesn't it? But I'm worried there won't be anyone my age to hang out with. They live in a smallish sort of town, and they don't have any kids themselves. It may sound weird, but I feel that whatever I decide, I'll probably regret it later! Can you help? I hope so.

B DRUMMER BOY

I got this drum set for my 16th birthday. There's a band at my school. They're great, but their drummer, Luca, is leaving at the end of the school year – his family is moving to another town. The band has asked me if I want to audition, and Luca has offered to teach me. But I'm not sure I'll be good enough. I don't think I should get my hopes up. I'd be so disappointed if I didn't get in.

1 ☐ Hmm. Yes, I understand that's not an easy situation. But I don't think that means you should just sit around complaining that everything's gloomy. Maybe what Anne Frank said will help you to be more optimistic: "How wonderful it is that nobody needs to wait a single moment before starting to improve the world."

2 ☐ Look, this is for you, and it's by Mahatma Gandhi. I'll say no more. It's all in the quote. "Man often becomes what he believes himself to be. If I keep on saying to myself that I cannot do a certain thing, it is possible that I may end by really becoming incapable of doing it. On the contrary, if I have the belief that I can do it, I shall surely acquire the capacity to do it even if I may not have it at the beginning."

3 ☐ My quote for you is by Winston Churchill: "A pessimist sees the difficulty in every opportunity; an optimist sees the opportunity in every difficulty." Even if you are right, there are probably about a million things you can do there that you can't do at home! So I'd say, go. And remember the rainbow!

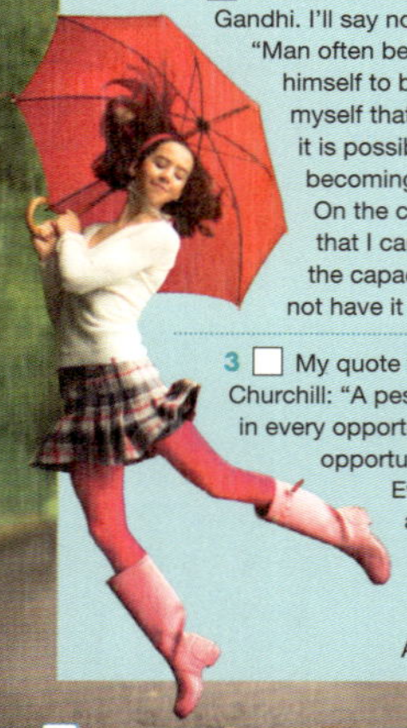

READING

1 **Read this webpage quickly. Who is it for? What are the two worries mentioned by the people who posted on the website?**

2 🔊 7.03 **Read and listen to the webpage again. Match the answers with the worries. There is one extra quote.**

3 **Read the webpage again and answer the questions.**
1 What does the writer have in common with the two worriers?
2 What is the difference between the writer and the two worriers?
3 Are the two worriers equally pessimistic? Why (not)?
4 What is the writer referring to in the third answer by saying, "And remember the rainbow!"?

4 SPEAKING **Work in pairs and discuss the questions.**
1 What kind of person is the owner of this website? Would you like to get to know them? Why (not)?
2 Do you think quotations can cheer you up when you're down?
3 How would you react if you were in the situation of one of the two worriers?
4 Look at the extra quote. What kind of problem could this quote be an answer to?
5 Which of the three quotes do you like most? Why?

70

Culture notes

Charlie Chaplin (April 16, 1889–December 25, 1977) was an English comic actor and director. His most famous movies were *The Kid* (1921), *Modern Times* (1936), and *The Great Dictator* (1940).

Anne Frank (June 12, 1929–1945) was a German Jewish teenager who fled with her family to Amsterdam to escape Nazi persecution during the Holocaust. The family went into hiding for two years. During that time, Frank wrote a diary of her experiences. In 1945, the family was discovered and sent to concentration camps where Anne died at the age of 15, probably from typhus. Her diary was published in 1947 as *The Diary of Anne Frank*.

Mahatma Gandhi (October 2, 1869–January 30, 1948) was the leader of the Indian independence movement until India became independent from Great Britain in August 1947. He was an advocator of non-violent revolution.

Winston Churchill (November 30, 1874–January 24, 1965) was a British politician. He was Prime Minister of the United Kingdom from 1940 to 1945 and from 1951 to 1955. He was named the Greatest Briton of all time in a 2002 poll.

TH!NK more

Workbook
Reading p68, Ex.1–4

5 Give a couple of your own ideas as examples before students work in pairs.

6 Set a one-minute time limit to encourage students to read quickly and to focus on overall meaning rather than specific vocabulary.
A an important sports game
B going back to college as a mature student C an exam
D a visit to the dentist

7 While students are working, recreate the two columns on the board for use during feedback.
expressing optimism: I have a really good feeling about I feel really positive about
expressing pessimism / worry: I'm feeling very apprehensive
I'm unsure about
I just have a bad feeling about
I just don't know where to start
It's a nightmare – I'm really worried
I'm getting so worked up

8 You may like to ask students to write answers so that you can monitor and check that they are being used correctly.

Workbook p66

9 During feedback, elicit or explain the meaning of the six phrases and give further examples as necessary to clarify meaning.
1 I hope so 2 so-so 3 So far
4 so what 5 so not 6 or so

10 During feedback, work on pronunciation and intonation of the sentences.
1 So what 2 so-so 3 so not
4 or so 5 so far 6 I hope so

Workbook p66

11 The notes for this exercise can be done in class, and the writing assigned for homework. Give students time to make some notes and then ask them to tell their stories to a partner. Ask students to give each other feedback. They should say how it could be made more interesting and point out any important elements that should be included. Give students time to revise their notes accordingly so that they are prepared for the main writing as homework.

VOCABULARY
Feelings about future events

5 SPEAKING Work in pairs. Make a list of five situations or events that can make you feel worried.

6 Read the following extracts from *Quotations for worriers*. What situation or event do you think each extract refers to?

A It's a big game, and **I'm feeling very apprehensive**. If we win, we'll be at the top of the league. I'm excited, but they're a good team, and in the last two games we were only so-so. So **I'm unsure about** our chances.

B **I have a really good feeling about** this. **I'm really looking forward to** it, and **I feel really positive about** it. If I'm honest, I'll probably be old enough to be the other students' mother, but so what? It's something I really want to do. Any suggestions for how I can bridge the age gap with my new classmates?

C **I just have a bad feeling about** this. I'm sure I'm going to fail. I haven't done any studying, and **I just don't know where to start** … **It's a nightmare – I'm really worried** about it.

D **I'm dreading** this, but I'm not sure why **I'm getting so worked up**. I've seen him lots of times before, and he's really good, but I just have a bad feeling about it this time. I think he'll need to pull one of my teeth.

7 Look at the phrases in bold and use them to complete each list. If needed, use a dictionary to help you with meaning.

expressing optimism	expressing pessimism / worry
I'm really looking forward to …	*I'm dreading …*

8 Match the phrases from Exercise 7 with the events you listed in Exercise 5 in which you might use them.

→ workbook page 66

WordWise: Expressions with *so*

9 Look at these sentences from the unit so far. Complete them with phrases from the list.

I hope so | or so | so far | so not | so-so | so what

1 A Can you help?
B ______________ .
2 In the last two games we were only ______________ .
3 ______________ , all the feedback's been positive!
4 That will feel a bit weird, but ______________ ?
5 I'm ______________ looking forward to this.
6 They've invited me to go there for a month ______________ .

10 Complete the sentences with the expressions from Exercise 9.

1 A Andrew isn't going to like this.
B ______________ ? I'm not worried about Andrew.
2 I'd hoped the movie would be really good, but it was only ______________ .
3 I'm going to read a different book. I'm ______________ enjoying this one.
4 My mom's gone to Chicago for a week ______________ , to work.
5 I'm taking guitar lessons, and ______________ I'm really enjoying them.
6 A Do you think we're going to have fun at the beach?
B ______________ , I really need some relaxation.

→ workbook page 66

WRITING
A short story

11 You are going to write a story (200–250 words) that finishes with the words, "Every cloud has a silver lining."

Think of:
- an unfortunate incident
- an unexpected positive outcome
- how it changed the main character's life.

71

Homework

You could assign the writing task in Exercise 11 for homework. As a follow-up in the next lesson, ask students to exchange their stories with another student for them to make comments and suggestions. Tell them not to correct every error, but to look for the following:
What further information would you like to know?
In what ways could vocabulary be improved?
What punctuation and spelling mistakes are there?

Activity idea Extension

If students have access to the internet in the classroom, you may like to divide the class into four groups and ask each group to research one of the four famous people quoted on the webpage. When they have made notes on their findings, regroup into groups of four for students to share information.

TH!NK more

Workbook
Vocabulary p66, Ex.4
WordWise p66, Ex.5
Developing Writing p69

Worksheets
Vocabulary Worksheets 7

Developing Speaking; Phrases for fluency; Functions; Pronunciation

Warmer

Ask students to think about their three favorite actors. In small groups, students discuss who they like, responding with *So do I, Neither do I*, etc. Hold a class vote to find out who the most popular actors are. Then ask: *If you had to decide who to cast in a movie, how would you decide?* Listen to some of their ideas and try to elicit *an audition*.

1 7.04 Tell students to cover the dialogue and discuss the question in pairs before listening to check their answers.
Suggested answer: He's in a play. / He's at an audition.

2 7.04
1 He was late, he read the wrong lines, and he started coughing.
2 Because he's unsure of himself.
3 By saying he has nothing to lose and that he should try again.

3 Monitor to help with any difficulties, but do not interrupt as this is a fluency activity.

4 Write the underlined sentences/ phrases from the dialogue on the board. Ask students for a translation before they complete the sentences in English. During feedback, say the sentences for students to repeat.
1 A for a start; B Fair enough
2 A put my name down; B get your hopes up
3 A make a real fool of myself; B Anyway

5 Allow students six to eight minutes to prepare their role-plays. Monitor to make sure all students are on task. If students have access to a recording device (their cell phones, for example), they could record their conversation and play it back to check their own pronunciation and intonation. They can then repeat the exercise and listen for improvements.

DEVELOPING SPEAKING

1 7.04 **Look at the photo. What do you think Matt is doing? Read and listen to check.**

Zoe: Hey, Matt. What's up? You look terrible.
Matt: Hi, Zoe. Well, I had an audition this afternoon – you know, for a part in a play. It was awful.
Zoe: Come on, Matt, cheer up! I'm sure it wasn't that bad.
Matt: Oh, it was! It really was. For a start, I was late, and I read the wrong lines, and then I started coughing. I made a real fool of myself! Am I a fool? Am I a terrible actor?
Zoe: Well, to be honest it sounds like you might have prepared better. But don't let it get you down. One bad audition doesn't mean you don't have talent.
Matt: I guess. But I really wanted that part. I need parts to have a better chance of getting into drama school.
Zoe: Well, let's look on the bright side. There'll be more auditions, won't there?
Matt: Yes, sure. In fact, I put my name down for another audition next week, but I don't think I want to go.
Zoe: No, Matt. Go for it. You don't have anything to lose.
Matt: I just don't want to get my hopes up for nothing.
Zoe: Fair enough. Getting turned down isn't easy. But you have to hang in there!
Matt: I know. Thanks, Zoe. You always manage to cheer me up; I really appreciate it. Anyway, how was your day?
Zoe: Well, nothing special, but it was better than yours, I think! Come on, let's get some ice cream!

2 7.04 **Read and listen to the dialogue again and answer the questions.**
1 What went wrong at Matt's audition?
2 Why is Matt thinking of not doing the audition next week?
3 How does Zoe encourage Matt?

3 SPEAKING **Discuss the statements in pairs. Do you agree with them?**
1 One bad [audition/day/exam/game] doesn't mean you don't have talent.
2 Matt should "hang in there."

Phrases for fluency

4 **Find the underlined expressions in the dialogue and use them to complete the conversations.**
1 A Well, there are lots of reasons I don't want to go there. It's very expensive, ______________.
B ______________. We'll have to think of another place to go, then.
2 A There's a singing competition at school next month. I thought I might ______________.
B Well, don't ______________. Sophie Kenny's bound to win it.
3 A So have you decided to try out for the team?
B No, I decided not to. I'm not good enough and I'd only ______________.
A That's disappointing and I'm sure that wouldn't happen.
B ______________, even if I did get in, they play on Saturday mornings and I like to sleep in on Saturdays.

5 SPEAKING **Work in pairs. One of you is Zoe; the other is Matt. Imagine it is five years later and you meet again. Act out two scenarios.**
1 Matt has taken his acting career further.
2 Matt has given up acting.

FUNCTIONS
Cheering someone up

KEY LANGUAGE
Cheer up!
Don't let it get you down.
There's light at the end of the tunnel.
Hang in there!
Look on the bright side.

6 **Complete the sentences with phrases from the Key Language box.**
1 ______________ up! Things will seem better after a good night's sleep.
2 ______________ there. Your exams will be over soon.
3 Don't let ______________. It's not the end of the world.
4 I can see that losing the game is really bothering you, but try to look ______________ side – it's early in the season.
5 I know this year of high school can be really difficult, but there is ______________ tunnel!

7 SPEAKING **Work in pairs. Think of situations in which someone would need cheering up. Write short dialogues using the language from the Key Language box. Then act them out.**

PRONUNCIATION
Intonation: encouraging someone
Go to page 121.

72

6 As an alternative, you could ask students to cover the Key Language box and try to guess what key words complete the sentences. During feedback, say each expression for students to repeat and check pronunciation.
1 Cheer 2 Hang in 3 it get you down 4 on the bright 5 light at the end of the

7 You could move on to pronunciation at this stage prior to doing the speaking task.

Pronunciation
Intonation: encouraging someone

Student's Book p121

TH!NK more

Workbook
Pronunciation p120

Warmer

Write *being tactful* on the board and elicit the meaning in this context (careful not to say or do anything that could upset someone). Ask students to give themselves a score between 0 and 10 for their ability to be tactful. Does their ability to do this change, depending on who they are interacting with?

▶ 19 Life Lessons: Being tactful

1 ▶ 19 Ask students to compare their ideas with a partner. Elicit or explain that *a jumper* is a word in British English for *a sweater*.
a jumper, a hat, and a scarf

2 ▶ **19 Check/clarify:** *dreaded, tack, knitting.*
Ask students to try to answer the questions from memory before watching the video again to check.

3 After a few minutes, invite students' reactions in open class, prompting them to try to explain their answers.

4 As a follow up, ask students to rank the three responses from the most to the least tactful. Discuss as a class and agree on a definitive list.

5 You could put students in two groups and give each group one of the texts to read and share ideas on.

6 Give students three or four minutes to think about their answers. Encourage them to make notes.

7 Monitor and prompt students to keep talking, but as this is a fluency activity, do not interrupt to correct mistakes. While monitoring, write down any common errors to review together at the end.

ROSE-TINTED GLASSES UNIT 7

LIFE COMPETENCIES

It's important to be honest with your friends, but sometimes being too sincere can upset or offend people. In these situations, we need to use tact and show sensitivity to how others may be feeling.

1 ▶ 19 **Watch the vlog. What three presents did Chloe get from her aunt?**

2 ▶ 19 **Watch the vlog again and make notes about:**
a Chloe's truthful thoughts
b things she could say to be tactful.

3 SPEAKING **Work in pairs. Think of three more things Chloe could have said to be tactful.**

4 SPEAKING **Read the situation and the responses. Work in pairs and discuss which response is the most tactful.**

A friend has bought a new outfit for the school dance and wants your opinion on it. The outfit was expensive, and they think they look great in it. However, you don't agree. You think the clothes are out of style and don't suit your friend at all. What do you say?

A Whatever you do, don't wear them. They're so ugly, and you look terrible in them.
B You look great in them. You'll be a big success.
C Can I be honest? I think blue is a better color for you.

5 **Read the situation. In pairs, think of a reply that is tactful. Then compare your ideas with another pair.**

1
You are on a team of four, working on an important project for school. While three of you are working your hardest to get the best result possible, the other member is not doing their fair share of the work. You want to say something before it's too late, but what?

2
You're in a band with a couple of friends from school. You've been together for about a year and are now pretty good. You've played several shows and are getting more popular. Your best friend wants to be part of the action and has asked if he could join the band as a singer. You know that his voice isn't very good. What do you say?

Me and my world

6 **Think of a time when you found yourself in an awkward situation (e.g., someone showed up at a party that they hadn't been invited to) and make notes.**
- Who did it involve?
- What did they want?
- Why was it awkward?
- Would you do things differently if it happened again?

7 SPEAKING **Work in pairs and tell your partner about the situation. Then discuss these questions below.**
1 Is it sometimes better to just be honest? Can you think of an example?
2 Who's the most direct person you know? What sort of things do they say?
3 Do you consider yourself to be tactful? Give examples.

TIPS FOR BEING TACTFUL

- Before giving negative feedback, think about how you would react if someone gave you similar news.
- It's always a good idea to try to focus on something positive first – this will make it easier to deliver the negative comments afterwards.
- It is possible to be too tactful. Make sure your message isn't lost in too much tact.

73

Homework

Ask students to write a short text describing a time when they found themselves in an awkward situation. They can use the notes they made in Exercise 6.

Activity idea Mixed-ability

In Exercise 5, stronger students could discuss both situations. Weaker students could discuss just one.

Emotional Development
Showing empathy for the feelings of others
Shows understanding of other people's perspectives and feelings.

TH!NK more

Practice Extra
Unit 7 Master it!

Worksheets
Life Lessons: Being tactful

Tests
Unit, extension, and skills test 7

Reading

Warmer

Ask: *How do you organize your studying before exams? How do you make sure you don't forget to do any homework? What can you do to be more organized?* Students discuss the questions in pairs or small groups. Invite students to report back on their discussions in open class.

▶ 20 Get **TH!NK**ing

Play the video and discuss the question with your class.

1 Put a copy of the four photos up on the board. Elicit what the jobs are (possible answers: A teacher, architect, engineer; B engineer, pilot; C architect, engineer, builder, surveyor; D surgeon, nurse) and do the exercise as a class before students open their books.

2 Set a two-minute time limit to encourage students to read quickly.
a checklist

3 🔊 **8.01 Check/clarify:** *manifesto, procedure, infection, reckon, inquiry.*
Ask them to underline the parts of the review that helped them choose their answers.
A 2 B 3 D 1 E 4 F 5
(extra title: C)

4 Give students time to read the questions. Encourage them to underline the key information in the questions that they will be looking for in the review. Students then read the review in more detail to find the answers. Suggest that they underline the parts of the review that support their answers.
1 the fact that no one was wearing a mask
2 There were almost no infections over 27 months, and it was estimated that around eight lives were saved.
3 a plane could crash; a skyscraper could fall down
4 A lot of them weren't very enthusiastic because they thought it would be too difficult to use. Students' own answers.
5 Because it's relevant for everyone to avoid making mistakes.

5 Make sure all students are speaking and encourage quieter students to give their opinions, too. Nominate one or two students to report back to the class.

8 LIST IT!

OBJECTIVES

FUNCTIONS: saying "yes" and adding conditions

GRAMMAR: conditionals (review); mixed conditionals

VOCABULARY: phrasal verbs (2); alternatives to *if*: *suppose, provided, as long as, otherwise, unless*

Get TH!NKING
Watch the video and think: what kinds of lists do you make?

A

C

B

D
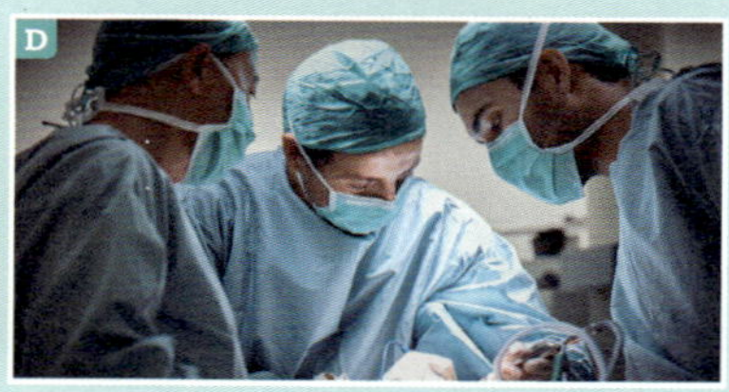

READING

1 SPEAKING **Look at the photos. Work in pairs and think about the things in the list below. Then compare your ideas with other people in the class.**
1 three ways in which the jobs are different
2 three things the jobs have in common
3 something that connects *all* of them

2 **Read the book review quickly. What does Atul Gawande recommend using to ensure procedures are followed?**

3 🔊 8.01 **Read and listen to the review. Match the paragraphs with the titles. There is one extra title.**
A Lives can be saved ☐
B It's not just for the medical profession ☐
C Mistakes don't really matter ☐
D Holes in the system ☐
E Not everyone agrees ☐
F A book for everyone ☐

4 **Read the review again and answer the questions.**
1 What surprised the doctor who went into the operating room?
2 What was the result of an experiment in an important American hospital?
3 What examples does Gawande give of what could happen if engineers and pilots didn't follow checklists?
4 How did many of the doctors react to the idea of using checklists? Why do you think they reacted this way?
5 Why does the writer of the review recommend the book?

5 SPEAKING **Work in pairs and discuss the questions.**
1 Can you think of any other jobs where checklists should be compulsory?
2 Have you ever made any checklists for yourself? What for? Were they useful?
3 Do you agree with the last sentence in the review? Why (not)?

74

Objectives

Functions and speaking Saying "Yes" and adding conditions
Grammar Conditionals (review); mixed conditionals
Vocabulary Phrasal verbs (2); alternatives to *if*: *suppose, provided, as long as, otherwise, unless*
Values Lists
Culture Wonders of the world

Resources for this unit

All available online

Videos
- Get **TH!NK**ing: *What kinds of lists do you make?*
- Grammar video!: Mixed conditionals
- Culture: Wonders of the world

Tests
- Unit, extension, and skills test 8

Worksheets
- Grammar and vocabulary: Basic, Standard, and Extension Worksheets
- Project: Top ten list
- Communication: Making lists
- Literature Worksheets: *Poetry*
- Get **TH!NK**ing and Grammar video! video Worksheets

Culture note

Atul Gawande is a practicing endocrine surgeon, public health advisor, and a professor at Harvard Medical School. He is also founder and chair of Lifebox, a non-profit organization making surgery safer globally. Since 1998, Atul has been a staff writer for *The New Yorker* magazine and has written four *New York Times* best-selling books. He is the winner of several awards for writing about science.

6 Check/clarify: *approach, discipline.*
Give students time to read through the ideas (a–h) and the checklist.
a 5 b 3 c 5 d 1 e 2, 4, 5 f 2 g 2, 3 h 2

7 As you monitor, make a note of some interesting checklists to come back to during feedback. Allow students to compare ideas in small groups and encourage them to give each other ideas on how to improve their checklist, e.g., do they need to be more specific?

Homework

Ask students to make a list of goals for the week and to keep a journal detailing what they need to do to achieve their goal, their progress each day, and whether or not they achieved it by the end of the week.

Activity idea Extension

Ask: *What goals have you set for yourself in the last year? Have your parents ever set goals for you? What goals have they set? Why is it important to set goals?* Students discuss the questions with a partner. Invite volunteers to report back to the class on their discussions and encourage reactions from the rest of the class.

LIST IT! UNIT 8

THE CHECKLIST MANIFESTO BY ATUL GAWANDE

1 A doctor in a large hospital walked into an operating room where an operation was being performed. Everything seemed to be going well, but the doctor picked up on one disturbing fact – no one was wearing a face mask. He was a little shocked – wearing a face mask is basic hospital procedure. But he didn't say anything. The operation was a success, but a few days later the patient came down with a fever. It turned out that she had a serious infection, probably because the doctors and nurses hadn't followed a simple rule. If they'd worn their masks, the patient wouldn't have been infected.

2 Someone who'd be interested in that story is Atul Gawande, who wrote a book called *The Checklist Manifesto: How to get things right*. Gawande is a doctor himself, and in his book he suggests that if surgeons run through a simple checklist before every operation, then lives will be saved. And he has the numbers to prove it. In 2001, at an important American hospital, there was an experiment that required doctors to use a five-point checklist before they carried out specific procedures. The checklist was just a list of routine things doctors should normally do without thinking – for example, wearing rubber gloves, washing hands before and after every patient, and so on. By making sure that the checklist was followed, there were almost no infections over the 27 months of the experiment, and they reckon that around eight lives were saved. When the checklist was tried out again in hospitals in Michigan, in the US, infections went down by 66 percent.

3 In his book, Gawande looks at other professions, too, to support his argument that checklists reduce accidents and improve success rates. He points out that people like engineers and pilots use checklists all the time, and he comes up with some good examples. Just imagine that an airplane crashed because the pilot had failed to follow basic procedures. Suppose a skyscraper fell down because the engineers hadn't remembered to do some important calculations. There would be an immediate inquiry to look into these events. So Gawande's question is: if pilots and engineers use checklists, why don't doctors use them?

4 But when Gawande talked to doctors at eight hospitals about a checklist that he had developed, he found that a lot of them weren't very enthusiastic. Twenty percent of the doctors that Gawande talked to said that the list was too difficult to use and that it wouldn't help to save lives. But, when they were shown the statement, "If I had surgery, I'd want the surgeon to use this list," 93 percent of the same doctors agreed with it! So it's hard to work out why they don't want to use it themselves.

5 *The Checklist Manifesto* is a really interesting and well-written book. It reminds us to do basic things to avoid problems. It's relevant for all of us, not just for doctors. We should all use checklists every now and then, otherwise we'll make mistakes.

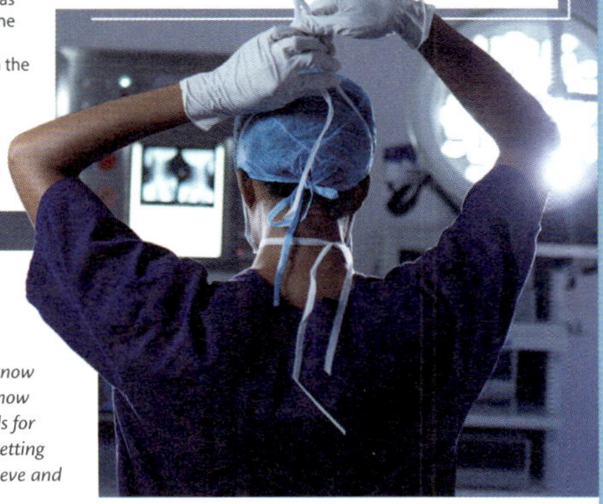

Train to TH!NK

The "goal-setting" checklist

When you go on a journey, you wouldn't say to yourself, "I don't know where to go to but I'll start my journey anyway." You will never know if your destination is where you wanted to be, if you don't set goals for yourself. This is important for all of our journeys in life. The goal-setting checklist helps you think clearly about what it is you want to achieve and how you're going to achieve it.

6 Max has a new project. He wants to learn to play the piano. Look at these ideas that Max has written and match them with items 1–5 in the checklist. (Some include more than one idea, and some could go in more than one place on the checklist.)

a I'll be able to play about 20 songs. ☐
b approach it as something to be enjoyed ☐
c I'll feel really good about my achievement. ☐
d learn to play the piano ☐
e positive comments from family and friends ☐
f a friend who will teach me ☐
g discipline to practice daily ☐
h lessons streamed from the internet ☐

1 What I want to achieve
2 Things I need in order to achieve this goal
3 How I need to act or behave in order to achieve this goal
4 Things that tell me I have achieved this goal
5 Results of achieving this goal, for myself and for others

7 SPEAKING **Think of something you want to achieve. Use the checklist to help you define your goals more clearly. Compare your ideas with a partner.**

75

Activity idea Extension

Point out that goal-setting is often done in groups as well as by individuals. Divide the class into small groups and tell students they are going to set a goal for the group as a whole. Give examples: *form a band, organize an end-of-year party, set up a study group, start a tennis club*, etc. Students work together to create a checklist to help them achieve their goal. Regroup for students to share their ideas.

TH!NK more

Worksheets
Project Top ten list
Communication Making lists
Get **TH!NK**ing *What kinds of lists do you make?*

Learning to Learn
Taking control of own learning
Setting goals and planning for learning.

Grammar; Vocabulary

Warmer

Write a list on the board outlining what you are going to do / have done in the lesson today. Ask: *Do you think this is a useful list? Who for? Why?* Students discuss in pairs or small groups. Listen to some of their ideas in open class. Ask: *Would you like me to write up a list like this at the beginning of every lesson?*

1 During feedback, ask concept-check questions to help clarify meaning and usage of each type of conditional, e.g., *What does sentence 1 refer to: the past, present, or future? Or does it refer to an imaginary situation? Does sentence 2 refer to the past or present? Were they wearing masks?*

1 run; will be 2 'd worn; wouldn't have been 3 use; don't … use 4 had; 'd want
RULE: 5 simple present 6 1 7 simple present 8 future 9 4 10 simple past 11 2 12 would(n't)

2 1 b 2 d 3 c 4 a

3 If you are short on time, assign this exercise for homework.

1 If you read books, you learn things about life.
2 You'll discover interesting things about pilots and doctors if you read it.
3 If Gawande wasn't a doctor, he wouldn't understand so much about this.
4 I wouldn't have found out about the importance of checklists if I hadn't read it.

Workbook p72

Get it Right!

would

Student's Book p125

4 1 picked up on 2 came down with 3 turned out 4 run through 5 carried out 6 tried out 7 points out 8 comes up with

THINK more

Workbook
Grammar p72, Ex.1–4
Vocabulary p74, Ex.1–3
Vocabulary Extra p75, Ex.1–3

Worksheets
Grammar Worksheets 8
Vocabulary Worksheets 8

GRAMMAR
Conditionals (review)

1 Write the correct form of the verbs in parentheses and check in the review on page 75. Then complete the chart.

1 If surgeons __________ (run) through a simple checklist before every operation, then lives __________ (be) saved.
2 If they __________ (wear) their masks, the patient __________ (not be) infected.
3 If pilots and engineers __________ (use) checklists, why __________ doctors __________ (use) them?
4 If I __________ (have) surgery, I __________ (want) the surgeon to use this list.

RULE:

Type of conditional	Example sentence	*If* clause	Main clause
Zero	3	simple present	5 ______
First	6 ______	7 ______	8 ______
Second	9 ______	10 ______	*would(n't)* + infinitive
Third	11 ______	past perfect	12 ______

2 Match the four sentences a doctor might say to a patient with situations a–d.

1 If people take this medicine, they don't get headaches. ☐
2 If you take this medicine, you won't get headaches. ☐
3 If you took this medicine, you wouldn't get headaches. ☐
4 If you had taken this medicine, you wouldn't have gotten headaches. ☐

a The patient didn't take the medicine.
b The doctor is telling the patient a general fact about the medicine.
c The patient isn't taking the medicine and gets headaches.
d The doctor is telling the patient about a future result of taking the medicine.

3 Write sentences using the type of conditional specified.

1 Reading books is a great idea. (0 conditional) If you / read books, you / learn things about life.
2 I think you should buy the book. (1st conditional) You / discover interesting things about pilots and doctors if you / read it.
3 Gawande's a doctor. (2nd conditional) If Gawande / not be a doctor, he / not understand so much about this.
4 I read this book a week or two ago. (3rd conditional) I / not find out about the importance of checklists if I / not read it.

→ workbook page 72

VOCABULARY
Phrasal verbs (2)

4 Complete the sentences with the phrases in the list. Then check your answers in the review on page 75.

came down with | carried out | comes up with | picked up on | points out | run through | tried out | turned out

1 The doctor __________ one disturbing fact.
2 The patient __________ a fever.
3 It __________ that she had a serious infection.
4 If surgeons __________ a simple checklist before every operation, then lives will be saved.
5 There was an experiment that required doctors to use a […] checklist before they __________ specific procedures.
6 When the checklist was __________ again in hospitals in Michigan, US, infections went down by 66 percent.
7 Gawande __________ that people like engineers and pilots use checklists all the time.
8 He __________ some good examples.

5 SPEAKING Work in pairs and discuss the meaning of the phrasal verbs from Exercise 4.

6 Use the correct form of seven of the verbs from Exercise 4 to complete the short story.

It was two days before the school camping trip. The teacher gathered everyone in the school auditorium because she wanted to [1] __________ some things. She gave us all a list she had [2] __________ of things we needed. Someone [3] __________ that this was a bit late, but she didn't [4] __________ on this. She just continued talking. She was like an army general about to [5] __________ an important attack. She had everything planned out, every last detail. The camping trip was getting less attractive by the minute. I looked at the list. How was I going to get all these things in 48 hours? Well, it [6] __________ I didn't need to worry. The next day, the teacher [7] __________ with the flu and the whole thing was called off.

→ workbook page 74

5 Encourage students to brainstorm other situations in which the verbs could be used.

6 During feedback, ask: *What is different about the verbs* run through, point out, *and* carry out? Elicit/explain that all the phrasal verbs are inseparable, apart from these three.

1 run through / point out 2 come up with 3 pointed out 4 pick up 5 carry out 6 turned out 7 came down

Workbook p74

Activity idea Fast finishers

Ask students to write about what they would do if they found a million dollars. Remind students to use conditional structures.

Activity idea Mixed-ability

In Exercise 4, ask students to cover the phrasal verbs in the list. Stronger students can complete each sentence with a phrasal verb, while weaker students complete them with any verb that makes sense. All students then uncover the phrasal verbs. Stronger students check their answers, while weaker students choose a phrasal verb to replace each verb they've come up with.

7 Check/clarify: *parachute, continent, novel.*
Give your own answers as an example before hearing from the students.

8 🔊 **8.02**
Parachute out of a plane G
Visit every continent T
Write a novel T
Meet a famous person T

9 🔊 **8.02** Ask students to try to complete the sentences from memory before playing the audio again to check.
1 disappointed 2 else's expectations
3 miss out on enjoying

10–11 Give students some time to work individually and to think about their answers before they discuss in pairs.

▶ 21 Grammar video!
Mixed conditionals

12 🔊 **8.03**
1 was; would have 2 had; would

13 Remind students that it is possible to start conditional sentences with the *would* clause.
RULE: 1 Sentence 2 2 Sentence 1

14 If you are short on time, assign this exercise for homework.
1 If Anna and Dan hadn't had a big argument, they would be talking to each other.
2 If we'd left early, we wouldn't be late now
3 If I had a good memory, I wouldn't have forgotten her birthday.
4 If I had eaten breakfast, I wouldn't be hungry now.
5 If he'd paid attention, he'd be able to do the homework.

15 Do the first item with the whole class as an example. Divide the class into mixed-ability pairs. Adapt the time limit according to the level of your class.

Workbook p73

Pronunciation
Weak forms with conditionals
Student's Book p121

LISTENING

7 SPEAKING Work in pairs. Look at this list. Which of these things would you be interested in doing?

Things to do before you are 25:
Parachute out of a plane ☐
Visit every continent ☐
Write a novel ☐
Meet a famous person ☐

8 🔊 8.02 Listen to Tom's great-grandfather giving a talk at Tom's school. Next to the items on the list above, write T (for things on Tom's bucket list) and G (for things his great-grandfather has done).

9 🔊 8.02 Listen again and complete Mr. Hardeman's concerns in four words or less.
1 Tom might feel ________________ if he doesn't complete his list.
2 The ideas on the list are not really Tom's, but someone ________________ .
3 If Tom focuses too much on his list, he will ________________ everyday life.

10 SPEAKING Work in pairs. Which of the concerns above do you agree with? Why?

11 SPEAKING Complete this bucket list for you. Then compare your list with a partner's list.
Five things to do before finishing school:
1 ________________
2 ________________
3 ________________
4 ________________
5 ________________

GRAMMAR
Grammar video ▶21
Mixed conditionals

12 🔊 8.03 Complete the sentences from the talk with the words or phrases in the list. Listen and check.

had | was | would | would have

1 If I ________________ younger, I ________________ known what a bucket list was.
2 If I ________________ made a list, what ________________ be on it?

13 Look at the sentences again. Underline the second and third conditional parts in each one. Then match them to the sentences in the rule.

RULE: Sometimes we mix second and third conditional forms so that we can connect present and past actions.
- To talk about the present result of an unreal or imagined past action, we use: *if* + *had* + past participle, *would ('d)* + infinitive. Sentence [1] ________________
- To talk about the past result of an unreal or hypothetical present situation or fact, we use: *if* + simple past, *would ('d) have* + past participle. Sentence [2] ________________

14 Write mixed conditional sentences to describe these situations.
0 I don't have any money. I didn't buy that phone.
If I had some money, I'd have bought that phone.
1 Anna and Dan had a big argument. They aren't talking to each other.
2 We didn't leave early. That's why we're late now.
3 I don't have a good memory. I forgot her birthday.
4 I didn't eat breakfast. Now I'm hungry.
5 He didn't pay attention. He can't do the homework.

15 Work in pairs. Complete the sentences. How many different mixed conditional examples can you make in five minutes?
1 If I hadn't ________________ yesterday, I wouldn't be ________________ now.
2 If I was ________________ , I would have ________________ .
3 I wouldn't have ________________ if I didn't like .
4 I would ________________ if I had ________________ at school.

→ workbook page 73

PRONUNCIATION
Weak forms with conditionals Go to page 121.

Homework
Ask students to choose one of the sentences in Exercise 14 and write further *would* clauses to continue a story. You might like to give them an example:
3 If I had a good memory, I wouldn't have forgotten her birthday.
If I hadn't forgotten her birthday, we would still be friends.
If we were still friends, I could/would have asked her to …

Activity idea Extension
In Exercise 11, encourage students to mingle to find someone who has the same ideas on their list. Ask students to make notes and report their findings back to the class. Encourage them to use the phrase "So does he/she/[student's name]."

TH!NK more
Practice Extra
Unit 8 Practice it!

Workbook
Listening p78, Ex.1–3
Grammar p73, Ex.5–7
Pronunciation p120

Worksheets
Grammar Worksheets 8
Grammar video! Mixed conditionals

Reading

Warmer

Elicit the names of ten school subjects and write them on the board. Divide the class into pairs for students to rank their lists from most to least interesting, useful, or difficult. You could start them off by tasking them to rank them by "most interesting" and then assign "most useful" and/or "most difficult" to any fast finishers.

1 Nominate one or two students to share their ideas with the class.

2 🔊 8.06 Before listening, set a three-minute time limit to encourage students to read the blog quickly for this initial reading-for-gist task.
1 because no one sent her a list
2 in the blog archive 3 She wants them to send her lists.

3 **Check/clarify:** *crushed, buried, ostriches, wrestling, volcano, Lego, cement, calligrapher.*
Point out that students need to decide which of the top ten lists the sentences might be found in.
a 6 b 8 c 1 d 7 e 3

4 Listen to some of the students' choices and have a show of hands to find out which lists were most popular.

5 Encourage students to be as funny and imaginative as possible when choosing and creating their lists.

Culture note

On the internet, more and more articles are written as lists. The editorial phenomenon – *listicles* (a portmanteau of *list* and *article*) – is incredibly popular. They appeal because they are easier to read than an ordinary article – they reduce the subject into a manageable number of facts, they are perfect for skimming, and the title tells you what to expect. If you're reading an article online and it's more than a single screen long, you can't be sure when it's going to end, whereas a listicle encourages you to keep going by helpfully letting you know how much there is left.

Elisa's LIST BLOG

As you know, every week I post a top ten list here that someone has sent me. Well, this week, no one sent me anything, so I'm offering you a top ten list of … my favorite top ten lists! And here they are.

1 Ten of the world's strangest sports
Everything from extreme ironing to cheese rolling and toe wrestling. You won't see any of these sports at the Olympics.

2 Ten crazy hotels
Suppose you wanted to spend a night in a volcano … Or how about in a sandcastle or inside a giant wooden dog? There's plenty of inspiration for your next vacation here.

3 Top things you never knew your brain could do
Did you know you can learn while you're asleep? And that you can predict the future? Or know what's happening behind you without looking? Well, you can. And there's a lot more your brain can do, too.

4 Ten amazing ways that animals communicate
Elephants use their heads and tails to communicate. Honeybees dance, and mushrooms have their own "internet." The facts will fascinate you, as long as you're interested in nature.

5 Amazing things people have found on the beach
Thousands of rubber ducks, an enormous tree, two-meter-tall Lego men … You just never know what might turn up when you take a walk along the shoreline!

6 Ten criminals who needed to call 911 to escape
A burglar who got stuck in a chimney. A gas station robber who got his arm stuck in a window. A car thief who got stuck in a car. Read all about them here – unless you have something better to do.

7 Everyday inventions from Victorian times
Cement, chocolate, flushing toilets, the sewing machine, the subway, the radio, and the X-ray – all invented in Victorian times, but we couldn't live without them today.

8 Ten superhero powers you could actually learn
Want to be a superhero? Well, here are the powers you could learn to help you on your way, provided you have the time. Powers include super strength, speed, and agility. And mind control!

9 Before they were famous
They weren't always mega-famous: before turning her hand to acting, Meghan Markle was a calligrapher (that means she wrote things in nice handwriting), Beyoncé swept hair from the floor of a salon, and Brad Pitt wore a chicken costume to advertise a restaurant. Well, we all have to start somewhere.

10 Ten amazing facts about the world around us
The amount of water in our world never changes. It just gets recycled. That means that cup of water you drank this morning might have been drunk by a dinosaur 350 million years before. And that's just the least interesting fact! Fascinating!

So, that's it for this week. You can find these lists in my archive. Lastly – please send me a list, people, otherwise I won't have anything for next week.

READING

1 SPEAKING **Work in pairs and discuss what "top ten" lists you have seen (or written) recently.**

2 🔊 8.06 **Read and listen to the blog. Answer the questions.**
1 Why is Elisa posting her own list this week?
2 Where can you see the complete lists?
3 What does Elisa want her readers to do?

3 **Read the blog again. Which list do each of these sentences come from? Write a number (1–10) in the boxes.**
a One man wasn't so lucky. While trying to rob a bank, the safe fell on him and crushed him to death. ☐
b Wim Hof set a world record when he buried himself in freezing ice for 72 minutes, wearing only a pair of shorts. ☐
c Everyone has heard of horse racing – but in some parts of the world people race on ostriches. ☐
d Perhaps the most remarkable of all, though, was the telephone, which changed the way people communicate with each other forever. ☐
e You can even learn to play the piano just by imagining you're playing it. ☐

4 SPEAKING **Which three lists would you like to read in full? Compare your ideas with a partner.**

5 SPEAKING **Choose one of these ideas, or use your own idea, to write a new top ten list. Then compare your lists in groups.**
- My top five most interesting …
- My top five worst …
- My top five strangest …
- My top five funniest …

78

A listicle is also much easier to plan and write than a regular article because the order and structure of the points are less important, updates are easier to make, and new points can be slotted in without disruption.

However, listicles have also become controversial. They assume the public wants quick hits of information, but more importantly, they demonstrate the shift in power between traditional print and online. To many, not only are they a "dumbing down," but they are the result of cost-cutting and redundancies in the traditional newsrooms.

Activity idea Extension

If students have access to the internet, ask them to do a search for one of the lists in pairs. Give students time to make notes on the information they find. Put pairs together to make groups of four to share the most interesting information they found.

TH!NK more

Workbook
Reading p76, Ex.1–4

THINK Values; Vocabulary; Functions

6 Students can choose more than one.

7–8 Encourage students to give reasons for their choices and to try to use conditional sentences in their discussions where possible.

9 To focus students on the vocabulary, write the five alternatives to *if* on the board and ask: *What do these words mean? What do they have in common?* (They are all alternatives to *if*.)
1 c 2 b 3 e 4 a 5 d

10 Refer students to the sentences in Exercise 9 to help them.
1 provided 2 suppose 3 unless 4 otherwise

11 During feedback, check understanding by asking students to rephrase the sentences using *if*. If you are short on time, students can finish this for homework.
1 provided 2 otherwise 3 provided 4 unless 5 provided 6 Unless

Workbook p74

12 Give students time to read the sentences before they begin discussing. Tell them there is no one correct answer. Encourage stronger students to think of various situations for each sentence.

13 Tell students to refer to the vocabulary section for help if necessary. You could do the first one together as an example.
1 You can borrow it as long as you drive really carefully.
2 Yes, you can go to the party, provided you promise to be home by eleven o'clock.
3 I'll get a really bad grade unless you help me. / Unless you help me, I'll get a really bad grade.
4 I'll fix it as long as you let me play games on it.
5 Close the door, otherwise it'll get cold in here.
6 Yes, you can practice, provided you don't make a lot of noise.
7 Suppose you could play the guitar – what kind of music would you play?

Critical THINKing
Evaluating ideas and arguments
Evaluating arguments as a whole.

Critical THINKing
Understanding and analyzing ideas and arguments
Identifying and classifying information.

THINK values

Lists

6 **Check (✓) the sentences you agree with.**
1 ☐ I never waste my time reading top ten lists.
2 ☐ Top ten lists aren't meant to be taken seriously – just enjoy them!
3 ☐ Some top ten lists can be very useful.
4 ☐ People who write top ten lists must have a very high opinion of themselves.

7 SPEAKING **Compare your choices in pairs.**

8 **Which of these top ten lists would interest you? Put a check (✓) or a cross (✗). Add one more thing of your own that you think would make for an interesting top ten list.**
- someone's favorite songs ☐
- things to do before you're 20 ☐
- ways to make money ☐
- things to do to relax and be happy ☐
- ______________________

VOCABULARY
Alternatives to *if*: *suppose, provided, as long as, otherwise, unless*

Look
To hypothesize about the present: *suppose* + simple past, *would* + infinitive
To talk about a future possibility and its results: *as long as* / *unless* + simple present, *will* + infinitive

9 **Match the sentence halves.**
1 **Suppose** you wanted to spend ☐
2 The facts will fascinate you, ☐
3 Read all about them here ☐
4 Here are the powers you could learn to help you on your way, ☐
5 Please send me a list, ☐

a **provided** you have the time.
b **as long as** you're interested in nature.
c a night in a volcano …
d **otherwise** I won't have anything for next week.
e – **unless** you have something better to do.

10 **Match the words in bold in Exercise 9 with these meanings.**
1 but only if: *as long as* / ______
2 imagine: ______
3 if … not …: ______
4 because if not: ______

11 **Complete with *unless, provided,* or *otherwise*.**
1 I don't mind going to the movies alone, ______ it's a movie I really want to see.
2 I think I should go home now, ______ my parents will be worried.
3 You'll do fine on the test, ______ you study enough.
4 I'll never speak to you again ______ you say sorry right now!
5 OK, I'll tell you what happened, ______ you promise not to tell anyone else!
6 ______ you start to work harder, you won't pass the exam next month.

→ workbook page 74

FUNCTIONS
Saying "Yes" and adding conditions

12 SPEAKING **Work in pairs. Read the sentences and discuss who is talking to whom and what they are talking about.**
1 You can borrow it if you drive really carefully. (as long as)
2 Yes, you can go to the party, if you promise to be home by eleven o'clock. (provided)
3 If you don't help me, I'll get a really bad grade. (unless)
4 I'll fix it if you let me play games on it. (as long as)
5 Close the door, or it'll get cold in here. (otherwise)
6 Yes, you can practice if you don't make a lot of noise. (provided)
7 Imagine you could play the guitar – what kind of music would you play? (suppose)

13 **Rewrite the sentences in Exercise 12, using the words in parentheses.**

14 **A friend asks you these things. For each one, on what conditions would you say yes? Make notes.**
1 Can I use your phone to make a call?
no international phone calls / no long phone calls
2 Will you come shopping with me?
3 Please come to the soccer game with me.
4 Can I borrow your jacket, please?

15 SPEAKING **Use your notes from Exercise 14 to write your answers. Then work with a partner and act out the conversations for the situations.**

Yes, of course – as long as / provided you don't make any long calls on it.

14 Ask students to try to think of at least two conditions for each one.

15 Allow students six to eight minutes to prepare their dialogues. Monitor to make sure all students are on task.

Homework
Students write one of the top ten lists mentioned in Exercise 8 and make a poster. If you have space, display them on the walls and ask pairs to circulate and discuss whether or not they agree with the choices.

Activity idea Extension
Ask students to review Grammar Exercise 14 on page 77 and to decide which of the sentences could be rewritten using alternatives to *if* and rewrite them.

THINK more
Workbook
Vocabulary p74, Ex.4–5

Worksheets
Vocabulary Worksheets 8

Warmer

Write the following on the board: *Where is the most beautiful natural environment that you have ever visited?* Students discuss in pairs.

▶ 22 TH!NK
Wonders of the world

1 Before students open their books, put a copy of the seven photos up on the board and write the names, mixed up. Ask students to match the photos with the places.

2 🔊 **8.07** Ask students to predict the answers by looking at the photos on the board before they open their books. Play the audio to check.

1 Mount Everest
2 The Great Barrier Reef

3 **Check/clarify:** *carve out, wilderness, life cycle, witness, particles, thunders, reef, hemispheres, border.*
Ask students to underline the language in the article that helped them choose their answers. Tell them not to worry about difficult vocabulary at this stage as this will come up later.

1 Rio de Janeiro Harbor
2 Aurora Borealis / Aurora Australis
3 The Great Barrier Reef
4 The Grand Canyon 5 Mount Everest 6 Paricutín 7 Victoria Falls

TH!NK
Wonders of the world

Culture

1 SPEAKING Work in pairs and look at the photos. Discuss what you know about these places.

2 🔊 8.07 Read and listen to the article and answer the questions.
1 Which wonder is the highest? 2 Which wonder is the longest?

Seven Wonders of THE NATURAL WORLD

The seven wonders of the natural world will inspire amazement from anyone who sees them. They are a constant reminder of the fragile beauty of our planet.

THE GRAND CANYON, ARIZONA, US

Around 17 million years ago, the Colorado River started to carve out its course through the Arizonian wilderness and the Grand Canyon was born. The Canyon is more than 450 km long, around 28 km at its widest point and around 1.5 km at its deepest. It is one of America's most visited natural wonders.

PARICUTÍN, MICHOACÁN, MEXICO

There are many impressive volcanoes all over the world. But what makes Paricutín so special is that it was born, grew up, and went extinct all in about 20 years, giving scientists a unique opportunity to study the life cycle of a volcano. Paricutín quickly grew to a height of 423 m. Then, in 1952, after 19 years of eruptions, it went quiet.

AURORA BOREALIS, AURORA AUSTRALIS

Visitors to the Earth's polar regions may get to witness a spectacular display of colorful lights in the night sky. The Northern Lights (Aurora Borealis) and Southern Lights (Aurora Australis) are the result of particles from outer space entering into the Earth's atmosphere. The closer you are to the poles, the more vibrant the displays will be.

VICTORIA FALLS, AFRICA

They're not the tallest or widest waterfalls in the world, but if you are measuring the amount of water that falls over them each second, they are certainly the biggest. These waterfalls, found on the Zambezi River as it enters Zimbabwe from Zambia, were named by the British explorer David Livingstone after Queen Victoria. These days the local name Mosi-oa-Tunya ("the smoke that thunders") is preferred by many.

RIO DE JANEIRO HARBOR, BRAZIL

When Portuguese sailors first sailed into Guanabara Bay on January 1, 1502, and landed on the shore, they gave it the name Rio de Janeiro (river of January) as they believed they were at the mouth of a large river. In fact, they were in a bay that stretched for almost 30 km.

THE GREAT BARRIER REEF, AUSTRALIA

More than 3,000 reefs and nearly 1,000 islands make up the Great Barrier Reef, and at around 2,250 km in length, it's the only natural object on Earth that is visible from outer space. These days the reef receives special protection from the Australian government to ensure its survival.

MOUNT EVEREST, THE HIMALAYAS

Mount Everest is one of the most well-known natural features of our planet. Standing at over 8,500 meters, it is the highest mountain in the world. Since it was first conquered by Tenzing Norgay and Edmund Hillary in 1953, thousands have climbed to the summit.

3 Read the article again and complete each sentence with one of the seven wonders.

1 ______________ was mistaken for being something else.
2 ______________ can be seen in both of the Earth's hemispheres.
3 ______________ can be seen by astronauts from the Space Station.
4 ______________ is more than 17 million years old.
5 ______________ was first climbed in 1953.
6 ______________ was formed very quickly.
7 ______________ is on the border between two countries.

80

Culture note

The Seven Wonders of the Ancient World is a list of monuments and constructions that are a testament to the creativity and skill of human beings. The list was featured in a work by Philo of Byzantium written in 225 BCE called *On The Seven Wonders* and included the Great Pyramid of Giza, the Hanging Gardens of Babylon, the Temple of Artemis at Ephesus, the Lighthouse of Alexandria, the Colossus of Rhodes, the Mausoleum at Halicarnassus, and the Statue of Zeus at Olympia.

In 2007, a campaign was launched by Swiss adventurer Bernard Weber and his organization New7Wonders to create a list for the modern day. Tens of millions of people voted for the UNESCO World Heritage Sites built between 220 BCE and 1931 with the final seven being: The Great Wall of China; Petra, Jordan; The Colosseum in Rome, Italy; Chichen Itza, Mexico; Machu Picchu, Peru; The Taj Mahal, India; Christ the Redeemer statue, Rio de Janeiro, Brazil.

In recent years, other lists of seven have been created: New7Wonders of Nature, New7Wonders Cities, Seven Wonders of the Underwater World, Seven Wonders of the Industrial World, and Seven Wonders of the Solar System.

4 When students have seen the highlighted words being used in context, ask them to try to work out the meaning of the phrases. Compare their meanings with the definitions in the book.
1 vibrant 2 course 3 summit 4 shore 5 fragile 6 visible 7 went extinct 8 eruptions

5 Monitor and help with vocabulary and ideas as necessary. After students have discussed in pairs, regroup them into small groups for students to report back on their discussions and to share opinions. Hold a class vote to decide which natural wonder is the most popular.

1 Set a two-minute time limit to encourage students to read quickly for gist and to focus on the questions. Encourage them not to focus on every word for now.
one of the most beautiful sunrises in the world

2 This can be done as a class competition with pairs competing to be first to find the mistakes.
spelling: 7 verb tense: 8 connecting word: 1 preposition: 3 missing word: 2

3 Remind students that they only need to write corrections for numbers 1, 2, 3, 7, and 8.
1 but 2 the 3 out 7 one 8 were killed

4 This exercise is designed to get students thinking about the mistakes they make when writing. Ask students to work individually and make a note of their answers to each question. If available, ask students to refer to pieces of writing they have recently produced to help them create a checklist.

5 Divide the class into small groups so that they can share ideas and make notes in preparation before writing individually (they could do this for homework).

6 Encourage students to make a plan before they begin writing their essays, and to organize their writing as outlined in the instructions. Remind students that they should refer to their checklist of past mistakes once they've written their essay.

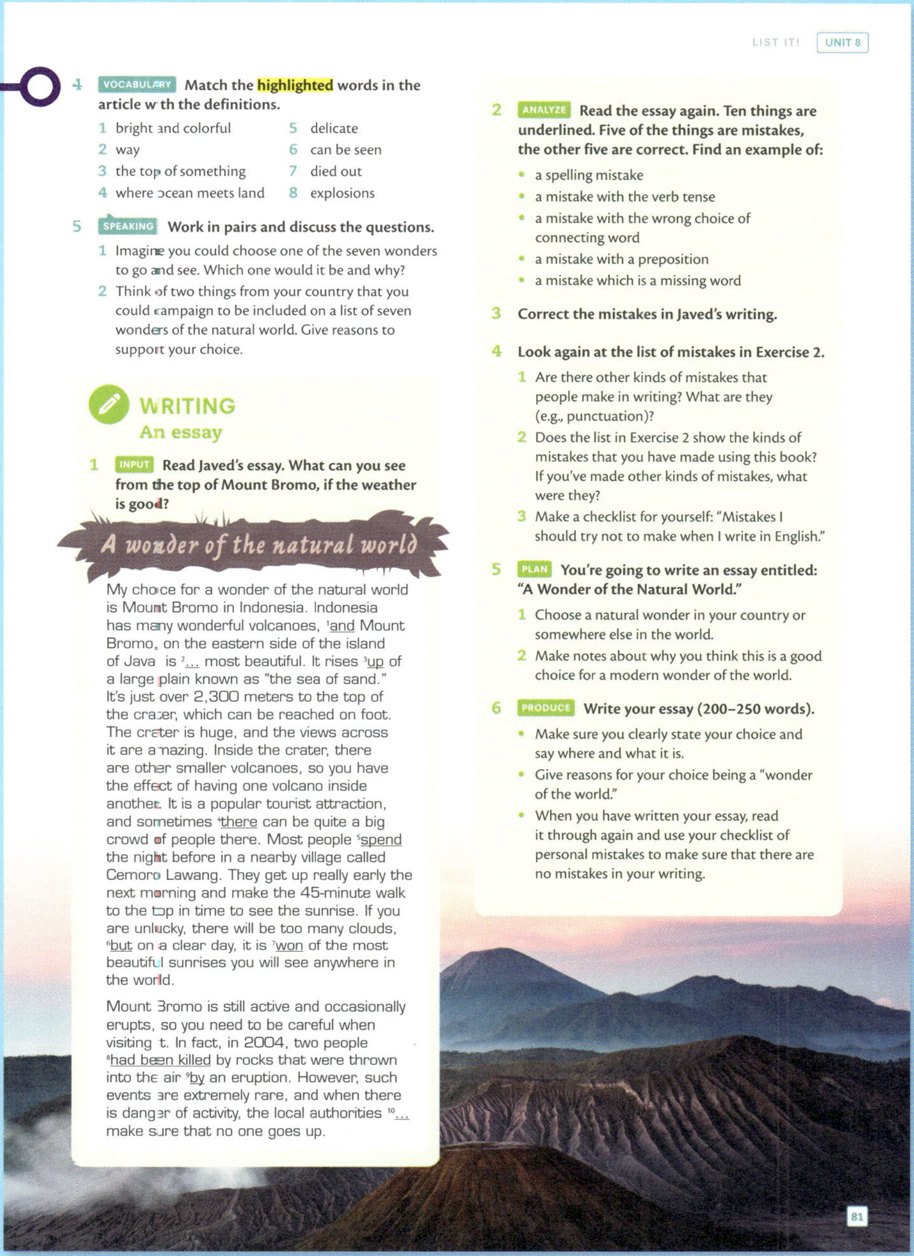

LIST IT! UNIT 8

4 VOCABULARY Match the highlighted words in the article with the definitions.

1 bright and colorful
2 way
3 the top of something
4 where ocean meets land
5 delicate
6 can be seen
7 died out
8 explosions

5 SPEAKING Work in pairs and discuss the questions.

1 Imagine you could choose one of the seven wonders to go and see. Which one would it be and why?
2 Think of two things from your country that you could campaign to be included on a list of seven wonders of the natural world. Give reasons to support your choice.

WRITING
An essay

1 INPUT Read Javed's essay. What can you see from the top of Mount Bromo, if the weather is good?

A wonder of the natural world

My choice for a wonder of the natural world is Mount Bromo in Indonesia. Indonesia has many wonderful volcanoes, [1]and Mount Bromo, on the eastern side of the island of Java is [2]… most beautiful. It rises [3]up of a large plain known as "the sea of sand." It's just over 2,300 meters to the top of the crater, which can be reached on foot. The crater is huge, and the views across it are amazing. Inside the crater, there are other smaller volcanoes, so you have the effect of having one volcano inside another. It is a popular tourist attraction, and sometimes [4]there can be quite a big crowd of people there. Most people [5]spend the night before in a nearby village called Cemoro Lawang. They get up really early the next morning and make the 45-minute walk to the top in time to see the sunrise. If you are unlucky, there will be too many clouds, [6]but on a clear day, it is [7]won of the most beautiful sunrises you will see anywhere in the world.

Mount Bromo is still active and occasionally erupts, so you need to be careful when visiting it. In fact, in 2004, two people [8]had been killed by rocks that were thrown into the air [9]by an eruption. However, such events are extremely rare, and when there is danger of activity, the local authorities [10]… make sure that no one goes up.

2 ANALYZE Read the essay again. Ten things are underlined. Five of the things are mistakes, the other five are correct. Find an example of:

- a spelling mistake
- a mistake with the verb tense
- a mistake with the wrong choice of connecting word
- a mistake with a preposition
- a mistake which is a missing word

3 Correct the mistakes in Javed's writing.

4 Look again at the list of mistakes in Exercise 2.

1 Are there other kinds of mistakes that people make in writing? What are they (e.g., punctuation)?
2 Does the list in Exercise 2 show the kinds of mistakes that you have made using this book? If you've made other kinds of mistakes, what were they?
3 Make a checklist for yourself: "Mistakes I should try not to make when I write in English."

5 PLAN You're going to write an essay entitled: "A Wonder of the Natural World."

1 Choose a natural wonder in your country or somewhere else in the world.
2 Make notes about why you think this is a good choice for a modern wonder of the world.

6 PRODUCE Write your essay (200–250 words).

- Make sure you clearly state your choice and say where and what it is.
- Give reasons for your choice being a "wonder of the world."
- When you have written your essay, read it through again and use your checklist of personal mistakes to make sure that there are no mistakes in your writing.

81

Homework

You could assign the writing task for homework. As a follow-up in the next lesson, ask students to exchange their essays with another student for them to read and make comments and suggestions. Tell them not to correct every error, but to look for the following:

What further information would you like?

In what ways could vocabulary be improved?

Are there any corrections from the checklist that could be made?

Activity idea Mixed-ability

The essay in Exercise 6 could be done as a collaborative writing activity in class with pairs of students writing their essays together.

TH!NK more

Practice Extra
Unit 8 Master it!

Workbook
Developing Writing p77

Tests
Unit, extension, and skills test 8

1 In B2 First Reading and Use of English Part 2, candidates have to fill eight gaps in a text using only one word in each gap. This part of the exam tests candidates' understanding and knowledge of grammatical structures, phrasal verbs, and common phrases.

Encourage your students to do the following when they approach this task:

- Skim the text to find out the topic and general meaning.
- Think of a possible word that makes sense in each gap.
- Check if the word fits the meaning and grammar of the sentence and the whole text.
- Check that the spelling is correct
- Read the completed text again to check that it makes sense.

1 on 2 if 3 by 4 have 5 out 6 an 7 long 8 will

Workbook p71

2 In B2 First Reading and Use of English Part 3, candidates have to read a text containing eight gaps. At the end of some of the lines there is a stem word in capital letters. Candidates need to form an appropriate word from the given stem word to fill each gap. This part of the exam tests understanding of structure, lexis, and more specifically, how prefixes, suffixes, and compounds are used.

Encourage your students to do the following when they approach this task:

- Skim the text to have a sense of the topic and general meaning.
- Read the text more carefully. Think of a possible word which makes sense in each gap.
- Check which part of speech is needed and if the word needs to be singular or plural, positive or negative.
- Check if the word fits the meaning and grammar of the sentence and the whole text.
- Check that the spelling is correct.
- Read the completed text again to check that it makes sense.

1 beneficial 2 central 3 sadness 4 belief 5 dissatisfaction 6 expectations 7 pleasantly 8 addition

Workbook p107

B2 First for Schools

READING AND USE OF ENGLISH

Part 2: Open cloze

→ workbook page 71

1 For questions 1–8, read the text below and think of the word which best fits each gap. Use only one word in each gap. There is an example at the beginning (0).

Reasons to be cheerful

Despite [0] ___*what*___ you may hear on the news, the future is looking bright for British teenagers. According to a government report, the economy is [1] ______ the point of making a dramatic recovery. And [2] ______ the report is correct, those who will benefit most are the young. In fact, it predicts that [3] ______ the time today's 13-year-olds leave school, unemployment will [4] ______ fallen to an all-time low. The report, which was carried [5] ______ by a leading employment agency, predicts that this growth will principally be in IT technology, because of constant technological innovation. It strongly recommends [6] ______ increase in the funding of science and technology and points out that failure to do this will mean that the UK will fall behind its competitors. The message is clear: as [7] ______ as the country continues to take education seriously, tomorrow's school leavers [8] ______ enjoy a prosperous future.

Part 3: Word formation

→ workbook page 107

2 For questions 1–8, read the text below. Use the word given in capitals at the end of some of the lines to form a word that fits in the gap in the same line. There is an example at the beginning (0).

The benefits of being an optimist

It is [0] ___*commonly*___ believed that it's better to be optimistic than	COMMON
pessimistic. But is that always true? Some people think that there are	
times when being pessimistic can be [1] ______ .	BENEFIT
Philosopher Alain de Botton starts with a [2] ______	CENTRE
question: what is it that causes us to be unhappy?	
And he thinks that often our [3] ______ comes from too	SAD
much hope. His [4] ______ is that in the modern age,	BELIEVE
we have learned to hope for so much that we cannot deal with the	
[5] ______ that comes when the things we hope for don't	SATISFY
happen. In this way we get put more and more pressure on ourselves.	
On the other hand, if we start from a pessimistic viewpoint, and	
have negative [6] ______ for the future, we can be	EXPECT
[7] ______ surprised when events turn out better than we'd	PLEASANT
hoped. In [8] ______, we don't feel so bad if things don't	ADD
turn out so well.	

82

1 1 down 2 about 3 up
4 unless 5 worried 6 Suppose
7 apprehensive 8 through
9 forward 10 point

2 1 would be 2 will have 3 are going
4 will 5 would have 6 will be

3 1 It's Diana's birthday next Friday, and she ~~will have~~ is having a party on Saturday.
2 I would have been happy if he ~~would have~~ had come.
3 If I hadn't made so many mistakes, I would ~~win~~ have won the tennis match.
4 This time tomorrow, ~~I'm~~ I'll be lying on a beach in the sun.
5 If I ~~had been~~ was / were taller, I wouldn't need the ladder. / If I had been taller, I wouldn't ~~need~~ have needed the ladder.
6 We must finish cleaning the kitchen before our parents ~~are arriving~~ arrive.

4 1 no; bright 2 provided; a good
3 unless; cheer 4 if; as long

TEST YOURSELF UNITS 7 & 8

VOCABULARY

1 Complete the sentences with the words in the list. There are four extra words.

about | apprehensive | as long as | down | dread | forward | point
succession | suppose | through | unless | up | worked | worried

1 Mike had lots of problems, but he didn't let them get him ________________ . He stayed cheerful.
2 Sally is excited. She's ________________ to go paragliding for the first time.
3 When we were planning the trip, Leo came ________________ with some good ideas.
4 Mom said we couldn't go to the concert ________________ we took a taxi home, because it'd be late.
5 He seems so down all the time. I'm really ________________ about him.
6 ________________ you could go anywhere in the world right now – where would you go?
7 I'm feeling very ________________ about the exam tomorrow. Math is my worst subject.
8 The organizers wanted to run ________________ the arrangements for the president's visit again.
9 I'm tired. I'm really looking ________________ to the school break.
10 Kate was on the ________________ of leaving the house when Mr. Hill called to cancel the meeting. /10

GRAMMAR

2 Complete the sentences with the words in the list. There are two extra words.

are going | don't | will | will be | will have | won't | would be | would have

1 If Juliana had accepted the job offer, she ________________ living in New York now.
2 By the end of the festival, I ________________ seen about 15 movies.
3 Watch out! You ________________ to hit that cyclist!
4 Don't stay on the computer all night, or you ________________ feel exhausted the next day.
5 If I were taller, I ________________ been chosen for the basketball team.
6 While my parents are away on vacation, I ________________ looking after the dog.

3 Find and correct the mistake in each sentence.

1 It's Diana's birthday next Friday, and she will have a party on Saturday.
2 I would have been happy if he would have come.
3 If I hadn't made so many mistakes, I would win the tennis match.
4 This time tomorrow, I'm lying on a beach in the sun.
5 If I had been taller, I wouldn't need the ladder.
6 We must finish cleaning the kitchen before our parents are arriving. /12

FUNCTIONAL LANGUAGE

4 Choose the correct options.

1 A Darn, I have *no* / *every* chance of saving enough money to fly to Mexico.
B Come on, look on the *better* / *bright* side. If you don't go to Mexico, you can buy that new phone you want.
2 A Yes, you can use my computer *unless* / *provided* you finish before six o'clock.
B That's fine! There's *any* / *a good* chance I'll only need it for half an hour.
3 A Dad won't let me watch the game *unless* / *as long as* I clean my room first.
B Oh, *cheer* / *hang* up. Cleaning your room won't take long – I'll help you!
4 A Yes, you can borrow my video camera *if* / *as long* I can use your computer for a couple of hours.
B OK, *as long* / *provided* as you don't spill anything on it. /8

MY SCORE /30
22–30 10–21 0–9

83

The Cambridge Life Competencies Framework

Creative Thinking
Generating ideas
Watch this video for a tip on developing your students' creative thinking skills.
Scan the QR code here.

Reading

Warmer

Draw a line on the board with *I always find it hard to make decisions* on the far right of the line and *I never find it hard to make decisions. I just do it!* on the far left. Ask students to copy the line and to mark on the line to show how much they think before making a decision. Divide the class into small groups and ask students to compare and give examples to explain their response. Come back to this later in the lesson.

▶ 23 Get TH!NKing

Play the video and discuss the question with your class.

9 TAKE CHARGE

OBJECTIVES

FUNCTIONS: asking someone politely to change their behavior

GRAMMAR: *I wish* and *If only; I would prefer to / it if …, It's time, I'd rather / sooner*

VOCABULARY: life's ups and downs; work and education

Get TH!NKING
Watch the video and think: do you find it hard to make decisions?

A

C

B

D

READING

1 **Look at the photos. Match each of the thoughts below to the people in the photos.**

1 *"This is so boring."*

2 *"College life is so exciting, but I could be making money right now."*

3 *"I'd rather spend time with my friends than go to the gym."*

4 *"I have the rest of my life to work."*

2 SPEAKING **Work in pairs. Compare your answers from Exercise 1. Think of one piece of advice you could give each person.**

3 **Read the article quickly. Choose the best alternative title for the article. Discuss your ideas with a partner.**

- Decisions, Decisions, Decisions
- Keep Life Simple
- There's Always a Plan B

4 9.01 **Read and listen to the article again. Match thoughts A–G with paragraphs 1–7. Paragraphs can match with more than one thought.**

A It's better to make a decision in the morning and not at night. ☐
B I wish we didn't have to make these decisions now, while we are still so young. ☐
C You think everyone is enjoying themselves except for you. ☐
D I wish I hadn't put my social life first. ☐
E Pretend it is your friend's problem and not yours. ☐
F It is a hard decision because I'd like both things. ☐
G Things are not going well for you. ☐

5 SPEAKING **Work in pairs and discuss the questions.**

1 Which of the four pieces of advice do you think is the best? Why? Which, if any, do you disagree with?
2 Which piece of advice would be the easiest to follow, and which do you think would be the hardest?

84

1 You may like to put a copy of the four photos up on the board before students open their books. Ask students to work in pairs to describe the pictures before they match them with the thought bubbles, but do not give answers yet.

2 You may like to give an example of your own to get students started on this.
A 2 B 1 C 4 D 3
Students' own answers

3 Set a three-minute time limit to encourage students to read quickly and get the gist in order to choose a title. Clarify that the question is about students' opinions – there are no right or wrong answers. Have a quick vote to see which titles students chose.
Students' own answers

4 9.01 **Check/clarify:** *unfair, major, blame yourself, stepping back, overthink.*
Before students read the article again, get them to read through headings A–G. Ask students to underline the language in the article that helped them choose their answers.
A 7 B 1 C 6 D 3 E 3 F 4 G 5

5 Give students some time to discuss the questions in pairs and then hold a class vote to decide what they feel are the most and the least useful pieces of advice.

Objectives

Functions and speaking Asking someone politely to change their behavior
Grammar *I wish* and *If only; I would prefer to / it if, It's time, I'd rather / sooner*
Vocabulary Life's ups and downs; work and education
Literature *The Remains of the Day*

Resources for this unit

All available online

Videos
- Get **TH!NK**ing: *Do you find it hard to make decisions?*
- Grammar video!: *I would prefer to / it if, It's time, I'd rather / sooner*

Tests
- Unit, extension, and skills test 9
- End of term test 3

Worksheets
- Grammar and vocabulary: Basic, Standard, and Extension Worksheets
- Project: Making decisions
- Communication: Be your own life coach
- Grammar presentation: *I wish* and *If only*
- Literature Worksheets: *Poetry* and *Bill the Bloodhound*
- Get **TH!NK**ing and Grammar video! video Worksheets

6 Check/clarify: *hasty.*
Do the first item with the whole class as an example.

1 Many Brazilians love soccer.
2 A lot of teenagers get up late.
3 It often rains on the weekend.
4 People who live in big cities can be less caring than people who live in the country.
5 Almost everyone loves a box of chocolates as a present.
6 Math is sometimes hard for people who are good at languages.

7 Give some of your own examples before students do the exercise. Monitor and prompt students to keep talking, but as this is a fluency activity, do not interrupt to correct mistakes. While monitoring, write down any common errors to review together at the end. At the end of the exercise, listen to some of the students' ideas and encourage open class discussion.

Homework

Ask students to keep a journal for two or three days, with a record of any hasty conclusions they or members of their family jumped to. Who or what did they make the hasty conclusion about? Did they correct themselves? If not, why not? If this is too sensitive a topic, they could make up some ideas.

Activity idea Extension

Set up a role-play. Divide the class into small groups. Half the group are adults who make hasty conclusions about teenagers. The other half are teenagers who must respond to the conclusions and say why they are not true. This can be done as a mingle with students changing partners every time you clap your hands. This gives the activity more spontaneity and encourages students to think on their feet.

Making difficult decisions

1 We face decisions, big and small, throughout life. It seems unfair that there are so many major ones early on in life: exams, relationships, work, where to live … And young people are often facing these kinds of decisions for the first time, which makes it all the harder.

2 There are two good questions to ask yourself to help you focus: "What is the worst that can happen?" and "What is my Plan B if Plan A doesn't work out?" So, let's look at some difficult decisions that you might have to make.

SCENARIO A

3 You don't want to take that amazing new course or go to a sports club on the other side of town because you'll get home late and that will get in the way of your social life. But later, will you think, "If only I had taken that course"? Imagine you're advising a friend. It will help you to make a rational decision rather than an emotional decision. Learning something new or exercising will do you good, and you may make new friends there, too.

SCENARIO B

4 You have a more complex and less emotional decision to make. Imagine you're saving to buy a car when you are 18. Then, you see the most amazing new video game. You really want to buy it, and you have enough money saved for it. However, if you buy the expensive video game, you will use your savings for the car. You wish you could afford both, but you can't. You have to make a choice. Your heart says one thing, and your head says another, which is tricky. How about making a list of pros and cons for both? Writing things down can be a great help. You could even color code your notes to make sure that you're considering everything.

SCENARIO C

5 Now imagine feeling like you've let everyone down, including yourself, because you failed your exams. If only you had studied harder! But what now? Should you look for a job or repeat your exams? More studying feels like a waste of time, and you're afraid you'll fail again. But now, you might end up with a low-paying, boring job and be stuck in it forever. Think through some of the possible scenarios and then try to change the way you're thinking. For instance, you might end up in a job you weren't expecting to do, but there might be advantages, too. They might even offer training or days off so you can study. If you did go back to studying and really tried your hardest, you're more likely to succeed, having learned from your mistakes.

SCENARIO D

6 You've been feeling down this year, and things just don't seem to be working out the way you'd like them to. The worst thing is, you don't know how to move past it, because you can't stop thinking about it and you blame yourself for it. You keep saying, I wish I was like everyone else – they all seem to be having a great time. Try stepping back and looking at things in a simpler way. Focus on yourself and not on others. Make small decisions, one at a time. Eat breakfast, go for a walk, go to class, separate each action, don't overthink, just do.

7 In all scenarios, it's sensible to sleep on decisions. Think, think again, and then act. And remember, if you've made the wrong decision, there's always Plan B!

Train to TH!NK

Jumping to a hasty conclusion

People sometimes jump to conclusions without any evidence. Take Stefania, for example. She argued with a friend on the way to school. At school, a teacher was not happy with her homework. When she got home, she had an argument with her mom. Five minutes later, she was sitting in her room, thinking, "nobody likes me." But of course, this isn't true. To spot hasty conclusions, watch out for clue words such as all, none, most, many, always, everyone, never, sometimes, usually, hardly ever, *etc.*

6 Read through these hasty conclusions. Why are they hasty? How can you make them true?

1 All Brazilians love soccer.
2 Every teenager gets up late.
3 It always rains on the weekend.
4 People who live in big cities are less caring than people who live in the country.
5 Everyone loves a box of chocolates as a present.
6 Math is hard for people who are good at languages.

7 SPEAKING **Work in groups and tell each other about some of the hasty conclusions you have heard about teenagers.**

TH!NK more

Worksheets
Project Making decisions
Communication Be your own life coach
Get **TH!NK**ing *Do you find it hard to make decisions?*

Critical TH!NKing
Understanding and analyzing ideas and arguments
Identifying and classifying information.

Social Responsibilities
Showing intercultural awareness
Interacting with others across cultures.

Warmer

Write the following on the board: *Things I would like to do in the future. Things I wanted to do in the past, but didn't.* Give students three minutes to copy the headings and to write a few items under each. Students can use their notes for the homework task.

1 Ask students to try to complete the sentences from memory before referring back to the article.
1 was 2 had taken
3 had studied 4 could
RULE: 5 simple past 6 past perfect

2 If you are short on time, assign this exercise for homework.
1 didn't criticize 2 hadn't told
3 hadn't stayed 4 won 5 hadn't given 6 hadn't lied 7 didn't eat / wouldn't eat 8 had invited

3 Monitor to help with any questions, encourage creativity and check that students are using *I wish* and *if only* correctly.

Workbook p82

Get it Right!
wish

Student's Book p125

Get it Right!
wish / if only

Student's Book p126

Pronunciation
Linking: intrusive /w/ and /j/

Student's Book p121

4 Ask students to race to find expressions 1–8 in the article and to underline them. Ask them to try to work out the meaning of the phrases from the context.
1 h 2 f 3 a 4 b 5 g
6 c 7 d 8 e

5 1 get in the way of 2 tricky
3 let (them) down 4 dwell on
5 tried (my) hardest 6 not worked out the way I'd like them to
7 blame 8 go my way

Workbook p84

TH!NK more

Workbook	Worksheets
Grammar p82, Ex.1–4	Grammar Worksheets 9
Pronunciation p120	Grammar presentation: *I wish* and *If only*
Vocabulary p84, Ex.1–2	Vocabulary Worksheets 9

GRAMMAR
I wish and *If only*

1 **Complete the sentences with the correct forms of the verbs in the list. Check in the article on page 85. Then complete the rule.**

be | can | take | study

1 I wish I ______________ like everyone else.
2 If only I ______________ that course.
3 If only you ______________ harder.
4 You wish you ______________ afford both.

RULE: To talk about how we would like things to be different now or in the future, we often use *I wish* or *if only* and the [5] ______________ tense (Sentences 1 and 4).
To talk about regrets we have about things we did in the past, we often use *I wish* or *if only* and the [6] ______________ tense (Sentences 2 and 3).

2 **Complete the sentences using the correct form of the verbs in parentheses.**

1 If only my parents ______________ me all the time. They just don't understand me. (not criticize)
2 If only the teacher ______________ my dad. He wouldn't be so angry with me now. (not tell)
3 I wish I ______________ up all night. I'm so tired now. (not stay)
4 If only my baseball team ______________ occasionally. Why do we always lose? (win)
5 I wish our teacher ______________ us so much homework today. I wanted to go out this evening, and now I can't. (not give)
6 If only I ______________ to Mom and Dad. They wouldn't be so upset with me now. (not lie)
7 I wish my brother ______________ with his mouth open. It's disgusting! (not eat)
8 I wish Annie ______________ me to her party. Lots of my friends were invited. (invite)

3 SPEAKING **Look again at the people on page 84. Write one wish for each person. Read the wish to a partner. Can they guess the photos?**

→ workbook page 82

PRONUNCIATION
Linking: intrusive /w/ and /j/ Go to page 121.

VOCABULARY
Life's ups and downs

4 **Match the expressions with their definitions.**

1 to (not) go your way ☐
2 to blame someone or something ☐
3 to let someone down ☐
4 to try your hardest ☐
5 to get in the way of something ☐
6 to dwell on something ☐
7 to (not) work out the way we'd like them to ☐
8 to be tricky ☐

a to disappoint someone
b to do your best
c to think about something for a long time (often meaning you can't make a decision about it)
d when the results of something are(n't) what we'd hoped for
e to be difficult
f to say something is someone's fault
g to obstruct or prevent something
h when things happen (or don't happen) the way you want them to

5 **Complete the text with the correct form of expressions of Exercise 4.**

OK, so I made a mistake. I shouldn't have been playing soccer in the house. Now the window is broken – that's certainly going to [1] ______________ my plans for a house party this weekend. It is a very [2] ______________ situation. Mom and Dad are going to say I've [3] ______________ them ______________ and that I'm not responsible enough to be left alone in the house. Well, I didn't [4] ______________ it for too long and decided to try to do something to make them proud. I decided to make dinner. I [5] ______________ my ______________, I really did, but things have [6] ______________, and the pie's a bit of a disappointment. I mean I thought it was going to be a beautiful golden brown color like in the book, but mine is black all over. I [7] ______________ the oven. I think it's hotter than it says it is. And then the deep-fryer. I mean how did that catch fire? Some days nothing seems to [8] ______________. Oh well, the table looks nice. Although that candle does look a little close to the curtains. Uh oh! I need some water. Quick!

→ workbook page 84

86

Language note *I wish* and *If only*

Remind students that if you want somebody else to do something, use *I wish* + subject + *would (not)* + infinitive, e.g., *I wish my brother would help me with my homework.*

Activity idea Extension

In pairs, ask students to take turns making a statement to which their partner responds with *I wish …* For example:

A: You don't have any money.
B: I wish I hadn't spent all my money.

Activity idea Mixed-ability

In Exercise 5, stronger students can try to complete the text without looking back at Exercise 4 and then refer to it to check. Weaker students can look back at Exercise 4 to complete the text.

6 Before students do the exercise, with books closed, ask: *Do all 19-year-olds go to college? If not, what do they do?* Give students time to discuss the questions in pairs, then listen to some of their ideas as a class. With books open, look at the photos and discuss what possible different life choices after school are shown. Some suggestions might be *further study, an apprenticeship*, or *work*, but accept all plausible answers.

7 **9.04**
a two-year degree program

8 **9.04** This exercise is closely modeled on Listening Part 4 of the Cambridge English: First exam. Ask students to read the questions and answer as many as they can based on memory and/or general knowledge. During feedback, encourage students to explain why they chose their answers and why other answers are not possible.
1 C 2 B 3 C 4 B 5 B

9 Before students do the task, ask them to cover the eight definitions and work with a partner to try to define the words. During feedback, ask students to mark where they think the main stress is on each word. Say the words for students to check and repeat.
1 b 2 d 3 h 4 e 5 g
6 f 7 a 8 c

10 Before students do the exercise, encourage them to read for a general understanding by asking: *What would the writer like to do after finishing school?* Give them two minutes to find the answer, ignoring the blanks (go to college, or have a year off).
1 work experience
2 high-school graduates
3 degree 4 graduate
5 two-year degree program
6 career advisor 7 life experience
8 launch my own business

Workbook p84

LISTENING

6 SPEAKING **Work in pairs. Look at the photos of three 19-year-olds and discuss the questions.**

1 What do they do?
2 How are their lives similar and how are they different?
3 How do you imagine they feel about their future?

7 9.04 **Listen to a radio show. Which of the three life choices in the photos in Exercise 6 does Jo, a career advisor, recommend that Alex pursues next year?**

8 9.04 **Listen again and choose the correct answer A, B, or C.**

1 What kind of job do approximately a third of students get?
A one that requires more training
B one that is boring
C one that doesn't require a degree

2 Why is college no longer a very tempting option?
A It takes longer to get a degree.
B It is very expensive.
C It is difficult to get a job after college.

3 What does Jo tell Alex?
A He should definitely go to college.
B He should follow his parents' advice.
C There is an alternative way to get a degree.

4 What do half of today's young people want to do?
A work in business management
B set up their own company
C get a degree in business studies at a college

5 What is Jo's advice to Gemma about setting up a business?
A to organize events for her customers
B to understand her customers and their likes and dislikes
C to follow her customers on Instagram and Twitter

VOCABULARY
Work and education

9 **Match the words with the definitions.**

1 work experience ☐
2 a high-school graduate ☐
3 career advisor ☐
4 two-year degree program ☐
5 a degree ☐
6 a college graduate ☐
7 life experience ☐
8 launch your own business ☐

a practical wisdom gained from living
b experience of having a job
c set up or start a company
d someone who has recently finished high school
e training while you work
f someone who has recently finished a college or university program
g a qualification you get from a college or university
h someone who gives advice about work and further studies

10 **Complete the paragraph using the words from Exercise 9. You can only use each word or phrase once.**

I won't finish school for another two years, but I'm already a bit worried about what to do. It would be good to get some [1] ________________, but there aren't a lot of good jobs for [2] ________________, so I think I'll go to college and try to get a [3] ________________. It'll be much easier to find work as a [4] ________________. I'm not sure what I want to study yet, and I've heard that an [5] ________________ might be a good option, as it involves on-the-job-training, so I'm going to see a [6] ________________ to get some advice about all of this. Anyway, I'm not sure I want to go straight into a career. It would be nice to have a year off and get some [7] ________________. Or maybe I'll see if I can [8] ________________. I have lots of ideas, and I think it's a great way to make lots of money – if you do it right.

→ workbook page 84

SPEAKING

11 **Read the sentences and write A (agree) or D (disagree). Discuss the statements in small groups.**

1 It's a good idea to get work experience when you're still in school. ☐
2 All students should see a career advisor before they finish school. ☐
3 College isn't for everyone. ☐
4 It's important to get a good degree to be successful in life. ☐
5 Doing a degree program is too expensive. ☐

11 Encourage students to justify their opinions and challenge each other's.

Homework
Ask students to write six sentences of their own using *I wish* and *if only* – one related to how they'd like things to be different in the present and one relating to the past. If students made notes during the Warmer, they could use these to help them.

Activity idea Mixed-ability
To simplify Exercise 8 for weaker students, for each question, tell them one option which isn't correct.

TH!NK more

Workbook
Listening p88, Ex.1–3
Vocabulary p84, Ex.3–5
Vocabulary Extra p85, Ex.1–3

Worksheets
Vocabulary Worksheets 9

Warmer

Write the following questions on the board: *What magazines do you read? Have you ever seen a multiple-choice quiz in a magazine? What was it about? What are typical features of a magazine quiz? Who does them? How much do you believe the answers?* Students discuss their answers with a partner. Listen to some of their answers with the whole class.

1. 🔊 **9.05 Check/clarify:** *gossiping, practical advice, cafeteria.* Students should answer individually.
2. Encourage them to give reasons for their choices. Ask: *How similar were your answers?*
3. As feedback, hold a vote to find out who agrees with their description and why.
4. Allow students six to eight minutes to prepare their questions. Ask some of the pairs to read out their questions for the rest of the class to answer.

Activity idea Extension

Elicit suggestions about why or in what circumstances *c* might not be the best answer to number 1. In pairs, students discuss instances where *a* or *b* might be better responses to the remaining questions. They could also suggest alternative responses. Follow up with a class discussion on alternative best responses, encouraging students to give reasons to support their opinions.

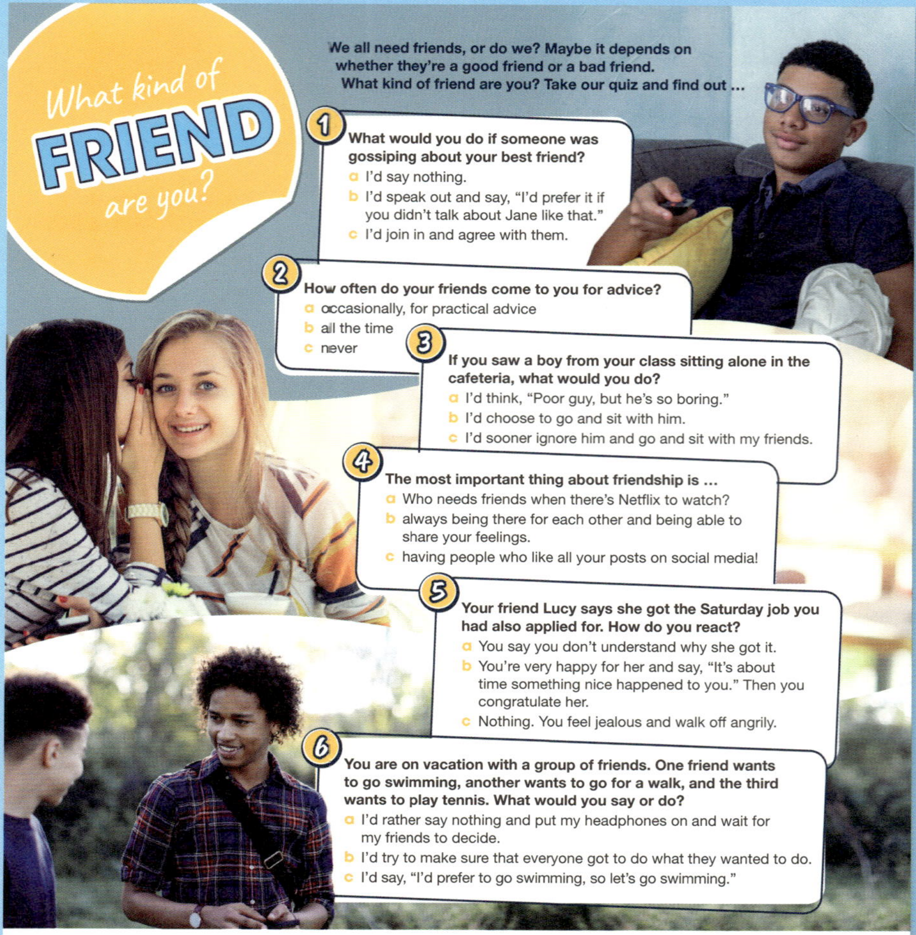

What kind of FRIEND are you?

We all need friends, or do we? Maybe it depends on whether they're a good friend or a bad friend. What kind of friend are you? Take our quiz and find out …

1 What would you do if someone was gossiping about your best friend?
a I'd say nothing.
b I'd speak out and say, "I'd prefer it if you didn't talk about Jane like that."
c I'd join in and agree with them.

2 How often do your friends come to you for advice?
a occasionally, for practical advice
b all the time
c never

3 If you saw a boy from your class sitting alone in the cafeteria, what would you do?
a I'd think, "Poor guy, but he's so boring."
b I'd choose to go and sit with him.
c I'd sooner ignore him and go and sit with my friends.

4 The most important thing about friendship is …
a Who needs friends when there's Netflix to watch?
b always being there for each other and being able to share your feelings.
c having people who like all your posts on social media!

5 Your friend Lucy says she got the Saturday job you had also applied for. How do you react?
a You say you don't understand why she got it.
b You're very happy for her and say, "It's about time something nice happened to you." Then you congratulate her.
c Nothing. You feel jealous and walk off angrily.

6 You are on vacation with a group of friends. One friend wants to go swimming, another wants to go for a walk, and the third wants to play tennis. What would you say or do?
a I'd rather say nothing and put my headphones on and wait for my friends to decide.
b I'd try to make sure that everyone got to do what they wanted to do.
c I'd say, "I'd prefer to go swimming, so let's go swimming."

READING

1 🔊 9.05 Read and listen to the quiz from a teen magazine and choose your answers.
2 SPEAKING Compare your answers in pairs.
3 Read the key. Do you agree with the advice? Do you think this is a fair description of you? Why (not)?
4 WRITING Work in pairs. Write three more questions for the quiz.

Mostly a's
You're not such a good friend because you're a bit of a loner. You don't like drama, and you are not a very supportive friend.

Mostly b's
You're very kind and considerate. In fact, you're the kind of friend everyone needs.

Mostly c's
Oof. You really aren't a very good friend at all. You are really pretty selfish. You always put yourself before your friends.

88

TH!NK more

Workbook
Reading p86, Ex.1–4

Grammar; Functions; Speaking

▶ 24 Grammar video!
I would prefer to / it if, It's time, I'd rather / sooner

5 Ask students to work with a partner to choose the correct options before checking answers in the quiz.
a say b ignore c happened
d didn't e to go
RULE: 1 c 2 a, b 3 e 4 d

6 If you are short on time, assign this exercise for homework.
1 played 2 didn't tell 3 went
4 didn't invite 5 eat 6 leave
7 learned 8 to stay in

Workbook p83

7 Ask students to speculate about what is happening in the picture. During feedback, say each phrase with polite intonation for students to repeat.
1 didn't use 2 didn't eat 3 put

8 Allow students six to eight minutes to prepare their dialogues. Monitor to make sure all students are on task. Encourage them to use the key language.

9 **Check/clarify:** *diplomatic, offend.* Describe a situation in which you would need to be diplomatic, e.g., your friend has had a bad haircut. Ask: *What do you say to your friend?* Elicit ideas. Monitor and prompt students to keep talking, but as this is a fluency activity, do not interrupt to correct mistakes. While monitoring, write down any common errors to review together at the end.

Homework
Ask students to keep a journal for two or three days with a record of times when they had to be diplomatic. If this is too sensitive a topic, they could make up some ideas.

GRAMMAR Grammar video ▶ 24
I would prefer to / it if, It's time, I'd rather / sooner

5 **Choose the correct option. Check your answers in the quiz on page 88. Then read the rule and match each point to the five sentences.**

a I'd rather *say / said* nothing.
b I'd sooner *ignore / ignored* him and sit with my friends.
c It's about time something nice *happen / happened* to you.
d I'd prefer it if you *don't / didn't* talk about Jane like that.
e I'd prefer *to go / going* swimming.

> **RULE:** To say we think someone should do something, we can use:
> *It's time* + subject + simple past sentence [1]__
> To talk about our own preference, we can use:
> *I'd rather / sooner* + base form sentence [2]__
> *I'd prefer* + infinitive sentence [3]__
> If the subject of the second verb is different from the subject of *'d rather / sooner / prefer*, we use:
> *I'd rather / sooner* + subject + past tense
> *I'd prefer it if* + subject + past tense sentence [4]__

6 **Complete the sentences with the correct form of one of the verbs in the list.**

eat | go | learn | leave | not invite | not tell | play | stay in

1 I'm not really excited about listening to opera in the car. I'd rather you ________ something else.
2 It's a secret. I'd prefer it if you ________ anyone else.
3 I'm tired. It's about time I ________ to bed.
4 I don't really like Tim. I'd sooner you ________ him to the party.
5 We had Italian food last week. I'd rather ________ at the Chinese restaurant tonight.
6 I don't want to miss the train. I'd sooner ________ the house a little earlier.
7 Can't you make yourself something to eat? It really is time you ________ to cook.
8 I don't really want to go out. I'd prefer ________ tonight.

→ workbook page 83

FUNCTIONS
Asking someone politely to change their behavior

7 **Look at the picture and complete the conversation with a suitable verb.**

Mom Josh. I'd rather you [1]________ your phone at the table.
Josh Sorry, Mom. I won't be a minute.
Mom And I'd sooner you [2]________ with your mouth open.
Josh I'll try not to.
Mom And I'd prefer it if you [3]________ your feet on the floor, not on the table.
Josh OK, Mom. Is there anything I can do?
Mom Yes, you can improve your table manners!

8 WRITING **Use the picture below and the expressions in Exercise 7 to write a short conversation between the passenger and the driver.**

SPEAKING

It's not always good to be entirely truthful, especially when you could hurt someone's feelings or cause an argument. In these cases, it's better to try to find a way of being "diplomatic" and to say something that won't offend anyone.

9 **Work in pairs. Decide on the best way to handle each of these situations. What would you say in each one?**

1 Your mom and dad have made plans for a family visit to your grandparents this Saturday. They forgot that you have a school soccer game that day.
2 You're at a friend's house having dinner. His father serves you fish. You really don't like fish.
3 Your friend wants to join the school volleyball team, but you know they aren't good enough to play for the team.
4 Your teacher asks the class to come up with ideas for a school trip. A friend comes up with an idea, but you don't think it's a good idea, and you think you have a better one.

Activity idea Extension
Write the pairs of phrases below on the board. Ask students to work individually and to choose which option from each pair they'd prefer to do, then think of a reason for their choice. They should express their choice using *I would prefer/rather/sooner*. Put students into pairs for them to compare preferences.

go to Tokyo	go swimming	eat spaghetti
go to London	play tennis	eat salad

Activity idea Extension
In Exercise 8, ask students to practice their conversations in pairs. Focus on using appropriate intonation and also encourage students to be polite in their responses. Invite one or two pairs to perform their conversations for the class.

TH!NK more

Practice Extra
Unit 9 Practice it!

Workbook
Grammar p83, Ex.5–7

Worksheets
Grammar Worksheets 9
Grammar video! *I would prefer to / it if, It's time, I'd rather / sooner*

Warmer

Ask students to make a list of five sad novels or movies and to discuss what happens in them in pairs or small groups. Elicit a few ideas in open class.

1 **Check/clarify:** *butler, pier.*

2 Tell students not to worry about difficult vocabulary at this stage as this will be covered later. Set a three-minute time limit to encourage students to read quickly and to focus on the question.

b

3 🔊 **9.06**

1 LD 2 S 3 M 4 LD 5 M and S

Culture notes

Kazuo Ishiguro (November 8, 1954) was born in Japan to Japanese parents. His family moved to England in 1960. He has written seven novels. His second novel, *An Artist of the Floating World*, won the 1986 Whitbread Book of the Year Award. He received the 1989 Man Booker Prize for his third novel *The Remains of the Day*, which was made into a movie, starring Anthony Hopkins and Emma Thompson.

The Remains of the Day was published in 1989 to critical acclaim. The novel recounts the memories of a butler who has spent most of his working life in the employment of an upper-class English family. The butler tells stories of his working life and of his love for a housekeeper who is now married with children. The movie adaptation received eight Oscar nominations, but won no awards.

Literature

1 **Look at the photos and read the introduction to the extract. Do you think you would like to read the book?**

The Remains of the Day by Kazuo Ishiguro

Stevens has spent his life as a butler, working for Lord Darlington. He is now an elderly man. At the end of the book, he finds himself sitting alone on a bench, on a pier by the ocean. A stranger begins to talk to him, and Stevens starts to tell the man about his life and his feelings about Lord Darlington.

"You must have been very attached to this Lord whatever. And it's three years since he passed away, you say? I can see you were very attached to him, mate."

"Lord Darlington wasn't a bad man. He wasn't a bad man at all. And at least he had the privilege of being able to say at the end of his life that he made his own mistakes. His lordship was a courageous man. He chose a certain path in life, it proved to be a misguided one, but there, he chose it, he can say that at least. As for myself, I can't even claim that. You see, I trusted. I trusted in his lordship's wisdom. All those years I served him, I trusted I was doing something worthwhile. I can't even say I made my own mistakes. Really – one has to ask oneself – what dignity is there in that?"

"Now, look, mate, I'm not sure I follow everything you're saying. But if you ask me, your attitude's all wrong, see? Don't keep looking back all the time, you're bound to get depressed. And all right, you can't do your job as well as you used to. But it's the same for all of us, see? We've all got to put our feet up at some point. Look at me. Been happy as a lark since the day I retired. All right, so neither of us are exactly in our first flush of youth, but you've got to keep looking forward."

And I believe it was then that he said:

"You've got to enjoy yourself. The evening's the best part of the day. You've done your day's work. Now you can put your feet up and enjoy it. That's how I look at it. Ask anybody, they'll all tell you. The evening's the best part of the day." […]

It is now some twenty minutes since the man left, but I have remained here on this bench to await the event that has just taken place – namely, the switching on of the pier lights. As I say, the happiness with which the pleasure-seekers gathering on this pier greeted this small event would tend to vouch for the correctness of my companion's words; for a great many people, the evening is the most enjoyable part of the day. Perhaps, then, there is something to his advice that I should cease looking back so much, that I should adopt a more positive outlook and try to make the best of whatever remains of my day. After all, what can we ever gain in forever looking back and blaming ourselves if our lives have not turned out quite as we might have wished? […] What is the point in worrying oneself too much about what one could or could not have done to control the course one's life took? Surely it is enough that the likes of you and me at least try to make our small contribution count for something true and worthy. And if some of us are prepared to sacrifice much in life in order to pursue such aspirations, surely that is in itself, whatever the outcome, cause for pride and contentment.

2 **Read the extract quickly and decide what seems to confirm the theory that the evening is the best part of the day.**

a the switching on of the pier lights
b the fact that the people on the pier are enjoying themselves
c knowing that your day's work is done

3 🔊 9.06 **Read and listen to the extract again. Who do these sentences refer to? Write LD (Lord Darlington), S (Stevens), or M (the man).**

1 He made his own mistakes in life. ☐
2 He didn't choose his own path in life. ☐
3 He is happy in his retirement. ☐
4 He died three years ago. ☐
5 He is no longer a young man. ☐

90

Writing

4 1 dignity 2 contribution 3 aspirations 4 passed away 5 butler 6 pursue 7 misguided 8 worthwhile

5 Monitor, but do not interrupt as this is a fluency activity.

1 Write the following on the board: *Is it important to get work experience before going to college? What sort of work experience can teenagers get?* Ask students to discuss in pairs and then discuss in open class.
1 She agrees with the statement and questions/challenges the reader to think about their own life.
2 Graduates are feeling the pressure because they are looking for the same jobs at the same time. Mature students with some experience may be far more attractive employees.

2 She asks questions in the first paragraph, and then uses the imperative in the final paragraph. This makes it feel like the essay addresses you personally, which makes you think about it more.

3–4 Give students an example on the board based on the model article. Ask: *How would Eve's plan have looked?* Divide the class into small groups to share ideas before writing individually.

5 If you are short on time, assign this exercise for homework.

Homework

If you are short on time, students can do Writing Exercise 5 for homework. If you have done this in class, ask students to exchange their articles with another student for them to read and to give feedback on content and structure. Students could check if the article uses the same structure as the template. They should also decide which the most/least interesting part of the article is.

4 VOCABULARY **Match the highlighted words in the extract with the definitions.**

1 the quality of a person that makes him or her deserving of respect
2 the part someone plays to make something successful
3 things you hope to accomplish
4 died
5 the male head of a household staff
6 try to achieve something
7 wrong because of bad judgment or false information
8 meaningful

5 SPEAKING **Work in pairs and discuss the questions.**

1 Does Stevens have a positive or negative outlook? Give examples.
2 What can he do to change his outlook? Do you have any advice for him?
3 Is there anything you look back on and regret? Why?

WRITING
A magazine article

1 INPUT **Read Eve's article and answer the questions.**

1 Does she agree with the statement?
2 What are her main arguments to support her position?

Students should try to get some work experience before they go to college

Do you really want to spend the rest of your life either studying or working? Wouldn't you like the chance to do a little more with your life and find out what it is you really want?

Most young people who have decided to go to a university or college go straight from school. A few people may take a gap year to see the world or earn some money, but how many take five or six years, or even longer, before they go on to study more?

These days, young people are led to believe that the pressures in the labor market are so high that they cannot afford to waste any time doing things that won't directly help them get a good job. They feel that if they haven't graduated by the age of 22, they will be too old to be successful.

This is simply not true. Graduates are feeling the pressure precisely because so many of them are looking for the same jobs at the same time, and there's very little for an employer to choose between them.

Anyone who is brave enough to wait a few years before they go to college will – as long as they have used their time well – be far more attractive as an employee. Their extra experience of life will mean they can offer companies so much more than any fresh-faced 22-year-old can. Besides, the fact that they've taken time to decide exactly what it is they wanted to do, shows that now they really want to do it.

So go on. Be brave. Delay. Go out and find out a little more about life. After all, you have the rest of your life to work.

2 ANALYZE **Look at the first and last paragraphs of the article. What technique does Eve use in each one? What effect does this have on the reader?**

3 PLAN **Choose one of the topics below. What is your position? What are your main arguments to support your position? Write notes.**

- Doing a degree program is a waste of money.
- The government should pay for all students to study at a college or university.

My position	
Argument 1	
Argument 2	
Argument 3	

4 **You're going to write an article for your school magazine about the topic you chose in Exercise 3. Think carefully about how to start and finish it.**

1 Think of two direct questions you could use to start the article.
2 Think of two imperatives to conclude your article.

5 PRODUCE **Write your article (200–250 words).**

Language note Similes, metaphors, and expressions

put your feet up – to relax, especially by sitting with your feet off the ground

as happy as a lark – extremely happy. A lark is a bird that is known for its beautiful singing.

in the first flush of youth/success/freedom – to be at the start of something (youth, success, freedom, etc.) at the time when something is new and exciting

Activity idea
Peer correction

Ask students to exchange their articles with another pair for them to evaluate on the basis of **content** (How interesting were the ideas?); **organization** (Did each paragraph include a distinct idea?); **communicative purpose** (Were you convinced by it?); and **language** (Were questions and imperatives used correctly?).

TH!NK more

Practice Extra
Unit 9 Master it!

Workbook
Developing Writing p87

Tests
Unit, extension, and skills test 9
End of term test 3

Warmer

Tell students about an interesting piece of news you have heard recently and then ask: *What's the most interesting news you've heard this week?* Make it clear that this could be news from a friend/family or from a newspaper/TV. Ask students to discuss in pairs.

▶ 25 Get TH!NKing

Play the video and discuss the question with your class.

1 Before students discuss, you could write the following on the board for them to match with the photos: *newspaper, TV, letter, online, internet, email, social media,* and *text message,* plus a few extra words: *postcard, magazine, radio,* and *phone.*

2 Students will speak more if they disagree, so you could tell one of each pair to say that the opinions are advantages, while their partner says they are disadvantages.

3 Make groups of four for pairs to compare their answers.

4 **🔊 10.01 Check/clarify:** *trustworthy.*
Set a two-minute time limit to encourage students to read the article quickly and to focus on gist understanding.
1 We start believing something if we read or hear it enough times.
2 Our knowledge is a strong factor in what we believe or disbelieve.
3 Fake news spreads much more quickly than real news.
4 Truthful tweets take six times longer to spread than fake ones.

5 1C 2A 3F 4G 5D 6B
(extra phrase: E)

10 UNBELIEVABLE NEWS

OBJECTIVES

FUNCTIONS: making a point; introducing news

GRAMMAR: reported speech (review); reported questions and requests

VOCABULARY: sharing news; reporting verbs

Get TH!NKING
Watch the video and think: is gossiping always bad?

A B C D E

READING

1 Look at the photos. How are these people getting or giving news? Can you think of any other ways of giving or getting news?

2 SPEAKING Work in pairs. Match these opinions with the photos in Exercise 1. They can go with more than one photo. Is each one an advantage or a disadvantage?
1 It takes ages.
2 You can read what you want, when you want.
3 You can share information easily.
4 You can trust the information you get.
5 You have to be careful what you read and write.
6 You can't always get reception.

3 SPEAKING With your partner, think of more advantages and disadvantages related to each of the different ways of sharing news in Exercise 1. Compare with another pair.

4 🔊 10.01 Read and listen to the magazine article. What are the four main research results about "fake news"?

5 Read the article again. Six phrases have been removed. Complete the article with the correct phrase A–G. There is one extra phrase.
A the research results are a little disturbing
B unless the research confirms it
C that they are not fooled by it
D assessing whether something is true or not
E because you saw it one place
F showing that it spreads way faster than the truth
G they touch people's hopes and fears

6 SPEAKING Work in pairs and discuss the questions.
1 What most interested/surprised/concerned you in the article?
2 Do you always believe what people say on social media? Do you check important information that comes to you through social media? How?
3 Should people be worried about "fake news"? Why (not)?

92

6 Give students time to think about their answers prior to their discussions.

Culture note

Twitter is a microblogging and social networking service on which users post messages known as "tweets." These are short (maximum 280-character) messages which registered users can read and resend. As of 2021, Twitter has more than 353 million monthly active users.

Objectives

Functions and speaking Making a point; introducing news
Grammar Reported speech (review); reported questions and requests
Vocabulary Sharing news; reporting verbs; **WordWise:** Expressions with *way*
Life Competencies Laughing at yourself

Resources for this unit

All available online

Videos
- Get **TH!NK**ing: *Is gossiping always bad?*
- Grammar video!: Reported questions and requests
- Vlog: Laughing at yourself

Tests
- Unit, extension, and skills test 10

Worksheets
- Grammar and vocabulary: Basic, Standard, and Extension Worksheets
- Project: Fake or real?
- Communication: Spreading the news
- Grammar presentation: Reported speech
- Literature Worksheets: *The Time Machine*
- Get **TH!NK**ing, Grammar video!, and Life Lessons video Worksheets

7 **Check/clarify:** *impartial* (point out that we would normally use *biased* as the opposite rather than *partial*); *suit their own agenda*.
Ask students to read the introductory paragraph and answer these questions: *What is the doctor's agenda/reason for making this statement? What about the politician's?* Give students time to look at the jobs and the statements.
Check/clarify: *abbreviations, helplessness, spread, efficiently, effective.*
Encourage students to give reasons for their choices.
a3 b1 c4 d2 e5

Homework

Ask students to fact-check a well-known fake story and produce evidence as to why it is fake, based on their checklist.

Activity idea Extension

In groups, ask students to brainstorm ideas and come up with a checklist for assessing the credibility of a news article. Help by giving the following ideas if they are struggling:

- *Who reported the story? Do they say they are a news company or journalist?*
- *Does the webpage look normal? Does the web address look normal?*
- *Is the writing formal, with correct spelling and punctuation?*
- *Does the headline match what the report is actually about?*
- *Are the facts supported by evidence (such as quotes, images, or statistics)? Are there quotes from real sources? Does the story use a real photograph that shows the event, with a caption and a credit?*

Choose an age-appropriate item from one of the main news stories of the day that everyone can investigate. In pairs, ask students to follow their checklist and investigate the story. Compare findings and the effectiveness of the checklist.

UNBELIEVABLE NEWS UNIT 10

The rise in the last decade or so of "fake news" has also led to increased research into what it is, how it spreads, and what its effects are.

Many people believe that they can spot "fake news" and [1] ________________ . One of the most worrying research discoveries is that this is not really true. Many studies have shown that we become more willing to believe something if we read or hear it enough times – and that includes things that we start off not believing. Back in 2015, some researchers in the US gave students statements which they were told were very likely to be false. When the statements were repeated several times, however, many students became uncertain. The lead researcher said that repeating something often enough made some students begin to think it was true. The "good news" from the research is that our knowledge is still a strong factor in determining what we believe or disbelieve. However, since there's so much fake news going around these days, [2] ________________ .

What adds to the feeling that we should be worried about fake news is further research [3] ________________ . A ten-year study with three million Twitter users followed the spread of over 120,000 Twitter stories (a "story" was a tweet that made a statement about something outside the user's own life – the statements were fact-checked by independent organizations). A researcher said that they had found some frightening things – especially the fact that truthful tweets took six times longer to spread to other Twitter users than fake ones.

It's clear that people who produce fake news know that people love headlines and statements that shock, that disgust, that are scary. This is one reason why people are more likely to share them – [4] ________________ . One researcher said that people often share something, not because they necessarily thought it was true, but because it would make friends and people in their network react strongly.

But surely, now, after about two decades of the internet and social media, people are much better at [5] ________________ ? Apparently not. Recently, American high-school students were given a photo of a damaged flower. The researchers told them it was a flower from near a damaged nuclear power plant, but did not tell them what the source of the photo was. Forty percent of the students thought the photo was good evidence about the state of the area around the nuclear plant, even though they had no idea where it came from.

So if you want to get real, not fake, news, check where it comes from. If it's a shared piece, who's sharing it with you and why? If it's from a website, have a look at the stories on the site – if they're all shocking or scandalous stories, be careful. And generally, never accept something's true [6] ________________ : see if you can find it in other – trustworthy – places, too.

Train to TH!NK

Recognizing the source of a statement

It's good to get an idea of the background of the person who says or writes something. Are they an impartial expert or are they someone who wants to change your opinion to fit their own agenda? For example, this statement about a flu epidemic, "Patients can already spread the virus a day before they feel sick themselves," is more likely to have come from a doctor than from a politician. On the other hand, "We have to stop people who are carrying the virus from getting into the country" is more likely to come from a politician. By knowing who is providing a piece of information, you're better able to decide how much importance to give it and whether you can really trust what they say.

7 SPEAKING **Read these statements about social media. Match them with the person you think said them. Which do you think is the least trustworthy? Why? Discuss in pairs.**

1 a psychologist | **2** a politician | **3** a linguist
4 an IT expert | **5** an advertising executive

a We have noticed that people use fewer abbreviations on Twitter than in texting, and tweets seem to show more creative word use.
b Young people sometimes make things public that they regret later. This can cause emotional problems as well as a feeling of helplessness.
c We're trying to develop a system that will help people to upload multiple photos faster.
d We use social media in order to spread our key messages more efficiently.
e Twitter – quite simply the most effective way to reach our target consumers.

93

Activity idea Extension

You may like to do more work on understanding and navigating the news. *The Guardian* newspaper has a lot of useful resources and lesson plans in its NewsWise unit of work section, from spotting fake news and identifying fact and opinion to producing balanced reports and analyzing bias.

Project Look Sharp also has free media literacy lessons.

There are several fact-checking websites that you might like to explore with your students such as Full Fact and Snopes (although make sure you have the legitimate ones – there are now fake websites made to look like some of these).

Critical TH!NKing
Understanding and analyzing ideas and arguments
Identifying and classifying information.

TH!NK more

Worksheets
Project Fake or real?
Communication Spreading the news
Get **TH!NK**ing *Is gossiping always bad?*

Warmer

In pairs, ask half the class to make a list of sections in a newspaper and the other half a list of types of items on a news broadcast. Start with a couple of examples, e.g., *business*, *sports*. Create a list on the board. Make sure *international/foreign news* is on the list for later in the lesson.

1 Discuss any changes between direct and indirect speech.
1 It's a flower from near a damaged nuclear power plant.
2 We have found some frightening things. / We found some frightening things.
3 Often, people don't share something because they necessarily think it's true.
RULE: 4 past continuous
5 past perfect 6 past perfect
7 would 8 could 9 then 10 that
11 that day 12 the next day
13 the day before 14 that night

2 1 He said he'd be in town later that evening
2 They said they'd had a great time at my house the day before
3 She said she was missing me, and she couldn't wait for the next day
4 John's mom said John had missed his train, and he was going to be late
5 Becca said she was seeing Eva that night and would tell her when she saw her
6 Lucas said the baby was due that day

3 Monitor and encourage students to use a variety of tenses in their messages.

Workbook p90

Get it Right!
Reported speech

Student's Book p126

GRAMMAR
Reported speech (review)

1 **Read these examples of reported speech and rewrite them in direct speech. Then complete the rule.**

1 The researchers told them it was a flower from near a damaged nuclear power plant.
2 A researcher said that they had found some frightening things.
3 One researcher said that people often share something, not because they necessarily thought it was true, but because it would make friends and people in their network react strongly.

RULE: When we report what someone has said we often change the verb tense.

simple present	→	*simple past*
present continuous	→	[4] ______
present perfect	→	[5] ______
simple past	→	[6] ______
will	→	[7] ______
can	→	[8] ______

We also change certain other words.

here	→	there
now	→	[9] ______
this	→	[10] ______
today	→	[11] ______
tomorrow	→	[12] ______
yesterday	→	[13] ______
tonight	→	[14] ______

Don't forget to change any pronouns so that they agree with any subject changes, e.g., *my* → *his/her/their*.

2 **Report these messages that you've received.**

1 I'll be in town later this evening.
He ______.
2 We had a great time at your house yesterday. Thanks.
They ______.
3 I'm missing you. I can't wait for tomorrow!
She ______.
4 John missed his train. He's going to be late.
John's mom ______.
5 I'm seeing Eva tonight. I'll tell her when I see her.
Becca ______.
6 The baby's due today!
Lucas ______.

3 WRITING **Write four messages about your day and plans for the future for a partner to report.**

→ workbook page 90

VOCABULARY
Sharing news

4 **Match the phrases with their meanings.**

1 I'll let you know as soon as I hear anything. ☐
2 If you see Ling, can you pass along the message? ☐
3 An old friend of mine got in touch with me on Instagram the other day. ☐
4 It's so easy to keep in touch with all your friends these days. ☐
5 When you tell her, break the news gently. ☐
6 His followers retweeted his message more than 10,000 times. ☐
7 I'll drop you a line when we get there. ☐
8 Give me a call when you get home. ☐

a tell him
b stay in contact
c sent on / forwarded (via Twitter)
d send you a message
e call me
f tell you
g made contact
h tell her what happened

5 **Complete the questions with suitable verbs.**

1 If you're going to be home late, how do you ______ your parents know?
2 How do you prefer to ______ good or bad news to other people?
3 How do you ______ in touch with your friends from elementary school?
4 How do you ______ in touch with old friends who you're not currently in contact with?
5 What's the best way to ______ bad news?
6 Have you ever ______ someone else's message on Twitter?
7 When was the last time you ______ someone a line and what did you say?
8 Do you always ______ your best friend a call on their birthday? I usually send them a text.

6 SPEAKING **Work in pairs and discuss the questions from Exercise 5.**

→ workbook page 92

PRONUNCIATION
Linking: omission of the /h/ sound
Go to page 121.

4 During feedback, clarify that the object pronouns (*you*, *me*, etc.) can be replaced by other objects or names and give some examples, e.g., *I'll let him know. Break the news* is used when giving bad news. We *get in touch with* people we haven't contacted for some time.
1 f 2 a 3 g 4 b 5 h 6 c 7 d 8 e

5 1 let 2 break / pass along 3 keep / stay 4 get 5 break 6 retweeted 7 dropped 8 give

6 Prompt students to keep talking, but do not interrupt to correct mistakes.

Workbook p92

Pronunciation
Linking: omission of the /h/ sound

Student's Book p121

THINK more

Workbook
Grammar p90, Ex.1–4
Vocabulary p92, Ex.1–2
Pronunciation p121

Worksheets
Grammar Worksheets 10
Grammar presentation: Reported speech
Vocabulary Worksheets 10

Language note Reported speech (review)

The past perfect and *would* do not change in reported speech. We do not change the other words in the list if the time or place of speaking remains the same. For example, "I will finish it today" is reported as "He said he would finish it today" if it is being reported on the same day as the original direct speech.

7 Write some of the students' ideas on the board, but do not comment at this stage.

8 🔊 **10.04**
1 T 2 F (Her work is dangerous some of the time, but not all the time.) 3 F (She couldn't imagine working in an office.) 4 T 5 T 6 T

9 🔊 **10.04** Ask students to answer as many of the questions as they can from memory before you play the audio to check.
1 get close to the action 2 She's helped by drivers, translators, and people who arrange interviews. 3 She has to train. 4 running ten kilometers with a heavy pack on her back
5 Yes. She says it's a fantastic job.

10 Discuss any interesting points as a class. Ask: *Do you think foreign correspondents are necessary? Why (not)?*

▶ 26 Grammar video! Reported questions and requests

11 Remind students they may need to change pronouns and add auxiliaries when transforming sentences from indirect to direct speech.
1 question 2 request 3 question
a your job dangerous
b you run ten kilometers
c do you do that/your job
RULE: 4 yes/no questions
5 wh- questions 6 requests

12 1 One of the students asked her which newspaper she worked for.
2 One of the students asked her where she was going next.
3 One of the students asked her if/whether she had ever been scared in her job.
4 One of the students asked her if/whether her job was well-paid.
5 One of the students asked her who her boss was.

Workbook p91

13 Before students do the task, elicit names of famous people that students would like to meet.

14 Allow students six to eight minutes to prepare their interviews. Encourage students to get into character and give detailed answers.

LISTENING

7 SPEAKING **You are going to listen to an interview with Janice Gordon, a foreign correspondent. What do you think her job involves? Compare your ideas in pairs.**

8 🔊 10.04 **Janice is being interviewed about her work by a group of students at a career fair. Listen to the interview and mark the sentences T (true) or F (false).**

1 A lot of the time, Janice is not at home. ☐
2 Her work is always dangerous. ☐
3 Sometimes, she would prefer to be a reporter in an office. ☐
4 In some cases, it's important that she's physically fit. ☐
5 Not everyone trusts that her reports are an accurate reflection of what happened. ☐
6 She thinks she is lucky to have her job. ☐

9 🔊 10.04 **Listen again and answer the questions.**

1 What does a correspondent have to do to "get a really good story"?
2 How does Janice rely on the help of local people in her work?
3 What does she sometimes have to do in order to get fit?
4 She mentions one thing she didn't enjoy. What was it?
5 Does she recommend her job? Why (not)?

10 SPEAKING **Work in pairs and discuss the questions.**

1 Would you like to be a foreign correspondent? Why (not)?
2 Which place(s) do you think would be the most difficult for Janice to go to right now? Why?

GRAMMAR
Grammar video ▶ 26
Reported questions and requests

11 **Here are three sentences from the interview with Janice. Which are questions and which are requests? Write the direct questions and complete the rule with *requests*, *yes/no questions*, or *wh- questions*.**

1 You asked me if my job was dangerous.
2 He asked me to run ten kilometers.
3 Just now, someone asked me why I do [this job].

a "Is ______________________ ?"
b "Can ______________________ , please?"
c "Why ______________________ ?"

RULE: In reported [4] ______________________ , we use *if* or *whether* and the same word order as in a statement.
In reported [5] ______________________ , we use the question word and the same word order as in a statement. We do not use auxiliaries.
In reported [6] ______________________ , we use *asked* + person + infinitive.

12 **Here are more questions the students asked Janice. Write them as reported speech. Be careful with the word order.**

0 "When did you start this job?"
One of the students asked her when she had started that job.
1 "Which newspaper do you work for?"
2 "Where are you going next?"
3 "Have you ever been scared in your job?"
4 "Is your job well-paid?"
5 "Who is your boss?"

→ workbook page 91

SPEAKING

13 **Work in groups of four. Imagine you are journalists. You are going to interview some well-known people you have never met before. Agree together on four people. For each person, write four or five questions to ask them.**

14 **Act out the interviews. One of you is the famous person. The others ask questions and write down the answers.**

15 **Each group reports to the class about the group's interviews.**

We talked to Harry Styles.

We asked him when he started singing. He said he had always sung …

WRITING
A magazine article

16 **Write a magazine article about one of your interviews. Make sure you do these things. Write 200–250 words.**

- Give a short introduction to the person.
- Say why you chose to interview this person.
- Include reported questions and statements.

15 Give students time to change the sentences into reported speech.

16 Students can do the preparation in class and complete the writing at home. Clarify that students should use reported questions and statements.

Homework

Ask students to report the questions from Exercises 9 and 10, starting with *My partner asked me …*

Activity idea Extension

Ask students to write three questions and two requests about next weekend. Students work in pairs and take turns asking a question or making a request. Their partner then puts the question or statement into reported speech.

TH!NK more

Practice Extra
Unit 10 Practice it!

Workbook
Listening p96, Ex.1–2
Grammar p91, Ex.5–8
Developing Writing p95

Worksheets
Grammar Worksheets 10
Grammar video! Reported questions and requests

Warmer

Write the following on the board: *Which celebrities do you see most photos of? Where do you see the photos? What are the celebrities doing in the photos? Where do the photos come from?* Divide the class into pairs or small groups for students to discuss the questions. Listen to some of their ideas in open class as feedback.

1 Before students open their books, check/clarify *paparazzo/ paparazzi* and write it on the board. Give students just two minutes to discuss before hearing from some of the students.

2 **10.05 Check/clarify:** *dishonest, editor, ashamed, invaded, publicity, ethical.* Ask students to underline the language in the article that helped them choose their answers.
1 E 2 C 3 F 4 A 6 D 7 B (extra title: 5)

3 **Check/clarify:** *sued.* Clarify that even though the information in some sentences may be true, they should put *doesn't say* if the information does not appear in the text.
1 F (He worked with a local photographer, then for a newspaper, and that's how he learned.)
2 T 3 F (No, he says you have to be technically good at taking photographs from a distance.)
4 F (He says they don't, because they like publicity.) 5 T 6 DS

4 Monitor to help with any difficulties, but do not interrupt as this is a fluency activity.

The Secret Paparazzo

We continue our "secret professional" series with an offering from an anonymous paparazzo.

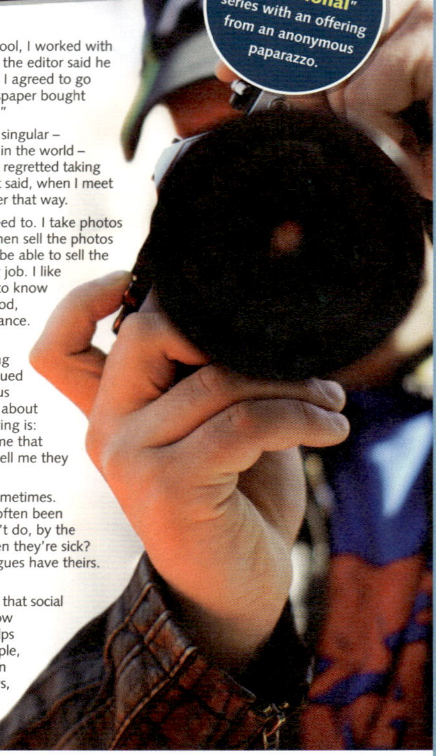

A I've always loved cameras and photographs. After I finished school, I worked with a local photographer, then a bit later for a newspaper. One day, the editor said he wanted some photos of a famous person who lived nearby, and I agreed to go and get them. I got some good photos, and a big national newspaper bought them, too. I thought, "OK, this is how I can make good money."

B That's how my life as a paparazzo started. (By the way, that's the singular – "paparazzi" is plural.) Paparazzi are not the most popular people in the world – especially after what happened to Princess Diana – but I've never regretted taking up the profession. And I've never denied being a paparazzo. That said, when I meet people, I just say I'm a photographer and leave it at that. It's easier that way.

C I never apologize for doing what I do, because I don't think I need to. I take photos of famous people (often without them knowing, it's true) and then sell the photos to magazines. If people didn't buy those magazines, I wouldn't be able to sell the photos. I provide a service, and I'm not ashamed of it. I love my job. I like the money, but I also like the challenge, the fact that you have to know where the celebrity's going to be. You have to be technically good, too – not everyone can take a good photo of someone at a distance.

D People have accused me of doing an unpleasant thing – but I honestly don't think it is. I take photos and sell them. Am I telling lies? Stealing? Attacking people? No, and in fact I've always argued that celebrities don't mind as much as you might think. A famous person once admitted to me that they often leaked information about where they were so the paparazzi could get photos. The old saying is: "All publicity is good publicity," and they know it. You can tell me that celebrities don't want their private lives invaded, but you can't tell me they don't love publicity.

E I can understand, though, why paparazzi get some bad press sometimes. Not all of my colleagues are as ethical as they could be. We've often been criticized for taking photos of young children – something I don't do, by the way – and rightly so. And should we take photos of people when they're sick? When they're at a funeral? I have my views; some of my colleagues have theirs. But then we're just like bankers or lawyers, aren't we?

F The profession is different now. A colleague warned me years ago that social media would change things, and she was right. I use it a lot. I follow celebrities' posts, and they help me find out where they are. It helps with legal issues, too. It used to be much harder for us! For example, celebrity X finds a photo of themselves somewhere and posts it on social media – only, the photo was taken by a paparazzo who says, "That photo's mine, and you need permission to use it! So, be prepared to pay for it, or you can't use it!"

READING

1 SPEAKING **You are going to read an article by a member of the paparazzi. What do you know about paparazzi? Tell a partner.**

2 10.05 **Read and listen to the article. Match paragraphs A–F with titles 1–7. There is one extra title you do not need to use.**

1 Morally OK? ☐
2 Why I love it ☐
3 Things have changed ☐
4 Starting out ☐
5 The future of paparazzi ☐
6 It isn't dishonest ☐
7 No regrets ☐

3 **Read the article again and mark the sentences T (true), F (false), or DS (doesn't say). Then correct the false sentences.**

1 He learned about cameras and photography at school. ☐
2 He avoids telling people he's a paparazzo. ☐
3 He thinks anyone could do what he does. ☐
4 He believes that celebrities hate being photographed. ☐
5 He doesn't take photos of sick children. ☐
6 He has sued celebrities who used his photographs. ☐

4 SPEAKING **Work in pairs and discuss the questions.**

1 What questions would you ask the paparazzo if you met him?
2 Do you know of any controversial events concerning paparazzi?

96

Culture note

Diana, Princess of Wales (born Diana Frances Spencer) was a member of the British royal family. She became well-known with her engagement to Prince Charles, the eldest son of Queen Elizabeth II, but their fifteen-year marriage ended in 1996 with a very public divorce. Throughout her life, Diana was renowned for her unconventional approach to charity work, centering on children and young people, cancer and AIDS patients, and people affected by mental illness. She also campaigned for the removal of landmines. Diana died in a car crash in Paris in 1997, while trying to escape paparazzi. Her death led to an unprecedented public outpouring of grief, and her televised funeral was watched by millions around the world.

TH!NK more

Workbook
Reading p94, Ex.1–4

5 Before students complete the rule, write sentence 5 on the board. Elicit that the word that follows *accuse* is an object, and the object is followed by a preposition (*of*) and a gerund (*being*).
1 agreed 2 regretted 3 denied
4 apologize 5 accused 6 argued
7 admitted 8 criticized 9 warned
RULE: 10 admit 11 warn 12 agree
13 deny 14 criticize 15 accuse

6 1 He/She admitted taking the/my sandwich.
2 He/She denied stealing the money.
3 He/She accused me of telling Jim his/her secret.
4 He/She warned me not to touch the dog.
5 He/She regretted saying those things.
6 He/She apologized for breaking the/my phone.
7 He/She criticized me for driving too fast/so badly.
8 He/She agreed to take me to the party.
9 He/She argued that it was important to always tell the truth.

Workbook p92

7 10.06
Editor 2 wants to run the story.

8 10.06
Editor 2 wants to run the story because their readers like controversy. Editor 1 doesn't want to run it because the woman is not really famous now, so it's not news.
Students' own answers

9 10.06 During feedback, point out the strong stress on *really*, *no way*, *exactly*, and *definitely* to emphasise the speaker's opinion.
1 There's no way this is a news story.
2 I'm really against running this story.
3 My mind's made up.
4 This is exactly the kind of story we want.
5 We're definitely going with this story.
6 And that's final.

10 1 way too 2 all the way
3 have it both ways 4 In a way
5 One way or another 6 no way

11 Encourage students to look at the six phrases in the sentences in Exercise 10 and try to deduce meaning from context before completing this exercise.
a one way or another b way too
c no way d all the way
e have it both ways f in a way

Workbook p92

VOCABULARY
Reporting verbs

5 Complete the examples with verbs from the list, using the article to help you. Then complete the rule with the verbs.

accused | admitted | agreed | apologize | argued | criticized | denied | regretted | warned

1 He ______________ to go and take some photos for the newspaper.
2 He has never ______________ deciding to become a paparazzo.
3 He's never ______________ being a paparazzo.
4 He doesn't ______________ for doing what he does.
5 People have ______________ him of being part of an unpleasant profession.
6 He's always ______________ that celebrities aren't too worried about being photographed.
7 A celebrity ______________ that they wanted the paparazzi to know where they were.
8 Paparazzi have been ______________ for taking photographs of children.
9 A friend of his ______________ him that things were going to change.

RULE: Different reporting verbs are followed by different verb patterns. Here are some of the more common ones.

pattern	examples
+ (*that*) + clause	argue / [10] ______________
+ [person] + (*that*) – clause	[11] ______________
+ infinitive	[12] ______________
+ gerund	regret / [13] ______________
+ *for* + gerund	apologize / [14] ______________
+ [person] + *of* + gerund	[15] ______________

6 Report these sentences using the verbs in parentheses.

1 It was me. I took your sandwich. (admit)
2 I didn't do it. I didn't steal the money. (deny)
3 You did it. You told Jim my secret! (accuse)
4 Don't touch that dog. It bites! (warn)
5 I wish I hadn't said those things. I really do. (regret)
6 I'm really sorry I broke your phone. (apologize)
7 You drive so badly. Can't you slow down? (criticize)
8 Sure, I'll take you to the party. (agree)
9 I think it's important to always tell the truth. (argue)

→ workbook page 92

FUNCTIONS
Making a point

7 10.06 Read the news story below. Listen to two different newspaper editors saying what they think about it. Which editor, 1 or 2, wants to run the story?

A woman, who was once on a reality TV show and has kept her name in the papers ever since by saying outrageous things, has caused controversy again by tweeting something rude about the president.

8 10.06 Listen again. How do the editors justify their views? Who do you agree with more?

9 10.06 Put the words in order to make sentences. Then listen again and check.

1 news / way / There's / story / this / is / no / a
2 story / really / running / against / I'm / this
3 up / My / made / mind's
4 want / is / exactly / of / This / the / kind / story / we
5 definitely / We're / with / story / going / this
6 final / that's / And

WordWise: Expressions with *way*

10 Look at these sentences from the unit so far. Complete them with phrases from the list.

all the way | have it both ways | in a way | no way | one way or another | way too

1 I think it's ______________ easy to make that kind of criticism.
2 I'm with you ______________ on that, Pete.
3 You can't ______________, you know.
4 ______________, it's the same thing as inventing stuff, isn't it?
5 ______________, we're talking about dishonesty.
6 There's ______________ this is a news story.

11 Match the phrases in Exercise 10 with these meanings.

a partly ☐
b very/really ☐
c no possibility ☐
d completely/as much as possible ☐
e benefit from two completely opposite things ☐
f from one perspective ☐

→ workbook page 92

97

Homework

Ask students to look back through the unit to find more expressions with *way*, put them in a sentence, and provide a definition. They can bring them to the next lesson for partners to read and match. They could also include any other expressions with *way* that they might know, or you could give them these to research, e.g., *in a bad way, in a big way, it cuts both ways, the only way to go, way off (base), that's the way the cookie crumbles, way out, Way to go!*

Activity idea Extension

Ask students to write questions using the expressions from Exercise 10 in pairs. Put pairs together to make groups of four to ask and answer their questions.

TH!NK more

Workbook
Vocabulary p92, Ex.3
Vocabulary Extra p93, Ex.1–3
WordWise p92, Ex.4

Worksheets
Vocabulary Worksheets 10

1 🔊 **10.07** Tell students to cover the dialogue and discuss the question in pairs before listening to check their answers.
Someone is being interviewed on camera.

2 🔊 **10.07 Check/clarify:** *current affairs.*
1 because he didn't know a new shopping center was planned
2 that Luke didn't know about the shopping center
3 about things like climate change and world politics

3 Encourage students to use the language from the dialogue when giving their answers.

4 During feedback, say the sentences for students to repeat. Drill sentences to ensure correct pronunciation.
1 on earth 2 at least
3 don't bother 4 or something
5 in any case
6 none of your business

5 Allow students six to eight minutes to prepare their role-plays. Monitor to make sure all students are on task.

6 As an alternative, you could ask students to cover the Key Language box and try to guess which words complete the sentences. During feedback, drill the phrases, not being afraid to exaggerate slightly, and encourage students to use wide-ranging intonation as they say them.
1 Guess 2 know 3 believe
4 heard

7 Monitor to help with vocabulary and ideas. Encourage students to use exaggerated intonation to express surprise.

DEVELOPING SPEAKING

1 🔊 10.07 **Look at the photo. What's happening? Read and listen to check.**

Bea: Hi Luke. You're late. What kept you?
Luke: It's none of your business, Bea.
Bea: Wow! You're in a bad mood. Did you get some bad news or something?
Luke: No, not bad news, but you're right; I'm not in a good mood. I'm embarrassed and angry at myself. You'll never guess what happened to me. I got stopped in the street, and that local TV news station was there with a camera crew and an interviewer. She said, "So, what do you think about the plans for the new shopping center?" And all I could say was, "What new shopping center?" Everyone laughed. It was so embarrassing. My big chance to be on TV and I blew it!
Bea: Ha, ha, ha! That's so funny! "What new shopping center?" Hilarious! Oh come on, Luke – you have to try to see the funny side of it.
Luke: I guess, but it's not easy when you've made a fool of yourself.
Bea: Oh, don't worry. No one knows about it – except me, of course! But how on earth do you not know about the shopping center plans? Don't you follow the news?
Luke: I do. Well, I look at things on Twitter sometimes, at least. But I've been so busy lately, what with exams and everything. In any case, why haven't we been discussing it at school? There's a current affairs lesson every week, isn't there?
Bea: Those lessons aren't about local stuff, you know that. We talk about climate change and world politics, not new shopping centers. But I can tell you all about it if you like.
Luke: Don't bother. It's too late now. I mean, they're not going to ask me again, are they?
Bea: No, but you might want to know what's going on in your own hometown.

2 🔊 10.07 **Read and listen to the dialogue again and answer the questions.**
1 Why was Luke embarrassed by his answer?
2 What is Bea surprised about?
3 What are the current affairs lessons at their school about?

3 SPEAKING **Discuss the statements in pairs. Do you agree with them?**
1 What happened to Luke was really embarrassing.
2 Teenagers should follow local news as well as global news.

Phrases for fluency

4 **Find the underlined expressions in the dialogue and use them to complete the sentences.**
1 Why ______ did you dye your hair green?
2 Can you lend me $20? Or $5, ______?
3 There's no Wi-Fi in the camp where we're going, so ______ writing me any emails.
4 I'm bored. Let's go swimming ______.
5 I don't really want to go to the party, and ______, I haven't been invited.
6 Stop asking me questions! It's ______!

5 SPEAKING **Work in pairs. Student A is someone who thinks it's important to follow the news. Student B doesn't watch or listen to the news. Write a short conversation and then act it out.**

FUNCTIONS
Introducing news

KEY LANGUAGE
You'll never believe … Did you know that …?
Have you heard (about) …? Guess what?

6 **Complete each sentence with one word.**
1 ______ what? I got 90 percent on the test!
2 Did you ______ that Maura's moving to Australia?
3 You'll never ______ what happened to me yesterday.
4 Have you ______ about Mike? He broke his leg.

7 SPEAKING **Work in pairs. Think of three surprising pieces of news (real or invented). Then follow the instructions below. Use the phrases in the Key Language box.**
- A tells some news to B using a phrase above.
- B replies.
- Then switch roles.

Activity idea Extension

In Exercise 5, if students have access to a recording device (their cell phones, for example), they could record their conversation and play it back to check their own pronunciation and intonation. They can then repeat the exercise and listen for improvements.

Warmer

Write *laughing at yourself* on the board and elicit what it might mean. Encourage students to try and clarify its meaning through examples or explanation, rather than through a translation. Ask students to read the introductory paragraph to check their ideas. Elicit examples of people laughing at themselves in Unit 10.

▶ 27 Life Lessons: Laughing at yourself

1 **▶ 27** Ask students to compare their ideas with a partner.
The bear says, "I don't know. I guess I just always had them." The joke is that "pause" and "paws" are pronounced the same.

2 **▶ 27** Ask students to try to answer the questions from memory before watching the video again to check.
1 to show that he can laugh at himself / his own jokes 2 his mother 3 He hasn't understood what "laughing at yourself" really means.

3–4 Give students two minutes to read the stories and to put them in order. Encourage students not to focus on every word.

5 Tell students that there are no wrong answers.

6 Give students time to reflect and make notes. Monitor and help with vocabulary as necessary.

7 Monitor and prompt students to keep talking, but as this is a fluency activity, do not interrupt to correct mistakes. While monitoring, write down any common errors, focusing on relative pronouns, to review together at the end.

Homework

Ask students to interview a family member about a time when they have laughed at themselves. As a follow-up, students can present this to the class in the next lesson.

Emotional Development
Understanding emotions
Discusses what makes them feel different emotions.

LIFE COMPETENCIES

We all do or say foolish things sometimes, and people laugh at us – a healthy reaction to such situations is to laugh at yourself, too. Laughing at yourself can help you stop feeling embarrassed.

1 ▶ 27 **Watch the vlog. What is the punchline to Will's final joke?**

2 ▶ 27 **Watch the vlog again and answer the questions.**
1 Why does Will start by telling jokes?
2 Who calls him halfway through the vlog?
3 What "mistake" did Will make?

3 **Read the stories. Imagine you are the person in each one. Put the situations in order of how embarrassing you think they are.**

A One day, I got on an empty bus with my headphones on. I closed my eyes and started singing along. Suddenly someone tapped me on the shoulder, and a lady said, "Can you sing more quietly, please?" There were about five other people on the bus now, all laughing or smiling. I felt really stupid! MAGGIE

B I was in a clothes store with my family. I found a pair of jeans, and I went over to where my dad was paying for some things. I put the jeans down and said: "Can you pay for these, too?" The man turned round, smiled, and said: "Well, I'm very sorry, but no!" Of course, it wasn't my dad. I looked away and saw my sister, laughing like crazy. CARLOS

C My dad bought a new car and drove to the supermarket. After doing the shopping, he pressed the key fob to open the car – nothing. He put the key in the lock – nothing. Dad got angry and kicked the tire of the car. Just then a woman came up and asked him what he was doing. Dad looked at her and then at the license plate – it wasn't his car. ANDREA

4 SPEAKING **Work in pairs. Compare your ideas from Exercise 3.**

5 SPEAKING **Read the responses below. With your partner, choose the best response for each person, A, B, or C. Say why you think it's the best one.**

Maggie
A get off the bus as quickly as possible
B smile and say, "Sorry, I'm a terrible singer!"
C put your headphones back on and start listening again without singing

Carlos
A tell your sister to stop laughing at you
B turn around and walk away
C smile and say, "Well, I feel really silly, I'm sorry!"

Andrea's dad
A laugh and tell the woman you've made a mistake
B run to your car and drive away quickly
C say you thought there was a problem with the tire on her car and were trying to help

Me and my world

6 **Think of a time when you did or said something foolish or embarrassing and make notes.**
- What happened?
- Why was it embarrassing?
- How did you react? Do you think it would have been better if you had reacted differently?

7 SPEAKING **Work in pairs and tell your partner about the situation. Then discuss these questions.**
1 Why might laughing at yourself be the best response?
2 Do you know anyone who is good at laughing at their own behavior or embarrassment?
3 How do you usually react when you have done or said something embarrassing?

TIPS FOR LAUGHING AT YOURSELF

- If you do something embarrassing and people laugh, remember that they're laughing at what happened more than laughing at you.
- Try to smile first – this helps you deal with the embarrassment.
- If you can laugh at something you've done, remember: other people will then be laughing with you, not at you.

Activity idea Extension

Ask students to imagine they are reporters and to write about the situation that their partner talks about in Exercise 7. Remind them to use reported speech and encourage them to refer to the reporting verbs on page 97. Their partner can read it and check for accuracy of both details and language.

TH!NK more

Practice Extra
Unit 10 Master it!

Worksheets
Life Lessons: Laughing at yourself

Tests
Unit, extension, and skills test 10

1 10.08 In B2 First for Schools Listening Part 4, candidates have to listen to a longer interview and answer seven three-option multiple-choice questions. This part of the exam tests understanding of the detailed meaning of the text, attitudes, and opinions.

Encourage your students to do the following when they approach this task:

- Read and listen to the instructions carefully.
- Read all the questions and options and think about the context.
- On the first listening, try to understand the gist and choose the best option.
- On the second listening, check that the answers are correct and focus on detailed understanding of the attitudes or opinions.

1 B 2 A 3 B 4 C
5 B 6 C 7 B

Workbook p89

2 In B2 First Writing Part 2, candidates are given a choice of four tasks, one of which is to write a review of about 160 words. For the review, they are given a short text and must write a response. This part of the exam tests the candidates' ability to write well-organized texts with a real communicative purpose and a good range of language.

Encourage your students to do the following when they approach this task:

- Candidates should read all the tasks and consider the topic and the language that is needed in each before choosing the task that best suits them.
- For the chosen task, identify what is required, who it is for, and what kind of information is needed.
- Make a plan, referring closely to the question.
- Look for opportunities to develop ideas and show a range of language.

Workbook p25

B2 First for Schools

LISTENING
Part 4: Multiple choice → workbook page 89

1 10.08 **You will hear an interview with a teenager called Diana Hollingsworth about the 'Good News Project'. For questions 1–7, choose the best answer (A, B or C).**

1 Diana's main reason for starting the project was that she
A was fed up of hearing only bad news.
B was determined to stop people complaining about the news.
C wanted to change the way her school magazine reported stories.

2 What did the local newspaper initially agree to do?
A to see if it would be popular with their readers
B to teach her about journalism
C to publish five stories each week

3 What does Diana say she enjoys about preparing stories for the radio station?
A finding unusual ideas
B making people laugh
C hearing her voice on the radio

4 What does Diana find most difficult about the project?
A co-ordinating her team of reporters
B deciding which stories to give to the newspaper and radio station
C checking that the stories are true

5 What should someone do if they have a story for the project?
A write it up and send it in
B be sure that it is recent
C give it to one of the pupils at Diana's school

6 How has Diana's opinion of the world changed?
A She has realised there are more good people than bad people.
B She now feels more optimistic about the future.
C She has become confident she can make a difference.

7 What are Diana's favourite kind of good news stories about?
A funny things that pets do
B helping people in the local community
C people overcoming serious problems

WRITING
Part 2: A review → workbook page 25

2 **You have seen this advert on a website for teenagers. Write your review in 140–190 words in an appropriate style.**

Reviews wanted

We are looking for reviews of a news website that you use regularly. Tell us why you use it and what type of information you can find on it. Is the website easy to use? Who would you recommend it to and why?
The best reviews will be published next month.

100

1 1 degree 2 way 3 drop
4 apologize 5 regretted 6 career
7 let 8 admitted 9 live 10 break

2 1 hadn't 2 had 3 would
4 didn't 5 was 6 wouldn't

3 1 I'd sooner ~~had~~ have a quick salad and then go back to work.
2 I wish he ~~doesn't give~~ hadn't given me so many presents – it was so embarrassing.
3 Correct
4 Correct
5 I'd rather you ~~come~~ came over to my house, if that's possible.
6 He accused me ~~to break~~ of breaking his camera.

4 1 A believe; B to join
2 A rather; B prefer
3 A didn't; B to sit
4 A heard; B know

TEST YOURSELF UNITS 9 & 10

VOCABULARY

1 Complete the sentences with the words in the list. There are four extra words.

admitted | apologize | break | career | degree | drop
front | give | let | live | living | pass | regretted | way

1 Maddy wants to work in finance, so she is studying for an economics ________________ at college.
2 The show was kind of interesting, but I thought it was ________________ too long.
3 As soon as you have any news, please ________________ me a line.
4 Mrs. Davies' car broke down, so she had to ________________ to the class for being late.
5 The book was terrible – I really ________________ buying it.
6 My ________________ advisor did a good job in helping me choose my major.
7 I don't know when we'll be arriving, but I'll ________________ you know as soon as I can.
8 When I confronted her, she ________________ losing the earrings I had lent her.
9 The hotel looked great on the website. But unfortunately, it didn't ________________ up to our expectations.
10 It's such bad news, and I don't know how to ________________ it to him.

/10

GRAMMAR

2 Complete the sentences with the words in the list. There are two extra words.

didn't | had | hadn't | was | wasn't | will | would | wouldn't

1 I feel sick. If only I ________________ eaten so much!
2 Davide said he ________________ seen Haruki the day before.
3 Elena asked Mike if he ________________ be at the basketball game that afternoon.
4 I'm sure I'd understand if only they ________________ speak so fast.
5 My friend asked me why I ________________ looking so down.
6 She called to say that unfortunately, she ________________ be able to attend the meeting.

3 Find mistakes in four of the sentences and correct them.

1 I'd sooner had a quick salad and then go back to work.
2 I wish he doesn't give me so many presents – it was so embarrassing.
3 Nell said the movie at the movie theater was excellent.
4 They announced that the president would make a speech before tomorrow's ceremony.
5 I'd rather you come over to my house, if that's possible.
6 He accused me to break his camera.

/12

FUNCTIONAL LANGUAGE

4 Choose the correct options.

1 A You'll never *know / believe* what Harry said to me.
B What? Did he ask you *to join / joining* his band?
2 A I'd *rather / prefer* you played that music more quietly.
B Well, I'd *rather / prefer* it if you went to your own room.
3 A I'd rather you *didn't / don't* hang around in the house all day.
B But I don't want to go out! I'd prefer *to sit / I sat* and watch TV here.
4 A Have you *heard / seen* about Jack's accident?
B Yes, I have, but do you *hear / know* what really happened?

/8

MY SCORE /30
22–30 | 10–21 | 0–9

101

The Cambridge Life Competencies Framework

Social Responsibilities
Showing intercultural awareness
Watch this video for a tip on developing your students' awareness of social responsibilities.
Scan the QR code here.

Warmer

Write the words *solar system* on the board. In pairs, ask students to make a list of as many of the planets in our solar system as they can. Give them four or five minutes for this and then elicit a few ideas. Ask students if they can put them in order from the sun (Mercury, Venus, Earth, Mars, Jupiter, Saturn, Uranus, and Neptune).

▶ 28 Get TH!NKing

Play the video and discuss the question with your class.

1–2 Give pairs two or three minutes to discuss. Write some of their ideas on the board.

3 Tell students not to try to understand every word, but to focus on answering the questions and on getting a general understanding of the article.

4 **11.01 Check/clarify:** *expedition, radiation, cross-contamination, planetary, all-time high, collaboration, at the forefront, isolation, protective.* Before students read the article again, get them to read the questions through.
1 because Mars was closer to Earth 2 because it's too much money for one country to spend 3 It can be reused. 4 They could have a range of activities. 5 It prepares astronauts for conditions on Mars. 6 using protective covering and faster rockets 7 If we go to Mars, we will bring microbes from Earth, and they might be catastrophic for Mars. 8 because we might do the same damage to Mars that we are doing to Earth

5 Encourage students to express themselves in English and to use any vocabulary they have learned from the article.

11 SHOOT FOR THE STARS

OBJECTIVES

FUNCTIONS: sympathizing about past situations

GRAMMAR: speculating (past, present, and future); cause and effect linkers

VOCABULARY: space idioms; adjectives commonly used to describe movies

Get TH!NKING ▶28

Watch the video and think: why are people so fascinated by space?

A

B

READING

1 **What can you see in the photos? What do you know about Mars?**

2 SPEAKING **Work in pairs and discuss the questions.**
1 Do you think humans will land on Mars in the next 30 years?
2 Why might a Mars landing be a good thing, and why might it be a bad thing?

3 **Read the article quickly. Does it mention any of your opinions? Do you agree with the opinions in the article?**

4 11.01 **Read and listen to the article again and answer the questions.**
1 Why would 2018 have been a good year to try to get to Mars?
2 Why will any Mars expedition probably involve more than one country?
3 How is Falcon 9 different from other rockets?
4 What could be done to help stop crew members getting bored?
5 How is the Hi-Seas project helping research?
6 What ideas are being explored to help overcome the problem of radiation?
7 What is cross-contamination and how might it affect Mars?
8 Why should we think twice before trying to inhabit Mars?

5 SPEAKING **Work in pairs and discuss the questions.**
1 If it became possible for humans to travel to or live on Mars, would you want to go?
2 If you were living on Mars, what would you miss the most about Earth?

102

Objectives

Functions and speaking Sympathizing about past situations
Grammar Speculating (past, present, and future); cause and effect linkers
Vocabulary Space idioms; adjectives commonly used to describe movies
Culture Being an astronaut

Resources for this unit

All available online

Videos
- Get TH!NKing: *Why are people so fascinated by space?*
- Grammar video!: Speculating (past, present, and future)
- Culture: Being an astronaut

Tests
- Unit, extension, and skills test 11

Worksheets
- Grammar and vocabulary: Basic, Standard, and Extension Worksheets
- Project: Tomorrow's world
- Communication: Space and beyond
- Literature Worksheets: *The Time Machine*
- Get TH!NKing and Grammar video! video Worksheets

Reading; Train to TH!NK

Culture notes

Mars is much smaller than Earth, but in many other ways is very similar. It has volcanoes, valleys, deserts, and polar ice caps. One Martian day lasts 24 hours and 37 minutes, while a year is equivalent to 687 Earth days. Also known as the Red Planet due to its reddish color, which comes mainly from iron oxide on its surface, the atmosphere on Mars is thin, while the surface temperatures are, on average, around -63 degrees Celsius.

Dennis Tito, born in 1940, is an American engineer and entrepreneur. In 2001, he made history as the world's first private citizen to fly to the International Space Station by paying for his own flight. He was in space for seven days.

6 Explain/elicit the meaning of *flawed* (describes something which is not perfect or doesn't work properly). Before students match, divide the class into groups of three and ask each student to read one of the three explanations A–C, then summarize it for their partners.
1 C 2 B 3 A

7 Read through the example flawed argument for statement 1 in the speech bubble and elicit which type of argument, A–C, it is (C). Elicit flawed arguments A and B for statement 1 from the class before students do the rest in pairs. Ask: *Which types of flawed argument are most convincing?*

SHOOT FOR THE STARS UNIT 11

A MISSION TO **MARS**

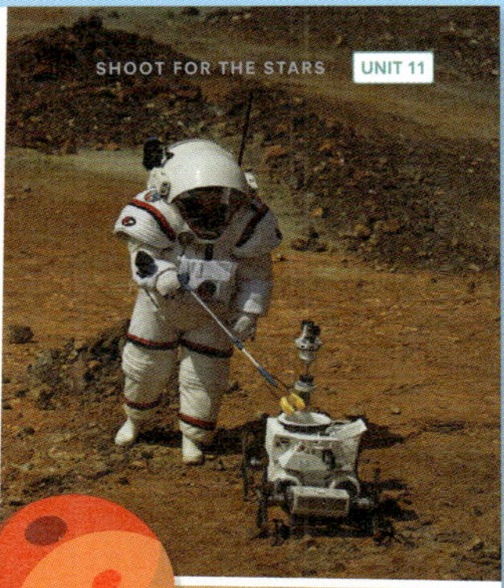

Back in 2001, Dennis Tito made a name for himself by becoming the first ever space tourist. Twelve years later, he launched his Mars Project with the idea of sending a couple on a flight around Mars. It never happened. The technology wasn't ready. 2018 may have been our best chance to get to Mars from Earth for some time, as the two planets were at their closest, meaning the 56-million-km journey might have taken as little as 200 days. Huge advances in science over recent years have meant that interest in reaching our closest planetary neighbor is at an all-time high, and we might not have to wait too long before it becomes a reality. The next time the two planets will come closer again is in 2033. The race for Mars is on. However, any space project wishing to touch down on the red planet will first have to overcome three major problems.

First, there is the expense. Current estimates for a round trip range from $100 billion to as much as $500 billion. Clearly this is a lot of money for any one government to find, which means a mission to Mars is sure to be an international collaboration. One way of bringing the cost down is to work on developing reusable rockets. SpaceX, one of the companies at the forefront of space exploration, believes their Falcon 9, which has already successfully been launched and landed, might be the answer to this.

Another problem that needs overcoming is the psychological effects of such an ambitious voyage on the astronauts. Medical experts are worried that the long time spent in a confined space can't be beneficial to the mental health of the crew. They advise that spacecrafts should be fitted with a wide range of activities to keep the astronauts busy. There is also the question of how well the astronauts will cope with the desert-like Martian landscape. The Hi-Seas project aims to help prepare for this and sees would-be astronauts spending up to eight months in isolation on the side of a Hawaiian volcano.

The final problem is perhaps the most serious. A trip to Mars is bound to expose crew members to extremely high levels of radiation, which is highly likely to lead to a number of illnesses. Ideas being worked on to fight this include the development of protective covering and the possibility of faster rockets to cut down on travel time.

Although human exploration of Mars seems certain at a future date, some say there are several reasons why this might not be such a good idea. Perhaps the greatest fear is that of cross-contamination: no matter how sterile the spaceships landing on Mars might be, the astronauts walking out on to the surface will bring with them millions of Earth microbes, and the effect of these on any potential Martian ecosystem may well be disastrous. Maybe we'd be better off concentrating on looking after the world we currently have, so that there will never be any need to find an alternative home.

Train to TH!NK

Spotting flawed arguments

There are many different ways in which people can try to convince you that something is true without using actual evidence. Here are three common ways.

A ***The ignorance argument:*** *Not being able to disprove something doesn't mean it's true. Something is only true if there is evidence for it.*

B ***Judging by emotions:*** *Just because someone has strong emotions doesn't always mean that what they say is true. Think carefully before you are persuaded by their argument.*

C ***Quoting an authority:*** *Sometimes an expert or their work is quoted, and this is used as evidence that something is true. But these people can make mistakes, too. They're not always right. Or their work could be taken out of context. Be careful – "experts" are often used in advertising to try to sell things to you!*

6 **Read the quotations and match them with explanations A–C.**

1 I saw this scientist on TV. He says that we should eat more fatty foods. ☐
2 I really dislike politicians and never believe anything they say. ☐
3 **A** I didn't take it. I wasn't even there.
B You must have taken it if you were there on your own. ☐

7 SPEAKING **Work in pairs. For each of the statements below, create three different flawed arguments (A, B, and C) to support it.**

1 Spiders make good pets.
2 Tall people are healthier.
3 Money always brings unhappiness.

The man at the pet store says I should buy a tarantula from him because they are really easy to take care of.

103

Homework

Ask students to research one of the planets in the solar system. They can find a picture and write a description in English. If students do not have access to the internet, they can use their own ideas and make up a planet.

Activity idea Extension

Write on the board: *The world spends billions of dollars on space programs every year. What are the advantages and disadvantages?* Ask students to discuss in pairs and make a list of the advantages and disadvantages of space exploration.

Activity idea Mixed-ability

In Exercise 7, put students into pairs roughly according to level. Ask weaker students to focus on one statement and think of three flawed arguments to support it. Stronger students can create three flawed arguments for all three statements.

Critical TH!NKing
Evaluating ideas and arguments
Evaluating specific information or points in an argument.

Critical TH!NKing
Evaluating ideas and arguments
Evaluating arguments as a whole.

Critical TH!NKing
Understanding and analyzing ideas and arguments
Identifying and classifying information.

Activity idea Extension

Make small groups. Ask students to take turns expanding on one of the flawed arguments they came up with in Exercise 7 and trying to convince their groups that their argument is correct.

TH!NK more

Worksheets
Project Tomorrow's world
Communication Space and beyond
Get **TH!NK**ing *Why are people so fascinated by space?*

Warmer

Write the following on the board: *2001, 9, 35 million, 100, 2018, 200, 12, 2033, 500*. Tell students that the numbers come from the article about Mars from the last lesson. Give students three minutes to try to remember as much as they can about the numbers in pairs. Listen to some of their ideas and then give them another three minutes to find the numbers in the article and what they refer to.

▶ 29 Grammar video! Speculating (past, present, and future)

1 Look at the seven phrases and ask: *What do these have in common?* (They are all used to speculate or express different levels of probability.) Ask students to try to answer the questions from memory before referring back to page 103 to check.

1 may have 2 might not have to 3 sure to 4 might be 5 can't be 6 bound to 7 highly likely
RULE: 8 could 9 can't 10 must 11 have 12 the infinitive without *to* 13 certain

2 If you are short on time, assign this exercise for homework.

1 must 2 can't 3 might 4 sure to 5 is bound to 6 likely 7 must 8 can't

3 You could move on to pronunciation prior to doing the speaking task.

Workbook p100

Pronunciation
Stress on modal verbs for speculation

Student's Book p121

GRAMMAR
Grammar video ▶ 29
Speculating (past, present, and future)

1 Look back at the article on page 103 and complete the sentences with the words from the list. Then complete the rule.

bound to | can't be | sure to | highly likely | may have | might be | might not have to

1 2018 ______________ been our best chance to get to Mars for some time.
2 We ______________ wait too long before it becomes a reality.
3 A mission to Mars is ______________ be an international collaboration.
4 SpaceX ... believes their Falcon 9 .. ______________ the answer to this.
5 ... the long time spent in a confined space ______________ beneficial to the mental health of the crew.
6 A trip to Mars is ______________ expose crew members to extremely high levels of radiation.
7 ... radiation, which is ______________ to lead to a number of illnesses.

RULE: To speculate we often use the modal verbs *might, may, could, must,* and *can't*.
- *might, may,* and [8]______________ refer to possibility.
- [9]______________ refers to a perceived impossibility.
- [10]______________ refers to a perceived certainty.

When we refer to past events, the modals are followed by [11]______________ + past participle.
When we refer to present or future events, the modals are followed by [12]______________.
We can also use *be + bound to* / [13]______________ *to* / *likely to* to speculate about past, present, and future events.
- *be + bound to* / *sure to* express greater certainty than *be likely to*.

2 Choose the correct answers.

1 They *must* / *can't* have gotten lost. Otherwise they'd be here by now.
2 They *might* / *can't* have gotten lost. They know the way.
3 They *might* / *must* have gotten lost. Or maybe they left home late.
4 Lea is *sure to* / *can't* know what to do. She always has good advice.
5 Bram *must* / *is bound to* be late. He always is.
6 It is *likely* / *sure* to rain today. You might need an umbrella.
7 You *must* / *can't* be hungry. You haven't eaten all day.
8 You *can't* / *might* be hungry. You've just eaten.

104

3 SPEAKING **How possible do you think these things are? Discuss with a partner and put them in order of probability.**

- humans landing on Mars in the next ten years
- a world free of pollution
- you going abroad on vacation this year

→ workbook page 100

PRONUNCIATION
Stress on modal verbs for speculation
Go to page 121.

FUNCTIONS
Sympathizing about past situations

4 Match the sentences and the replies.

1 Alex didn't pass his driving test. ☐
2 So when I went to check in, I realized I'd left my passport at home. ☐
3 The store had already closed when they got there. ☐
4 Dad wrecked Mom's car yesterday. ☐

a Oh, no. She can't have been happy about that.
b What a shame. They must have been disappointed.
c Poor him. He must have been upset.
d How terrible. You must have been so annoyed.

5 Put the conversation in order.

☐ **Amy** I wasn't. I didn't even have a book with me.
1 **Amy** You won't believe what happened to me on my way home.
☐ **Amy** I didn't get home until midnight. My mom was waiting up for me.
☐ **Amy** It was. And to make things worse, my phone battery was dead.
☐ **Amy** She was. But of course, I couldn't call her and let her know.
☐ **Amy** I missed my train and had to wait three hours for the next one.
☐ **Tom** Oh, no. You had to wait for three hours? How terrible. That must have been boring.
☐ **Tom** What? Poor you. You can't have been happy about that.
☐ **Tom** Oh, gosh. She must have been worried.
☐ **Tom** What happened?
☐ **Tom** So you must have gotten home really late.

6 Think of something annoying that happened to you recently. Make notes about what happened.

7 SPEAKING **Work in pairs. Tell each other your stories from Exercise 6 and sympathize.**

4 1 c 2 d 3 b 4 a

5 After feedback, ask students to practice the dialogue with a partner. Monitor to make sure students sound sympathetic when responding.
7, 1, 9, 5, 11, 3, 4, 6, 10, 2, 8

6–7 Talk about an experience of your own as an example to get students started on this. Encourage them to refer to replies a–d in Exercise 4 and to sympathize with speculative language.

THINK more

Workbook
Grammar p100, Ex.1–3
Pronunciation p121

Worksheets
Grammar Worksheets 11
Grammar video! Speculating (past, present, and future)

Language note Modal verbs for speculation

Remind students that the opposite of *must be* when making deductions is *can't be*, not *mustn't be*. *Could/might/may* have similar meanings when used to speculate. Point out that *may* is more formal and less commonly used than *could* or *might*.

Activity idea Extension

Students write five sentences about themselves using the modal verbs from the rule box.

Listening; Vocabulary

8 Put a copy of the two photos up on the board and do the exercise as a class before students open their books. Write a few of their ideas on the board, but do not comment at this stage.

9 🔊 **11.04**
It's a special plane that takes a smaller plane to the edge of the Earth's atmosphere. The smaller plane then flies above the Earth in space at very fast speeds before landing back on Earth like a normal plane.

10 🔊 **11.04** Ask students to answer as many of the questions as they can before they listen again.
1 C 2 C 3 A 4 C 5 C 6 C

11 Invite students to share their answers with the rest of the class during feedback.

12 Encourage students to use the context provided by each sentence to help them to deduce the meaning and to guess answers if they are not sure, by elimination.
1 e 2 f 3 a 4 b 5 c 6 d

13 Before students do the exercise, write the italicized phrases a–f on the board. Ask: *Is there a similar phrase in (your L1)?* During feedback, clarify that we use *over the moon* to describe somebody's reaction to a certain situation. It does not describe somebody's happiness over a long period of time.
1 over the moon 2 down to earth 3 out of this world 4 It's not rocket science. 5 once in a blue moon 6 starry-eyed

Workbook p102

Homework

Ask students to research and write three questions for a quiz on the topic of space, each with A/B/C answer options. They can bring them to the next lesson for partners to read and respond to.

LISTENING

8 **Look at the photos. What do you think is special about this vehicle?**

9 🔊 11.04 **Listen to the podcast to check your ideas.**

10 🔊 11.04 **Listen again and choose the correct answer, A, B, or C.**

1 What happened in the years after Denis Tito became the first space tourist?
A Flights were stopped altogether.
B There was a mad rush of people going into space.
C Not as many people as expected followed his example.

2 How many people can the VSS Unity take into space at one time?
A two B six C eight

3 How long will space tourists on the VSS Unity spend in space?
A around two hours
B less than two hours
C six days

4 Why is the White Knight Two aircraft needed?
A to take the VSS Unity on its 14,000 m trip into space and back
B to help land the VSS Unity
C to get the VSS Unity off the Earth's surface

5 Which of these things can tourists do on board the VSS Unity?
A take photos of the wonderful views
B help land the plane
C enjoy being weightless for a while

6 How many people have already paid for flights into space?
A 20 B 200 C 700

11 SPEAKING **Work in pairs and discuss the questions.**

1 Do you think space vacations on the moon will be commonplace one day? Why (not)?
2 If you had the money, would you like to go on a trip like this? Why (not)?
3 What else could you better spend this money on?

VOCABULARY
Space idioms

12 **Match sentences 1–6 with follow-up sentences a–f.**

1 Jen's been accepted by Cambridge University. ☐
2 You'll like Mike. ☐
3 The special effects in the new *Star Wars* movie are amazing. ☐
4 Anyone can boil an egg. ☐
5 We very rarely go to the movies. ☐
6 He thinks every city he visits is the most perfect place in the world. ☐

a They're *out of this world*.
b *It's not rocket science*.
c Maybe *once in a blue moon*.
d He's very *starry-eyed*.
e She's *over the moon*.
f He's very *down to earth* and easy to get along with.

13 **Match the expressions from Exercise 12 with the definitions.**

1 really happy
2 normal (not pretentious at all)
3 incredible
4 It's very simple.
5 hardly ever
6 overly romantic / overly optimistic

→ workbook page 102

Activity idea Extension

Put students into small groups to discuss the following questions:

1 When did you last see or hear something out of this world?
2 Give an example of a time when you might use the phrase "It's not rocket science."
3 Name something you do once in a blue moon.
4 Do you know anybody who is starry-eyed? How do they behave?
5 When did you last feel over the moon about something?
6 Do you know anybody who is down to earth?

Language note A Blue Moon

According to modern folklore, a Blue Moon is the second full moon in a calendar month. Usually, months only have one full moon, but because they are separated by 29 days, it is possible to fit two full moons in a single month. This happens every two and a half years, on average, so the phrase *once in a blue moon* means only occasionally.

TH!NK more

Workbook
Listening p106, Ex.1–3
Vocabulary p102, Ex.1–2
Vocabulary Extra p103, Ex.1–3

Worksheets
Vocabulary Worksheets 11

Reading

Warmer

Ask: *How many movies about space can you think of?* Divide the class into small groups and assign a three-minute time limit to list as many space movies as possible. Invite the group that came up with the most to read their list to the class.

1 Set a two-minute time limit for students to read and answer the question. Tell them not to worry about any difficult language at this stage, as this will come up later.
The Martian

2 🔊 **11.05 Check/clarify:** *linguist, decipher, codes, aliens, mission, base, consequently.*
Before playing the audio, give students just two minutes to scan the blog quickly. Encourage them not to focus on every word for now but just to find the answers, then listen and check. Ask them to underline the parts of the blog that support their answers.
1 Gravity 2 Arrival
3 The Martian 4 First Man
5 The Martian 6 First Man
7 Gravity 8 Arrival

3 Ask students to discuss the merits of any movies they mention and to describe the plots of any movies other students have not seen. Monitor to help with vocabulary and ideas. During feedback, invite students to share their favorite space movie with the class and perhaps hold a vote to find out the class's favorite space movie.

Top four SPACE MOVIES of the 21st century

NASA's InSight's thrilling touchdown on the surface of Mars got me thinking a lot about space. So, with that in mind, I've decided to come up with a list of my four favorite space movies of the 21st century so far. It wasn't easy choosing just four (and you might not agree with me), but here they are.

1 ARRIVAL (2016)

Arrival isn't exactly action-packed. Not much happens, but it still leaves you thinking about it for days and days afterwards. It stars Amy Adams as Louise Banks, a linguist who is asked by the American military to try to help them communicate with an alien spaceship. It is one of 12 ships that have landed in various locations around Earth. Because of increased tensions between these countries, Louise must work quickly to decipher the codes the aliens are sending and discover exactly why they are here. It is a memorable movie and was considered by many critics to be one of 2016's top movies.

2 GRAVITY (2009)

I saw this one in 3D on the big screen, and it blew me away. In a word, it's stunning. The shots of outer space are so breathtaking that you spend the whole time thinking you are actually up there yourself. I don't want to give away too much of the plot, but due to a run of incredible bad luck, the astronaut played by Sandra Bullock finds herself all alone in the International Space Station, with little hope of ever getting home. Will she or won't she? Watch and you'll find out. *Gravity*, which also features George Clooney – all too briefly – was a huge box office success, but also a hit with the critics. It won a total of seven Academy Awards.

3 FIRST MAN (2018)

This one differs from my other choices because it's based on a true story. Neil Armstrong is the First Man referred to in the title of this movie: the first man on the moon. He is played brilliantly by Ryan Gosling in this biopic of America's most famous astronaut. It's full of fascinating details and things you never knew. It's very moving at times, especially when dealing with the death of Armstrong's young daughter. At times, it gets a little sentimental, perhaps as a result of having Steven Spielberg as an executive producer. It's a must for all space travel fans and highly recommended for everyone else.

4 THE MARTIAN (2015)

I've saved the best until last. Matt Damon plays astronaut Mark Watney, who is part of a space mission to explore Mars. He gets caught up in a huge storm, and the rest of his crew, deciding that he must be dead, return home without him. Watney must now somehow survive everything the planet can throw at him and try to find a way of making contact with his base back on Earth. The plot might seem a bit far-fetched, but scientists agree that the movie gets a lot right about Mars. The special effects are amazing, and consequently, this movie is best seen on the big screen. But even on a small screen, this is easily the best space movie of all time.

READING

1 **Read the blog quickly. Which movie does the writer consider to be the greatest space movie of all time?**

2 🔊 11.05 **Read and listen to the blog again. Complete the sentences with the names of the movies.**

1 ____________ is about someone faced with an impossible journey.
2 ____________ has a long-lasting effect on its audience.
3 ____________ takes place on another planet in our solar system.
4 ____________ is mostly likely to make you cry.
5 ____________ should really be seen at a movie theater.
6 ____________ is about a real person.
7 ____________ won a lot of awards.
8 ____________ involves someone trying to understand a different language.

3 SPEAKING **Work in pairs and discuss the questions.**

1 Which of these movies have you seen or would you like to see?
2 Which movies do you think are missing from the list?
3 Why does the writer refer to these movies as space movies rather than sci-fi movies?
4 What do you think is the best sci-fi movie of all time?

106

Culture notes

Science-fiction movies, and particularly those about space, appeared very early in the silent cinema era. *Le Voyage dans la Lune* (*A Trip to the Moon*), created by Georges Méliès in 1902, is considered to be the first. It used stop-motion and other techniques that were ground-breaking at the time. The 1920s and 30s saw many cinematic portrayals of imagined worlds, while post-WWII science-fiction movies offered visions of alien invasion. Since the moon landings of the 1960s, travel in space has been at the center of the movie industry with titles such as *2001: A Space Odyssey* being held up as a masterpiece of science-fiction, influencing countless other movies such as *Star Wars*, *Alien*, *Gravity*, and *Interstellar*.

TH!NK more

Workbook
Reading p104, Ex.1–4

Activity idea Extension

If you feel your students need extra writing practice, ask them to write a blog entry describing a movie of their choice. First, ask them to underline collocations and expressions that they like in the blog on page 106 and to try to incorporate them in their own blog. They should include information on the lead actors, a brief outline of the plot, and their reasons for liking the movie. This could either be done individually, or as a collaborative writing activity, with students working in pairs or small groups.

4 Ask students to try to answer the questions from memory before referring back to page 106 to check.

1 Because of 2 due to
3 as a result of 4 consequently
RULE: 5 because of 6 Consequently

5 This exercise is closely modeled on Reading and Use of English Part 4 of the Cambridge English: First exam. Ask students to read the instructions and example.

1 result of eating 2 due to (the) bad weather 3 because of a bad 4 as a result of 5 due to (a)

Workbook p101

Get it Right!
Cause and effect linkers
Student's Book p126

6 During feedback, say the words for students to repeat and check pronunciation. Write the words on the board to elicit and mark the stress on each word. Point out the stress on *fetch* in *far-fetched*.

1 moving 2 stunning 3 thrilling
4 sentimental 5 far-fetched
6 action-packed 7 breathtaking
8 memorable

7 **Check/clarify:** *on the edge of my seat, close to tears, car chases, dull.*
If you are short on time, assign this exercise for homework.

1 thrilling 2 sentimental
3 moving 4 action-packed
5 far-fetched 6 stunning
7 memorable 8 breathtaking

8 During feedback, listen to some of their ideas and ask: *Which adjectives was it easier to think of example movies for? Why?*

Workbook p102

9 Give a couple of your own examples to get students started on this. Encourage them to go into detail when giving their reasons for choosing movies and challenge them to use all of the adjectives in Exercise 7. When students have completed their lists, put pairs together to make groups of four. Ask them to compare and agree on a list of four for each category. Listen to some example lists and, as a class, decide on the best movies in each category.

GRAMMAR
Cause and effect linkers

4 Complete the sentences. Then look back at the blog to check your answers and complete the rule.

1 ______________ increased tensions between these countries, Louise must work quickly.
2 ... ______________ a run of incredible bad luck, the astronaut played by Sandra Bullock finds herself all alone.
3 ... it gets a little sentimental, perhaps ______________ having Steven Spielberg as an executive producer.
4 The special effects are amazing, and ______________, this movie is best seen on the big screen.

> **RULE:** We use linkers such as *due to, as a result of, because of,* and *consequently* to link actions and their consequences.
> *Due to, as a result of,* and [5] ______________ can come at the beginning of a sentence or in the middle between the two clauses. They are followed by the reason for an action or event.
> These linkers are usually followed by a noun phrase.
> *Due to* and *as a result of* are more formal than *because of.*
> [6] ______________ generally comes at the beginning of a new sentence or clause. It introduces the effect of the cause mentioned in the previous sentence. It is followed by a clause (subject and verb).

5 Complete the second sentence so that it has a similar meaning to the first sentence, using the word in parentheses. You must use between two and five words, including the word given.

0 Olivia didn't have time to study for the test. Consequently, she didn't do very well. (because)
Because of lack of time to study, Olivia didn't do well on the test.
1 Paul ate too much. He felt sick. (result)
As a ______________ too much, Paul felt sick.
2 The weather was bad so the race was canceled. (due)
The race was canceled ______________.
3 Jack had a bad cold. He didn't go to school. (of)
Jack didn't go to school ______________ cold.
4 The police got some information and arrested the man. (result)
The man was arrested ______________ information given to the police.
5 No one was interested so the concert was canceled. (due)
The concert was canceled ______________ lack of interest.

→ workbook page 101

VOCABULARY
Adjectives commonly used to describe movies

6 Match the highlighted words from the blog with the definitions below.

1 causing strong feelings ______________
2 really beautiful ______________
3 really exciting ______________
4 overly emotional ______________
5 difficult to believe ______________
6 full of action ______________
7 really exciting and really beautiful ______________
8 something you won't forget ______________

7 Choose the correct word to complete each sentence.

1 The ending of the movie was really *thrilling / sentimental.* I was on the edge of my seat.
2 I was surprised that the ending of the movie was so *stunning / sentimental.* It was a horror movie, after all.
3 It's a *moving / far-fetched* movie. I was close to tears at the end.
4 It's full of explosions and fights and car chases. It's a really *action-packed / moving* movie.
5 I know it was a fantasy movie, but for me the story was so *far-fetched / memorable* that it just seemed ridiculous.
6 The characters were a little dull, but the costumes were *thrilling / stunning.*
7 It's a really *sentimental / memorable* movie. I'm sure I'll be thinking about it for days.
8 The opening scenes of the movie are *action-packed / breathtaking.* They're absolutely beautiful.

8 SPEAKING **Work in pairs. Think of a movie as an example for each of the sentences in Exercise 7.**

→ workbook page 102

SPEAKING

9 Work in pairs. Choose one of the categories below and think of four movies for it. As you discuss your choices, use the adjectives in Exercise 6 to help you describe your movies and agree on your final list.

- the four greatest comedies
- the four greatest romantic movies
- the four greatest action movies
- the four greatest horror movies

Homework
Ask students to try to rewrite the sentences in Exercise 7 so that they make sense with the other adjective, e.g., *1 The ending of the movie was really sentimental. I don't mind a happy ending, but this was too much!*

Activity idea Fast finishers
Ask students to transform the sentences in Exercise 5 in different ways using the other linkers.

Activity idea Mixed-ability
Stronger students can find the words in the blog and try to deduce meaning from the context, without looking at the definitions in Exercise 6. They then look at the definitions to check their answers.

TH!NK more

Practice Extra
Unit 11 Practice it!

Workbook
Grammar p101, Ex.4–6
Vocabulary p102, Ex.3–5

Worksheets
Grammar Worksheets 11
Vocabulary Worksheets 11

Warmer

Ask students to imagine that they are going to space for six months. They can only take one small backpack. Ask them what six items they would take with them. Allow students time for pairs to discuss and to put the items in order of importance. Hold a class vote to decide which they feel are the most and the least important.

▶ 30 TH!NK
Being an astronaut

1 Tell students that they need to scan the text for specific information, so they do not need to read every word of the text in order to successfully complete the exercise. Set a two-minute time limit to encourage them to read quickly. Listen to some of their ideas in open class, but do not comment at this stage.

2 🔊 **11.06** Tell students not to worry about difficult vocabulary at this stage as this will come up later.
1 the US, Russia, Canada, Europe, and Japan (as well as Italy, Brazil, Malaysia, and South Africa) 2 It's uncertain (beyond 2024/2028).

3 Ask students to underline the parts of the text that support their answers.
1 the size of an American football field 2 piece by piece, using the NASA space shuttle to transport the pieces, which were assembled by robots and astronauts 3 a combination of English and Russian. It's used when the astronauts socialize with each other. 4 They travel on a Russian Soyuz spaceship. 5 They range from growing plants to observing the effect of life in space on the human body and testing products to see how they perform in zero gravity. 6 to make repairs to the station

TH!NK
Being an astronaut

Culture

1 Scan the text to find the answers to these questions.
1 What countries are engaged in space exploration these days?
2 What is the future of the ISS?

2 🔊 11.06 Read and listen to the text to check your answers.

A multinational enterprise

Somewhere up there in the skies, 400 km above your head, a huge metallic structure the size of an American football field is orbiting the Earth every hour and a half, as it travels at speeds of up to 28,000 km/h. Inside, you will find several sleeping areas, two bathrooms, a gym, and a 360° window offering some of the most spectacular views you can imagine. You will also find people!

It's the International Space Station (or ISS for short), and as its name suggests, it truly is the result of a huge collaboration between many different countries. The main financial contributors are the US, Russia, Canada, Europe, and Japan. Although it is constantly being added to and adapted, the main construction of it was completed between 1998 and 2011. It was taken up into space piece by piece, using NASA's space shuttle to transport most of the larger pieces. Once up there, these pieces were assembled by robots and astronauts.

Since November 2, 2000, it has been called home by 230 astronauts from 18 different countries. The majority (145) have been from the US, with Russia sending the second most (46). Other countries that have sent astronauts include Italy, Japan, Brazil, Malaysia, and South Africa.

Although English is the official language of the Space Station, astronauts are also expected to learn Russian, as technical commands are given in that language. This has led to the creation of "Runglish" – a mixture of the two – that many of the astronauts use to socialize in their everyday life on board the station.

These days, the ISS generally has a crew of three to six people living on it. Their journey begins on board a Russian Soyuz spaceship, which transports them from Earth to the station where they spend on average six months before returning home. In case of emergency, they can always evacuate the station using one of the two Soyuz spaceships that are docked to the ISS.

During their time there, crew members have a number of different responsibilities. One of the main reasons they are there is to conduct scientific experiments in space. These range from growing plants, to observing the effect of life in space on the human body, in order to understand the challenges humans will face if they want to explore further into the solar system. They also test products such as 3D printers and coffee makers to see how they perform in zero gravity. But the astronauts are also responsible for making sure the ISS is in full working order, and they will often need to make repairs that might involve spacewalks to access the exterior of the station. They also put aside two hours each day for exercise and to make sure they are taking care of themselves.

But the ISS might well not be there forever. At the moment, there are plans to keep it in operation until at least 2024 and possibly until 2028, but after that, its future is not so certain. It might be taken out of orbit permanently or broken up into parts to be used on future space stations. But whatever happens to it, let's hope the spirit of international cooperation will continue as mankind explores further and further into space.

3 Read the article again and answer the questions.
1 How big is the ISS?
2 How was it built?
3 What is Runglish? When is it used?
4 How do astronauts get to the ISS?
5 What kinds of experiments do astronauts do on the ISS?
6 Why might an astronaut need to make a spacewalk?

108

Culture notes

The International Space Station (ISS) is the second brightest object in our night sky, after the moon. You don't even need a telescope to see it zoom overhead, and the NASA app lets you find out when and where to spot the ISS. Astronauts on the International Space Station can see 15 sunrises and 15 sunsets a day with an average of one every 45 minutes. On September 3, 2017, the astronaut Peggy Whitson set the record for spending the most amount of time living and working in space at 665 days.

4 During feedback, say the words for students to repeat. Check that they're placing stress on the correct syllable.

1 collaboration 2 evacuate 3 gravity 4 in operation 5 orbiting 6 docked 7 exterior 8 assembled

5 Monitor and help as necessary, encouraging students to express themselves in English and to use any vocabulary they have learned from the article.

1 Set a two-minute time limit to encourage quick scanning.

Problem: computer malfunction due to food spillage Solution: ban all liquid food

2 Encourage students to underline the parts of the report that support their answers.

1 a brief description of what the report is about 2 an outline of the problem 3 suggestions for changes

3 Monitor to check how well students are able to do this and to make a note of any repeated problems. During feedback, pay attention to the use of the words in parentheses and elicit/clarify rules regarding punctuation and position in the sentence.

1 The computer had stopped working as a result of being covered in a thick orange liquid.

2 The computer had stopped working because of being covered in a thick orange liquid.

3 The crew was able to run the back-up computer. However, the incident has raised serious concerns about dining habits.

4 Despite the crew being able to run the back-up computer, the incident has raised serious concerns about dining habits.

4–5 The planning for this exercise can be done in class and the writing assigned for homework. Before students begin writing, encourage them to underline collocations and expressions in the model in Exercise 1 that they could use in their report. Remind them that they should also use linkers of cause and effect.

4 VOCABULARY Match the highlighted words in the article with the definitions.

1 a partnership/working together
2 to leave somewhere in a hurry (usually because of danger)
3 the force that keeps us on the ground
4 working
5 circling around an object
6 attached to
7 the outside of a building/structure
8 put together

5 SPEAKING Work in pairs and discuss the questions.

1 Would you like to spend time in a space station if it was possible?
2 What experiment would you like to conduct most?
3 What do you think would be the most difficult aspect of living on the ISS?

WRITING
A report

1 INPUT Read the report. What problem does it report and what solution does it suggest?

1 The aim of this report is to discuss a problem recently encountered during the Admiral 9 mission to the International Space Station and to make suggestions about what can be done to prevent this from happening in the future.

2 On September 3rd of this year, commander Captain Jade Logan reported a serious computer malfunction in the dining quarters of the International Space Station. On further inspection, it appeared that the computer had stopped working due to it being covered in a thick orange liquid. Logan questioned members of her team only to discover that the problem had occurred when engineer Ian Coyne's carrot soup had leaked from its container and found its way to the computing area.

3 Although the crew was able to run the back-up computer, the incident has raised serious concerns about dining habits. Consequently, while a more detailed report is being prepared, we suggest an immediate ban on all liquid food aboard the Space Station until safer procedures can be introduced.

2 ANALYZE Match the paragraphs with their main function. There are two extra functions.

- [ ] say who is responsible
- [ ] a brief description of what the report is about
- [ ] suggestions for changes
- [ ] talk about the cost of making changes
- [ ] an outline of the problem

3 Rewrite the sentences from the report, replacing the underlined words with the words in parentheses.

The computer had stopped working due to it being covered in a thick orange liquid.

1 (as a result of)
2 (because of)

Although the crew were able to run the back-up computer, the incident has raised serious concerns about dining habits.

3 (however)
4 (despite)

4 PLAN Read through the situation below and make notes.

Last Friday, there was a school trip to the space museum. The bus was supposed to leave at 9 a.m., but didn't leave until 10 a.m. because five students were late. As a consequence, the group had an hour less to spend at the museum.

Problem: ___

Solution: ___

5 PRODUCE Write a report about the problem with the school trip (200–250 words). Remember to do these things:

- say what the report is about
- outline the problem
- suggest a solution

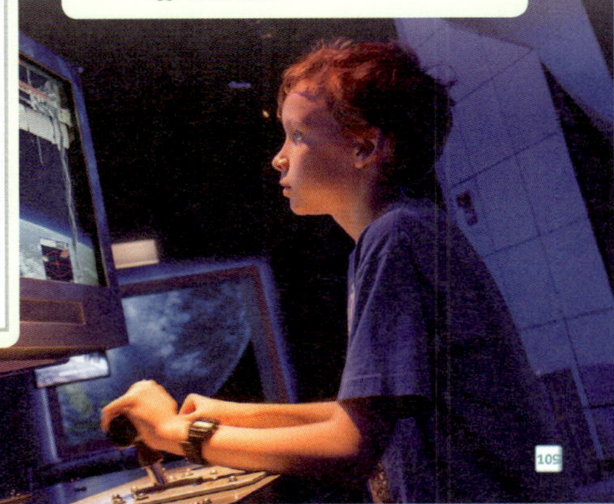

Homework

If you are short on time, students can do Writing Exercise 5 for homework. If you have done this in class, ask students to exchange their reports with another student for them to read and to give feedback on content and structure. Students could check if the report uses the same structure as the model. They should also decide if the solution to the outlined problem is a good one or not.

Activity idea Extension

On completion of the writing task, ask pairs to swap reports and read and evaluate each other's writing on the basis of **content** (How interesting was the report?), **organization** (Did the report follow the structure of the model text?) and **language** (Did they use a variety of linking words?).

TH!NK more

Practice Extra
Unit 11 Master it!

Workbook
Developing Writing p105

Tests
Unit, extension, and skills test 11

Warmer

Ask: *Do you like visiting foreign countries? If you could go anywhere in the world, where would you go?* Give student pairs three minutes to agree on a list of the five most exciting destinations in the world. Nominate students to share their lists with the rest of the class.

▶ 31 Get TH!NKing

Play the video and discuss the question with your class.

1 Put a copy of the four photos up on the board and do the exercise as a class before students open their books.

2 Assign a three-minute time limit and tell students to read quickly and not worry about understanding every word, but just focus on checking their answer to Exercise 1.
A The Dead Sea – Jordan B The Mirador Basin and Tikal National Park – Guatemala C The Chacaltaya Glacier – The Andes (Bolivia) D The Nazca Lines – Peru The Chacaltaya Glacier doesn't exist anymore.

3 🔊 **12.01 Check/clarify:** *glacier, summit, inject, carbon dioxide, ruins, Mayan civilization, pyramids, Peruvian, archaeologist, chalk, litter, vandalism, scrolls.*
Before students read the article again, get them to read the questions through. Ask them to underline the parts of the article that gave them their answers.
1 They're gradually being ruined by global warming and man-made disasters. 2 It was the highest ski run in the world. 3 climate change 4 He took the first photographs of the ancient Mayan city. 5 The area is (said to be) losing 400 km² a year. 6 barriers on the road that runs through them 7 Tourism has brought litter and vandalism. 8 because people use water from the Jordan River

4 You could put students into small groups to discuss the questions and assign a quieter student the role of note-taker. Make sure all students are contributing to the discussion and encourage quieter students to voice their opinions, too.

12 OFF THE BEATEN TRACK

OBJECTIVES

FUNCTIONS: speaking persuasively

GRAMMAR: passive report structures; the passive: verbs with two objects

VOCABULARY: geographical features; verb + noun collocations

Get TH!NKING
Watch the video and think: how important is tourism where you live?

A

C

B

D

READING

1 Look at the photos. What do they show? In which parts of the world can they be found? Which do you think don't exist anymore?

2 Read the article quickly to check your ideas.

3 🔊 12.01 Read and listen to the article again. Answer the questions.
1 What is happening to many beautiful and ancient destinations around the world?
2 What was the Chacaltaya Glacier's claim to fame?
3 What caused the Chacaltaya Glacier to disappear so quickly?
4 What was important about Sir Alfred Maudslay's trip to Tikal?
5 What is happening to the forests around the Mayan ruins of Tikal?
6 What might help protect the Nazca Lines?
7 What part does tourism play in the destruction of the Nazca Lines?
8 Why is the Dead Sea shrinking so rapidly?

4 SPEAKING Work in pairs and discuss the questions.
1 What can be done to stop these places and other amazing places from disappearing?
2 Can you think of any places in your own country which are in danger of disappearing?
3 Which of the places in the article would you most like to visit? Why? Do you think you should?
4 Do you think there are other places in the world where tourism should be limited?

110

Objectives

Functions and speaking Speaking persuasively
Grammar Passive report structures; the passive: verbs with two objects
Vocabulary Geographical features; verb + noun collocations
Values Human activity and the natural world
Literature *The Lost World*

Resources for this unit

All available online

Videos
- Get **TH!NK**ing: *How important is tourism where you live?*
- Grammar video!: The passive: verbs with two objects

Tests
- Unit, extension, and skills test 12
- Final test

Worksheets
- Grammar and vocabulary: Basic, Standard, and Extension Worksheets
- Project: Endangered animals
- Communication: More to explore
- Grammar presentation: Passive report structures
- Literature Worksheets: *The Time Machine*
- Get **TH!NK**ing and Grammar video! video Worksheets

Culture notes

The Mayan civilization began as early as 2000 BCE in Mesoamerica (a huge area in modern-day southeast Mexico, Belize, Guatemala, and Honduras) and lasted until 1697 CE. Hundreds of cities were built in the rainforests, each governed by its own king or queen. After 800 CE, many of the Mayan states began to collapse. The Spanish conquest in the 16th century resulted in centuries of population decline and cruelty towards the Mayan people. However, today there are over seven million Maya, some of whom maintain their traditions.

The Dead Sea Scrolls are the remains of about 850 ancient manuscripts that were found inside several large pottery jars by a young Bedouin shepherd in 1947 on the shore of the Dead Sea in Jordan. Most of the manuscripts date from the 3rd–1st century BCE. The texts have great historical, religious, and linguistic significance, particularly within the history of Judaism, because some contain parts of one of the earliest versions of the Hebrew Bible.

5 Tell students that we sometimes use "hidden message" language when we want to avoid being direct. For example, statement 4 might be used as a "polite" way of accusing somebody of copying.

6 Encourage students to practice responding in such a way that the true message is hidden. During feedback, listen to some of their responses and ask the rest of the class to decide if the answers sound authentic.

Homework

Ask students to research another place that is in danger of disappearing from around the world. They can find a picture and write a description in English. If students do not have access to the internet, they can make up a fictional place.

Critical TH!NKing
Evaluating ideas and arguments
Evaluating arguments as a whole.

Communication
Using appropriate language for register and context
Using language appropriate for the situation.

Emotional Development
Empathy and relationship skills
Showing empathy for the feelings of others.

OFF THE BEATEN TRACK UNIT 12

Saving great discoveries!

Many places discovered by explorers in past centuries are now in danger of disappearing, and many have already disappeared. Sadly, forests, lakes, glaciers, and ancient ruins are gradually being destroyed by global warming and man-made disasters. What can we do to save them?

The Chacaltaya Glacier

5,300 m up in the Andes
STATUS: disappeared

The Chacaltaya Glacier in the Andes was once the highest ski resort in the world. The summit was in fact higher than the base camp at Mount Everest.
The glacier, which is believed to be 18,000 years old, was 0.22 km² in length in 1940. It shrank to 0.08 km² in 1996, before finally disappearing completely in 2005.
So why did it disappear? The answer is climate change. Scientists predicted that it would disappear in 2015. In fact, it melted a lot more quickly.
Climate change is destroying other glaciers, too. In Iceland, it is believed scientists have found a solution. They inject carbon dioxide into rock. The carbon dioxide gas then turns to rock, too. This helps to stop temperatures from rising and the ice from melting.

The Nazca Lines

Ancient chalk drawings in Peru
STATUS: in danger of disappearing

Peruvian archaeologist Toribio Mejia Xesspe was the first to study the Nazca Lines. He discovered them while he was exploring the area, in 1927. These ancient chalk drawings show more than a hundred different figures, including flowers, animals, and humans, and are the oldest of their kind in the world. The largest figures stretch more than 200 meters across. It is believed that they date back to a time between 500 BCE and 500 CE.
In recent years, however, tourism has brought litter and vandalism. To help protect the Nazca Lines, barriers could be built on the road that runs through them. This would protect the drawings from cars and trucks which sometimes drive onto them.

The Mirador Basin and Tikal National Park

Forest home to Mayan ruins in Guatemala
STATUS: losing 400 km² of forest a year

The Mirador Basin and Tikal National Park in Guatemala are home to the amazing pyramids and ruins of the Mayan civilization. In 1881, the explorer Sir Alfred Maudslay took the first photos of the ancient Mayan city. Nowadays, the area is said to be losing 400 km² of forest a year. It's being burned for farms. One solution to this is to ask villagers to help protect the land.

The Dead Sea

A salt-water lake in Jordan
STATUS: 24 meters shallower than 40 years ago

The Dead Sea Scrolls are very important pieces of writing discovered in the area around the Dead Sea. Sadly, the Dead Sea has decreased in size by a third in the past 40–45 years, and it is known to have sunk over 24 meters since the 1980s. If countries around the sea continue to use water from the Jordan River, it is thought that the sea will not exist in 50 years' time. Action must be taken now to change the way people use the water from the Jordan River so that we can save this beautiful salt lake.

Train to TH!NK

Exploring hidden messages

People don't always say what they mean. For example, imagine you show a short story you've written to a friend and ask for their opinion. What do you think when they tell you, "I thought the beginning was great."? Was the beginning really good, or are they trying to hide the fact that they didn't really like the rest of it? People do this for a number of reasons: they don't want to be rude; they're not brave enough to tell the truth; or they don't really have an opinion.

5 **Look at the sentences below. What do you think the speakers might really be hiding?**
1 That's an interesting sweater you're wearing.
2 There's an earlier train you could catch, if you want.
3 Joe always has a lot to say for himself.
4 Your homework reminded me a lot of Simon's.

6 SPEAKING **Work in pairs. Read the situations. What could you say without being too direct?**
1 Your dad cooked something new that you really don't like.
2 Your best friend asks you what you think about their new haircut. You think it's awful.
3 Your aunt's annoying dog keeps barking.

111

Activity idea Extension

Tell students that if two people do not get along, they may have conversations with a lot of hidden messages. Students may enjoy creating dialogues containing a variety of hidden messages. For example:

(at Anne's party)

A: Hi, Anne. Great party! I like parties without too many people. (Few people showed up to your party.)

B: The music's good – I haven't heard this song since I was about ten. (You like children's music.)

Ask students to create dialogues with a partner, then act them out for another pair, who have to guess the true meaning of the statements.

TH!NK more

Worksheets
Project Endangered animals
Communication More to explore
Get **TH!NK**ing *How important is tourism where you live?*

Warmer

Do a brief review of the passive. Write these sentences on the board:

1 Only 2% of the ocean floor has been explored.

2 Villagers are being asked to protect the land.

3 It's easy to think that everything that could be discovered already has been.

Ask: *What do these sentences have in common?* (They are all in the passive.) Ask students to work in pairs to name the passive forms (1 present perfect passive; 2 present continuous passive; 3 modal passive, present perfect passive).

1 Before students do the exercise, ask: *Which of the sentences are facts and which are opinions?* (1, 2, 3, and 5 are opinions; 4 is a fact) During feedback, ask: *When and why do we use passive report structures?* (mostly in written language; to make language more formal; to avoid starting sentences with impersonal subjects such as *people* or *experts*)
1 It is believed that they date back to a time between 500 BCE and 500 CE.
2 … it is thought that the sea will not exist in 50 years' time.
3 The glacier, which is believed to be 18,000 years old …
4 … it is known to have sunk over 24 meters since the 1980s.
5 … the area is said to be losing 400 km² of forest a year.
RULE: 6 present 7 past 8 written

2 1 is believed to be disappearing 2 is said to be 500 meters deep 3 in the deep ocean are thought to be blind 4 is known to have contained water only 5,000 years ago 5 are believed to have existed for millions of years

Workbook p108

Get it Right!

been and *being*

Student's Book p126

TH!NK more

Workbook
Grammar p108, Ex.1–3
Vocabulary p110, Ex.1
Vocabulary Extra p111, Ex.1–3

Worksheets
Grammar Worksheets 12
Grammar presentation: Passive report structures
Vocabulary Worksheets 12

GRAMMAR
Passive report structures

1 Find and <u>underline</u> the sentences in the article which have the same meaning as 1–5. Then complete the rule with *written*, *past*, or *present*.

1 People believe that they were drawn 1,500 to 2,500 years ago.
2 People think that the sea will disappear completely in the next 50 years.
3 Experts believe that this ancient glacier is thousands of years old.
4 We know that the Dead Sea has sunk over 24 meters since the 1980s.
5 People say that the area is losing hundreds of square kilometers of forest every year.

RULE: An example of a passive report structure is:
*Thousands of caves **are thought to exist** in China.*
We can also say:
***It is thought** that thousands of caves exist in China.*
These structures use reporting verbs like *say, think, believe, know,* and *consider.*
If we use a passive report structure to talk about beliefs or knowledge of [6] ______ actions, we use the correct form of *be* + past participle of the reporting verb + *to* + infinitive:
*She **is said to be** one of the greatest explorers of all time.*
***It is said** that she is one of the greatest explorers of all time.*
If we use a passive report structure to talk about beliefs or knowledge of [7] ______ actions, we use the correct form of *be* + past participle of the reporting verb + *to* + *have* + past participle:
*Many people **are known to have died** on the expedition.*
Passive report structures are more often used in [8] ______ or more formal language, e.g., newspaper reports.

2 Rewrite the following sentences using passive report structures.

0 Experts know that Death Valley is the hottest place on Earth. Death Valley *is known to be the hottest place on Earth*.
1 We believe that the ice in Antarctica is disappearing.
The ice in Antarctica ______.
2 People say that this cave is 500 meters deep.
This cave ______.
3 Experts think that most fish in the deep ocean are blind.
Most fish ______.
4 We know that the Sahara Desert contained water only 5,000 years ago.
The Sahara Desert ______.
5 Experts believe that some deep-sea creatures have existed for millions of years.
Some deep-sea creatures ______.

→ workbook page 108

VOCABULARY
Geographical features

3 Match the words with the photos. Write 1–8 in the boxes.

1 bay | 2 canyon | 3 dune
4 glacier | 5 mountain range
6 reef | 7 volcano | 8 waterfall

4 Complete each sentence with a word from Exercise 3.

1 There's often snow on the top of a very high ______.
2 It can be difficult to run up a ______ because it's all sand.
3 When water goes over the edge of a ______, it often looks white.
4 A ______ can be dangerous for ships, because it's just below the surface of the water.
5 If a ______ is active, it sometimes erupts and can be very dangerous.
6 It can take a very long time for a ______ to move even as little as ten centimeters.
7 A ______ is sometimes a good place for ships to stop, because it's protected by land on three sides.
8 There's usually a river at the bottom of a ______.

5 SPEAKING **Work in pairs. You have three minutes to think of as many famous examples of the features in Exercise 3 as you can. Then compare your ideas with another pair.**

→ workbook page 110

112

3 During feedback, say the words for students to repeat and pay attention to the long vowel sounds in *bay*, *volcano*, and *glacier*.
A 6 B 1 C 3 D 2 E 8 F 5 G 7 H 4

4 **Check/clarify:** *surface, erupts.*
1 mountain range 2 dune 3 waterfall 4 reef 5 volcano 6 glacier 7 bay 8 canyon

5 Make the activity into a competition to see which pair has the most examples.

Workbook p110

Activity idea Extension

Write the following verbs on the board. Tell students that they can be used with the structure *it is* + past participle + *that*: *agree, announce, believe, calculate, claim, consider, discover, estimate, expect, feel, hope, know, report, say, show, suggest, think, understand.*

In pairs, students write six sentences about their country using some of the verbs in the passive report structure. They should write three sentences that are true and three that are false. Ask them to share their sentences with another pair and work out which sentences are true and which are false.

6 Check/clarify: *pocket.*
Put a copy of the four photos up on the board and do the exercise as a class before students open their books.
A 4 B 2 C 1 D 3

7 Students' own answers

8 🔊 **12.02** Ask students to listen to find the answer to Exercise 7 (the gibbon) before eliciting the answer to Exercise 8.
They've recently been discovered.

9 🔊 **12.02** Give students time to read through questions 1–5 before playing the audio again.
1 It has a pocket-like feature just near the fins below its head. 2 80 years ago 3 Their eyebrows are thinner and farther apart, and the shape of their skulls and teeth is different from other gibbons. 4 It's yellow and green. 5 We need to stop habitats from being destroyed.

10 🔊 **12.03** Ask students to try to complete the extract from memory. Play the audio to check.
1 *endangered* 2 *human beings* 3 *don't act* 4 *vital* 5 *don't you*

11 To check understanding of terminology (adjectives, adverbs, question tag, conditional clause) elicit examples of each from the class.
1 *rapidly, vital* 2 *don't you?* 3 *If we don't act now*

12 Refer students to the extract in Exercise 10 as an example. Check that students are including examples of the structures in Exercise 11 to make their points strongly. Put students into small groups to take turns giving their speeches. Students could vote on the most persuasive speech.

Pronunciation
Linking: intrusive /r/
Student's Book p121

13 Encourage students to use bullet points to make notes and to write down any interesting vocabulary.

LISTENING

6 Match the photos and the names. Write 1–4 in the boxes.

1 giant rat | 2 gibbon | 3 pocket shark | 4 rainfrog

A

B

C

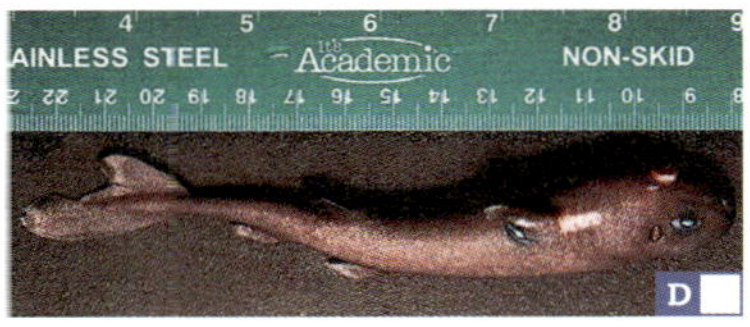

D

7 Which of the creatures do you think is named after a *Star Wars* character? Why?

8 🔊 12.02 Listen to someone giving a talk about animal species. What is true about all of the creatures?

9 🔊 12.02 Listen again and answer the questions.
1 Why is the tiny shark called a pocket shark?
2 When was the last time a new rat species was found in the South Pacific?
3 What three things are different about Skywalker gibbons?
4 What makes this frog eye-catching?
5 What can we do to protect these animals?

FUNCTIONS
Speaking persuasively

10 🔊 12.03 Listen again to the end of the talk. Complete the text.

"... all these animals are [1] ________________. Their habitat, that is the places where they live, is being destroyed rapidly, and it is [2] ________________ who are doing this. If we [3] ________________ now, to stop habitats from being destroyed, many animals will disappear, and future generations will only see them in books. I think it's [4] ________________ for humans to find ways to live well and without harming other living creatures, [5] ________________?"

11 In the extract in Exercise 10, underline these things.
1 adjectives and adverbs used to make a point strongly
2 a question tag
3 a conditional clause to show urgency

12 WRITING Write two or three sentences for a speech in which someone wants to persuade listeners about these things.
1 Traffic has to be reduced in a town.
2 Having a new supermarket in a town is a bad idea.
3 A recreation center is needed in a town.

PRONUNCIATION
Linking: intrusive /r/ Go to page 121.

TH!NK values
Human activity and the natural world

13 Read what the speaker says at the end of the talk. Then think about the questions. Make notes.

... forests are being turned into fields to grow food, and trees are being cut down to get wood, and rivers are being used by more and more boats, and so these animals find it harder and harder to live.

1 Can you give any real-life examples of what she's describing?
2 What other problems can human activity cause? (not just problems for animals)
3 Do you think there might be problems if people explore the deep ocean? What kind of problems?

14 SPEAKING Work in pairs or small groups.
1 Use your notes from Exercise 13. Decide on the question you are most interested in.
2 Together, prepare a two-minute presentation entitled "Human activity and the natural world."
3 Give your presentation to the class.

14 Before students begin, elicit/clarify that they should include a brief introduction before giving their opinions and ending with a strong conclusion. Remind students to use the kind of persuasive language used in Exercise 10.

Homework
If you are short on time, students can prepare their presentation in Exercise 14 for homework and give the presentation in the next lesson.

Activity idea Mixed-ability
In Exercise 12, stronger students can complete the exercise alone. Weaker students can work with a partner.

TH!NK more
Workbook
Listening p114, Ex.1–3
Pronunciation p121

Social Responsibilities
Understanding global issues
Discussing a range of global issues.

Warmer

Ask: *How do you travel to … (city near the school)?* Elicit answers in open class. Ask: *How could you travel if there were no roads? How long would it take?* Ask students to discuss with a partner before eliciting some of their ideas.

1 If students have access to the internet, give them time to research their answers before discussing them.

2 Before students read the article, get them to cover it, look at the title and pictures, and answer the question. Then set a three-minute time limit for them to skim the article quickly.

Rondon built many roads and telegraph lines across Brazil. He also spent his life protecting the interests, cultures, and lives of many of the native peoples of Brazil.

3 🔊 **12.06**

1 T 2 T

3 F (He became friends with them.)

4 T 5 DS 6 T

4 Make sure all students get an opportunity to speak.

Activity idea Fast finishers

Ask students to write two more statements about the article for their partners / the class to decide if they are true, false, or not in the article.

Activity idea Extension

Ask student pairs to write five questions based on the article. Put pairs together to form groups of four to ask each other their questions. Students score two points if they can answer correctly from memory, and one point if they can find the answer after looking at the article for no longer than 15 seconds.

EXPLORERS

Almost every country on our planet has been explored and mapped and all of these have roads, railways, and lines of communication. So it can be hard for us to imagine the people who went there without all the infrastructure that we now take for granted.

This series celebrates the men and women who opened the world up and risked their lives to protect the people and environments they discovered along the way. This week, we profile a man not well-known outside his own country and continent – Cândido Rondon.

A FRIEND TO NATIVE PEOPLE CÂNDIDO RONDON

In 1865, in a small village in the state of Mato Grosso, Brazil, a boy was born. His father was of Portuguese ancestry, and his mother was a native Brazilian. Who could have known that his origins would play such a big part in helping to connect so many cultures in very real and visible ways?

He decided to join the army as an engineer, and when he was only 25, he was involved in the building of a road from Rio de Janeiro to Cuiabá, a journey that previously could only be made by boat. He was later given the monumental task of placing telegraph lines from Brazil to Bolivia and Peru. This was a difficult job through rough and unexplored terrain, so it required a skilled engineer. Rondon opened paths through uncharted territory, and he came into contact with the Bororo, a tribe he had family connections with on his mother's side. Rondon established a friendly and respectful relationship with the Bororo people, and the telegraph lines were completed with their help.

Next, Rondon was given the job of extending the telegraph system from Mato Grosso to the Amazon. This time, he came across and made friends with the Nambikwara, previously thought of as a timid but hostile tribe. Rondon got to know many tribes during his expeditions, and he was a great friend to them. He was disturbed and ashamed to learn about the terrible way that they were often treated by outsiders. He fought long and hard to protect them and their right to follow their own beliefs, traditions, and customs.

However, some people still considered him an outsider. During his expeditions in Amazonia, Rondon was attacked several times, and once he was wounded by an arrow. Other members of the expedition wanted to take revenge on the native people who had attacked them, but Rondon said, "Die if necessary, but never kill." Years later, Rondon set up Brazil's Indian Protection Service, an agency to safeguard the interests and support the cultures of native peoples. Rondon's famous words became its motto.

Rondon died in 1958 and is remembered as a hero in Brazil. A state in Brazil (Rondônia) was named after him, as well as the airport in Cuiabá and several roads.

Next week: Abel Tasman

READING

1 SPEAKING **Work in pairs. Discuss what you know about when the main roads, railways, and telephone lines were built in your country. Think about these things:**

1 how and when the main roads (and/or railways) were built and by whom
2 how communications, such as telephone lines, started and when
3 any difficulties people had when building the roads, telephone lines, etc.

2 **Look at the title of the article and the pictures. What do you think Rondon achieved? Read the article quickly to check.**

3 🔊 12.06 **Read and listen to the article again. Mark the sentences T (true), F (false), or DS (doesn't say). Then correct the false sentences.**

1 Cândido Rondon was half Portuguese and half Brazilian. ☐
2 Rondon was considered a good engineer. ☐
3 The Nambikwara were not friendly to Rondon. ☐
4 Rondon was upset by the way strangers treated the tribes. ☐
5 Rondon's motto came from one of the tribes. ☐
6 Many people in Brazil still appreciate what Rondon did for the country. ☐

4 SPEAKING **Work in pairs and discuss the questions.**

1 What do you understand by Rondon's motto, "Die if necessary, but never kill."?
2 What places in your country are named after famous people?
3 Who would you name an airport after in your country?

114

Culture notes

The Bororo are indigenous people living along the upper Paraguay River in southern Brazil. It is estimated that they have been living in this area for at least 7,000 years. The term *Bororo* means "village court," and their houses are traditionally in a circular position around a central court where ceremonies are held. During rainy seasons, the Bororo abandon their villages and move to higher ground, subsisting mostly by hunting, gathering, and fishing, but also some farming. They probably number a little more than 1,000.

The Nambikwara are the indigenous people of Mato Grosso in Brazil. In the early 20th century, Cândido Randon estimated the population to be around 10,000 people, but by 1930, due to introduced diseases such as measles and smallpox, this had been reduced to only 500. Their language is apparently unrelated to any other.

Indian Protection Service (Serviço de Proteção aos Índios, abbreviated as SPI) was the first Brazilian government agency to be charged with protecting Indian peoples from persecution and extermination. Founded in 1910 in response to international pressure and accusations of indigenous genocide from Cândido Randon, the organization was disbanded in 1967 and replaced by the National Indian Foundation (Funação Nacional do Índio or FUNAI), which is still active today.

TH!NK more

Workbook
Reading p112, Ex.1–4

▶ 32 Grammar video! The passive: verbs with two objects

5 Give students two minutes to read the article and find the sentences.
Sentence 3 is used in the article.
RULE: 4 indirect 5 direct 6 person

6 Clarify that both are grammatically possible, but one of each pair is more common.
1 B 2 A 3 A 4 A

7 1 My mom was offered a job.
2 My dad was owed a lot of money.
3 He was given some medicine.
4 We were promised a free trip.
5 I was shown the right way to do it.

Workbook p109

8 Remind students to put the verbs into the correct form.
1 made 2 made 3 take 4 play

9 If you are using an IWB, prepare a board with the nouns written in individual text boxes. During feedback, ask individuals to come to the board and drag and drop words into the correct column.
make: a complaint, a deal, a decision, a joke, a journey, a speech, amends, a wish, an effort, friends, fun of someone, good, money, progress
take: a joke, a journey, a photo, advantage, advice, a test, an exam
play: a joke, a role, a part, the fool
do: favor, exercise, good, research
give: a speech, advice, a test, an exam, an example, an interview, money

10 Encourage students to first read the story and ignore the blanks in order to get a general understanding.
1 take/make 2 gave 3 making 4 gave 5 made 6 done 7 taken 8 made 9 made 10 take 11 make 12 take

11 The notes for this exercise can be done in class, and the writing assigned for homework. Give students time to make some notes and then ask them to tell their stories to a partner. Ask students to give each other feedback. They should say how it could be made more interesting and point out any important elements that should be included.

Workbook p110

GRAMMAR Grammar video ▶32
The passive: verbs with two objects

5 Check which of these three sentences is in the article on page 114. Then complete the rule with *person*, *direct*, and *indirect*.

1 They gave Rondon the job of extending the telegraph system.
2 The job of extending the telegraph system was given to Rondon.
3 Rondon was given the job of extending the telegraph system.

RULE: Some verbs (like *give, offer, ask, promise, read, show, write, buy*, etc.) can be followed by two objects (a person and a thing).
1 Verb + indirect object + direct object:
The teacher read the children a story.
2 Verb + direct object + indirect object:
The teacher read a story to the children.
There are also two ways of making the passive construction:
1 *The **children** were read a story.*
([4]__________ object as subject)
2 *A **story** was read to the children.*
([5]__________ object as subject)
It is more common to have the [6]__________ as the subject of the passive construction, not the object.

6 In each pair of sentences, check (✓) the one that is more common.

1 A A lot of money was paid to her. ☐
B She was paid a lot of money. ☐
2 A I was told a lie. ☐
B A lie was told to me. ☐
3 A We were promised a big party. ☐
B A big party was promised to us. ☐
4 A I was bought a new pair of shoes. ☐
B A new pair of shoes was bought for me. ☐

7 Rewrite the sentences using the passive. Use the person as subject.

0 They told me a secret.
I was told a secret.
1 They offered my mom a job.
2 People owed my dad a lot of money.
3 They gave him some medicine.
4 Someone promised us a free trip.
5 Someone showed me the right way to do it.

→ workbook page 109

VOCABULARY
Verb + noun collocations

8 Complete the sentences about the article on page 114 with the correct verbs.

1 Rondon __________ friends with the Nambikwara tribe.
2 Before that, the journey could only be __________ by river transportation.
3 They wanted to __________ revenge on the native people.
4 Who could have known that his origins would __________ such a big part in helping to connect so many cultures?

9 Complete the table with nouns from the list to make collocations. Some nouns can go into more than one column.

advantage | advice | amends | a complaint
a deal | a decision | an effort | an exam
an example | exercise | a favor | the fool | friends
fun of someone | good money | an interview
a joke | a journey | a part | a photo | progress
research | a role | a speech | a test | a wish

make	take	play	do	give

10 Complete the story with the correct form of the verbs in Exercise 9.

When I got to the small jungle town, I [0]__*made*__ friends with some of the locals and told them that I wanted to [1]__________ a journey up the river. They thought I was crazy! One of them [2]__________ me some advice – he said, "Don't go! It's dangerous." At first, I thought he was [3]__________ fun of me, but then he [4]__________ me some examples of the dangers I would face.
But I had [5]__________ my decision – I wanted to explore. I had [6]__________ some research about the diseases I could catch, and I had [7]__________ some medical tests to make sure I was in good health. I had worked for years and [8]__________ a lot of money, so I [9]__________ a deal with three of the men to come with me.
I needed to leave soon, to [10]__________ advantage of the good weather and to [11]__________ as much progress as I could before the rains began. So, the next morning, we met at the port. I put my phone in my pocket (I could use it to [12]__________ photos) and got into the small boat. I looked at the river – would I make it?

11 WRITING **Work in pairs. Write the next paragraph of the story in Exercise 10. Try to include some more collocations from Exercise 9.**

→ workbook page 110

Homework

Allocate students one of the five verbs in the table in Exercise 9 and ask them to make a poster of the verb + noun collocations for that verb group for display in the classroom.

Activity idea Mixed-ability

In Exercise 7, ask weaker students to underline the direct objects and circle the indirect objects before they rewrite the sentences taking the indirect object as subject.

TH!NK more

Practice Extra
Unit 12 Practice it!

Workbook
Grammar p109, Ex.4–6
Vocabulary p110, Ex.2–5

Worksheets
Grammar Worksheets 12
Grammar video! The passive verbs with two objects
Vocabulary Worksheets 12

Warmer

To review verb + noun collocations from the last lesson, give a student a noun and ask them to say the correct verb to score a point, e.g., *A: a speech, B: make a speech.* Do this two or three times with different collocations and then ask students to play "collocations tennis." In pairs, one student says a noun, and the other person must reply with the correct verb as quickly as possible.

1 Check/clarify: *plateau.* Before students open their books, ask: *Can you think of any novels or movies about dinosaurs? What happens in them?* Students discuss the questions in pairs. Listen to some of their ideas and write any repeated themes on the board.

2 Set a three-minute time limit to encourage speed-reading. Tell students not to worry about difficult vocabulary at this stage, as this will come up later.
2

Culture note

Sir Arthur Conan Doyle, born in 1859, was an author from Edinburgh, Scotland. At the age of nine, he was sent to boarding school in England, where he realized he had a talent for storytelling, and he would often make up stories to tell the younger students. He trained as a doctor, gaining a degree from the University of Edinburgh in 1881.

Following a voyage to the Arctic as a ship's surgeon and to Africa as a medical officer on a steamer, Doyle returned to England to open his own practice in Portsmouth. He divided his time between writing and medicine.

In March 1886, Doyle started writing *A Study in Scarlet*. It catapulted him to fame and introduced the world to Sherlock Holmes and Dr. Watson. In 1891, Doyle abandoned his medical career and wrote many more stories featuring Holmes. By 1893, frustrated that his other work was being largely ignored, he decided to "kill off" Sherlock Holmes to concentrate on other works. There was a public outcry, but Doyle wrote a number of other novels, including *The Lost World* along with many non-fiction works before resurrecting Holmes in 1903. He ran unsuccessfully for MP for Edinburgh Central and in later life became very interested in spiritualism. He died in 1930 surrounded by his family, having published over 200 stories and articles throughout his career.

Literature

1 Look at the photo and read the introduction to the extract. Do you think you would like to read the book?

2 Read the extract quickly and choose the best ending for the statement.

The narrator feels worried about …
1 what will happen when the sun comes up.
2 the noise of drums that he can hear.
3 the animals in the jungle around them.

The Lost World by Arthur Conan Doyle (1912)

Professor George Challenger and his friend Lord John Roxton, together with a reporter and some local guides (one of whom is named Gomez), travel up the Amazon River to find a plateau. Challenger claims he has visited the plateau before, and that there are prehistoric creatures living there. Also with them is another professor who dislikes Challenger and doesn't believe his claims. The reporter narrates the story.

The very next day we did actually make our start upon this **remarkable** expedition. We found that all our possessions fitted very easily into the two canoes, and we divided our personnel, six in each, taking the obvious precaution, in the interests of peace, of putting one professor into each canoe. […]

At dawn and at sunset the monkeys screamed together and the parrots started making their high-pitched noise, but during the hot hours of the day only the loud noise of insects, like the beat of a distant surf, filled the ear, while nothing moved amongst the **solemn** views of huge tree-trunks, **fading away** into the darkness which held us in. Once some creature, an ant-eater or a bear, walked clumsily amid the shadows. It was the only sign of life which I had seen in this great Amazonian forest.

And yet there were **indications** that even human life itself was not far from us in those mysterious dark corners.

On the third day out, we were aware of a strange, deep, rhythmic beat in the air, coming and going on-and-off throughout the morning. The two boats were moving within a few yards of each other when we first heard it, and our guides remained motionless, as if they had been turned to bronze, listening intently with expressions of terror upon their faces.

"What is it, then?" I asked.

"Drums," said Lord John, carelessly, "war drums. I have heard them before."

"Yes, sir, war drums," said Gomez. "Native people, **aggressive**, not friendly; they watch us every mile of the way; kill us if they can."

"How can they watch us?" I asked, gazing into the dark. Gomez shrugged his broad shoulders.

"The native people know. They have their own way. They watch us. They talk the drum talk to each other. Kill us if they can."

By the afternoon of that day – my pocket diary shows me that it was Tuesday, August 18th – at least six or seven drums were beating from various points. Sometimes they beat quickly, sometimes slowly, sometimes in obvious question and answer, one far to the east breaking out in a high-pitched beat, and being followed after a pause by a deep roll from the north. There was something **incredibly** nerve-shaking and threatening in that **constant** noise, which seemed to shape itself into the words that Gomez used and endlessly repeated them: "We will kill you if we can. We will kill you if we can." No one ever moved in the silent woods. All the peace of quiet nature lay in that dark curtain of vegetation, but away from behind, there always came the one message from our fellow-man: "We will kill you if we can," said the men in the east. "We will kill you if we can," said the men in the north. […]

That night we tied our canoes with heavy stones for anchors in the centre of the stream, and made every preparation for a possible attack. Nothing came, however, and with the dawn we pushed upon our way, the drum-beating **dying out** behind us.

Adapted from *The Lost World* by Arthur Conan Doyle

116

Reading; Writing

3 🔊 **12.07 Check/clarify:** *personnel, precaution, high-pitched, tree-trunks, clumsily, amid, rhythmic, motionless, bronze, nerve-shaking, threatening, fellow-man.*
1 F (They were in separate boats to avoid any conflict.) 2 T 3 F (They only saw a few animals.) 4 T 5 F (There was no attack.)

4 Stronger students can look at the words in the extract and try to deduce meaning from context before referring to the definitions.
1 constant 2 remarkable 3 solemn 4 indications 5 incredibly 6 dying out 7 fading away 8 aggressive

5 After students have discussed in pairs, regroup them into small groups for students to report back on their discussions and share opinions.

1 **Check/clarify:** *ANC (African National Congress), presidency, a stroke.*
Ask students to quickly read the biography and answer the questions.
1 education and law 2 Zambia and London 3 Because he had a stroke and could not work any longer.

2 Point out that the information in the biography is presented chronologically.
A fourth paragraph B second paragraph C first paragraph D third paragraph

3 Elicit the names of some places in students' cities which are named after famous people and write them on the board. In pairs, students choose a subject they are both familiar with and plan their biography. If students have access to the internet, they can do the research in class. If not, this could be done at home.

4 Encourage students to use the biography about O. R. Tambo as a model.

OFF THE BEATEN TRACK UNIT 12

3 🔊 12.07 **Read and listen to the extract again. Mark the sentences T (true) or F (false). Then correct the false sentences.**

1 There was not enough room for both professors to sit together. ☐
2 The noise of the insects sounded like the sea. ☐
3 They saw some wild animals hiding among the trees. ☐
4 The guides were terrified when they heard the drums. ☐
5 The violent attack came at dawn. ☐

4 **Match the highlighted words in the extract with the definitions.**

1 never changing, always the same
2 not ordinary, amazing
3 very serious and a little sad
4 signs
5 difficult to believe
6 decreasing to nothing
7 stop existing
8 fierce and eager (wanting) to fight

5 SPEAKING **Work in pairs and discuss the questions.**

1 What about this text tells you it was written more than 100 years ago? Give reasons.
2 Which attitudes of the narrator are outdated today?

WRITING
A short biography

1 INPUT **Read Joel's biography of Oliver Tambo and answer the questions.**

1 What did Tambo study during his life?
2 Where did he live, apart from in South Africa?
3 Why did he give the ANC presidency to Nelson Mandela?

2 ANALYZE **Which paragraph is which? Write letters in the boxes in the text.**

A Conclusion
B Early life
C Introduction to the person
D Main achievements

3 PLAN **You're going to write a short biography.**

1 Think of something in your country (e.g., a street, an airport, a square) that is named after a famous person.
2 Make notes about the person's life. Do research on the internet if you need to.
3 Decide which information is most important to include in a biography.

4 PRODUCE **Now write your biography (200–250 words).**

- Make sure that you include information that makes it clear why the place was named after the person.
- Follow the structure of the biography about Tambo.

☐ Johannesburg is my home city, and the international airport here is called O. R. Tambo airport. It is named after Oliver Tambo, who not many people know much about. Almost everyone has heard of Nelson Mandela, but Tambo is not as well known around the world.

☐ Oliver Reginald Tambo (everyone knew him as O. R.) was born in 1917, in an area of South Africa now known as the Eastern Cape. As a young man he studied education, and for a while, he was a teacher. Later, he gave up teaching to study law, and in 1952, he joined Nelson Mandela's law firm.

☐ These were the years of apartheid in South Africa. Tambo, like Mandela, was part of the African National Congress (ANC), which was an illegal organization at that time. Mandela was sent to prison on Robben Island, and Tambo left the country – he lived in Zambia and London at different times. He was the "president in exile" of the ANC and worked very hard to get support from other countries in the struggle to end apartheid.

☐ He went back to South Africa in 1990, when the ANC became legal. But he had a stroke and could not work any longer, so he passed the presidency of the ANC to Mandela. Tambo died in 1993, before he could see the first black government of his country. In 2006, the airport was renamed after him to honor his achievements. And to sum up, I think that this honor rightly recognized the very important role that Tambo played in the development of the country he loved.

117

Homework

If you are short on time, students can do Writing Exercise 4 for homework. If you have done this in the class, ask students to exchange their biographies with another student for them to give feedback on content and structure. Students could check if the biography uses the same structure as the model. They should decide which the most/least interesting part of the biography is.

Activity idea Extension

Give students five minutes to work in pairs and search for as many adjectives as they can find in *The Lost World*. When time is up, elicit answers, but don't discuss meaning or what the adjectives refer to yet. Put students into groups of three pairs. Pairs take turns saying an adjective. The other two pairs race to say what the adjective refers to in the extract and the meaning.

TH!NK more

Practice Extra
Unit 12 Master it!

Workbook
Developing Writing p113

Tests
Unit, extension, and skills test 12
Final test

1 12.08 In B2 First for Schools Listening Part 2, candidates have to listen to a monologue and complete ten sentences. This part of the exam tests candidates' ability to listen for specific and detailed information. It also checks the spelling of common words.

Encourage your students to do the following when they approach this task:

- Read and listen to the instructions carefully.
- Read the sentences, think about the context, and predict the language and information.
- During the first listening, find and write down single words, numbers, or short noun phrases to complete the information. Use the order of the information on the page to follow the recording.
- During the second listening, check that the answers are correct and make sense. There will only ever be a maximum of three words to write in each gap. If the word was spelled in the recording, the answer must also be spelled correctly.

1 (sea) temperatures 2 plants 3 pollution 4 medicine(s) 5 sand 6 volcanic 7 95% 8 11,000 metres 9 (totally) silent 10 winds

Workbook p115

2 In B2 First Reading and Use of English Part 4, candidates have to read six questions. Each question contains three parts: a lead-in sentence, a key word, and a second sentence of which only the beginning and the end are given. Candidates have to fill the gap in the second sentence so that the completed sentence has a similar meaning to the lead-in sentence. This part of the exam tests lexical and grammatical structures and the ability to paraphrase.

Encourage your students to do the following when they approach this task:

- Read the first sentence to understand the meaning.
- Pay attention to any verb in the second sentence as it will often indicate whether to use a singular or plural noun.
- Write only the words that fill the gap.
- Check that the gap has between two and five words, including the key word.
- Check that the key word has been used in the same form as it was given.
- Read the completed sentence again to make sure it makes similar sense to the first one.

1 if he had an explanation 2 only order this book if 3 are said to cause 4 a good idea to watch 5 was given by 6 rather stay at

B2 First for Schools

LISTENING
Part 2: Sentence completion

workbook page 115

1 12.08 **You will hear a woman called Frances Williams talking about her work as an oceanographer. For questions 1–10, complete the sentences with a word or a short phrase.**

Frances believes oceanography is important for dealing with increased [1] ______ as a result of climate change.

Frances says that marine biologists study the impact of changes in the marine environment on [2] ______ and animals.

Chemical oceanographers try to find out more about the impact that [3] ______ has on the quality of the ocean waters.

Some chemical oceanographers try to find resources for new [4] ______ .

Physical oceanographers focus on movements of the sea, such as how [5] ______ is moved along coastlines.

Frances' job involves studying how the ocean floor changes as a result of [6] ______ activity.

Frances says that [7] ______ of the world's ocean floors have not yet been explored.

Challenger Deep is an area of the ocean that goes down to nearly [8] ______ .

Frances' research does not confirm the general belief that the ocean's deepest places are [9] ______ .

Oceanographers have also discovered that there are strong currents that can be compared to extreme [10] ______ .

READING AND USE OF ENGLISH
Part 4: Key word transformation

2 **For questions 1–6, complete the second sentence so that it has a similar meaning to the first sentence, using the word given. Do not change the word given. You must use between two and five words, including the word given. Here is an example (0).**

Example:

0 Kate has an interest in marine biology.
INTERESTED
Kate ______ a marine biologist.
Write the missing words in CAPITAL LETTERS.
Kate IS INTERESTED IN BECOMING a marine biologist.

1 'Have you got any idea why coral bleaching is happening, Nick?' asked Mia.
IF
Mia asked Nick ______ for coral bleaching.

2 You can't order this book unless they have an online store.
ONLY
You can ______ they have an online store.

3 Researchers say that high water temperatures cause coral bleaching.
SAID
High water temperatures ______ coral bleaching.

4 My friends were in favour of watching the documentary.
IDEA
My friends thought it would be ______ the documentary.

5 The researcher gave a fascinating talk.
GIVEN
A fascinating talk ______ the researcher.

6 I'd prefer not to join you.
STAY
I'd ______ home.

118

Units 11 & 12 Test Yourself

1 1 squeezing 2 solar 3 breathtaking 4 volcano 5 waterfall 6 reef 7 took 8 bonus 9 do 10 far-fetched

2 1 to have 2 consequently 3 can't have 4 to be 5 must be 6 was given

3 1 I'm sure a lot of people have met the new boy. Sofia ~~mustn't~~ can't be the only one.
2 Only a few people are thought to have ~~survive~~ survived so long alone in the desert.
3 Darn, I'm bound to ~~got~~ get / have gotten this all wrong – I didn't understand the question.
4 My father was brought up by his aunt after his parents ~~were~~ died.
5 Kate Jones is ~~know~~ known to have owned three houses, although she has always said that she's very poor.
6 I suppose it's possible – Cara might ~~be~~ have been at the party last night, but I didn't see her.

4 1 must; no 2 had been; terrible 3 believed; can't 4 thought; seen

TEST YOURSELF UNITS 11 & 12

VOCABULARY

1 Complete the sentences with the words in the list. There are four extra words.

action-packed | bonus | breathtaking | do | far-fetched | gave | make | reef | solar | squeezing | star | took | volcano | waterfall

1 My baby cousin drew a picture of me by ______ toothpaste onto the mirror in the bathroom.
2 Jack has an image of the ______ system projected on the ceiling of his bedroom.
3 The effect of the fireworks and the music was really ______ .
4 Flights were disrupted when a ______ erupted and filled the sky with ash.
5 We climbed up to the top of the ______ and watched the water pouring down.
6 The water in the bay is always calm because it's protected by a ______ .
7 Pete's dad gave him some good advice, but I don't think he ______ it.
8 We weren't expecting good weather on our vacation, so the sunshine was a real ______ .
9 Christina's presentation is next week, so she needs to ______ some research on the internet.
10 His excuse for being late was so ______ that no one believed a word of it. /10

GRAMMAR

2 Complete the sentences with the phrases in the list. There are two extra phrases.

can't have | consequently | due to | must be | must have | to be | to have | was given

1 Samuel L. Jackson is known ______ made more than $5 billion dollars as an actor.
2 Arlo was always eating fast food, and ______ , he put on a lot of weight.
3 Silvia is a terrible singer – she ______ won the singing competition!
4 London is known ______ one of the most expensive cities in the world.
5 Hafsa left half an hour ago – she ______ home by now.
6 Luis ______ two identical sweaters for his birthday.

3 Find and correct the mistake in each sentence.

1 I'm sure a lot of people have met the new boy. Sofia mustn't be the only one.
2 Only a few people are thought to have survive so long alone in the desert.
3 Darn, I'm bound to got this all wrong – I didn't understand the question.
4 My father was brought up by his aunt after his parents were died.
5 Kate Jones is know to have owned three houses, although she has always said that she's very poor.
6 I suppose it's possible – Cara might be at the party last night, but I didn't see her. /12

FUNCTIONAL LANGUAGE

4 Choose the correct options.

1 A I lost my phone! I *can* / *must* have left it on the bus.
B Oh *no* / *shame*, that is a problem.
2 A Last weekend, we couldn't find our cat. We thought she *was* / *had been* hit by a car.
B How *shame* / *terrible*! You must have been very worried.
3 A You know, in the past, being left-handed was *believed* / *known* to be unnatural.
B That *mustn't* / *can't* have been easy for left-handed people.
4 A In some countries, black cats are *thought* / *known* to be unlucky.
B Yes, but in other countries, they are *seen* / *looked* at as bringers of good luck. /8

MY SCORE /30

22–30 | 10–21 | 0–9

119

The Cambridge Life Competencies Framework

Critical THINKing
Evaluating ideas and arguments
Watch this video for a tip on developing your students' critical thinking skills. Scan the QR code here.

Get it Right!

Unit 1
Verb patterns
1 They wanted ~~going~~ to go sailing, but the weather conditions were too extreme.
2 I enjoy ~~to wander~~ wandering around outdoor markets when I'm on vacation.
3 Correct
4 Do you think you'll manage ~~completing~~ to complete the mountain climb?
5 Correct
6 Kate had hoped ~~reaching~~ to reach the glacier by early afternoon but slipped on the ice and broke her leg.
7 The children learned ~~building~~ to build a shelter during the survival course.
8 Megan was thrilled when she got her exam results as she'd expected ~~failing~~ to fail.

remember, forget, regret, try, and *stop*
1 to buy
2 to get
3 climbing
4 to climb
5 studying
6 going
7 to complete
8 to inform

Unit 2
that and *which* in relative clauses
1c The gray whale is the animal that swims about 18,000 km every year. (defining)
2e Domenico Lucano had an idea that saved his village. (defining)
3a Our teacher always praises us when we've done well on a test, which helps give us confidence (non-defining)
4f I spoke to him using Italian, which I had learned while working there. (non-defining)
5d Elena has decided to live abroad, which I think is very brave of her. (non-defining)

Relative pronouns
1 ✓
2 ✓
3 They went through a bad time which/that lasted a few months.
4 ✓
5 Those are the residents who/that live in that building over there.
6 The Bedouin are the people who/that are always on the move.

Unit 3
much vs. *many*
1 many
2 much
3 much
4 many
5 much
6 much

much and *most*
1 ~~The~~ Most of my teachers at school were very strict.
2 Correct
3 Correct
4 Sally tried on a few outfits, but ~~the~~ most of them were too big for her.
5 It would be interesting to know if most ~~of~~ people agreed with the strict new rules.
6 Were ~~the~~ most of your old school friends at the reunion?

Unit 4
used to
1 Liam ~~use~~ used to be very bad-tempered, but he's nicer now.
2 There's a lot of planning involved in my job, so I ~~use to be~~ am usually organized.
3 When I was in school, we ~~use~~ used to sit in a row for some classes.
4 They ~~use to~~ usually go to school by bus except for Tuesdays when they walk.
5 The man who ~~use~~ used to live there moved to Spain.
6 Sara ~~used to watch~~ usually watches a lot of TV when she doesn't have much homework.

Unit 5
should
1 A
2 A
3 A
4 B

Unit 6
Comparatives
1 harder
2 best
3 happiest
4 higher
5 hardest
6 better
7 highest
8 happier

Linkers of contrast
1 Despite the fact she confessed to the crime, the police didn't arrest her. / Even though she confessed to the crime, the police didn't arrest her.
2 We made an inquiry about the delivery. However / Nevertheless, no one got back to us. / Despite this, no one got back to us.
3 In spite of / Despite the fact that they made a complaint about the food, the chef didn't apologize.
4 The children took the move to the country in stride, despite the fact / in spite of the fact they had been happy living in the city.

Unit 7
Future continuous
1 ✓
2 I'll be seeing you sometime over the weekend, so I'll show you then.
3 ✓
4 I'll come to the airport to pick you up. I'll be waiting for you at arrivals.
5 Daphne won't be coming to the party on Saturday because she's busy.
6 This time next week, they'll be lying on a beach relaxing.

Unit 8
would
1 If they had run through the calculations, they would have realized their mistake. (extra word: would)
2 The meal wouldn't have turned out so well if you hadn't lent me your cookbook. (extra word: wouldn't)
3 She'll do it provided that we help her. (extra word: would)
4 If you don't wash your hands, you might get an infection. (extra word: would)
5 The cloth wouldn't have ripped if it had been stronger. (extra word: would)
6 It won't be a problem as long as you arrive on time. (extra word: would)

Unit 9
wish
1 wishes
2 hope
3 wants
4 wish
5 hopes
6 hope
7 hope

wish / *if only*
1 c 2 f 3 g 4 a 5 d 6 h 7 e 8 b

Unit 10
Reported speech
1 Simon asked me if I had remembered to pass along the message to the class.
2 ✓
3 Angela asked how efficiently the machine worked.
4 She asked if any politician could ever be impartial.
5 The students asked the speaker how big the impact of war had been.
6 The chief editor asked the journalist if he thought the article was newsworthy.

Unit 11
Cause and effect linkers
1 Due to
2 As a result
3 because of
4 consequently
5 so
6 because of

Unit 12
been and *being*
1 being
2 being
3 been
4 being
5 being
6 been

Unit 1

Diphthongs: alternative spellings

1.02 & 1.03 Students learn to identify and produce the diphthongs /aɪ/, /oʊ/, /eɪ/, /aʊ/, and /ɔɪ/ in words, e.g., *ice* /aɪs/, *snow* /snoʊ/, *late* /leɪt/, *town* /taʊn/, and *boys* /bɔɪz/. Ask students to listen to the recording and identify the sounds in the words in bold. Then ask students to say the words containing the diphthongs in the dialogue.

Unit 2

Phrasal verb stress

2.04 & 2.05 Students learn to identify syllables and stress within a phrasal verb. Ask students to read the dialogue and listen to the recording. Then ask them to count how many syllables each of the phrasal verbs has (*turned out*, *pick up*, and *hung out* have two; *run into* has three). Ask them to say these and stress the correct syllable to help them choose the correct option (1 primary, 2 secondary, 3 particle, 4 verb). Finally, ask them to listen again to the dialogue and repeat. Ask students to try to copy the stress patterns.

Unit 3

Adding emphasis

3.04 & 3.05 Students learn to identify and recreate emphatic stress in a sentence. Ask students to read the dialogue and listen to the recording, focusing on the stress of the words in bold. Ask students to say which words create the emphasis in each sentence (*such*, *so*, *did/do*). Ask them why the words in bold are emphasized (they make the meaning stronger). Ask students to act out the dialogue in pairs and to try to copy the emphatic stress on the words in bold.

Unit 4

Pronouncing words with *gh*

4.04 & 4.05 Students learn to identify and produce different sounds that are represented by *gh*. Ask students to listen to the recording and read the dialogue. If students are struggling to notice anything, tell them that in some of the words the *gh* is silent (*thought*, *through*, *brought*, and *right*) and ask them to identify the sound in the other two words (/f/ in *laugh* and *enough*). They then listen again and say the words with the *gh* spelling. Then ask them to listen and repeat the dialogue, focusing on the sounds.

Unit 5

The schwa /ə/ sound

5.03 & 5.04 Students learn to identify and produce words containing a schwa sound (/ə/) in words with a variety of spellings. Ask students to read the text and listen to the recording. Then ask them to read the dialogue out loud and to focus on the words with the short /ə/ sound (*the*, *to*, *a*, *or*, *an*). Finally, ask them to listen and repeat the whole text.

Unit 6

Linking words with /dʒ/ and /tʃ/

6.02 & 6.03 Students learn to discriminate between the /dʒ/ and /tʃ/ consonant sounds. Ask students to listen to the recording and read the dialogue. They then listen again and say the phrases with the /dʒ/ sounds (*Would you*, *Do you*, *Did you*, *told you*) and /tʃ/ sounds (*Didn't you*, *Don't you*), focusing on the difference between the two. Students then listen and repeat the whole dialogue, focusing on the linking sounds.

Unit 7

Intonation: encouraging someone

7.05 & 7.06 Students learn to identify and produce correct intonation when encouraging someone. Ask students to listen to the recording and read the dialogue. Then ask students to look at the blue phrases in the dialogue, listen again, and mark if the voice goes up or down. Ask them why the speaker does this (it makes the meaning stronger). Students then listen and repeat the whole dialogue, focusing on the intonation.

ˈdon't let it get you ˌdown

ˌLook on the bright side ˈIt'll be all ˌright!

I ˈknow you can ˌdo it!

Unit 8

Weak forms with conditionals

8.04 & 8.05 Students learn to identify and produce weak forms of the conditionals *would have* /wədəv/, *could have* /kədəv/ and *should have* /ʃəd əv/. Ask students to listen to the recording. Then ask students to say the words in blue. Ask them when the /v/ sound in *'ve* is pronounced (when the contraction is followed by a vowel sound, e.g., *should've asked* /ˈʃʊdəˈvæskt/). Students then listen and repeat the whole dialogue, focusing on the weak sounds.

Unit 9

Linking: intrusive /w/ and /j/

9.02 Students learn to identify and produce the intrusive sounds /w/ and /j/. Ask students to listen to the recording and read the dialogue. Ask them to listen again and identify the phrases with the /w/ sounds (*so angry*, *you ask*, *to explain*, *you always*, *to everything*, *so annoying*), and /j/ sounds (*me off*, *be able*, *be angry*, *be annoying*), focusing on the difference between the two. Students then listen and repeat the whole dialogue, focusing on the linking sounds.

Unit 10

Linking: omission of the /h/ sound

10.02 & 10.03 Students learn to identify silent *h* at the beginning of words, as well as practicing not pronouncing them. Ask students to listen to the recording and read the dialogue. They should then listen and underline the silent *h*. Ask students whether it is silent in stressed or unstressed words (it is silent in unstressed words, e.g., *he* and *her*). Students then listen and repeat the whole dialogue.

Unit 11

Stress on modal verbs for speculation

11.02 & 11.03 Students learn to recreate speculative intonation and stress within a sentence. Ask students to read the dialogue and listen to the recording, focusing on the stress of the underlined words. Ask students to say which words are emphasized (*might have dis**cov**ered*; ***might** have, I sup**pose***; *may have built some **vil**lages*; ***could** be true*; *may be the greatest ex**plor**ers in history*). Then ask students to listen and repeat the dialogue, focusing on the stress and intonation.

Unit 12

Linking: intrusive /r/

12.04 & 12.05 Students learn to identify and produce the intrusive /r/ sound. Ask students to listen to the recording and read the dialogue. Ask them to listen again and identify the phrases with the /r/ sound, focusing on how it links two words. Students then listen and repeat the whole dialogue, focusing on the linking sounds.

2 We're going far away to explore amazing places.

3 We hope to learn more about our incredible Earth.

4 We'll remember our adventure forever!

5 Join us on our adventure – follow our excellent blog!

Unit 1

1.04

Man Hello, everyone. Well, here in Britain, it's exam time again – that time of the year when thousands of schoolkids sit their exams, and for many it's a very important time because, right or wrong, the results of some exams, like A-levels, will determine whether they go to university or not, and what they'll do next. So, lots of stress around and here to talk about this stress and how to survive it is educational psychologist Janet Greaves.

Woman Hello.

Man Janet, the build-up to exams, the days and weeks before the exams actually start – this is perhaps the most difficult part, isn't it? I mean, my exams were a few years ago, but I still remember having sleepless nights.

Woman Yes, me, too! It's a difficult time in every young person's life. And a big question in the days before the exam is studying – how much, when, what kind, and so on. Um, I have to say that I didn't study enough for my exams, so I didn't actually do very well. I really regret not taking it more seriously.

Man But you survived, right? And you're doing OK?

Woman Yes, that's right. Everyone knows that exam results aren't everything. Life is much more than that! But of course, exams are really important when you're doing them.

Man Yes, indeed. So what advice can we give young people who are about to take these exams?

Woman Well, I'd say don't forget to take care of yourself! Remember to eat regularly and well – that's the first thing. And make sure to get lots of sleep, too. Tiredness always makes stress worse.

Man How much studying should they do?

Woman Well, that depends on all kinds of things. I think it's important to maintain a balance – study, sure, but keep doing things that you enjoy as well. And try to avoid comparing yourself with your friends – some of them will do more studying, some will do less. You have to do the right amount for you.

Man That's interesting, because I tried studying together with my friends, but it wasn't a great success. All that happened was we made each other feel more desperate!

Woman Well, yes, that can happen. You know, I think it's nice to study with your friends, but try not to get pulled into doing things in a way that doesn't suit you.

Man One last piece of advice?

Woman OK – be flexible! It's good to have a timetable and try to stick to it – but if you oversleep one morning, that's OK – it's not the end of the world! Don't feel guilty!

Man Absolutely. Well, I regret to say that we've run out of time. Janet, thanks for being with us. And good luck to all you exam-takers out there!

Unit 2

2.02

Host Hello and welcome back to "The Great Nature Quiz." It's the semi-final, and after two rounds, Dee has three points, and James has four. This round is all about migration. I'll describe an animal famous for its migration, and you buzz in when you think you know what it is. One point for a correct answer, but be careful. Give me the wrong answer, and you'll lose a point. So, fingers on buzzers. Let's play.

Host What am I? Each year I fly about 11,500 kilometers from New Zealand to Northern China. This is not the longest migration of a bird – that belongs to the Arctic Tern, but, believe it or not, I don't stop … Yes, Dee.

Dee Are you a bar-tailed godwit?

Host Yes, I am a bar-tailed godwit. Well done. As I said, what's most impressive about the bar-tailed godwit's migration is that it doesn't stop to feed, drink, or rest. Instead, it uses strong winds to help it complete its journey as quickly as possible. And would you believe me if I told you they do this in as little as two or three days? So fingers back on buzzers. I am born in a part of the western Atlantic Sea called the Sargasso Sea and then spend about two years getting to the rivers of the UK. Yes, James?

James Are you a freshwater eel?

Host I am indeed. Very impressive. What else can you tell us about the migration of the freshwater eel, James?

James Well, I know that when they get to the UK, they spend about twelve years inland growing until they are big enough to breed. Then it's all the way back to the Sargasso Sea where they lay their eggs and die.

Host Wow, you certainly know your eels, James. OK, question three. What am I? Each year I make a journey of up to 1,000 kilometers across the North American arctic regions, from the forests to the tundra and back again to escape the heaviest snows. My journey is made on foot and … Yes, Dee.

Dee Are you a caribou?

Host Yes, I am a caribou. Now did you know that although the caribou doesn't make as long a migration as the eels or the godwits, its journey is arguably more difficult as walking takes a lot more energy than either flying or swimming? So, at the end of round three Dee and James, you both have five points. The final round will decide the winner …

Unit 3

3.02

Hello, and welcome to *True Tales*. I have a *very* moving story to share with you today. It's the story of an American father from Michigan, Ricky van Beek, and his thirteen-year-old daughter Madison. The two share a love of the outdoors, and they have competed in many outdoor races together. Now, I know this may sound like an average father and daughter story, but it is much more than that. Madison has cerebral palsy, and van Beek is a devoted father who has carried his daughter across many kilometers of land and water. Together they have completed some of the most difficult triathlons.

When they began training for their first marathon in 2008, van Beek was a heavy smoker and very unfit. But seeing just how much joy Madison got from being bumped along roads in a cart really motivated him to get fit. For them both, the Grand Rapids Marathon was a life-changing event. Van Beek gave up smoking, and Madison found something that she truly loved.

Madison was diagnosed when she was just two months old, and learning that his daughter would never walk or talk was heart-breaking for Ricky. It was in fact one of the worst days of his life. Since then, he has been her legs, and she has been his motivation.

The Sanford and Sun sprint triathlon of 2012 is one of many events they have competed in together as "Team Maddy." Van Beek swam 500 meters, pulling his daughter through the water behind him in a kayak. He completed the 20-km bike ride pulling Madison behind him in a cart. He then ran 5 kilometers pushing Madison in a running chair. Seeing them participate together has been an inspiration to loads of people.

Together, they have competed in more than seventy events, some half-marathons, some triathlons, all very intense and all with one aim – to make Madison happy. This devotion and love for his daughter has resulted in people calling van Beek "the father of the century."

For van Beek, the motivation is love, and he says, "That will never fade. She is my heart, and I am her legs, though someday she might not physically be able to be there with me, she will always be in my heart, quietly cheering me on."

Their story has touched many people, and I think you'll agree, his determination to make his daughter happy is an inspiration to us all.

Unit 4

4.02

Phoebe What are you reading, Lewis?

Lewis Oh, hi, Phoebe. It's a challenge thing in this magazine. "How imaginative are you?" You have to think of things to do with old CDs. They want you to think of six.

Phoebe Oh, that's easy. I mean, you can use them as coasters – you know, put cups and glasses on them.

Lewis Oh, yes, that's right.

Phoebe What things have you thought of?

Lewis Well, none, to be honest.

Phoebe Let's think about it. Well, you could put one under a candle, and then the wax won't drip onto the table.

Lewis But most candles don't drip nowadays, do they?

Phoebe No idea, but it's only a game, right? Let's see – oh, you could use it to draw a perfect circle – in fact, two perfect circles, because there's the hole in the middle, too.

Lewis Well, that's three things – I guess.

Phoebe Yes, three. So far, so good. But I'm not sure I can think of three more!

Lewis Hang on – you could use them like Frisbees. Throw them and get your dog to bring them back.

Phoebe I don't have a dog.

Lewis Oh, you know what I mean. This is getting boring.

Phoebe Don't be so impatient, Lewis!

Lewis Let's try the other one. Come on, Phoebe, help me with this picture. You have to find lots of different things. I've been looking at it for ages, but it's no good, I can't see anything at all.

Phoebe Seriously? I mean, there's a tree …

Lewis Well yes, of course there's a tree!! I mean, I can't see anything else.

Phoebe Well, look at the trunk, there are two faces looking at each other.

Lewis Oh, yes! Aren't you clever!? Anything else?

Phoebe Umm …

Lewis Oh, oh! A piece of broccoli …

Phoebe OK … hmm, yes, OK, I <u>think</u> I can see that. I think!

Lewis Oh, come on, Phoebe, give me a break, it's the only thing I've managed to see!

Phoebe OK, I'll accept broccoli, if you'll accept … a human brain.

Lewis A brain? What? Oh, hang on, yes. The top part. Way to go, Phoebe! What else?

Phoebe Nothing else! I'm getting bored now. Who makes these things up? Are they supposed to tell you something about yourself?

Lewis Well, they're supposed to show you how imaginative you are. And I'm not very good at them, so I guess I'm not very imaginative!

Phoebe No, don't be so hard on yourself. What's so creative about thinking of things to do with an old CD?

Lewis You have a point, I guess. It's a good thing there aren't any tests on creative thinking, isn't it?

Phoebe That's true!

Lewis And you know what? I don't like this magazine now. I'm going to stop buying it for good.

4.07

You will hear people talking in eight different situations. For questions 1–8, choose the best answer (A, B, or C).

One

Woman 1 Seriously? This is the first time you've ever been to the theatre?

Man 1 Yes! I'm not sure why you're so surprised though.

Woman 1 Sorry, it just seems odd that … well, I guess I thought everyone has been to the theatre at least once.

Man 1 Well, growing up, apart from seeing student productions, I never really had the opportunity as we lived so far from a theatre. I wasn't that bothered anyway because I became obsessed with cinema in my early teens.

Woman 1 Well, I hope you enjoy this!

Man 1 I'm sure I will – it's really nice of you to invite me. I hope the tickets didn't cost too much.

Two

Girl 1 Hi, Sally. It's Julia here. How are you? Sorry I missed you. The reason I'm calling is, um, you know the new guy at school, Ralf, he's from Germany? Well, his parents are having a kind of party at their place, this Friday, so they're having over new friends they've made since they arrived here. Ralf was wondering if you'd like to go, but he hasn't got your number. So can you get back to him? His number's 07913 656 009. OK? If you call him, then he'll have your number, too. Right, that's it. Bye!

Three

Woman 2 So, last night we went to that Indian restaurant you recommended.

Man 2 The Taj Experience? Did you like it? The food's fabulous, isn't it?

Woman 2 Yes, we had a really nice meal. My curry was one of the best I've ever eaten!

Man 2 Brilliant. I'm glad you liked it. Quite expensive though, isn't it?

Woman 2 Well, not cheap, but not too bad. I have to say, though, that if we go back, I hope the service is a bit better. We waited too long for the food and the bill!

Man 2 Oh? I guess we were luckier than you, then. No complaints about the waiters when we went.

Four

Man 3 It was exciting to be invited to be in this film. The fact is, erm, I was worried that people didn't remember who I was, or had started to think that I could only play characters that are basically evil. You know, in my last three films I played that kind of part, but I do actually have more range than that! So to be asked this time to take on the part of someone sympathetic, like Jed, the character I play in the film, was a relief, and now hopefully people will see that I can be nice as well as nasty!

Five

Woman 3 I've been looking at how prices can vary around shops, and it's remarkable how things differ. Take for example a simple healthy cereal bar, with honey and oats. Now, I went into one shop in the high street and bought one for 60p. Another shop, I bought exactly the same bar, but paid 65p. But, if you go to the supermarket just outside the town, you can buy five for two pounds fifty – that's 50p each. Of course, the supermarket can only sell so cheaply because they can afford just to make a very small profit, or indeed no profit at all. But town centre shops can't do that, so they have to sell at a higher price.

Six

Woman 4 Our next caller is James Wood. What are you calling about, James?

Man 4 Good morning. I'd like to talk about all the potholes around where we live. They're everywhere, and last month someone in my street had to buy a new tyre for his car after it went through one. Every time it rains the holes get worse, and sometimes new ones start to appear.

Woman 4 Have you complained to the council?

Man 4 Certainly, and more than once. But they just give excuses about not having enough money. Typical – you pay the city council, but you get nothing back.

Woman 4 Well, perhaps they're listening and will do something soon.

Seven

Woman 5 Jean Scott, congratulations on your team's performance today. You must be happy.

Woman 6 Overall, yes. 2–1 isn't a bad result for us, but it could easily have been one all if our last goal hadn't been allowed. To be honest, I think we might have got a couple more goals, in fact, we really should have, some good chances missed, so that's something we'll have to work on. But we were lucky there weren't any injuries given the poor condition of the pitch after all the rain we had last week. There's a big game next week as you know, and everyone's fit for it. So, I'm happy and relieved at the same time!

Eight

Woman 7 So it sounds like your holiday was a good one.

Man 5 Best ever. So good I was really annoyed when I had to come back.

Woman 7 What was so great about it?

Man 5 Where to start? It was such a peaceful place, you know? During the night I never heard a sound – and you know what it's like at my flat with the traffic!

Woman 7 Yes, I do.

Man 5 And even during the day there was only birdsong and the sound of wind in the trees. So I could sit and read – and I put my phone on silent almost all the time, too.

🔊 4.08

Girl 1 I've been into art as long as I can remember. When I was a little kid, I was always colouring in and cutting out and making things. It's my favourite subject at school by a long way, and I know that when I leave school, I'm definitely going to art college. So this club was always going to be for me. It's been really interesting and a good chance to learn about different ways of doing things. The teacher is absolutely amazing, and he really brings out the best in me. I've made a massive improvement, and it's all thanks to him.

Boy 1 There's a huge emphasis at our school on sport, and we're really encouraged to get involved. There are clubs for loads of different sports, and most kids want to get into at least one team. Being into art is most definitely not cool so if you're creative like me, you usually don't talk too much about it. When I heard our art teacher was starting an art club after school, I got really excited because it was my chance to find out if there were any other secret artists like myself at school. It turns out there are, and I've made loads of new friends.

Boy 2 I'd always thought of myself as a bit of a maths geek. I mean, I already know that I want to work in IT when I leave school. I never really thought of myself as having much imagination, so I've been really surprised at how much I actually like drawing and that I'm actually quite good at it. I'm really proud of some of the work I've produced. In truth, I only went to art club because I wanted to make new friends, not because I was particularly interested in art. I've met some really nice people, but what has surprised me most is how much I'm enjoying being creative.

Girl 2 I consider myself to be a really creative person, and I love painting and drawing so this was the perfect after-school club for me. It's run by the new art teacher, who's really young and friendly, so it's fun. What's really great is that we don't just do painting and drawing, which I've never been any good at. We've done sculpture, photography – we've even made a short film, too, and we're encouraged to experiment. I can't wait to see what we do next. I really enjoy the class; even the short lectures about famous artists aren't too bad.

Boy 3 If I'm honest, I didn't really want to do extra art classes, but my parents made me because they didn't want me in the house on my own after school. I'd rather have gone to a history club, but there isn't one. But it's not as bad as I thought it would be, because the teacher gives us quite a bit of art history, too. It's good to learn about which famous artists were doing what and when. I'm not really a very creative kind of person so I don't really enjoy the practical side of the lessons, although we do do different stuff, which makes it less boring.

Unit 5

🔊 5.02

Aaron And now here with this week's latest tech news is Shauna. Shauna, what do you have for us this week?

Shauna Well, I think I have something you will absolutely love.

Aaron Why's that?

Shauna I think it's fair to say that you, Aaron, are a man of fashion. But you also have a terrible sense of direction.

Aaron Unfortunately, that is true.

Shauna So what you need is this pair of stylish shoes that tell you exactly in which direction to walk.

Aaron Tell me more.

Shauna These shoes are the invention of a man called Dominic Wilcox, and he was inspired by the movie *The Wizard of Oz*. In that movie, the heroine, Dorothy, had a pair of red shoes, and whenever she wanted to go home, she just clicked the heels together, and her shoes magically took her there. So Dominic decided to design a pair of shoes to take you wherever you want to go.

Aaron Wow. So, how do they work?

Shauna Well, first you need to plug a USB cable into the heel of the left shoe where the GPS is located and upload your destination using specially designed mapping software. Then click your shoes together, just like Dorothy, and the shoes will show you where you need to go. They're so simple to use that I didn't need to read the manual.

Aaron And how do they do that?

Shauna Well, the left shoe has a circle of small lights on the top of it. There are eight of these lights in total, and they act as a sort of compass. The light shows you the direction you need to go.

Aaron I'm not sure I understand.

Shauna OK, so if you need to go straight ahead, then the light at the top of the circle will light up. If you need to turn left, then the light on the left-hand side lights up, and so on.

Aaron So if I'm going completely the wrong way, then the light at the bottom of the circle will light up and tell me to turn around.

Shauna Exactly.

Aaron Brilliant.

Shauna Isn't it? But that's not all. On top of the right shoe, there is a straight line of five small lights. These lights are a sort of progress bar. They show you how close you are to your destination. The more lights that are lit, the closer you are to where you want to go.

Aaron But how does it do that if the GPS is in the left shoe?

Shauna The GPS transmits this information using wireless technology.

Aaron Wow, these shoes really are high tech. I don't need to worry about ever getting lost again.

Shauna No, you don't!

Aaron So I needn't have downloaded that GPS app for my phone. I should have just got a pair of these shoes instead.

Shauna Absolutely.

Unit 6

6.04

DJ Today's story on *Best Buddies* comes from Carlotta, and she's here to tell us about her friendship with Lily. Please welcome Carlotta. Now, Carlotta, I know that you met Lily at school – in kindergarten, in fact.

Carlotta Yes, that's right. It was our first day of school. We were sitting next to each other, and we were wearing the same school sweaters. We had the same hairstyle and hair color, brown hair, tied back in a ponytail, and the same eye color, too – green. In fact, we looked like two peas in a pod. We found that we had the same hobbies, too. We got along like a house on fire. We shared secrets. We laughed at the same things. And if I needed a shoulder to cry on, Lily was always there.

DJ Your friendship went on for years.

Carlotta Yes, it did – all through elementary school, we did everything together. My mom used to say we were joined at the hip.

DJ But then something happened, didn't it?

Carlotta Yes … yes, it did. We had a falling out.

DJ And whose fault was that?

Carlotta Mine, actually. I did something terrible. When we were about nine, at the end of the school year, there was a costume competition. Lily was very excited about it. She told me all about her ideas for her costume. Then one day, our art teacher asked us all, "What are you going to make?" I wasn't very creative, and I had no ideas. It came to my turn and I said, "A dragon costume." Of course, that was Lily's idea for her costume. I described all the details Lily had described to me, and the teacher said, "That sounds amazing. Well done." Lily didn't say anything. She just looked very sad. She didn't speak to me after that.

DJ And did you bury the hatchet?

Carlotta Yes, we did, but it was several years later. We were on a school trip to the beach. It was a hot day, and everyone was swimming. I couldn't swim, but I decided to paddle. The water wasn't very deep, so I walked further and further out. Suddenly, I took a step and the water was up to my neck. I panicked and screamed. People waved at me and smiled. They didn't know I couldn't swim, but Lily knew. She knew me inside and out, you see. She knew all the things I loved and all the things I hated.

DJ So she saved your life?

Carlotta Yes, she did. But we didn't become friends again immediately. It took a while to clear the air and for her to trust me again. But we did it, and we're still good friends today.

Unit 7

7.02

Host Hello and welcome to *Silver Linings*, the show where our guests try to find a little good in everything. Well, we all know the expression: "Every cloud has a silver lining" – and that's exactly what my special guests Paul and Nadia are here to do; find the silver lining. I'm going to give them some potentially disastrous situations, and they're going to tell me why, in fact, they're actually really good things. A point goes to whoever gives the most imaginative answer. Paul, Nadia, all clear? Great. So let's play *Silver Linings*. So Paul and Nadia, round one. It's the first day of summer break, and you fall and break your ankle. The doctor says – no walking for at least three weeks.

Paul Well, that's so not a problem! I can be the ruler of the house! "Sorry, Mom, I can't clean my room!" "Sorry, Dad, I can't help you in the garden." And "Hey, Sis, can you get me another piece of cake, please?"

Host OK, Paul. Thanks. Well, I think that after six weeks of that, you'll have annoyed your entire family. Never mind. Now, Nadia, what's your silver lining?

Nadia OK, so, for a long time now I've had an idea for a novel. A really great, funny novel. Now I'll have the time to write it, with other people taking care of me. Every day, I'll be writing the novel that's going to make me rich and famous.

Host OK, thanks Nadia. So now over to the audience. If you think Paul's answer is best, press the green button. If you think Nadia should get the point, press the red button. And the winner is Nadia. Well done, Nadia – one point for you. OK, round two. You and your family are flying to Turkey on vacation. Halfway through the flight, the pilot says there's a technical problem and you have to land in Rome. When you land, the pilot tells everyone that they can only fly on to Turkey tomorrow. Nadia?

Nadia OK, so that's not great. But look, the airline will put us in a nice hotel, and soon I'll have taken a shower in a hotel room, and after that I'll be sleeping in a comfy bed. And hey! I'll have spent a day in Rome, too! So when I get home, I can tell my friends that I went to Rome as well as Turkey.

Host Sounds good. What about you, Paul?

Paul Well you know, I've always wanted to learn Italian, so when the airline puts us all in a hotel, I can start! When we take off the next day for Turkey, I'll have learned at least twenty Italian words. Well, ten words perhaps. But it's a start! And you know what? Because of this "technical problem," in a few years' time I'll have married an Italian woman, I'll be living in Italy, and I'll be the happiest man in the world!

Host Hmm. I'm not sure how likely that is! Anyway, what does the audience think? Who wins that round? Green for Paul, red for Nadia. And … it's Paul! Good job, Paul. OK, here we go for the deciding question …

Unit 8

8.02

Teacher It's not every day you get to meet someone who is 100, and that's one of the many reasons today's guest is so special. So please, let's have a huge round of applause for Tom's great-grandfather – Mr. Hardeman.

Mr. Hardeman Thank you. Now, when Tom asked me if I could come and talk to you as part of your age awareness week, I thought "What on earth do you young people want to listen to an old man like me for?" But then he explained to me about all the work you're doing making your bucket lists. Now if I was younger, I would have known what a bucket list was. But I didn't, so he had to explain and show me his list – ten things to do before you're 25, and he asked me what would be on my bucket list. Now, as I'm already very old, the idea of a bucket list for me might seem a bit strange. It's probably a bit late for me to start planning to climb Mount Everest or parachute out of a plane – although actually, I did do that when I was in the Royal Airforce. But it did make me think, if I was seventeen again, what would be on my list? I must admit I was finding it a bit difficult, so I had another quick look at Tom's list to help me. Well, it was full of some very ambitious plans – visit every continent, write a novel, meet a famous person – all sorts of exciting things, and if you all have lists like Tom's, I wish you good luck trying to tick all those things off. But the more I thought about it, the more something was troubling me about Tom's list. There was a lot of ambition on it. I was worried that if he doesn't manage to do all those things, he might feel disappointed. I also worried that these weren't really Tom's ambitions, but someone else's expectations. And finally, I was also worried that if Tom spends all his time trying to do these things, then maybe he will miss out on enjoying his normal everyday life as it happens around him. Now maybe I'm taking the idea of a bucket list too seriously, and it's just meant to be a bit of fun. So if I had made a list, what would be on it? Well, things I've already done; things like enjoying watching my wonderful family grow up around me, being there for a friend when they really needed me, trying not to make too much trouble in the world – that sort of thing. And now I can add one more thing – talking to a whole class of students at age 100. Thank you.

Unit 9

9.04

Chris Hi, I'm Chris Williams, and welcome to a special edition of *Radio Helpline*. Research shows that 28% of college graduates have jobs that do not require a degree. And when you consider that, in the US, college tuition for the average student is nearly $40,000 for a four-year degree, college is not as attractive an option as it used to be. I'm joined in the studio today by career advisor Jo Harvey who is here to take some of your calls and help you with decisions about your future. Jo, welcome and thank you. Let's go straight to our first caller. Hello, Alex. What would you like to ask Jo?

Alex Hi. I'm graduating from high school next July, and my family and teachers are all expecting me to go to college, but I'm not so sure it's such a good idea. It's so expensive, and I'd like to get some life experience, too.

Jo Hi, Alex. You'll be pleased to know there are other options you could consider. Have you thought about a two-year degree?

Alex No, I haven't. I just know I'm interested in engineering.

Jo There are some two-year engineering degree programs available. You'll be able to study at a community college, which is much more affordable, and you'll be able to start working in half the time. I think it's an option you could look into. It is a great alternative to doing a traditional four-year university degree.

Alex Oh, wow! Thanks, Jo. I'll certainly look into two-year programs.

Chris Let's move on to another caller. We have Gemma on the line. Hello, Gemma. What's your question for Jo?

Gemma Hello, Jo. I want to launch my own business, and I just wondered if you had any advice.

Jo Well, Gemma, 50 percent of high-school graduates born between 1995 and 2010 want to launch their own business, so you're not alone. And it's always good work experience for the future. However, there is a lot of competition, so your business needs to be very special and unique. I have three pieces of advice for you. (1) Do a lot of research and know who your customers are. What do they like? What don't they like? Who do they admire and who do they follow? (2) Use social media for marketing. Post interesting blogs and attractive photos on Instagram. Have conversations with your followers and reply to their comments and messages. Build good relationships with them. And (3) make sure you are organized. Download an online planner or organizer to keep all your plans on track and organized.

Gemma Thanks, Jo. That's great advice.

Jo You'll also find some good advice on my website. Have a look at that.

Gemma Thank you, I will.

Unit 10

10.04

Janice Hello, everyone. It's great to see so many of you here today. Well, I'm what's called a foreign correspondent. That means that I'm a reporter for my newspaper who reports on things that are happening abroad. So of course, I spend a lot of time away from home, I travel around the world, and I try to tell readers at home what's going on in other places. I'm here today to answer your questions, so I hope you have lots of them. Where should we start? The young man in the front row.

Boy 1 Do you travel to dangerous places?

Janice Yes. Sometimes you go to a war zone, for example, because to get a really good story, you have to get close to the action. And sometimes the action is in a place where there's fighting, and that's dangerous, of course. But often, it's more dangerous for the local people who help me – drivers, translators, even the people who arrange interviews for me. I might stay in the country for a few days or weeks, and then I come home, but they stay there because that's where they live, and it's obviously way harder for them. But you asked me if my job was dangerous. And, yes, it is some of the time.

Girl 1 So why do you do it?

Janice Good question! Well, I do it because I think it's important and helpful. And of course it's exciting. It's very, very exciting, and, in a way, you get hooked on it. I mean, I can't imagine working in an office, sitting behind a desk every day.

Boy 2 How do you prepare for each story?

Janice Well, you have to know a lot about the place you're going to. You have to spend time reading and talking to people and finding things out. And depending where you're going, sometimes you have to train physically, you know, you might be in a desert or up in the mountains, so you have to be physically fit. For one story I did, where I had to follow an army in the Sahara, I had two weeks of training with an army instructor; he asked me to run ten kilometers with a heavy pack on my back. I didn't like that much!

Girl 2 What's the most difficult part of your job?

Janice Right. Well, I'd say the most difficult part is trying to be objective, you know, to write about what you see, and not what you think you see or what you want to see. And sometimes people think your report isn't a fair representation of the facts.

Boy 3 Would you recommend your job to other people?

Janice Oh, yes, absolutely. I mean it isn't for everyone – just now, someone asked me why I do it, and it's not the first time I've heard that question! But it's a fantastic job, I love it and feel very privileged to have the opportunity to do the work I do.

10.06

Editor 1 I'm sorry, but there's no way this is a news story. I mean just because this woman was famous for a short while a few years ago doesn't mean that everything she says is news. I'm really against running this story. My mind's made up!

Editor 2 This is exactly the kind of story we want. This woman always causes controversy, and that's what our readers like to read. She sells papers. We're definitely going with this story. And that's final.

10.08

You will hear an interview with a teenager called Diana Hollingsworth about the "Good News Project." For questions 1–7 choose the best answer (A, B or C).

Interviewer We all like to complain that there seems to be nothing but bad news when we turn on the TV or open the newspaper, but do we ever think of doing something about it? One person who has decided to do just that is 16-year-old Diana Hollingsworth who is here with me today to tell us all about her "Good News Project." Diana, welcome. Tell us, just what is the Good News Project?

Diana The Good News Project is exactly what its name suggests. It's a project to hunt down and report stories that will make us feel happy about the world that we live in.

Interviewer And how did you come up with the idea?

Diana Well, all the depressing stories in the news were getting me down, but I was even more tired of hearing people going on and on about the same problems, and I thought to myself, "I should definitely do something about this." I was the editor of the school magazine so I decided that the next issue would contain nothing but good news. I also used the magazine to explain my idea to pupils. I was amazed by the response I got. Loads of them came forward with stories. That's when I thought I could do more.

Interviewer And now you print stories in the local paper. How did you get involved with that?

Diana My mum has a friend on the local newspaper, and she arranged for me to meet her. I took along some of the stories that I'd been given by people at school and explained my idea to the journalists there. They loved the idea and said that each week they would publish one of our stories to see how the public responded to it. It was such a success that after a few months we were publishing around five stories in each edition. I've learnt so much from this experience.

Interviewer And you're also on the local radio station? Tell us more about that.

Diana The producer of the radio station had seen our stories in the newspaper and really liked the idea of doing something similar. So now I produce a good news story for the broadcast at the end of their news bulletins. I love coming up with amusing stories that will cheer people up. I don't actually listen to myself though because I sound weird.

Interviewer It sounds like you're quite busy.

Diana I am. I mean I don't do all the work myself. I have a team of reporters who find the stories, but I'm the one who makes the final decision as to which stories we're going to pass on to the paper and the radio. It's actually quite a bit of responsibility because I need to be sure that the stories are 100% accurate, which can be challenging. It's probably the toughest part of the job.

Interviewer So who writes your stories? Are they all young people like yourself?

Diana Most of them are. Most of them are pupils from our school, but actually anyone can get in touch and send in a story. They can do it just once or they can contribute regularly. And they don't have to write the story. I'm happy to do that if I have all the facts. The only thing we ask any potential contributor is that their story should be either current or about something that's only just happened. And of course, it has to be uplifting.

Interviewer Has doing this project changed your opinion of the news in any way?

Diana Oh, definitely. Before I always saw the world as a dangerous place, and I felt powerless to do anything about all the problems the world is facing. I try not to think about those, and instead I focus on things individuals can do. I know there are things that people like me can do to make the world a better place.

Interviewer That's good to hear. And finally – can you give us some examples of your favourite types of stories?

Diana Oh my goodness. Where do I start? Animals always make good stories. Animals doing silly things, people finding their lost cats, that sort of thing. We also have lots of stories about people doing amazing things to raise money for people in our area – like building a skatepark, for example. I like those the most because everyone can get involved. Sport is also a good topic. We had an inspiring story the other day about an 82-year-old man who still plays football every week.

Interviewer Diana, it's been a pleasure. Thank you so much for telling us all about the Good News Project and good luck for the future.

Diana You're welcome and thanks for having me.

Unit 11

11.04

Host 1 Hello and welcome to *Science Today*. Well, believe it or not, it's been nearly twenty years since American businessman Dennis Tito paid an incredible $20 million dollars for a journey into space and a six-day stay on board the International Space Station.

Host 2 That's right. On April 28, 2001, Mr. Tito took a trip on a Russian Soyuz spaceship that was quite literally out of this world and became the first ever space tourist.

Host 1 Back then it seemed like that was going to be the start of a mad rush of space tourism, but things didn't quite move as quickly as everyone had imagined. Between 2001 and 2009, there were only a total of eight tourism flights, and then in 2009, these flights were stopped altogether.

Host 2 But don't worry all you starry-eyed space travelers, there are a few companies that have plans to put anyone who has the money up into space. One of those companies leading the way is Virgin Galactic, part of the massive Virgin Group created by the British entrepreneur Richard Branson.

Host 1 The Virgin Galactic's spaceship, known as the SpaceShipTwo VSS Unity, will carry six tourists along with its two pilots into outer space, and rather than the $20 million that Tito paid, the cost of this journey is a mere $250,000.

Host 2 But we should add that you won't be getting six days full board on the ISS for that money, and neither will you be going as far or spending as long in space. In fact, the whole trip on VSS Unity, from Earth to space and back again, will last just over two hours.

Host 1 Let me explain how it works. The VSS Unity is attached to another ship, the WhiteKnightTwo carrier aircraft. This blasts off from Earth and carries the VSS Unity to a height of around 14,000 meters above the Earth. At this height, the two spaceships separate, and the Unity will fire up its engines and travel at supersonic speeds to a height of 80,500 meters, where the rules of space take over and you become weightless. So, after a bit of floating around the spaceship and admiring the wonderful views of our planet, passengers will be returned to Earth where the VSS Unity will land on a runway, a bit like a regular airplane.

Host 2 And that's it. It's not exactly rocket science.

Host 1 Except that it is.

Host 2 You know what I mean. So, if you're interested and have the money, here's the bad news. The first flight, whenever it takes place, is already sold out.

Host 1 Indeed. In fact, there are around 700 people who have already bought tickets into space with one or other company who are waiting to get onto a flight. Some of them have been waiting for nearly twenty years.

Host 2 So, if you're in a hurry for an exotic vacation, then you might be better off going for something a little more down to earth for now. A trip to Antarctica maybe?

Unit 12

12.02

Well, good morning everyone. My name's Maggie Wilson, and I'm from an organization called *The Species Finders*. I'm here today to talk to you about a few of the new species of animals and insects we've only recently discovered.

Now, I don't know about you, but a lot of people think that we already know about all the animals, birds, fish, and insects on this planet. But in fact, that's simply not true. We're finding new species all the time.

So the first species I'd like to tell you about today is the American pocket shark. It's very cute! It was discovered in the Gulf of Mexico. It was caught in 2010, but it wasn't described as a new species until 2015. Now, it's very rare; only one or two of these sharks have ever been seen. Why do you think it's called a pocket shark? It's not in fact because it's tiny and only 14 cm in length. It's because it has a pocket-like feature just near the fins below its head. Isn't that adorable?

My next species is small and furry. For the first time in 80 years, a new rat species has been found in the South Pacific. In 2010, Tyrone Lavery heard rumors about a giant rat that could crack coconuts. It lived in the trees on Vangunu Island. There were even songs and children's rhymes about these rats. But Lavery couldn't find it. Then, in 2015, a ranger caught one of the rats as it ran out of a tree which was cut down. "As soon as I examined it, I knew it was different," Lavery said. It was indeed a new species.

The next new species is this cute gibbon which was discovered in the forests of the Gaoligong mountains in southwest Asia. It's been named after the famous *Star Wars* character, Luke Skywalker. This is because of the gibbon's high treetop home and the mysticism surrounding it in Chinese history. The Skywalker gibbons' eyebrows are thinner and farther apart, and the shape of their skulls and teeth are different from other hoolock gibbons. Sadly, although it has just been found, the Skywalker is already on the list of endangered species.

My final new species today is a very eye-catching yellow and green frog that was discovered recently in Ecuador's cloud forests. According to a new study, it is a new species of rainfrog. Ecuador is home to 570 frog species. It's really beautiful. It, too, is already considered to be endangered.

So, the good news is that we're finding new species all the time. We don't know how many more species are still out there. What we do know is that more will be found.

What's not so good, of course, is that all these animals are endangered. Their habitat, that is the places where they live, is being destroyed rapidly, and it is human beings who are doing this. If we don't act now to stop habitats from being destroyed, many animals will disappear, and future generations will only see them in books. I think it's vital for humans to find ways to live well and without harming other living creatures, don't you?

12.08

You will hear a woman called Frances Williams talking about her work as an oceanographer. For questions 1–10, complete the sentences with a word or a short phrase.

Frances: Thanks for the invitation to talk to you today. I'm a geological oceanographer, and when I mention this to people, I usually see that they have no idea what it entails. So first, let me give you a brief introduction to the field of oceanography. As the name suggests, it's the science of studying the world's oceans. This is of huge importance given the challenges the world faces because of rising sea temperatures caused by climate change. Oceanographers are doing essential research in order to find solutions to this problem.

There are many different types of oceanographers. Marine biologists look into the effect of changing conditions on plants and all types of fish and other sea creatures, and they collect data about them. Because of course it's not just humans that are being affected by climate change. There are a number of shark species that are in danger of becoming extinct – to give just one example.

Then we have chemical oceanographers. They look into the ways in which pollution is having an effect on the chemistry of the ocean waters. They also study the critical role the ocean plays in regulating the earth's climate by removing carbon from the atmosphere and providing oxygen. And they might be involved in exploring what kind of materials found in oceans could be used in the development of medicines.

Physical oceanographers, in turn, do research into all kinds of physical movements of the oceans, including waves, currents and tides and how these movements affect coastlines; for example, how sand is transported by the sea on and off the coast.

And last but not least, there are geological oceanographers, like me. What we do research into is the ocean floor and how its mountains and valleys were formed. My particular area of expertise is in the study of undersea volcanic activity. I've always found this really fascinating.

There are lots of new discoveries being made all the time. A recent study mapped about 20% of the sea floor of the Pacific Ocean, which led to the discovery of several new species. But 95% of the world's ocean floors are still to be explored – which is really exciting.

It's only recently that we've had the technology to explore the deepest parts of the ocean, such as the so-called Challenger Deep, a place that is almost 11,000 metres under the sea. It's significantly deeper than the height of the highest mountain, Mount Everest, which is about 9,000 metres. People always thought that the deepest parts of the oceans were totally silent. Well, in our research we have found that the opposite is the case. With the help of microphones that are fixed to special submarines that can go to these depths, we have recorded high volume sounds. These sounds are evidence of the enormous amounts of energy there are at work down there – there are rumbling sea-quakes, the equivalent of earthquakes as we know them, and extremely violent currents that have a similar effect on the seafloor that extreme winds such as hurricanes or tornadoes have on the surface of our planet.

Acknowledgments

The authors and publishers acknowledge the following sources of copyright material and are grateful for the permissions granted. While every effort has been made, it has not always been possible to identify the sources of all the material used or to trace all copyright holders. If any omissions are brought to our notice, we will be happy to include the appropriate acknowledgments on reprinting and in the next update to the digital edition, as applicable.

Key: WL = Welcome; U = Unit.

All third party texts are reused from *Think Second Edition British English Student's Book 4*; **WL–U12:** All photographs are reused from *Think Second Edition British English Student's Book 4*.

Cover photography by David Sacks/The Image Bank/Getty Images; Alex Tihonov/Moment Open/Getty Images

Teaching Tip videos produced by Honest ideas Ltd.

Adaptation by Zoltan Rezmuves